All shall be well

Alles, alles möge sich zum Guten wenden, and all manner of thing shall be well

Richard Essberger

Q

First Published in Great Britain in 2023 by
Quacks Books in a limited edition of 200 copies.

7 Grape Lane, Petergate, York YO1 7HU
Tel: +44 (0)1904 635967
Email: info@quacks.info
Website: radiusonline.info

Quacks Books is an imprint of Radius Publishing Ltd

A CIP catalogue record for this book is
available from the British Library.

ISBN (Paperback): 978-1-912-728-66-4
ISBN (E-Book): 978-1-912-728-67-1

Set in twelve point Baskerville with a page size of 250mm x 176mm printed by offset lithography on an eighty gsm book wove chosen for its sustainability.

Contents

To my mother and father,
Mary and Josef

Foreword

I felt privileged when I was offered the opportunity to review this tale, pre-publication. I have an advantage over some other readers in that I know the author, not least for his fastidious and sensitive approach to research. The product is awesome, and I congratulate him on his assembly of such a detailed, informative, and addictive tale.

I also know, only too well, that the Soviets continue to eliminate all opposition; they may call themselves 'Russian', but they are still 'Soviet' in their outlook, quite unable to respect the truth and freedom of choice, or rule by common consent. This is a compelling story that needs to be published.

Is it fact or is it fiction? The Author's note explains the difference in publishing terms; fiction writers, however, sprinkle fact around their tale, but this is thick with well-researched fact. The core story, leaving aside the romance, gives colour to the period's intelligence war; brutal and embarrassing, but true and in need of telling as much to inform today's generation as generations past. I suggest it should not be 'hidden' as fiction, but it should be sat on the history shelves as 'friction', any lack of proof being due to the opacity of official record-keeping and its selective omission or destruction.

I like the staccato style, *him, her, officialdom*. The text is punchy, and it's not a tale for speed-reading, life seldom rolls out like an essay. So, it needs its speed bumps, the commas that stop the reader tripping into the narrative. Yet the rapid-fire quotations from source material, with the frozen politeness of Civil Service English up against the greater honesty - if you want to believe it - of journalists, and the directness of the military, not to mention secret services, of five countries, carry the reader along at a gallop.

Wow, what a tale!

Christopher Beese, MBE - inter alios, explorer of the Empty Quarter

Glossary

- .38 – a Smith & Wesson revolver of this calibre used by the British Army
- 2IC – Second in Command
- 5 TGM – a Czecho-Slovak infantry battalion named after Tomáš Garrigue Masaryk, statesman and philosopher
- AA – Anti-Aircraft
- AIC Huyton – Alien Internment Camp, Huyton, Liverpool
- AMGOT – Allied Military Government for Occupied Territory, immediately post-WW2
- AMPC – Auxiliary Military Pioneer Corps, later the Royal Pioneer Corps
- Anschluß – 'connection' in German, the invasion of Austria in 1938 and its absorption into the German Reich
- ARP – Air Raid Precautions, hence ARP warden or patrol
- ASD – Austrian Social Democrats
- ATk Bty or A/Tk Bty – Anti-Tank Battery
- AWOL – Absent Without Leave
- BAOR – British Army of the Rhine
- BCRC – British Committee for Refugees from Czechoslovakia, later the CRTF
- Bde – Brigade
- BEF – British Expeditionary Force, at the beginning of WW2
- BIOS – British Intelligence Objectives Sub-Committee, see T Force
- BKVÙP – Baterie kanónu proti útočné vozbě, Czecho-Slovak term for an anti-tank battery
- BMP – Boyevaya Mashina Pekhoty, a Soviet tracked armoured personnel carrier
- Bonzos – German nationals trained by SOE for insertion into occupied Germany on hopeless missions
- BQMS – Battery Quartermaster Sergeant
- Br inf bn – British infantry battalion
- Bren LMG – the British Army Light Machine Gun developed in Brno, Czechoslovakia, and Enfield, Britain
- C/L – Conditional Landing, 'Admitted to the UK at the port of entry, subject to conditions'
- Capt – Captain
- CB – Companion of the Order of the Bath
- CC – Chief Constable
- CCE – MI6's Chief Controller Europe
- CCG – Control Commission Germany
- Cheka – Extraordinary Committee to Combat Counter-Revolution and Sabotage. 1917-1922. Soviet security
- CIOS – Combined Intelligence Objectives Sub-Committee, see T Force
- civ – civilian(s)
- civvies – civilian clothes

- CMG - Companion of the Order of Saint Michael and Saint George
- CO - Commanding Officer, most usually a lieutenant colonel's appointment
- Col - Colonel
- Comd - Commander
- COS - Chief of Staff, in the British and Czechoslovakian armies
- CPGB - Communist Party of Great Britain
- Cpl - Corporal
- CRTF - Czechoslovak Refugee Trust Fund, previously the BCRC
- Cz-Sl - Czechoslovakian/Czecho-Slovakian
- Demo - Demonstration
- DG - Director-General of MI5
- DGW or DW - 'Dick White', christened Dick. DG of MI5, then Chief of MI6; Sir Dick Goldsmith White, KCMG, KBE
- DLI - Durham Light Infantry
- DPW - Director of Prisoners of War
- EPES - Enemy Personnel Evacuation Service, see T Force
- FIA(T) - Field Intelligence Agency (Technical), see T Force
- GI - Government Issue, initials that became a nickname for enlisted men in the US armed forces
- GP - General Practitioner, a local doctor in the UK
- GPU - State Political Directorate. 1922-1923. Soviet security/intelligence
- GRU - Military Intelligence Service. 1918-until recently, Soviet/Russian army security/intelligence. 2010-2018 named GU. Distinct from the NKVD, KGB, etc
- GSO2 - General Staff Officer (Grade 2), usually a major's rank
- GS (R) or GS-R - General Staff Research, later MI (R) or MI-R, the Army forerunner of SOE
- GUGB - Main Directorate for State Security. 1941-1943. Soviet security/ intelligence
- Haganah - Defence, the main Jewish paramilitary organisation until 1948
- Hansard - the daily record of parliamentary proceedings at Westminster
- HE - High explosive
- HMS - His Majesty's Ship/Her Majesty's Ship
- HMT - Hired Military Transport, a Royal Navy term for impressed civilian transport ships
- HO - Home Office
- HOAD - Home Office Aliens Department
- Hot Axle - a verb for axle bearings being caused to overheat on railway rolling stock, an SOE technique
- HQ - Headquarters
- hvy arty - heavy artillery
- ID - Identification, used in ID Card, meaning Identity Card
- Int - Intelligence
- IO - Intelligence officer, in the British Army
- IRA - Irish Republican Army

- ISRB – Inter-Services Research Bureau, a cover name in the Second World War for SOE
- IWM – Imperial War Museum
- KBE – Knight Commander of the Order of the British Empire
- KFS – Knife, fork and spoon, a common military equipment
- KGB – Committee for State Security. 1954-1991. Soviet/Russian security/ intelligence
- kkStB – Kaiserlich-königliche österreichische Staatsbahnen – Austrian Imperial-Royal State Railways
- KPÖ – Kommunistische Partei Österreichs, the Austrian Communist Party
- k.u.k. – kaiserlich und königlich – imperial and royal, used by government in the Austro-Hungarian Empire
- LCC – London County Council
- LO – Liaison Officer, usually an army term
- Lt Col – Lieutenant Colonel, an army rank, usually addressed conversationally as 'colonel'
- M, MX and MYO – appointment code-names of various officers in SOE's Czechoslovakian Section, in descending order of importance
- M/S – Motor Ship
- M&B – used of an antibiotic, sulfapyridine, originally manufactured by May and Baker
- Maj – Major
- MC – Military Cross
- MD – Medical Doctor, in America and Canada
- MEDLOC – Mediterranean Lines of Communication, the British Military Train running post-war between Vienna and Italy
- MGB – Ministry of State Security. 1941 and 1946-1953. Soviet/Russian security/ intelligence
- MI Room – Medical Inspection Room, an army term
- MI-R – Military Intelligence (Research), a War Office team previously called GS (R), one of the foundation elements of SOE
- MI5 – Military Intelligence, Section 5, usually MI5, occasionally just 'Five', the British secret service, responsible for the UK and colonies
- MI6 – Military Intelligence, Section 6, usually MI6, SIS, occasionally just 'Six'; see also SIS, responsible for overseas intelligence
- Mil Gov Dets – Military Government Detachments, administering areas of occupied Germany post-WW2
- MOD – Ministry of Defence, London, from 1964, previously the War Office
- Mossad – HaMossad leModi'in uleTafkidim Meyu□adim – Israel's Institute for Intelligence and Special Operations
- MP – Member of Parliament
- MP – Military Police, in the British or US armies
- MTS – Motor Transport Ship, a rarely used term, but sometimes the SS Ettrick went under this title

- MV, mv or M/V – Motor Vessel or SS – Steamship
- MVD – Ministry of Internal Affairs. 1953-1954. Soviet/Russian security/ intelligence
- NAAFI – Navy, Army and Air Force Institute, shops and recreational establishments for the British armed forces
- NATO – North Atlantic Treaty Organisation
- NCO – Non Commissioned Officer, the ranks of lance-corporal and corporal, or their equivalents
- NFD or nfd – No Further Details
- Nippy – a waitress in the cafés and restaurants of J Lyons and Company
- NK or nk – Not Known
- NKGB – People's Commissariat for State Security. 1941 and 1943-1946. Soviet/ Russian security/intelligence
- NKVD – People's Commissariat for Internal Affairs. 1934-1941. Soviet/Russian security/intelligence
- NTR or ntr – Nothing To Report
- O gauge – a size for railway models, smaller than Gauge 1, introduced by Märklin
- OBE – Officer of the Order of the British Empire
- OBZ – Obranné zpravodajství, Czech Military or Defence Intelligence in the Cold War
- OC – Officer Commanding a squadron, battery or company, usually a major's appointment
- Oe or Ö – the sign used by the Austrian underground in 1945, standing for Österreich, or Oesterreich, a name banned by Hitler
- OGPU – All-Union State Political Board. 1923-1934. Soviet security/intelligence
- OR or ORs – Other Rank(s), the army term for private soldiers, sometimes for privates, NCO's, SNCO's and warrant officers
- Orbat or ORBAT – Order of Battle, the command structure and strengths of a military unit or formation
- OSS – Office of Strategic Services, a predecessor of the CIA
- Ostmark – the 'provincial' name that replaced 'Austria' after the anschluß
- PA – Protected Area, sometimes 'Prot Area', coastal strips or areas of military significance in any invasion
- PB 2, or 2 PB – 2nd Pionierbataillon – 2nd Pioneer Battalion. An Austrian Army railway engineer battalion in 1938
- PC – Pioneer Corps, initially Auxiliary Military Pioneer Corps, later Royal Pioneer Corps
- PCO – Passport Control Officer, a thin – very thin – pre-war 'cover' appointment for MI6 officers in embassies. So: PCO (V) was PCO (Vienna)
- PF – Personal File, sometimes P/File, of someone being monitored by MI5
- POW, PW or PoW – Prisoner(s) of War
- PPS – Principal Private Secretary, in the Civil Service, overseeing a minister's private office
- PT – Physical Training

- Pte – Private soldier
- PWE – Political Warfare Executive, split off from SOE to deal in political and economic warfare
- QM – Quartermaster, an officer in charge of stores
- QRF – Quick Reaction Force
- RA – Royal Artillery
- RAF – Royal Air Force
- RASC – Royal Army Service Corps
- RAVAG – Österreichische Radio-Verkehrs-Aktiengesellschaft – Austrian Radio Transmission Company
- RC – Roman Catholic
- RCMP – Royal Canadian Mounted Police, nickname, 'the Mounties'
- Redcaps – nickname for the Royal Military Police
- RMP – Royal Military Police
- RN – Royal Navy
- RSM – Regimental Sergeant Major
- Soviet/Russian state security/intelligence: variously Cheka, GPU, GRU, GUGB, KGB, MGB, MVD, NKGB, NKVD, OGPU, Soviet/Russian state security/ intelligence organisations, not necessarily in that order. Confused? You should be
- RV or R/V – Rendezvous
- S/S – Secretary of State, the Government minister in charge of the Home Office
- SA – Sturmabteilung, the Nazi party's paramilitary wing, most usually known as the Brownshirts
- Sanitorium, nicknamed 'The San' – the medical ward and facilities in some boarding schools
- SC – Staff Captain
- Section D – originally part of SIS, controlled by the Foreign Office. In 1940 it was merged with MI(R), from the War Office, i.e. the Army, as one of the founding elements of SOE
- Section X – SOE's department covering Germany and Austria, later it was enlarged and became AD/X, the German Directorate
- SIS – Secret Intelligence Service, or MI6
- Sitrep – Situation Report
- Sjt – Serjeant, and still used in some regiments; but more usually Sgt – Sergeant
- SMB – St Margaret's Bushey, a girls' (but now mixed) boarding school in Hertfordshire
- SNB – Sbor Národní Bezpečnosti, Czechoslovak Police in the Cold War
- SNCO – Senior Non-Commissioned Officer, a sergeant or colour-sergeant/staff-sergeant
- SOE – Special Operations Executive, jocularly known as the <u>S</u>tately '<u>O</u>mes of <u>E</u>ngland or, inter alia and more officially, by its cover name, IRSB
- SOS – Struck off Strength, transferred out of an army unit. The opposite of TOS
- SPÖ – Sozialdemokratische Partei Österreichs – Social Democratic Party of Austria

- SRN - State Registered Nurse
- SS - Schutzstaffel - Protective Echelon. Principal agency of security, surveillance and terror in Nazi Germany
- SS - Steamship
- SSgt - Staff Sergeant or CSgt/Colour Sergeant, sometimes SSjt or CSjt
- Stasi - Ministerium für Staatsicherheit, the feared (and hated) Ministry for State Security in East Germany
- StB - Státní bezpečnost - Czechoslovak State security
- STS - Special Training Schools of SOE
- T Force - Target Force, Allied post-war search for German scientific/industrial secrets; it incorporated BIOS, CIOS, EPES and FIA(T)
- TB - Tuberculosis
- Toc H - Talbot House, a soldiers' rest and recreation centre in WW1, 'Toc' being the then signaller's code for 'T'; 'Tango' in NATO's postwar signals alphabet
- TOS - Taken on Strength, transferred into an army unit. The opposite is SOS
- TUC - Trades Union Congress
- U-boat - U-boot, submarine in German, the abbreviation of Unterseeboot
- USAAF - United States Army Air Force
- USSR - Union of Soviet Socialist Republics, more usually known as the Soviet Union
- V diff - Very Difficult, a mountaineering term describing the grade of a climb
- V1 - Vergeltungswaffe 1 - Vengeance Weapon, often called the Doodlebug or Flying Bomb
- VC - Victoria Cross
- VE Day - Victory in Europe Day, 8 May 1945
- VGAD - Die Verstärkter Grenzaufsichtsdienst - The Reinforced Border Control Service, part of the SS
- voj - abbreviation of Vojin, the Czech army word for the rank of private
- WCIT - War Crimes Investigation Team, later WCIU - War Crimes Investigation Unit
- WEF or wef - With Effect From
- WIPA - Wiener Internationale Postwertzeichen Ausstellung - Vienna International Philatelic Exhibition
- WO - War Office, London
- WT or W/T - Wireless Telegraphy, wireless transmission by radio
- X - Head of Country Section X, Germany and Austria, in SOE
- X/A1 - Mrs Clara Holmes's appointment within Section X

Maps

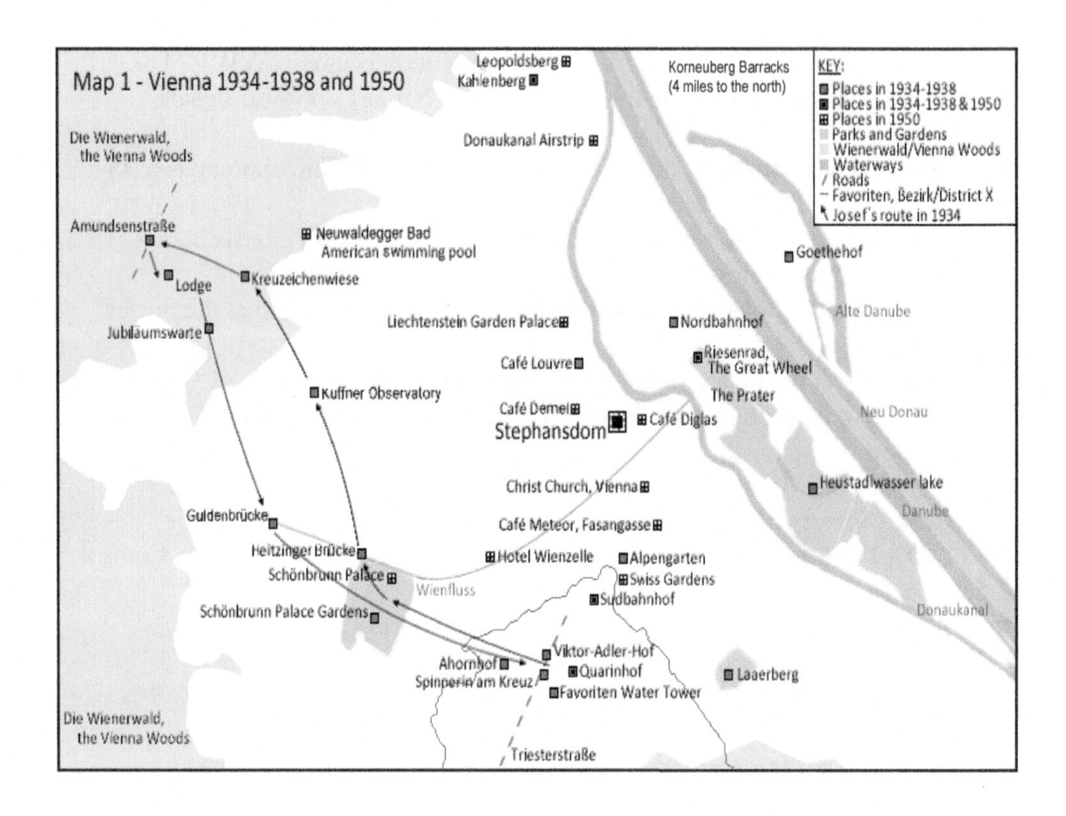

Map 1 - Vienna 1934-1938 and 1950
KEY:
Places in 1934-1938
Places in 1934-1938 & 1950
Places in 1950
Parks and Gardens
Wienerwald/Vienna Woods
Waterways
Roads
Favoriten, Bezirk/District X
Josef's route in 1934
Leopoldsberg
Kahlenberg
Korneuberg Barracks
(4 miles to the north)
Die Wienerwald,
the Vienna Woods
Donaukanal Airstrip
Amundsenstraße
Neuwaldegger Bad
American swimming pool
Lodge
Kreuzeichenwiese
Goethehof
Liechtenstein Garden Palace
Nordbahnhof
Alte Danube
Jubiläumswarte
Riesenrad,
The Great Wheel
Café Louvre
Kuffner Observatory
The Prater
Café Demel
Stephansdom
Café Diglas
Neu Donau
Christ Church, Vienna
Heustadlwasser lake
Guldenbrücke
Danube
Café Meteor, Fasangasse
Heitzinger Brücke
Hotel Wienzelle
Alpengarten
Schönbrunn Palace
Swiss Gardens
Wienfluss
Sudbahnhof
Schönbrunn Palace Gardens
Donaukanal
Viktor-Adler-Hof
Ahornhof
Quarinhof
Laaerberg
Spinperin am Kreuz
Favoriten Water Tower
Die Wienerwald,
the Vienna Woods
Triesterstraße

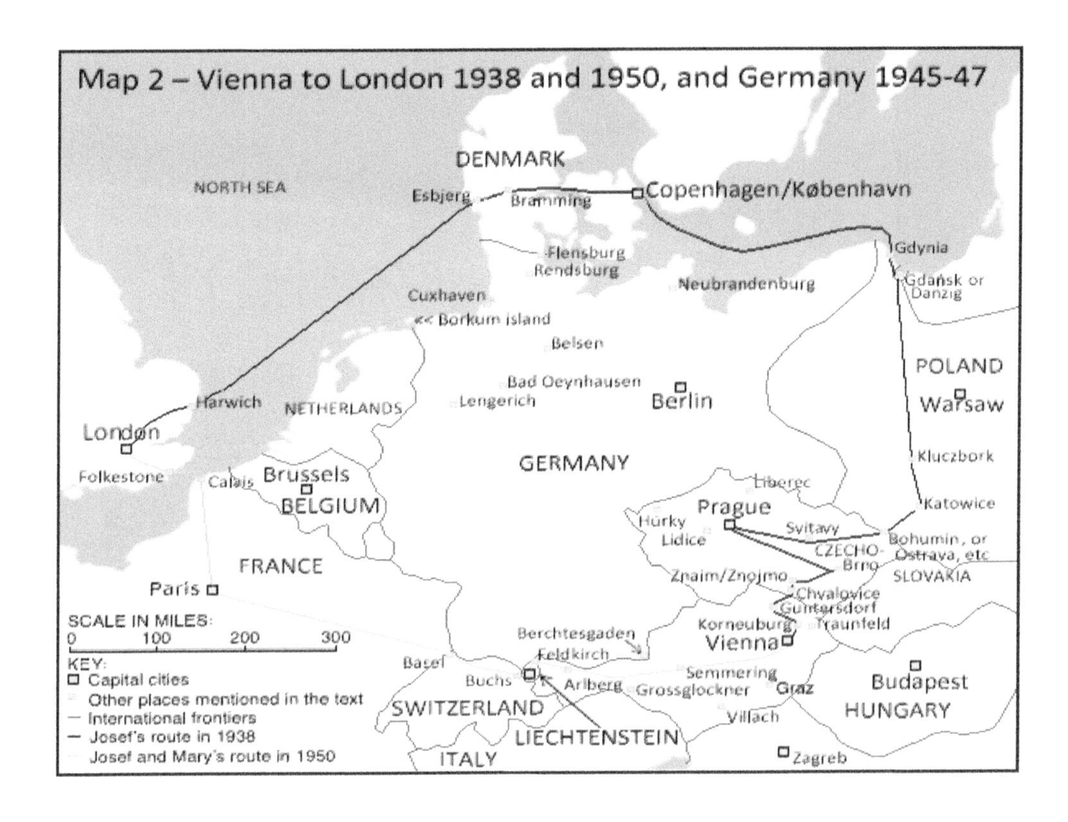
Map 2 – Vienna to London 1938 and 1950, and Germany 1945-47
DENMARK
NORTH SEA
Esbjerg
Bramming
Copenhagen/København
Flensburg
Rendsburg
Gdynia
Gdańsk or Danzig
Neubrandenburg
Cuxhaven
<< Borkum island
Belsen
POLAND
Bad Oeynhausen
Lengerich
Berlin
Warsaw
Harwich
NETHERLANDS
London
Kluczbork
GERMANY
Folkestone
Calais
Brussels
BELGIUM
Liberec
Katowice
Prague
Hurky
Lidice
Svitavy
Bohumin, or Ostrava, etc
CZECHO-
Brno
SLOVAKIA
FRANCE
Znaim/Znojmo
Paris
Chvalovice
Guntersdorf
Traunfeld
SCALE IN MILES:
0 100 200 300
Korneuburg
Vienna
Berchtesgaden
Feldkirch
KEY:
Capital cities
Other places mentioned in the text
International frontiers
Josef's route in 1938
Josef and Mary's route in 1950
Basel
Buchs
Arlberg
Semmering
Grossglockner
Graz
Budapest
SWITZERLAND
Villach
HUNGARY
LIECHTENSTEIN
ITALY
Zagreb

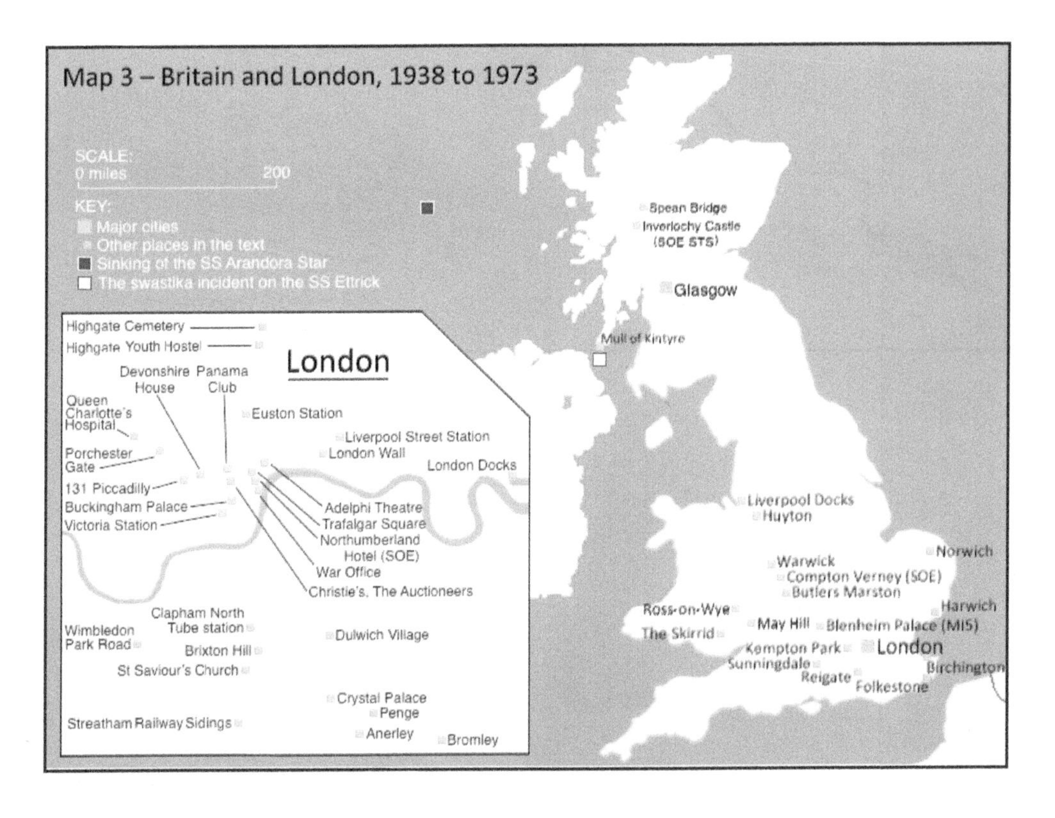
Map 3 – Britain and London, 1938 to 1973
SCALE:
0 miles 200
KEY:
Major cities
Other places in the text
Sinking of the SS Arandora Star
The swastika incident on the SS Ettrick
Spean Bridge
Inverlochy Castle (SOE STS)
Glasgow
Mull of Kintyre
London
Highgate Cemetery
Highgate Youth Hostel
Devonshire House
Panama Club
Queen Charlotte's Hospital
Euston Station
Liverpool Street Station
London Wall
Porchester Gate
London Docks
131 Piccadilly
Buckingham Palace
Victoria Station
Adelphi Theatre
Trafalgar Square
Northumberland Hotel (SOE)
War Office
Christie's, The Auctioneers
Clapham North Tube station
Wimbledon Park Road
Dulwich Village
Brixton Hill
St Saviour's Church
Crystal Palace
Penge
Streatham Railway Sidings
Anerley
Bromley
Liverpool Docks
Huyton
Norwich
Warwick
Compton Verney (SOE)
Butlers Marston
Harwich
Ross-on-Wye
The Skirrid
May Hill
Blenheim Palace (MI5)
Kempton Park
London
Sunningdale
Reigate
Folkestone
Birchington

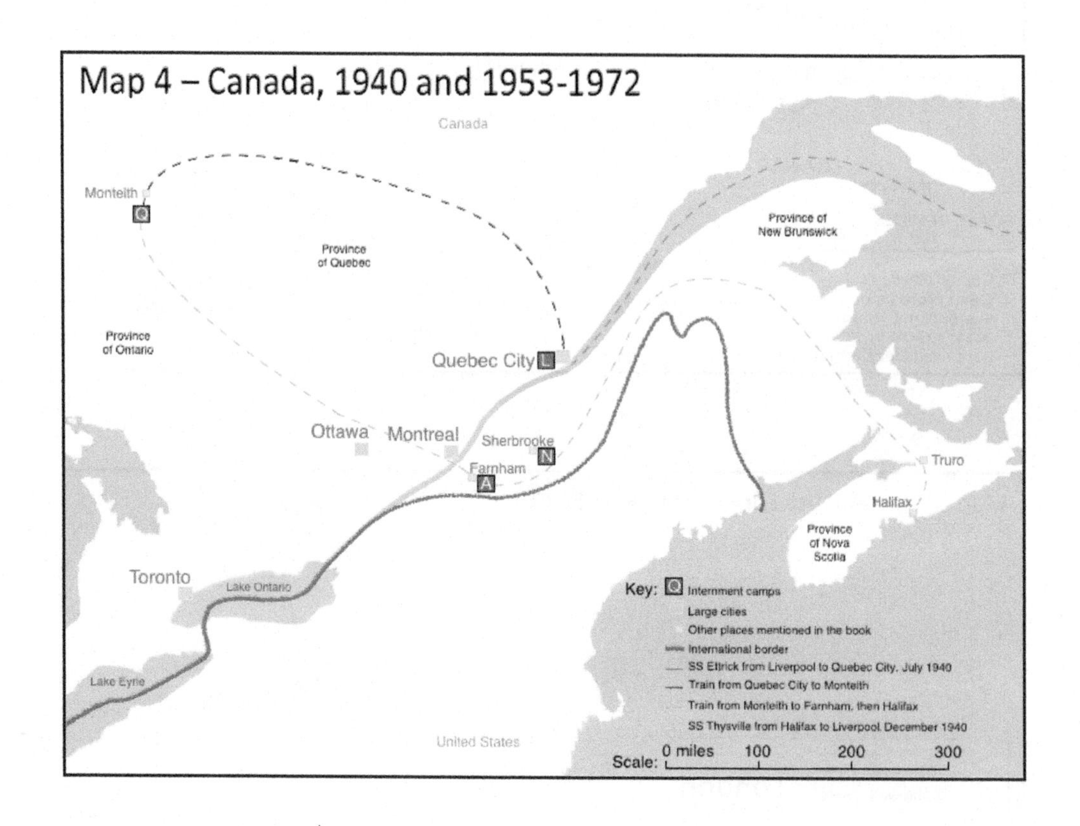
Map 4 – Canada, 1940 and 1953-1972
Canada
Monteith
Q
Province of Quebec
Province of Ontario
Quebec City
L
Ottawa
Montreal
Sherbrooke
N
Farnham
A
Province of New Brunswick
Truro
Halifax
Province of Nova Scotia
Toronto
Lake Ontario
Lake Eyrie
United States
Key:
Internment camps
Large cities
Other places mentioned in the book
International border
SS Ettrick from Liverpool to Quebec City, July 1940
Train from Quebec City to Monteith
Train from Monteith to Farnham, then Halifax
SS Thysville from Halifax to Liverpool December 1940
Scale: 0 miles 100 200 300

Chapter 1

From Favoriten to the Vienna Woods, by way of Schönbrunn Palace

Mary's story: The first thing I noticed was his politeness. In a sea of darting, suspicious eyes he held my gaze a moment longer, then, in halting English, he thanked me gently for the tea.

Was it at that moment I thought, 'He's the man for me'? Possibly; but certainly I haven't wavered in that belief from that day till this. I'll always remember that grey, damp November day in 1938 as the brightest of all my life.

.....

15th February 1916

Josef's story: In the big scheme of things it's unimportant, but in 1916 Josepha Bramminger gave birth to me in Vienna, calling me Josef, after my father.

My first memory is when I was two years old. We lived in such a tiny apartment that every night I was put to sleep in a drawer. You may laugh, but it wasn't even a large drawer!

When my brother Oskar was born he inherited the drawer and I was promoted to the small room, the *Kabinett*, where the rest of the family slept, Mama and Papa, Liza - my elder sister - and me, all in one not very large bed.

I also have memories of a nursery rhyme and I think the conversation might have gone like this... Mama, with me in her arms, saying, 'Now, young Josef, I'll read you that rhyme you love, *Leb', waiß ...*'

'Oh not again, Josefa! Growing up a Monarchist will do him no favours in Vienna.'

'Let him be, Peppi. If you have your way he'll end up a Communist and, in Austria, that would never do. It's only a rhyme.'

'You know I'm no Communist, they're as evil as the Nazis. I'm a Social Democrat, altogether finer. Anyway, that's no nursery rhyme. Some say one of those Emperors you worship wrote it in a wine cellar in Schloss Tratzberg, probably after drinking half its contents. Let him hear a real nursery rhyme.'

Mama was shocked. 'It was the great Emperor Maximilian, he was not drunk, and I do NOT worship him.' She turned to me and began reciting, in a gentle, sing-song voice,

Und stürb', waiß nit wann	*And die, I know not when*
Müß fahren, waiß nit wohin	*I must travel, yet know not where*
Mich wundert, das ich so fröhlich bin	*I'm astonished I am so happy*
Leb', waiß nit wie lang	*I shall live, I know not how long*

I heard it so often I shall never forget it.

I don't know how Vienna got through the 20's. Typhus, TB and Spanish flu raged, housing was terrible and overcrowding... well, Oskar wasn't the only one sleeping in a drawer. With so many people unemployed and inflation wrecking lives it's hardly surprising three-quarters of Vienna voted Social Democrat in 1919.

Papa, '*Herr Bahnlokführer*' to his neighbours - everyone in Vienna has a title - was an engine driver for *kkStB, Die Kaiserlich-königliche österreichische Staatsbahnen,* you'd say Austrian Imperial-Royal State Railways. The Habsburgs soon passed into history and the railways took on a simpler name, but Papa still had a job. In Austria the key thing was that even the humblest railwayman was a civil servant, meaning a job for life and an assured pension.

Papa was a fervent Social Democrat, he was a railwayman after all, the most committed of all trades unionists. Mama was quite the opposite, admiring the clerical party. She was so happy when Dollfuss declared democracy dead. I took after Papa, Liza took after Mama... things could be tense at home.

Mary: 'And your mother?'

Josef: Mama? She owned a shop in Lerchenfelderstraße, a grocer's, I think you say. Full of foodstuffs, many Hungarian, a riot of colour. Every other thing was red, red peppers, meats, sausages, *Debreceni*, *Virsli*, and delicious pastries, *Arany galuska*, *Palacsinta* pancakes. I loved it when she took me there, those sights and smells were intoxicating. Did her being a bit of a capitalist, a very little capitalist, offend Papa's Socialist beliefs? I don't know, but we - Liza, me and Oskar - were in a household with two incomes in a city where many had none.

We lived on Quellenstraße in Favoriten, Vienna's *Bezirk X,* the 10th District, south of *Die Innere Stadt,* the city centre. Mama took a tram to her shop in the city while Papa walked to work at Südbahnhof, from where his trains most often went to Italy and Switzerland.

Mary: 'Favoriten?'

Josef: It was one of the Habsburgian Empresses' 'favourite' garden, but now it's a tough area, working class through and through. 'It's boozing, brawling, politics and shooting', a policeman said, 'rougher and tougher the further you get from the city centre.' Austria's empire had had sixteen nationalities and even more languages, and in Favoriten half the families used Czech as their first language, although everyone spoke *Wienerisch...*

Mary: I was puzzled. 'Wienerisch?'

Josef: It's the language of Vienna, it's in the air, it's German with Italian, French and Spanish thrown in and, especially, a sense of humour, or mischief the Germans would say, although they're so solemn they wouldn't recognise humour if it bit them. A German might say, 'Things are serious but not hopeless', in Vienna we'd say, 'Things are hopeless, but not serious.' They can never make Austrians out, especially the Viennese.

Papa told the family legend of how, a century ago, an ancestor travelled south from a village called Bramming in Denmark, ending up in Vienna. They called him *Der Bramminger,* the man from Bramming. Mama's maiden name was Koci, so maybe her ancestors came from Hungary, where Kocsis means coachman. I saw a funny side in that, 'Maybe Mama's ancestor wasn't so very different from you, Papa, he drove a coach, you drive a train."' He laughed, Mama didn't.

Mama was always strict with us, more so with Liza than us boys...

Mary: 'You speak of it in the past tense, darling. Have you given up hope of returning?'

Josef: That took me aback, I had to think before I answered. 'Vienna? She's such a special place. The great hulk of Stephansdom towering over the city, dark and forbidding, that great tiled ridge, with the surrounding rooftops coated with snow in winter. But *Alt Steffl* – that's the steeple's nickname – is too steep for snow to settle on it, so as a child it always looked to me like a tower of strength, a shepherd protecting its huddled flock. And those great bells ringing out across the city... yes, I want to hear those again. But my family? I don't know. If you pressed me just now the truth would be...' I paused, then out it came, 'I never want to see them again.'

I don't know which of us was the more shocked, me or her.

At the age of five I went to school on Knöllgasse. It was dismal: stark white walls, a crucifix high up and the smells... in the classrooms wood polish, in the corridors tile polish and in the lavatories Beetz, a dark, oily disinfectant, every Austrian remembers that smell. If the iron stove in the classroom was unlit we would be as cold as ice, but when it was lit it was so red hot that we'd try to sit further away, only to be ordered back, '*Setzen Sie sich auf Ihre eigenen Bänke!,* Sit on your own benches!' If our teachers loved us they hid their feelings well.

In December Mama would take us to Christkindlmarkt, the great fair in Stephansplatz of toy stalls lit by naphtha lamps. She'd buy wonderful biscuits shaped like St Nicholas, covered in nuts and wrapped in foil. On 6th December, *Sankt-Nikolaus-Tag,* St Nicholas's Day, we went by train to stay with our grandparents, *Oma und Opa,* Granny and Grandpa, out in Traunfeld, the village north-east of Vienna where Papa grew up. All evening we'd sit there in great excitement, 'Would St Nicholas visit again this year?' Without fail, every year, there was a knock on the door. Oma would open it and there was the saint himself, in his bishop's flowing red robe, with mitre and beard, and carrying a great golden book. We knew that all year round angels had been writing our deeds in it, good and bad, and now St Nicholas read from it, praising us or admonishing us, reminding us that Christmas was soon to come and we must prepare our hearts for the Holy Child. Then, after a blessing, he'd be off. Not long afterwards Opa would come home; somehow he always missed St Nicholas's visit.

The next morning, in the shoes we'd left outside our bedroom, apples, nuts, sweets and small presents appeared. Once, I shall always remember, a pouch of stamps. Stamps from the old empire, Sarajevo, Trieste, Budapest, Prague, Zagreb, Krakow and Lemberg. They were the first stamps I'd ever noticed, and now I became a dedicated collector, well, as dedicated as my small pocket money allowed.

Vienna at Christmas: joy and peace, but fun as well. I loved it: snow, braziers, roasting chestnuts, dancers and musicians on the streets, Glühwein and iced champagne - for those who could afford it.

From our apartment in Favoriten I'd hear the whistles of trains running into Südbahnhof and my imagination ran riot... was that Papa's train? Or this one? Was that train heading west to Switzerland? No, the noise was disappearing southwards, it must be off to Zagreb. I could walk to the station in a few minutes, thrilled just to stand on the platforms and watch the great monsters puffing and hissing to a halt, carriage doors opening all at once and passengers surging out. I met the men he worked with, drivers, firemen and tickets collectors. To record Papa's journeys I begged, *'Kann Ich bitte einen Fahrplan haben?* Or, Can I have a timetable, please?' I don't know what fascinated me most, the people, the machinery or the signals, the tracks and junctions? I drank it all in.

One Christmas, when I was seven, I found a Märklin train under the tree. It was O gauge, a simple oval of tracks, *Ein Eisenbahn Personenzug mit Dampflokomotive,* a passenger steam train. Papa explained, 'Like the one I've driven for years, son. Take care of it.'

I'd goggled at it for weeks through Kober's toy shop windows on the Graben, enthralled by the electric lights in the carriages, doors that opened and closed. Mama was torn between smiling at our obvious pleasure or scowling at the expense. Papa said, 'I want him to enjoy railways. Maybe one day he'll drive a real one.' Well, for years he certainly drove my train often enough.

Then, next spring, 'Papa, there's an envelope for me, but there's nothing inside.'

'Look again.'

Ah, the stamp had a train on it! 'What train is it Papa? Is it YOUR train?' I was so excited.

'Look again. Where's it from?'

I spotted the postmark. 'Feldkirch', I said, dubiously.

'Don't look at me like that. Where's Feldkirch?'

'It's on the frontier with Switzerland. Ah...! Is that where the Arlberg Express enters Austria?'

'Exactly. Imagine a collection of stamps, postmarked from all the railway towns on our frontiers. Wait and see.'

And, over the following months, in they poured, envelopes postmarked Salzburg, Kufstein, Villach, Unterretzbach – 'Papa, where's Unterretzbach?' 'It's the last station in Austria, before the line to Znaim crosses into *Tschechoslowakei,* that's what we call Czechoslovakia. I go there sometimes. One day, if you're good, you'll come with me on the footplate, only don't tell your mother. She'd have a fit if she knew what we're plotting.'

He laughed. 'What you really need are stamps postmarked from the other side of the borders, foreign stamps. Now, across Europe all railwaymen are strong trades unionists and we look after one another. We have a tradition of formal hand shakes on handing over trains between countries, so I'll give the letters to fellow drivers for their stationmasters to post. With such a collection you might even start reading your atlas.'

1925

Our flat in Quellenstraße had just two rooms, one window, a bucket and wash-basin, no electric light or water, in winter a fire of waste wood we'd collected on foot from *Der Wienerwald,* those are the famous Vienna Woods. Twice a week we went to the public showers.

That all changed in 1925. The *Gemeindebauten,* the municipal tenement blocks, were built by the city, run then by the Social Democrats. They represented all that was good in Red Vienna, as everyone called it. You may have heard of them. Well, as a railwayman and an active Social Democrat, Papa was allocated one of the earliest flats. I was nine when we moved into just such a tenement block, the Quarinhof.

Our new flat had a lobby, three rooms and three whole windows, reflecting the city's motto for eradicating typhus: 'Healthy Living Equals Healthy People.' Also, untold luxury - even Mama had to admit - a balcony, shared with our neighbour. There was a communal nursery, a courtyard and children's garden, nineteen shops, a central laundry, a library, a shower bath and a training workshop. But what I remember are the four white chairs around our kitchen table, the blue-checked oilcloth, the smell of boiled new potatoes, and a window kept open all night. It was wonderful.

I also remember Mama's mantra: 'You can play in the courtyard, but I'll not have you playing on the street. Street kids are *Messerhelden,* dangerous cut-throats, their parents are not proper! They live underground, in cellars.'

'But Mama! Please, Mama!'

'No, Josef. You heard what I said. And as for you, Liza, my pet, girls <u>never</u> play on the streets, not with those gangs. Never, do you hear?'

She was probably right. *Räuber und Gendarm,* that's Robbers and Policeman in English, Favoriten's favourite game, sums it up. Every child on those streets she was so anxious to keep us off always wanted to be the robber, never the cop.

With Papa's job and Mama's shop we managed to scrape along and, with her watching *jeden Groschen,* every penny you'd say, we were more comfortable than many.

From 1925 my father sometimes took me on his footplate on trips to Budapest, Ljubljana, Venice... all over the empire. It was so exciting. In a siding I spotted a carriage with '*k.u.k.*' painted on it in faded gold. I asked Papa what it meant. 'It's *kaiserlich und königlich,* imperial and royal in English. It was on every train, every government department used it, you couldn't get away from it. But that's all past now, dead and gone.'

'*k.u.k*, it sounds *kuckuck,* cuckoo, to me', I joked.

Papa laughed with me. 'Very funny, son, you're a died-in-the-wool Socialist like me. But don't say it in front of your mother, she was attached to all that.'

My best friend was a girl, Frieda Reisner, aged ten, a year older than me, and the only other youngster on our staircase at Quarinhof. It was her family we shared that balcony with. Frieda had blue eyes, blonde hair and was very bright. I spent a lot of time with her, on that balcony or in the courtyard, playing around the stone fountain, in and out between the trees and bushes. We shared homework - which helped. I may have an excellent memory but I was never a scholar - we drew and painted together. Mama approved, it kept me off the streets. What she never realised was that Frieda was leading me astray - no, no, not like that, we were far too young - for Frieda told me she belonged to *die Roten Falken,* the Red Falcons, where Social Democrat youngsters met once a week. She took me to a meeting and I enthusiastically joined up.

I went out walking with them. Papa encouraged it, although Mama wanted me to join *Der Bund Neuland*, a Catholic youth group. She even enrolled me, paying the yearly subscription - doing me an important favour that I only discovered twelve years later - but I rarely went along, it was the Falcons that became important to me.

I liked their famous red neck scarves and parading behind their red flags at summer camps and on demonstrations. In school holidays we went camping, exploring little villages and the countryside. We cooked the most terrible food on fires of fir cones, got lost at night using compasses and the stars, fell asleep under blankets in the woods. We hiked into the mountains, studied nature, sang songs around camp fires and, if we could, raided other camps to steal their flags. There were outings in the Wienerwald, sometimes by torchlight, to Social Democrat party meetings and, every May Day, we marched in our tens of thousands around *Die Ringstraße,* Vienna's Ring Road. We went to annual camps in Czechoslovakia and Yugoslavia, exchanging gifts and badges with their Young Socialist groups (and stealing their flags if we could).

The organiser in Favoriten was Johann Svitanics, a trades union leader. He took me under his wing, encouraging me to learn motor-cycling, mountaineering and skiing through the Falcons. But after February 1934 he became a wanted man and had to escape to Prague. I believe he's in London now.

Mary: 'But, darling, why did you become a Socialist?'

Josef: It's very different here. No one in England thinks politics matters, but in Austria it can be a matter of life and death, or freedom at least. Well, my father was one, to start with at least, as were most of my friends. Later I realised for myself that Socialism was genuinely important, something worth fighting for.

1927

In 1927 the conservatives – in England you'd call these 'conservatives' fascists – ambushed a Socialist meeting in Schattendorf with rifles, killing three, including a small boy. Months later a Viennese jury acquitted them, so the workers across the city downed tools and marched on the Innere Stadt, breaking windows at *der Justizpalast,* Vienna's Palace of Justice and setting fire to it, although Frieda's uncle, a police lieutenant, saw an officer handing out red armbands, which Socialists were wearing, to plain-clothes policemen. It's still hotly debated who actually set the Justice Palace ablaze, was it a Socialist or an agent provocateur? Anyway, shots rang out and police on horseback rode into the crowd, firing, swinging sabres... they killed 89 people.

Until *Der Justizpalast Brand,* the Palace of Justice fire, I had dreamt of Social Democracy bringing justice and fairness to all. I was only 11 years old but that day, for the first time, I saw fascism in its true light. My naive political dreams were shattered.

Dreams... ! People picture Vienna as a happy-go-lucky place, glamorous Klimts, the Prater, its Ferris Wheel, lovely old buildings, hidden squares, with Stephansdom popping up above the city's roofs; Heurigers, wine, song, good food; waltzes, cuckoo clocks, paperweights that snow. All that's true, even if few Viennese can afford such things, and fewer still in Favoriten, where the daily experience was grinding poverty and unemployment. Things became pretty bleak.

1930

Then, politically, things went from bad to worse. Every party had its own armed force. We had *Der Republikanische Schutzbund,* or Republican Defence League, the Communists had their Red Brigades, but they were so few in number they amounted to nothing. The real threat came from the conservatives' *Heimwehr*, their 'Home Guard.' It had real money behind it, from Mussolini and Austrian industrialists, and aristocrats like Prince Ernst Rüdiger von Starhemberg. But they were poorly led, undisciplined, and their strength lay in the countryside, in Upper Austria, not in Vienna.

Then, in May 1930, the Heimwehr collectively swore their Korneuburg Oath, 'We reject the Party State and Western parliamentary democracy. We stand for the Leadership State', in a word, Fascism. The future didn't look good for democracy.

My school on Knöllgasse - named after Johann Knöll, who'd made a fortune as a *Fleischselcher*, that's a butcher who cures meat, soaking it in salt and brine and 'hot smoking' it, making smoked meats, salami and sausages - did me a favour. One day, walking to school past the local Fleischselcher's shop, the boy was setting out the trestles on the pavement. I'd walked past it hundreds of times but, perhaps it was the warm, musty smell of sawdust, or the sight of those rows of sausages and salamis, anyway, that day I stopped and asked many questions. After that, after school, I often spent hours inside watching the master butcher at work.

I learnt the usual subjects at school, plus some English, but I was never academic. Mama was always going on at me to learn a trade so, aged 14, off I went of to *Berufsschule,* in English you might say, I think, vocational school, to train for two years as a Fleischselcher.

We visited Vienna's *Fleischmarkt,* the Meat Market; that held my attention more than any classroom. Then, nearby, on Adlergasse, I spotted a stamp dealer's shop which held an even greater fascination for me. Whenever I saved up some money I'd go in and stare, eventually finding the courage to ask questions. Herr Weisz was a kindly man and occasionally he sold me a bag of stamps - I think he never charged the full price, just being glad to find a youngster interested in stamps.

On a visit to my grandparents I blurted out something that I didn't even know myself. I was walking across the fields with Mama and Oma, towards the railway line that skirted their village of Traunfeld. Oma pointed at a passing train and said, 'Perhaps your Papa is driving that.'

I turned to her and said, most seriously, 'No, Oma, that train goes to Nordbahnhof. Papa's train is at Südbahnhof.'

She laughed, 'So, you'll be an engine driver when you grow up?'

'No, I'm going to be a stamp dealer.'

Mama was pleased. To keep me 'off the streets' she paid 50 groschen annually for membership of *Briefmarkensammler Verein Favoriten,* the Favoriten Stamp Collectors Club, where we youngsters traded stamps like the adults. It met in Café Kellner, near the Quarinhof.

1932

Mama and Papa took us to the city centre to see some state ceremony, and

I asked, 'Papa, why is that man so small?' 'Shhh, keep your voice down', he replied. 'That is Herr Dollfuss. He is not a tall man, it's true. Herr Heffter told me he is 1.62 metres tall', then he whispered to Mama, 'before he steps into his high heels!' She laughed, but when it dawned on her that he was joking about 'her' Chancellor the smile froze on her face.

Training and jobs were important, but in Austria everyone had to profess a political leaning, like it or not. At Berufsschule there were brawls between the Nazis and the Blacks - well, the Christian Socialists and Monarchists - or between the Blacks and us Sozis, the Socialists.

So, I was glad when my training ended and I found a job with Fleischhauer Kästner. I started as *Die Fleischer Junge,* the butcher's boy, complete with blue-striped uniform, straw hat, bicycle and wicker basket, delivering meat to apartments in Favoriten and the Innere Stadt, including some grand old palaces.

It was hard work. Up at five to cycle to work, by six I'd have lit the big copper and dropped in the calves' and pigs' heads. As they rendered down I'd be packing the meat deliveries, next it was back to the copper to haul the heads out of the boiling water, then off on my rounds. I discovered the butchers' secret language, *zurück Slang,* 'back slang' as it's called, so we could talk amongst ourselves without customers knowing what we were saying. In Vienna, with so many languages and dialects, no-one noticed strange talk. Later I used something similar in my underground work.

Soon – this I really enjoyed – I learnt the real art of making sausages, certainly more about it than they ever taught us in college. What it all boils down to – ha ha – is whether you want cheap or tasty. For cheap, more water; for tasty, less.

But Herr Kästner was a staunch Social Democrat and a fair man. There was no side to him, he insisted apprentices call him Heinrich from day one, and only the best sausages would do in his shop.

Frieda and I were finding ourselves being drawn into political activity. Six of us would get up to all sorts, Hans Amsel, our leader (from my class at school), Frieda, Michael, Anton, Joachim, and myself, carrying messages, putting up posters and banners, acting as lookouts at party events. Soon we were being invited to attend illegal meetings.

They trained us on moving in groups across the city. If uniforms suddenly loomed up - whether police or Heimwehr patrols (both could land us in jail, but the Heimwehr always handed out a beating as well) – we knew what to do. Hans and Frieda walked at the back of the group, his arm about her waist, the rest of us earnestly debating football results, 'Rapid will wipe out First Vienna, you'll see!' 'Ha! Vienna will score four goals to Rapid's one. They'll hammer them.' Michael was a fan, he knew the teams inside out and the rest of us soon picked it up. We could 'talk football' across many *Straßen und Plätze,* the streets and squares.

If some eagle-eyed police sergeant took an interest, or a drunken Heimwehr patrol lurched too close, Hans would stop, put his arms around Frieda and kiss her – it was what the routine called for – while I split away from the other two, walked on and turned left at the next junction. Anton and Michael would start jabbing their fingers at one another until it seemed a punch would be thrown. It worked every time. The uniforms invariably looked at the kissing couple long enough for Michael and Anton's dispute to peter into nothingness, when they'd be off, turning right after two junctions. Then the courting couple would break away and walk on, also turning at the next junction.

The Heimwehr were too lazy to follow up, but throwing off the police took longer. Once we'd turned off our original route we'd join up again on a parallel road. If the police still followed we broke away, meeting later in a pre-arranged café, not a known Socialist haunt, or worked our way home. The routine varied, but we'd trained for it and it worked every time. We could slip through the city by day or night, like sand through a sieve.

At the end of 1932 I joined the Schutzbund. They only ever used Christian names and, at Johann's suggestion, I used a false one, Hans.

Unlike the Heimwehr we were tightly organised and well-equipped with weapons, stored since 1919, to defend the Republic against Monarchists, Communists and the Heimwehr. We saw ourselves as on the same side as the army and many of our firearms instructors were serving officers and NCO's. We intended to give a good account of ourselves.

Many a Saturday night I sat in cellars, half-asleep, half-listening to the old men – well, in their thirties or forties – talking endlessly about 'their war' on the Italian front, Isonzo, Gorlice, and so on, and on, and on. But their greatest triumph was after the war: by day handing their weapons and ammunition over to the Inter-Allied Military Commission then, by night, returning in trucks to take them away for burial around Vienna.

We really woke up if somebody turned up with sausages, that put us in the mood for the morning, when we'd march out to the Laaerberg for field training, grenade-throwing and the rifle and machine-gun ranges.

It may sound romantic, princelings, workers, aristocrats and home guard, but Mussolini was adding to their hidden stockpiles as much as Czechoslovak intelligence was to ours. The Heimwehr started holding demonstrations in our strongholds to terrify the workers, so we paraded to reassure them. We may not have been so colourful – blue overalls and leather caps, grey jackets, for those who could afford them – but our discipline was far, far better. We looked impressive, marching through our districts. We had 17,000 men under arms in Vienna, twice the army's strength, every district had three or more battalions.

One day Heinrich was giving me the customers' orders, 'This meat to this address, that to another...' when I surprised myself by interrupting him. 'No need to tell me. Frau Heinlin, she's at 17 Wahlengasse, District III. She always has a kilo of pork sausages, liver and chop ends.'

Heinrich gave me an odd look then said, 'It comes easy to you, remembering details?'

I tapped my temple, 'Once it goes in there, it stays there.'

A week later, when the shop was empty and Eugen and Vincent were out the back, Heinrich took me to one side, saying, 'Josef, young comrade, would you be interested in doing something more for the party than just the youth group, attending meetings and the Schutzbund?'

'What do you mean?'

'We think you could help in more specialist work. You'd be a party member, still attend meetings, if less often, but you'd receive training in certain tasks. Interested?'

'Tell me more.'

'Oh no, I'm just the messenger boy. I'll arrange a meeting.'

That was how I met Franz Emmerich, another Fleischelcher like Heinrich. He took me into the Schutzbund's Intelligence Section. Few people knew it existed, let alone how many men and women were in it or what it did.

Over time we underwent training by Franz and others. 'Security, security and nothing but security' was drummed into us. We lived it, slept it, trained for it and practised it, in our everyday lives, not just in training. You never knew when you were being examined, if the man or woman next to you on the tram, in the workplace, in the woods, was testing you. We learned not to trust anyone, no-one, not a single person... if you dropped your guard with the next comrade you met it could turn out that he or she was part of some test that they'd caused you to fail.

Next lesson: 'Never, never set a pattern. Vary your routine, your route, your behaviour, every time, every time.'

On and on it went. Eventually you develop a sixth sense, to trust to some internal instinct, if something didn't feel right, walk away.

We never really knew the small handful that we trained with; yes, we worked together like a team, and I discovered their weaknesses and strengths as they learnt mine, but I never knew their real names.

Once security training was over, we started 'real' training. Watching, recording, watching for watchers, shaking off watchers, working underground, communicating, interrogating and resisting interrogation, and... well, so much more. We were even taken down the sewers to see the storm drains, tunnels, valves, outfalls, weirs and manholes, to learn how the Police Sewer Brigade operated, where and when they entered the system. Fortunately for us, a handful of them were secretly Socialists.

We were taught communications. Using couriers - pedestrian and mobile, our motor scooters and bicycles amongst them - running dead letter drops, and meetings that don't look like meetings. Avoid telephones, the police are listening in. Avoid handwriting, their experts will identify your script. Use a typewriter, they can be just as traceable as your writing, but work around that... swap machines with legitimate machines from other offices and, vitally, rewind the ribbon every few sentences. The more you use the same stretch of ribbon, we were taught, the less 'they' could read it.

'We are NOT running an office so do NOT keep files and registers. If you need a copy type out three copies and immediately destroy the top one and the carbon papers. Immediately, and thoroughly! Carbon paper is your worst enemy, the traitor in your midst. Even the dimmest detective can spot the burnt ash from carbon paper. It looks, smells and tastes different from burnt paper, and who but an illegal burns carbon paper? So, burn it, break up the ashes and flush them down a sink or toilet. Remember: *BKS! Brennen, Zerknittern, Spülen,* that's BCF! Burn, Crumple, Flush.'

'Use gloves whenever possible, any sort of gloves. It's easy enough in winter, but to save your prints ending up in a police file find any excuse to wear gloves in summer.'

We often trained walking in the Wienerwald, where no-one could overhear. 'Classes' were never more than four, with another, shadowy figure, never introduced, hovering nearby. If this 'watcher' walked past us we would, in a moment, disperse to all points of the compass, our watcher, he or she, and each of us soon hidden by a fold in the ground, or lost in a crowd of Viennese out for a stroll.

I never trained with anyone from Favoriten. No one used his or her own name, only their illegal name. If we met outside of training there was never the slightest flicker of mutual recognition. It's a lonely place, that secret world.

Once Franz knew he could trust me he revealed he was in touch with Czechoslovakian military intelligence. They needed to know what was happening beyond their borders, and he asked me to act as his agent. I didn't need much persuasion as they were our only friend in the world. I'd already worked out it was them who supplied the Schutzbund's weaponry. So, any intelligence I gathered he fed to Prague.

But as well as such secret allies we had a host of deadly enemies. The police, yes, but almost more dangerous were the Communists, they were so active against us. In 1932 Johann warned me: 'They have few members or supporters but Moscow has issued them secret orders to throttle us. Be on your guard.' I remembered that warning when Fritz Hanke, who'd been with me in the Red Falcons, tried to enlist me into Favoriten's Young Communist League.

1933

In January Hitler came to power in Germany and, shortly afterwards the small Austrian Nazi Party started planting bombs.

In February Dollfuss, urged on by Mussolini, declared government unworkable, suspended parliament, introduced the death penalty, restricted the freedom of the press and the right of assembly, and made his *Die Vaterländische Front,* the Fatherland Front as you'd call it, the sole party of government. He banned the Schutzbund, the Nazi Party, the insignificant Communist Party and its Young Communist League. Overnight, Dollfuss arrogantly announced, our beloved country had become a fascist - 'Austro-Fascist, that is, not Nazi', he insisted - state.

The Schutzbund went fully underground. Overnight we fully became 'illegals', but our forbidden activities gained a real purpose. We rushed to hide paper, stencils, mimeographs and typewriters, removing the party funds and equipment we could lay our hands on, for the day when Dollfuss and his hated deputy, Major Fey, turned on our party.

A month later the government crushed the strongest trades union, the railwaymen. They'd gone on strike after discovering the Italian government was smuggling weapons into Austria to the fascists by train. Some lost their lives, many their jobs. I saw its effect on Papa, he was never the same man again.

But that year has one happy memory. In June I went to *WIPA 1933*, the Vienna International Philatelic Exhibition. I found myself rooted to the spot at the British stand, looking at the original printing die for the Penny Black, the world's very first stamp. I was so impressed.

1934

And so we come to 1934.

A few times in January Franz sent me with messages for an English newspaperman, Mr Gedye, at the Café Louvre, quite unforgettable with its dark brocade, marble-topped tables, cane chairs, and bamboo racks full of newspapers. Franz told me that Gedye (and his dog, Strupye, a great blond, bounding mongrel), was part of the café's *ihr Stammtisch,* their regulars' table. Here the greats of European and American journalism met, Gedye, John Gunther, William Shirer, Dorothy Thompson, Charles Knickerbocker and Marcel Fodor, all exchanging the latest news and gossip around their large table. I noticed a young Englishman hanging around. His name I didn't catch, but he had a slight stammer.

That January I was given my first operational Schutzbund task: sentry at a meeting at *Die Kreuzeichenwiese,* or the Cross Oaks Meadow, in the Vienna Woods. It was an exciting moment for me, I was only seventeen.

In early February the police – they had a turncoat in our ranks, we know that now – descended in force on the workers' districts, arresting many of our district commanders and uncovering many of our caches of weapons.

Faschingsamstag or Carnival Sunday, 11th February

The pressure was building on us, the opposition, but we were blind, we failed to see what was coming. Perhaps our thinking was numbed by the snows of winter, or perhaps it was because Vienna was celebrating *Fasching*, that pre-Lenten carnival of masked balls, extravagant behaviour and noisy, costumed parades. It culminates on Faschingsamstag, when Frieda and I went to a cabaret where, to cries of approval from the audience, a comedian extolled the virtues of the town called *Znaim*, or *Znojmo*, as Czechs say, across the border in Tschechoslowakei. 'In Znaim', he proclaimed, 'there is no Schutzbund, no Heimwehr. But, good friends', he continued, 'have no fears, in Vienna our problems are being seriously considered at the very highest level...'

You could have heard a pin drop. Did he have the ear of a cabinet minister? Was he about to reveal some deep political secret?

'Every night Herr Chancellor Engelbert Dollfuss is thinking them over, mulling over what steps he should take. He paces up and down, up and down...'

He paused – he had us in the palm of his hand – then quietly finished, '...under his bed.'

The room collapsed into loud, slightly hysterical laughter. It was the last laughter I heard for many months.

Monday 12th February

For me that Monday started like any other, dragging myself out of bed at five, making coffee and cycling to work over the last of the snow.

The conversation was the usual Monday morning chatter. Women gossiping about their weekend, hinting at mild affairs, the latest scandals, passing on news of yet more arrests and police searches early that morning...

'They took Herr Pokorny, you know, in Quellenstraße.'

'They searched the Weber Cinema and the two cellars in Laxenburgerstraße for buried weapons. They found nothing but, from the colour of them when they left, they'd shifted a lot of coal!' People chuckled; the police were never too popular in Favoriten.

All was well until five past nine. The telephone rang. Heinrich answered, listened for a long while, then a single question, 'And what are we to do?' Clearly dissatisfied with the answer he put the phone down, very deliberately took off his apron, said, 'Josef, take over here', and walked out of the shop. Eugen paused in wrapping the meat at the counter and Vincent's head appeared through the gap from the back room, both looking enquiringly at me. 'No idea, no idea at all. He'll be back soon enough.'

In the hour before he returned, rumour grew and grew. A customer came in and whispered to the woman waiting in front of her. People overheard the words 'Linz' and 'shooting', and turned to question the newcomer. Embarrassed, she turned and ran out. A buzz of speculation began. The next three people who entered were interrogated sharply, as if they were messengers, not housewives out shopping. Then Frau Feldman came in, excited, even more self-important than usual, waiting until she'd got everyone's attention before announcing, 'The police in Linz were fired on by the Schutzbund, some were killed. The railwaymen and tram drivers are discussing a strike.'

There were gasps of disbelief. Old Frau Wernher said emphatically, 'The railways won't lift a finger, Dollfuss squeezed them so tight last year they've taken fright. They won't risk their pensions.' Others stood in shock, two quietly slipped out. The oldest housewife turned and whispered urgently to Eugen, 'Double my order.'

Four days of civil war

What happened between Monday and Thursday? When it was over Frieda and I pieced this together...

Before 10.00 the party executive met to decide its response to the shootings in Linz. Our Socialist leader, Otto Bauer, argued for resistance, Berthold Koenig, head of the railwaymen, against. The decision should have taken five minutes but only after noon did they proclaim a general strike and issue orders for the Schutzbund to turn out with its weapons, 'only for use in self-defence.' By then, however, with no central orders, workers had started taking action and events spiralled out of the party's control.

At 11.20 lights across Vienna started to get dimmer. Then, at 11.47, a worker removed vital parts at the electrical works and all power was lost, the agreed signal for the Schutzbund's 'last stand.' But it occurred before the order had been issued. Confusion reigned across Vienna amongst workers and party officials. Well before midday Franz recalled seeing a line of trams halted on the Ringstraße and asking the drivers if it was a strike or a breakdown. They replied, 'You want the truth? We just don't know.'

Our mighty party machine had eight printing plants, hundreds of mimeographs and thousands of volunteers. But no-one had foreseen that when the manifesto arrived to be printed the electricity would be off. A handful were eventually produced on an old duplicating machine.

Dolfuss was more decisive. He dissolved the Social Democratic Party, its societies and trade unions, seized their assets and bank accounts, and announced martial law on radio. Outside the Opera troops erected barbed wire entanglements.

In his *Rathaus,* the City Hall, the Mayor told the Heimwehr, 'Clear out. I am the legally elected *Bürgermeister* and I yield to no threats, only to force.' So, force it was... they dragged him off to prison.

The atmosphere was extraordinary. Franz saw people walking towards the Reumannhof, some whom he knew were Schutzbündlers, wearing long overcoats to hide their uniforms. They were going to collect weapons, and he saw some exchanging glances with policemen along the route, while others staring fixedly ahead, avoiding eye contact with their soon-to-be enemies.

In the Gemeindebauten blocks uniformed Schutzbündlers began barricading the great gates with carts and rubbish bins. Men and women frantically dug up courtyards and broke down walls in search of their hidden weapons, but so many leaders – those who knew where the caches were hidden – had been arrested over the past two days that most weapons could not be found.

That afternoon the shooting began, sporadic rifle fire, later the tat-tat-tat of machine-guns. Finally, that night, came the sound of explosions from the suburbs, a sound that had the whole city in shock. No one believed that Major Fey, let alone Dollfuss, would turn artillery onto women and children in the apartment blocks. But it was true. Fey arrogantly proclaimed: 'I'll turn the Blue Danube red.'

Armed police and Heimwehr were soon on the streets, racing about, firing wildly at anyone who showed themselves. In Simmering they retreated into their police station because we held the power station, gas works, the Aspang railway station and many blocks. Battles raged around bridges over the Danube and most tenements, including Karl-Marx-Hof, Reumannhof and Schlingerhof. Men worked by day, fearing losing their jobs more than death itself, then, at night, joined their fellow Schutzbündlers on the front line.

That first night Dollfuss spoke on radio to a city in total darkness. Between Lehár's Merry Widow and the Radetzky March he proclaimed the two ringleaders had flown and the Government had the situation in hand. On Tuesday he broadcast that fighting had ended in Vienna, but through open windows everyone could hear the fighting across the city. Several times the police announced they had defeated us and withdrew, only for Schutzbündlers to re-emerge from the sewers. The army had to be brought in.

Favoriten's Laaerberg had been our rifle ranges and we'd constructed an excellent position of trenches for 2,000 men. They had no winter clothing, little food and few weapons, but one bright spark set up 'machine-guns' in the trenches. Machine-guns! Those broomsticks poked through cardboard held off five infantry battalions over three bitterly cold days and nights.

The Municipal Guard was the Schutzbund's best trained, elite unit. Its war role was defending the Combat Command HQ from Favoriten's *Wasserturm,* the Water Tower, just 250 metres from Quarinhof, where I lived, and near *der Spinnerin am Kreuz,* that's the stone monument, the Spinstress at the Cross. Early on our Guard arrived at the tower, armed with pistols, but no one had foreseen that the army would park its thirty-two howitzers in the park alongside the Spinnerin. Unable to discover the rifles and ammunition hidden around the tower the Guard sat there like mice in a trap, just 100 metres from those artillery pieces. A huge package of ammunition arrived at night, but it was all for rifles, which they had none of! When the nearby Trost army garrison demanded their capitulation, they had no choice but to march out, one by one, and surrender.

It was so depressing, some of my best friends were in the Guard.

Some Schutzbündlers held on through Wednesday, into Thursday, then retreated through the sewers, smashing to pieces any machine-guns they had to abandon. The army said it was closely watching the sewers, but their heart was never in it. The police's heart certainly was – they behaved brutally. Franz saw fighters, driven out of cellars onto the streets, being beaten by the police with rifles and insulted as *Kellerratten,* cellar rats. People shouted in disgust at the police from their windows, '*Schäm dich!* Shame on you!' Fortunately for us the Heimwehr's passion for beating and killing was still matched by their stupidity and cowardice.

'What did you do in the war?'

And what was I doing for those three days? On Monday Heinrich closed the shop soon after two, with the customers having scuttled-off home and no-one on the streets. His parting shot was 'Franz wants a word', so I went to my emergency RV in a nearby café.

My task, Franz said, was to be security around Viktor-Adler-Hof, on Triesterstraße. Just two blocks from our family's apartment and across the street from my old school, I'd known it since I was a youngster, every street corner, every alley and most of the people who lived there. It turned out it was the Schutzbund's communications centre, to which motor scooter men and bicycle couriers were carrying fighting reports from the Schutzbund in every district. A score of us covered every approach, walking nearby, hanging around or sitting in the three cafés that were still open. Any sign of police, Heimwehr or army approaching and we passed it on to the Adler-Hof.

That evening I was 'promoted' from security to foot messenger, taking messages from the Adler-Hof 200 metres south down Triesterstraße to Ahornhof, which I reckoned was our Combat Command headquarters. It was our highest secret. Any couriers captured at the roadblocks across the city would have led the police to think our leadership was in the Adler-Hof.

We foot messengers were the 'cut-out', so all I ever saw was Ahornhof's stony-faced caretaker. He simply took any message then shoo'ed me back out onto Triesterstraße.

I worked as a messenger all through Monday night, getting little sleep. And the same on Tuesday, the news getting bleaker by the hour, although messages still came and went. Each time I slipped past the Spinnerin I glanced nervously across the road, towards the Wasserturm. The army's artillery had disappeared, gone to bombard Karl-Marx-Hof and Sandleiten, but their lorries had stayed.

The remaining gunners seemed deliberately oblivious to the few remaining Schutzbündlers, some in uniform, just 100 metres away, up and around the tower, and to us messengers flitting past them into Ahornhof.

But, by late on Tuesday night, few couriers were getting through, and cyclist after cyclist sent out from the Adler-Hof failed to return. About midnight Franz sent me home for some sleep.

Our dispatch riders must have been brave. Many were captured and tortured, yet it wasn't until the Thursday that the police attacked the Adler-Hof and Ahornhof. They found nothing, by then they'd all escaped.

So, again, what did I really do in *Der Februar* (that's what Vienna now calls *Die Februarkämpfe,* the February War)?

Wednesday 14th February

My serious part began quite unexpectedly at eight on Wednesday morning with a knock on the door of our flat. Papa had gone to work – I'd tried to ask why, but he wouldn't discuss it – while Mama had closed her shop on Monday and was at home, but it was me who answered the door. Franz Emmerich was standing there. 'Let's go for a coffee', he said briskly, not pausing for his usual enquiry after my parents' health.

Soon, in Café Kellner, on a deserted Zur Spinnerin, we sat facing one another over two Kleiner Brauners. 'Ah, Josef, *Genosse...*' I braced myself, things were serious when he called me comrade.

Franz casually looked about him, checking that we couldn't be overheard, then continued, 'I have a task for you, you're going for a long walk. This afternoon an important meeting takes place in the Wienerwald, and you are part of its security, your name, *Birne,* that's Pear. Go through Schönbrunn to *Die Hietzinger Brücke,* the Hietzinger Bridge, the north side. Use the underground trick of meeting on a bridge, it looks so innocent, leaning over the parapet, gazing down into the Wienfluss, but it flushes out any "shadows." At twenty-eight minutes past ten you'll meet a redhead, codename *Apfel,* that's Apple. You say "*Gott sei Dank, der Fluss ist Niedrig,* Thank God the river's low"; her reply, "*Ja, kein Hochwasser in diesem Jahr,* Yes, no floods this year." She'll tell you the next place and time.

'The army and Heimwehr are still fighting us on the Margaretengürtel and around Sandleiten, so keep well clear. I know you will want to help them, but today's job is more important, do not get entangled in anything; anything. That is an order. If you are stopped on the way out you say your destination is Jubiläumswarte, you have no time for these Socialists, you're middle of the road. Mention your mother, her shop, her monarchist leanings, anything to put them off the scent. And', a slightly bitter smile crossed his face, 'for heaven's sake don't say your father's a railwayman!'

'Carry nothing, I repeat nothing, that could incriminate you. Do you have any friends, or acquaintances, in the Heimwehr?'

I hesitated... 'Three or four from school are with them. Two I still see around, one's in the stamp club.'

'Good. Carry their names with you, a letter, or something. If you're stopped and searched that's what they'll find.'

Then, looking me straight in the eye, he said quietly but with surprising force, 'This is important, I stress, *unhamlich wichtig,* absolutely vital, so give this everything you have. Now, enjoy your coffee.' Without waiting for a response, he got up and walked out, no friendly words, no turning his head in farewell. This really must be serious for Franz, normally so good-humoured, to be so serious, so abrupt; he was in a hurry.

I set off at 9.30 under an overcast sky. The occasional sound of far-off artillery told me the war was still being fought, with rifle fire a faint crackle to the north and, closer and much louder, occasional bursts of machine-gun fire. I wanted to head towards them but I had my orders. How would I ever explain myself to my friends, my comrades? None of them had an inkling I was part of Schutzbund intelligence. I'd have to face that when it came to it.

Triesterstraße was almost empty, no trams, carts or cars, occasional army lorries with soldiers in the back, helmeted, rifles upright between their knees. A few pedestrians scurried past, heads down, eyes averted; this wasn't the day for expressing one's feelings in public. It was the start of spring but, overnight, rain having fallen, the dirty snow heaped on the pavements was turning to ice.

I went across Schönbrunn Palace's gardens. They were too open for anyone to follow me without standing out. Little chance, really. The police and their plain clothes men must have their hands full fighting a real war. There was no sign of any followers.

As I strolled across those gardens I couldn't help recalling childhood days when my grandparents had brought us there: bright summer sunshine, warmth, carefree happiness, an ice cream to look forward to. Today was grey, chilly. My mind was full of turmoil. I tried to clear my head for the task ahead. But what would that task be? How was it connected to the life and death struggle going on, off to my right, up in the suburbs? How...? – 'No!' I forced myself to say, 'Concentrate, concentrate!'

I checked my watch, 10.25, just three minutes to cross Hietzinger Bridge. Then I noticed a red-headed girl standing near the far end. And she wasn't just any redhead, she was a very attractive redhead. A huge and grotesque bronze eagle, part-threatening, part-absurd, crouching on its stone pillar, towered above her, but she just stared down at the water. I strolled along the pavement, stopped about a metre from her and leant over the parapet, looking down into the Wienfluss. Then, as casually as I knew how, in my best 'flirting-with-attractive-redheads' voice, ventured, '*Gott sei Dank, der Fluss ist Niedrig*.'

Without turning she replied, '*Ja, kein Hochwasser in diesem Jahr*.'

Now she turned her head to look at me, and smiled. 'OK, Herr Birne, I'm Fraulein Apfel. At seven minutes to twelve you must be at the Kuffner Observatory, near the corner of Ottakring Cemetery. A man with a green jacket over his arm will enquire if anyone from your family is buried there. Reply that you're just going for a walk in the Woods.' She turned fully towards me, as if she was surprised by something I'd said, then suddenly flung her arms around me and kissed me on the lips. 'He'll tell you where to go. Have you got that?'

'How could I forget?' I replied, but it was to the back of her head, for she was already walking away from me, south, across the bridge. 'Everyone's in such a hurry today', I remember musing regretfully, then checked my watch and set off. I turned left at the end of the bridge and set off westwards alongside the Wienfluss. It was only 10.35 and my final destination could be several hours away. As I walked, I cursed the need for security, security, security. It would be so much simpler if they'd just tell me where I was headed for and what I had to do when I got there. Then I remembered an early lesson, only one person must ever know the whole operation. I was just another link in the chain, as was Apfel, however unforgettable. How many more contacts would there be before I arrived at the actual operation, whenever that might be?

I took a circuitous route to the cemetery. Off to the north, still, the noise of artillery, with smoke drifting along the horizon. 'We're getting a hammering at Sandleiten', I thought. 'Ottakring cemetery will be well used in the next few days.'

I crossed Johann-Staud-Straße. There he was, outside the Observatory, as she'd said he would be, a jacket draped over his arm. As I approached, he looked up and turned slightly. The jacket was green. 'Going to the cemetery?' he asked, 'My grandparents lie there, perhaps yours also.'

'No, I'm off for a walk in the Woods.'

'Follow round to the right, keep uphill. Be at the southern end of Kreuzeichenwiese by ten minutes past one.'

Relief coursed through my mind, 'I know it. I was there in January.'

'So, when they picked you, they knew what they were doing', adding, somewhat ruefully, 'for once.' It was the closest to a joke I'd heard in three days. He continued, 'At 12.20 you'll see *ein Jaeger,* a hunter, carrying a hunting rifle by the barrel, upside down. He'll say "No deer today, young man", and you reply, "I'm walking, not hunting." He'll know what you do next.'

All morning, as I'd walked, I'd heard intermittent gunfire in the background, the crackle of rifle fire, the chatter of machine-guns, like tearing paper or ripping cloth, and, every few minutes, the dreadful thump of artillery shook the earth. Here the sounds of battle were closer, and clearer. They were getting a beating, making me think of those comrades, my friends, who were under it. But now even those noises were dying away. 'Sounds as if the Sandleiten Schutzbund have escaped', I said. Then, more gloomily, 'or surrendered.'

Leaving Herr Green Jacket and the houses behind me, the Wienerwald was covered by cloud. Entering the trees, I became enveloped by dark and humid low-lying mist that muffled the gunfire – even now I can remember that smell of dampness. Things had an unearthly air, like the landscape in a dream – or nightmare more likely. I shook myself. I must keep my wits about me, I mustn't be late.

I went along the paths through the trees. I'd thought I'd remember them from my January visit, but they weaved back and forth, in the mist each junction looking the same. Soon I felt lost. Then it came back to me, Green Jacket had said, 'Follow round to the right, uphill.' I forced myself on. A tall water tower, one I'd seen in January, loomed out of the obscurity, half-hidden by grey tree trunks. Now I knew where I was. Next there'd be a clearing, a small meadow. The scent of *Schneeglöckchen,* beautiful snowdrops, came to me, I'd smelt them here before. Suddenly, through the carpet of dead leaves at my feet, there were their unmistakable flowers, somehow giving me confidence.

Ahead some brightness. Through the shifting murkiness I glimpsed a patch of sky. It was enough. I recalled several paths across this meadow, my path lay off to the left. A long-forgotten voice from the Red Falcons came into my head, 'If in doubt, aim off!' So I bore slightly right then, coming up to the trees at the meadow's far edge, turned left. Sure enough, a few metres on, there was the path. I relaxed, 500 metres of woodland and I'd be at the Kreuzeichenwiese.

Light began streaming in from a much bigger clearing. A few more paces and I was in the open. 'Don't stop', I told myself, 'don't hesitate, you're taking a walk in the woods, not on some secret mission. Act naturally, not furtively.' Twelve paces into the clearing and I began to ask myself if I'd missed my contact. I wanted to stop and look about me, but my training urged me, 'just keep on walking.' Then, off to one side, a voice called out, '*Grüß Gott!*' I looked over. A man dressed in the dull green and brown of a jaeger emerged from the tree line, a man in his early forties.

'Why am I surprised by the very thing I am expecting?' I asked myself. More calmly than I felt I replied, 'Grüß Gott.' As I took him in I saw he was carrying over his shoulder a hunting rifle, from my training on the Laaerberg I recognised it as a Mannlicher-Schönauer. Then it dawned on me, he was holding it by its barrel, it was upside down! Relief flooded over me.

'No deer today, young man.'

My head cleared. The response came back to me, 'I'm walking, not hunting.' A smile broke across his face. 'He's in as much danger as me', I thought, 'and just as relieved.'

'I'll talk as we walk', he said. We set off across the open space. At the end, with his free arm, he pointed to the corner of the meadow, 'Follow the track west one kilometre. Amundsenstraße crosses in front of you, it's tarmac, not a track, you won't miss it. Turn left, 350 metres. There you'll see Orange, he knows your codename. His challenge, "Not as warm as it could be", your response, "It's warm enough for me." He'll brief you. Walk, no running, nothing out of the ordinary. If you don't see Orange do not hang about, just get off the road at 350 metres, on the east side, out of sight amongst the trees and wait. Now, repeat to me what I've just told you.'

I did so, then immediately set off – there's no dawdling in such work, no time for idle gossip. Ten metres along the track I looked back, no sign of the jaeger, the mist had swallowed him up.

The stony track had trees on both sides, bare of leaves, looming from the mist like sentinels. Frantically I fixed my mind on my paces, 682, 683, 684... now a track joined this one, from behind my right shoulder, was this the road? No, just another track... 750 metres. Then, as I began doubting my pacing, a glimpse of a grey line to the right, 980 metres, there it was, just ahead of me, a metalled road.

Today everything worked, the contacts, the secret codes, even the distances. Behind me I could again make out the sounds of battle, muffled by the distance from the city and the mist, now thinning, but my Socialist pride was mixed with despair. 'Why can't we be as good at fighting as we are at these intricate underground routines?' I asked myself.

I shook myself – I suddenly felt really cold – turned left and began pacing again, heading south. No one in sight. Would Orange be there? Jaeger had not given me a time to be at the final RV. Was I early? What was the task? Who could be out here, in the middle of nowhere? What, who, could be so important? 300 metres. 325, 350 metres, I'd arrived. No sign of anyone. I glanced around, then, as casually as I could, walked off the road and into the trees to my left. 25 meters in I'd lost sight of the road and ahead of me some undergrowth beckoned. I decided to relieve myself, my excuse for being there. Then, not ten metres away, I heard my name being called, well, today's name at least, 'Birne!'

Cautiously I moved towards the sound, ready to run off at right angles, when I saw a man standing by a tree, a man in his early-twenties. Again the man spoke, 'Birne? It's not as warm as it could be.' I responded, 'It's warm enough for me.'

'Orange?' I asked.

'Yes. You are early, good. In thirty minutes an ambulance will come from the south', he pointed. 'Do not be surprised. It contains someone dressed as a wounded Heimwehr. He is one of us, codename *Clementine*. No need to know who he is and if you recognise him you must forget you ever saw him, that is <u>absolutely</u> vital, now and later. The driver is his guard, codename *Weintraube,* Grape. There's also a doctor with the ambulance, a real doctor, not one of us, but sympathetic and risking his life. Clementine and I will go east into the trees to a small forest lodge. You and *Kirsche,* Cherry, who's due any moment from Penzing', again he pointed down the road to the south, 'are the close perimeter guard, twenty metres from the lodge, under my command and out of sight. We told the other side, the Reds, to bring no security, we're responsible for that. So, two men only, codenames *Kohl,* Cabbage, that is, and *Salat,* Salad. They're on foot, coming from the north-east. I will meet them and take them to the lodge. They'll leave the way they came.'

'Come...', he walked off, bent down and pulled out of the bracken an automatic rifle and a pistol, handing them to me. He bent down again. In his hands were five magazines, two for the pistol, three for the rifle, all loaded. 'I've been told you've fired both weapons. Is that correct?'

'Yes, sir', I replied.

'Good. That sounds like Kirsche. Out of sight!'

A young man was coming through the trees and was challenged by Orange. All was clear and Kirsche was being given his rifle and pistol. Orange was thorough. He took us both to recce the lodge, our positions and our withdrawal route, then handed me a small wooden whistle and Kirsche a plainer tube, 'Try them', Orange ordered, 'use them at the first sign of danger'... for a few seconds the woods echoed to fair imitations of a goose and a deer calling.

Orange resumed his orders, 'A duck call – that's your Jaeger', he pointed to me, 'is one of several sentries a kilometre out from here – would give warning of enemy approaching. Immediately we would put Clementine in the ambulance and the three of us stay until he is clear away. If he is cut off from the ambulance the three of us accompany him on foot south-east through the forest', he pointed. 'You are to shoot anyone, soldier, police or Heimwehr, who is threatening Clementine but NOT, repeat NOT a Heimwehr with bandages on – that will be Clementine himself. You are here to defend him, nobody else. The rest, us and the Reds, just take our chances.'

'Is that clear?'

He recapitulated. 'Any threat or shots, the three of us fight until he has got away, then escape, throwing weapons and ammunition into the undergrowth. But if all goes to plan then the meeting takes place in the lodge, it finishes, the Reds go north, Clementine goes south in the ambulance and you two go southeast towards *Die Jubiläumswarte,* the Jubilee Tower. Your story... You walked out to Jubiläumswarte, then went on to the Schottenhof for a drink but found it closed, now you're walking home.'

He pointed Kirsche to a small thicket, 'To your post. Stay out of sight. Your arc of responsibility, the woods from north to south through east!' To me, 'Arc, the road to the west from north to south. Then he pointed, 'To your posts!'

We took up positions as silently as possible, gingerly loading and cocking our weapons as we did so. I lay still. It was bitterly cold. I remember wanting to reach out and pick a blackberry that hung there, a remnant, so tempting.

Fifteen minutes passed; I heard a vehicle away to the south, approaching along Amundsenstraße.

A decrepit grey van with a red cross on white painted on its side crept into sight through the trees. Wheezing like an old man it pulled to a halt. Orange went forward, spoke to the driver. It spluttered into life once more and moved deeper in until it was largely hidden by the scrub and a fold in the land. I heard it reverse, then reverse again. The engine stopped and silence reigned again. 'He's positioned it to face along its escape route. That driver knows what he's about', I thought.

I watched the road and listened. Nothing, no engine afar off, no sight or sound of pursuit. Over my left shoulder Orange was opening the ambulance's rear doors and helping out an old man, or so he seemed, in the hateful uniform of the Heimwehr. With his head bandaged and left arm in a sling, he looked confused, a touch shambolic. 'Who is he? He reminds me of someone.' They were joined by the driver and a white-coated man from the front of the ambulance. 'His guard and the doctor', I thought. Orange and Clementine set off towards the lodge, the driver and doctor got back into the ambulance.

Silence descended. Slowly the small noises of the woods came back, muffled by the mist. A slight wind stirred the branches. There was no goose call, no duck. Ten minutes passed. Then I heard, off to my right, 100 metres away through the trees, the swish and slight thump of footfalls. Then again, and again, there were more than one of them, clearly walking south down Amundsenstraße. Soon, from my hiding place, I could dimly make them out through the trees, forty metres away. Near me I sensed Orange getting up from his hiding place. Unseen, he watched the men for a few more metres, then began calling softly, 'Kohl! Kohl!'

He went forward and began talking to them, three of them. I saw them through my screen of bushes, twenty-five metres away, detecting from the tone of the whispered conversation and his fierce gesticulations that Orange was angry about something. He walked the visitors past my hiding place, his face thunderous, shepherding them off to my right. 'He doesn't want them to see the ambulance', I thought. The four of them passed within five metres of where I lay in the undergrowth. One of them I recognised immediately, Josef Dycka. He'd worked in Ottakring as a dental technician, years ago, becoming one of the Schutzbund's military experts but, in 1928, he turned Communist and disappeared to Moscow. Now, so café rumour had it, he held high rank in the Red Army.

The second man was older, in his 50's, with long, unruly reddish hair, moustache and short beard. He wore spectacles. He was a little man but had a commanding presence, patrician even. 'He carries himself with authority, not someone to argue with', I thought to myself.

The third man - 'But why three? There were meant to just be two, that's why Orange is so angry' - was young, well dressed, but there was something peculiar about his clothes. Then it dawned, 'I've seen him before', I thought to myself, 'he's that Englishman who hung around the Café Louvre.'

Talking amongst themselves they passed by me, unseen in the bushes. Next, behind me, I heard the murmur of introductions as they met Clementine outside the lodge.

Twenty minutes passed with, occasionally, a raised voice from the lodge. Way off to the north the dire symphony of civil war occasionally made itself heard, the dull 'crump, crump' of artillery fire, or were they explosions? Impossible to tell at this distance. Then, behind me, there was the distinct sound of a door opening and men coming out of the lodge. In a Viennese accent someone said dismissively, 'Leave us, we will discuss in private', and people were walking towards my small thicket.

They stopped within two metres of where I lay. I could distinctly make out their voices, one Viennese: Dycka. Another strongly accented German. What accent? It wasn't Polish. I listened, could it be Russian? No, not quite Russian... Ukrainian, that was it. His voice dominated the conversation, the one giving orders. Dycka was arguing, a mixture of anger and wheedling. The third one spoke less. He clearly knew less German and, from his accent, he was the Englishman. He was taking orders, not giving them.

The older man, the Ukrainian, 'No concessions. They are broken, they do not realise it yet.'

Dycka, 'We should supply them with ammunition. They are running out; we haven't used a single round. Explosives, they have some in Favoriten; none in Dobling, we could...'

'Not a single round or stick! DO you hear? Party orders: NO fighting! NO help! Let the Fascists finish them off. We'll pick up the pieces when it's over.'

The Englishman stammered, 'C-c-can we h-h-help them escape?'

'Escape to Tschechoslowakei? No, that is against Party orders. Make out it is so, of course. Talk it up, put on a show of it, yes, but no effort is to be made that actually supports it. Escape to Spain, on the other hand, yes, to the Soviet Union, definitely. There they'll be under our influence, our command.'

My mind was reeling at this cynical betrayal of socialist comrades. I listened all the more intently.

Again the Englishman spoke. 'And w-w-what are m-m-my orders?'

'Stay close to the Social Democrats, but make no promises, give no real assistance. Give them as much money as you choose, there is plenty, but only to the weak ones, the ones we can bend to our ways. Report all you find out through

Dycka here. Every murmur, every whingeing complaint about their party, every sign of disaffection, corruption or co-operation with the police. To those journalists the same, get close enough to discover each one's weaknesses, every point of pressure, let appearances be deceptive.'

'But I repeat, NO concessions to Bauer. We'll string him along, yes, but we will bury the Social Democrats here, in Vienna. And as to your Labour Party', he must have turned to the Englishman, 'in time we will bury them too!'

From the direction of the lodge came footsteps. The men immediately stopped talking and Orange called them back to the meeting. Barely five minutes later the lodge door opened again and people emerged. All of them. At once the three Communists disappeared northwards, then Clementine and Orange – no, no, not Clementine, I wanted to cry out at the discovery – 'it's Bauer! It's Otto Bauer! The Social Democrat leader! He's the one in the Heimwehr uniform' – but in a moment they had passed by me, Orange leading. Moments later the ambulance's engine started up, doors slammed shut and away it went.

I scanned my front. Nothing. No noise, except that engine fading southwards. Nothing coming down the road from the north. Suddenly I felt all alone in the light mist and surrounding trees. My hands were clammy on the butt of the rifle, a shiver passed down my spine. Was it all a dream? A nightmare? I was horror-struck, my head spinning, struggling with what I'd heard. Then, as when you wake from a bad dream, I heard Orange's voice, quiet but urgent, 'Birne! Birne!' Relief flooded over me. As I got to my feet there he was with Kirsche, beckoning.

Orange seemed distraught, no, furious. 'B...', he stopped himself. 'Clementine says we've been abandoned to our fate', he was struggling to contain himself. 'The Communists won't lift a finger to help us. I will never trust a Red again. They preach revolution but, when it comes, wrap themselves in "Party orders" and let us do the fighting. They can't even keep to simple underground rules. Two men, we said, they brought three. So, in that lodge it was three of them to two of us. And he wasn't even a guard or a guide, so what was he? Who the ...' He looked at us and must have seen two teenage faces staring at him, dumbfounded by his outburst. 'Enough! It's over, everything is over. You two, make your way home.' He led us away, towards the start of our escape route.

Before we parted company, he ordered us to keep quiet about what we'd seen. 'Not today, not tomorrow, not in a year's time are you to speak of what you saw here. I know how difficult it's been for you to stay away from your comrades in the front line, but suppress the need to talk about what you've done today. Not a word! Not to a comrade, your families, your girlfriends! *Stumm,* Dumb!

Do you hear? Give me those weapons, and the alarm calls, and be off with you. *Aufwiedersehn,* Goodbye.'

I remember little of walking home that day. I know I and Kirsche, unspeaking, together passed a couple of ponds half-hidden by overhanging trees, then crossed the meandering, treacherous *Moosgraben,* the Mossy Ditch. Its moss-covered banks, partly hidden by the last dreary drifts of snow, made a dismal contrast with the deep, colourful litter of leaves carpeting most of the Woods. Below the Jubiläumswarte we parted with a brief *'Pfüat di,* Goodbye.' Kirsche walked off east, I headed back south. I paced along the Linzerstraße, my head in a whirl, and crossed the Wienfluss by the Guldenbrücke – for reasons I could not define I wanted to avoid the Hietzingerbrücke – then back to Favoriten through Schönbrunn, then Meidling's Cemetery – ha! From palace gardens to cemetery, perhaps there was some Freudian significance in that. Anyway, it was after six that I arrived back at the door of the flat.

Like some things that day my homecoming is etched in my memory. Even as I approached the front door it was wrenched open from inside and there stood Mama; she must have been keeping watch for my return through the peephole. There was anger in her eyes and she immediately demanded, 'And where have you been? Not a word, with the whole city at war, people dying and wounded, soldiers and police everywhere. Where have you been?'

Her outburst wasn't just anger, she was probably struggling to hide the deep concern which must have been building all day long. I didn't have any answer to satisfy her, I just had to brave it out and let the storm break over me, it would pass.

I wanted to say, 'I have friends and comrades among those dead!' but contented myself with, 'My head was in a whirl, I needed to think. I went for a walk, the longest walk I ever took...' I needed a lie that contained enough truth to cover every eventuality, 'out beyond Jubiläumswarte...'

'You never even said you were going out. I made your lunch and now it's wasted. I've been worrying myself silly all day long', she wrung her hands, but her tone had become less harsh.

I remember smiling inwardly. I'd diverted the storm, but not stilled it. Then I remembered something that would throw her off the scent. 'And a beautiful girl kissed me, a redhead. Now THAT cleared my head more than any walking.'

Immediately her attention shifted. 'Who was she?' she demanded, more stridently than before. 'Do we know her? Is she one of those Socialist girls of yours, all boots and marches but no sense of responsibility, probably cannot cook or keep house!' Then, accusingly, 'Perhaps you spent the day with her, not walking.'

'I don't even know her, Mama. I saw her on the bridge in Hietzing and we got talking, then suddenly she turned, kissed me, then stormed off.' I wasn't sure what Mama was thinking but now I held the stage, so continued, a touch wistfully, 'Unfortunately she was going in the other direction, not to the Wienerwald. I think this war must have affected her mind!'

Chapter 2

From civil war to prison cell, by way of Chvalovice

15th February 1934

Josef: I had little to celebrate that birthday, my eighteenth, when fighting ceased, but the government certainly rejoiced over us. Visiting the Goethehof, von Starhemberg saw forty-two bodies laid out in its shattered wash-house. 'Far too few', he declared.

We will never forget that.

Soon the corpses were gone, the blood hosed away, the rubble, barricades and discarded weapons, the debris of war, all carted off. In the city centre plaster and paint were slapped on to hide bullet and shell holes from reporters. Working-class Favoriten, off any tourist trail, was left to wallow in the wreckage.

Silent crowds watched, expressionless, a hundred elaborate funeral corteges as they trailed through the streets, burying the government's dead with gun carriages and great ceremony. But the police ensured our one thousand dead, men, women and children, enjoyed no pomp. They executed eleven captured Schutzbündler, Dollfuss gloatingly celebrating 'the joyous hangings of wartime.' Other countries protested, so he promised to end hangings in Vienna and, as a good Catholic, he kept his promise; thereafter they only took place in Upper Austria.

Politics ground to a halt; what could anyone do? Many Clerical Fascists, wringing their hands and searching their consciences, retreated from supporting their party; we Social Democrats were angry with Dollfuss, the Heimwehr, the police, even the army. Can you imagine how baffled, how disenchanted we were? We had endless debates, as always. Some hotheads, wanting revolution, tore up their membership cards and joined the Nazis or the Communists. Most simply put their heads down and kept quiet.

Those of us that kept the faith, if that's the word, buried it deep. Our leadership sat quiet as figureheads in *Brünn* – Brno. Active socialists went underground, into pyramids of 'fives', cells of five that had no idea who any others were, so anyone arrested and tortured couldn't give away more names. It was a dangerous time for us, but if you're young you shrug off the risk.

Over black coffee at Siller's Café in March younger members, including the 'Illegals', our subterranean cadres, renamed the Social Democrats as the Revolutionary Socialists.

And me? Well, when you're already underground digging deeper is difficult. My family and friends didn't know I was an illegal, so I kept quiet about what I'd seen and got on with my day job. I expected to be attacked, verbally at least, by those who'd fought, but my apparent inactivity went unnoticed. The families of the dead were too grief-stricken to talk, most real Socialist heroes were dead, some had fled to Russia into Stalin's gulags, or into Spain's other civil war. Those who stayed in Vienna were cowed by unemployment, poverty and police brutality. People remained strangely reticent about what they'd done in '*Der Februar,*' as everyone called it. Three things had burned themselves into my memory: our utter betrayal by the Reds; Mama's greeting, of anger mingled with concern; and a beautiful redhead kissing me out of the blue.

We hid what weapons remained. Machine-gun parts, no longer carelessly hidden in family rucksacks, now were buried deeper under coal heaps in cellars, rifles deep in flower beds.

Franz raised the subject of Bauer's escape. 'Schuschnigg lies about it. He claims Bauer left our fighters in the lurch, fleeing with the party funds to Bratislava. His Reichspost newspaper reported that Bauer crossed into Czechoslovakia even before the fighting started. Now Bauer's own account says he was smuggled out on the 14th by a distinguished Vienna surgeon, disguised as a wounded Heimwehr man.'

He gave me a quizzical look. Was he trying to probe what I knew? 'Most Schutzbündlers don't believe a word the government says, but some do and it's damaging morale.'

All I could say, looking him straight in the eye, was 'Bauer's account sounds good to me.'

Those three Communists still nagged away at me. Cautiously, very cautiously, I asked around. People said Dycka had been in Vienna for ten days but then had dropped out of sight, probably back to Moscow.

I asked about the Ukrainian.

'He's Vladimir Alexeyevich Antonov-Ovseyenko, a hero of 1917, he led the Red Guards storming the Winter Palace. He's famous in the party, very senior, a close ally of Trotsky and the OGPU, so Stalin, fearing him, sent him into political exile as ambassador to Poland. The mystery, everyone said, was, 'what was so important that he showed up in Vienna?'

And that third man?

Franz told me. 'He's the Englishman who hung around the foreign correspondents in Café Louvre. Be very wary of him. He says he's from the British Labour Party, but every intelligence indication is that he's a Communist working for "The World Committee for the Relief of the Victims of German Fascism." That's a Communist front (they can't resist endless, wordy titles) in Paris but everyone knows it's controlled by Moscow. He's living in Leopoldstadt with his girlfriend, Litzi Friedmann. She's openly Communist, and many Socialists in Vienna think he's one too. My contact, Spiro, a journalist, knows this man and warned me. He claimed to Spiro that he had close ties to a senior Soviet officer, allied to OGPU who arrived in Vienna at the start of the civil war. It makes no sense. Why would an Englishman be in the company of such a man? In any event, steer clear, is my advice.'

'What's his name?'

'Philby.'

It meant nothing to me.

There was another Englishman in Vienna, Hugh Gaitskell. We had no doubts about him, he'd proved himself a genuine comrade. He brought funds from the British Labour Party to help families whose breadwinners had died. He bribed officials for false papers and acted as courier to the party's office in Brünn. 'He even took three underground leaders with him on the train to Prague', Franz said, 'that was brave, as that route's particularly hot, and it must have cost a fortune.' He helped over 170 escape. Another Briton praised him, 'He looks so innocent, so unsuitable for clandestine work, but underneath he's active and resourceful, calm and quiet. He has an uncanny ability to unmask traitors in our ranks. A good man.'

Franz himself was involved with those escape routes. He told me, 'We've made useful contacts, professional pepper smugglers and cucumber lorries, travelling between Retz and Znaim... they might prove useful in the future.'

Sometime after Franz's warning, the mystery Englishman married his girlfriend Litzi in the British Embassy, then they disappeared from Vienna. But the underground had already cut all ties with him because the *KPÖ,* the Austrian Communist Party, was riddled with police spies.

Things were terrible in Favoriten. No laughter, no joy, just treachery, fear, conspiratorial huddles, and tears, so many tears. Many men from the Gemeindebauten were 'gone', that hateful word. It could mean many things... escaped, imprisoned, dead or, worst of all, not knowing. In the bullet-scarred Goethehof, where we were distributing aid, a young woman whispered, 'My husband is safe in *Brünn, Gott sei dank,* Brno, thank God. Sixty have gone from this building, forty to Brünn, but eight were killed on the frontier!'

Around her lay her flat, smashed by gunfire, her furniture in splinters, her kitchen stove crumpled like tin foil, with children's books, Christmas decorations, half a doll and a hoop strewn amongst the debris. She said *'Ich bin stumm,* I can't speak.' We could only stand there with her, not knowing what to say. Frieda put her arm around her shoulder. *'Aber es ist meine Wohnung,* But it's my little house', she cried. That had affected Frieda back then, and even now I saw Mary dabbing away a tear from her eyes.

Flat after flat, family after family, heart-breaking stories everywhere. That evening we retreated to a café. The sheer horror of the day broke our silence, the first time we'd openly discussed the war. One comrade spoke up, 'The Communist Party scarcely took part in the battle...'

'Scarcely!' I couldn't stop myself from interrupting. 'They didn't fire a single shot, supply us with a single gun or bullet, or suffer a single casualty! It was *Unsere Genossen,* our comrades, who were killed and wounded, Social Democrats every one, not one Red died. "Scarcely" is scarcely the word for it!'

Around the café people applauded,

'Peppi, Peppi, I misspoke...'

Mary: 'Why did he call you Peppi?'

Josef: 'It's the Italian influence in Vienna, from Giuseppe, Italian for Josef. We Austrians liked it and stole it for ourselves; just as with Mary: a Viennese would call you Mitzi, if they liked you.'

Then somebody else broke in, 'Young Bramminger, you speak powerfully, but are you correct? I've heard Communists helped us in the sewers, and their propaganda daily proclaims how they got people away to Tschechoslowakei. Can you deny that, were you in every front line? Who can say they didn't take part in the battle? Can you?'

With a sudden bitter feeling in my stomach I realised I couldn't tell my story; I was sworn to secrecy. All I could think to say was, 'Well, each of our womenfolk fought and helped in the fight more than all the Reds in the city.'

Franz came up to me afterwards. He spoke quietly. 'Josef, that was well said, but a word of warning...', he looked around before continuing. 'In our world it's best to never draw attention to oneself. I don't know what you got up to that day after we met in the café, but whatever you saw or heard, keep to yourself. Keep your head down, and don't give cause for anyone, police or comrade, to ask what you did in the war. If people accuse you of being a coward, let them. Don't answer back. Inside you'll be crying out to tell the truth, to justify yourself. Don't! In a café, in a police cell, at home, stay silent, always.'

Maybe I should have stayed silent. Even now. It would be the safest way for everyone. Perhaps I should not even be telling you this.

Mary: 'No', I said, 'please. It's important to me.'

March to June

Josef: Now our little bands roamed at night, armed with tins of red paint, the city waking up to the Schutzbund's three red arrows and painted battle cries, 'Down with Fascism', or 'We'll be back!!!' On government posters we bloodied Dollfuss's hands with red ink, adding '*Mörder*, Murderer', put red pimples on Starhemberg's nose and, in cinema foyers, red carnations - our symbol - on Hedy Lamarr's bosom.

May Day was our special effort, flags, banners and leaflets reminding the citizens, 'We're still here!' We thought we saw a collective smile on faces in Vienna that morning.

Most got away with it, but those the police caught disappeared into the '*Liesl*', the prison on Elisabethpromenade, where they endured heavy beatings all over, but always on the genitals. Daily they were sustained, if that's the word, by little more than a slice of bread and the thinnest of coffees, *Kaffee schwitzen*, sweat coffee, we called it, the only coffee that's not on the menu in any Vienna café.

The chestnut trees always bloom in June but, in 1934, they didn't lift our spirits.

25th July

After months of detonating bombs, supplied by Berlin, in railway stations, the Nazis attempted a coup, storming RAVAG's radio studios in Vienna, broadcasting that Dollfuss had resigned and handed over the government. Another group, disguised in army uniforms, arrived in trucks at the Chancellery and bluffed their way inside, locking the great doors behind them and shooting Dollfuss dead. But when the coup collapsed most of the activists fled to Germany.

That week Hans and I started 'night climbing.' Papa, before the accident that saw him pensioned off from the railways, had taught me as a youngster the equipment and techniques for mountain climbing in the Wienerwald's Rodaun quarry. But it wasn't mountains we climbed, it was factory chimneys, pylons, bridges, railway signal gantries, anywhere we could lash a red flag or banner, disappearing into the crowds of spectators before the police turned up.

December

My secret lessons in intelligence and illegality increased, with 101 tricks and deceptions to stay hidden from the police. Number 1, always, 'Punctuality.' Number 2, 'Compartmentalise', concentrate totally on one thing at a time. On they went: use the telephone only in emergencies; part your hair differently; grow a moustache; wear a different hat; learn to jump on a tram, scan your fellow passengers for plain clothes detectives then, if necessary, jump off at the next stop; stay alert for a shadow; take a ferry across the Danube, never a bridge; never walk straight to your destination, set off in the wrong direction then retrace your steps; on a mission take risks early, never near the target.

We learnt about furtive meetings - the most dangerous moment - with informants and couriers at street corners, tram stops, in apartments. Have pre-arranged danger signs: a cactus in the window, or not, a doormat that isn't there, the wrong hand holding the handbag; plan for alternate meeting places. If your contact isn't there, walk past. At the slightest sign of the police, run, we're younger than them. Always having a story ready: pretend you're lovers, the football match you're on your way to, the library book you're returning. Always have a reason for being somewhere; anything to avoid a spell in the dreaded 'Liesl.' And confessions never lighten sentences, they only provide more evidence to the police and courts. Say nothing, at worst just 'yes, no, yes, no.'

When carrying something vital, Franz taught us, hide it well enough to resist casual street searches. He passed on smugglers' tips: hidden bottoms in rucksacks; how the Czechoslovakian diamonds funding our operations came concealed in toothpaste tubes. He told us of one matronly woman who tucked any list you gave her down her ample bosom. 'In it goes', she'd say, laughing, 'money, lists, letters, everything!'

One morning Frieda cheered me up. 'Last night', she said, 'the police went out with a list of ten wanted men. Four weren't at home, three, they later discovered, were already in police cells, one had been in jail for three months and one had died a year earlier. They ended up arresting just one man. They really are blockheads.'

But not a day went by when we didn't expect their hand on our shoulder.

November 1935

Economically things went downhill. Unemployment caught up with me when Heinrich Kästner had to close his shop. Franz gave me occasional work as a delivery boy, but there was little money in it. With three of four children unemployed, and little chance of finding jobs, Mama supported us somehow. It never dawned on her that I was 'working', but underground.

March 1936

One day in March Franz told me and Hans to meet him in the Café Centrale, not our usual haunt. 'Yesterday', he said, 'the Communists floated a balloon with a hammer and sickle on it over the Parliament Building. The Heimwehr failed to shoot it down but few people saw it because it drifted off towards the Alps.'

'A farmer's probably scratching his head up on Semmering, wondering why a balloon is draped over his mountain pasture. We need to seize back the initiative. I want to see a Socialist flag over Favoriten, one that lasts more than five minutes.'

'Leave it to us, Herr Emmerich. We promise...' Hans pointed upwards, 'tomorrow Favoriteners will be seeing red.'

So, that night, we tied our shoes around our necks and climbed the lightning conductor of Favoriten's Water Tower, and at dawn Favoriteners saw a huge red Socialist flag fluttering from its highest point, sixty metres up. All morning happy crowds watched police and firemen struggling with ropes, hooks and ladders to remove it, but the last ten metres was – as mountaineers call it – 'V diff', and defeated them. At lunchtime a patrol car set off for a professional steeplejack, but the only one available was half-way up Stephansdom. It took two more hours to get him down from there and up the Wasserturm, and longer still to get past the barbed wire we'd strung up after us.

Our flag flew for over five hours, and was the topic of conversation in Vienna's cafés for weeks.

Autumn

Frieda was quieter than usual, and often away. Like me she was an illegal but we never discussed that; we never asked each other if we were on some scheme. Then, out of the blue, she suggested a walk in the Wienerwald, collecting fruit for the winter, she said.

All morning we picked raspberries, bilberries, cranberries, everything we could see. We climbed the Jubiläumswarte, and stood, side by side, looking across Vienna. I sensed she was struggling to say something, so I put my arm around her shoulder and said, 'What is it, Frieda? You can tell me.'

Out it came, like uncorking a bottle. She'd met an Englishman, a Herr Kendrick... he worked in their embassy. She became bolder... they'd fallen in love... he'd asked her to marry him.

I was bowled over. We had always been the best of friends yet, for some reason, I'd never thought about Frieda romantically. But here I was, upset, jealous even. 'Does he have a name, this Herr Kendrick, a Christian name? What job has he? Did you say yes?'

She looked at me, perhaps surprised by my tone of voice, but then she smiled, a smile so wide that at that moment I knew I'd lost her. I didn't regret it, she clearly loved this Englishman.

'He's Harold, Harold Kendrick, he does something with passports in their embassy and, yes, I've agreed to be his wife. He is so kind, as *gemütlich* as any one of us...'

Mary: Gemütlich?

Josef: I saw her puzzlement and tried to explain. 'There's no English word for it, nor German to be honest. It's our Viennese mentality, careless, jolly, gay and easy-going, perhaps a touch of laziness.'

Mary: 'My Scottish Presbyterian ancestors wouldn't approve. My Grannie's love was frugality, not frivolity, she taught me to never tell a lie. Although' - I probably looked wistful - 'occasionally she had a twinkle in her eye.'

Tuesday 22nd June 1937

Austrian State Archives, Vienna Conscription Command: Bramminger, Josef. Height 177 cm, weight 69 kg, chest 84 cm. Fit for service, no infirmities. Born 1916, RC, single, lives with parents in Quarinhof. Butcher's assistant, unemployed since Nov 1935. Father State Railways pensioner.

...and Criminal Records: Of sufficiently good repute, nothing adverse on state files, no political activity detected, a paid-up member of Der Bund Neuland Catholic youth group. Not appeared before state courts. Nothing morally held against him. Proceed with conscription. Signed, City Captain.

Josef: My long-expected conscription papers arrived. Nervously I sliced open the envelope, Mama peering over my shoulder. 'Report to 2nd Engineer Battalion'...

'Ha!' Papa slapped me on the back. 'Officers with sense. A railwayman's son to a railway battalion, that's good.'

'A railway battalion?'

'*Eisenbahntruppen,* Railway troops, up at Korneuburg since the 1890's. They're engineers, specialising in laying tracks, building bridges and operating the Army's trains. I was under their orders once, my engine was sent from Südbahnhof to the Tyrol...'

'Yes, Papa.'

1st October

We new conscripts on the train to Korneuburg expected to leisurely amble to the barracks, clutching our suitcases and rucksacks. The army had other ideas. The moment our feet touched the platform a massive and loud sergeant descended on us and marched us – if that's the word – 300 metres to *Albrechtskaserne,* Archduke Albrecht Barracks.

An officer addressed us. 'Men', he said, 'I am *Oberst Ingenieur,* Engineer Colonel Janowsky, your Commanding Officer. I'll say only this: we are the *Schwarz Pionere,* Black Pioneers, because of', he pointed, 'these black collar tabs, but some in the army find it amusing to call us "*Dienstmädchen aller Berufe*"', maids of all work, I think you'd say. 'Let them laugh! If a job's too difficult for the cavalry, gunners or infantry, we do it for them. In August we provided flood relief in Niederrussbach, in November we'll be at the Alpine Engineering School learning to ski and build railways in the mountains, in December you'll learn demolitions near Tschechoslowakei. Could they do that?'

'No Sir!' we chorused.

'Can we?'

'Yes Sir!'

'By the time we've finished with you you'll be soldiers, infantrymen, mountain troops and engineers. But most importantly...' he paused, slowly turned his head, seemingly looking each of us in the eye, 'you'll be Eisenbahntruppen.'

How we cheered!

Two of the other conscripts in the platoon I'd known as comrades for years and we formed a cell: Leo Pröglhöf, a close friend from Favoriten who knew both me and Frieda; and Wilhelm Benko I'd remained in touch with as we'd worked together as butchers, I'd even walked out with his sister Ernestine. The cell's task? To watch and report to Franz every development and the mood of the battalion. Besides us, but unknown to me at first, there was another underground cell in the battalion.

They trained us as soldiers: drilling, saluting, polishing boots, all that; firing, field-firing, firing at night; as infantrymen: estimating ranges, crawling through barbed wire, ditches and every sort of mud. 'Mud', they told us, 'can be hard mud, soft mud, gravelly mud, bottomless mud, mud with ice in it, and the sort you can't tell if it's mud or dirty water. You'll get used to it!'

Finally, we started engineer training. Tools of every description. Wire, great spools of it, plain wire, signals wire and the dreadful *Stacheldraht,* barbed wire. Building railways, permanent way, junctions and bridges. The trains we'd operate on them, and the railway network across Austria and its one-time empire.

Next Captain Unger, our instructor, announced, 'You've learned to build railways, now you're going to demolish them! Over to you, Sarn't-Major.'

'Thank you, sir. Listen in! My name's Kühler, and my job's demolition. On the battlefield we build railways and bridges to advance over but sometimes, when we withdraw - and', glancing across at Unger, 'the Austrian army NEVER retreats, it only ever withdraws - we blow them up...' Then, in that mad army way, he taught us to destroy everything we'd built, as efficiently but considerably faster. They taught us explosive charges, detonating cord, exploder kits, how to booby-trap equipment and, for some dark, atavistic, Freudian reason we enjoyed demolishing things more than we ever had building them.

December

A company training day was announced, 'Delays and Demolitions', near the Czechoslovakian border, north of Vienna. In front of Hollabrunn station the sergeant-major shouted 'Off the trucks.' Then, on the platform, Captain Unger addressed us: 'Our task is to slow down invading armies, so we blow the bridges. Better still, if there's one handy, a tunnel. We'd use *Die Schienenwolf,* the Rail Wolf, an armoured plough that can rip through the sleepers, but we don't happen to have one with us. We could destroy this platform,' pointing down, 'the points, or cut the railway track. What's the best track to cut?' He looked around us... 'Bramminger?'

'A curve, Sir.'

'Why?'

'Takes longer to replace than a straight rail, Sir.'

'Good answer, that man. The aim's to slow 'em down, slow 'em down! Five minutes spent on demolition to slow their advance by five hours is time well spent. Back on the trucks!'

Soon we were in the back of the trucks watching passing countryside. Something from an old Schutzbund lesson was nagging at me, 'Keep your eyes open! Remember this!' In my head, I started to take note of all I was seeing...

Our route northwards took us through a small town, Guntersdorf, with its great *schloß,* or castle, a prominent church tower and steeple, then we turned off northwards along what was once the Prague road, I suspected, now just a lane. Next, at a white shrine on the roadside, we branched half-left into an avenue of lime trees. Minutes later we'd stopped on a verge beside a tarmac road, a railway embankment looming over us.

'Off the trucks', chorused the sergeants.

We climbed steps of wooden sleepers staked against the embankment. Sergeant Gloeckner pointed at them, 'What do you call those?' No-one answered.

'Spare timber *für das Eisenbahntruppen,* for railway engineers. Remember that', he said.

'Get a move on!'

January to February 1938

In January 1938 our training for an unlikely war with Czechoslovakia suddenly turned into training for a more likely real one, and against a more dangerous enemy. General Jansa, the Chief of Staff, devised *Betrieb Zeitgewinn,* Operation Saving Time, a strategy to resist the German Wehrmacht long enough to allow Austria to obtain foreign military allies. Destroying bridges and roads with explosives, laying mines and tank traps was just what we'd trained for so morale rose – apart from that of the few Nazi sympathisers in our ranks.

On 1st February a Nazi coup seemed likely, even though less than 5% of soldiers or officers in the army belonged to the Nazi's *Soldatenring,* or Soldiers' Ring, but the Bundesheer was ordered to increase readiness and double all guards. On the 12th, when Schuschnigg went to Berchtesgaden to meet Hitler, the army's morale was excellent; if ordered to fight we would. I reported all this to Franz.

At Berchtesgaden, Schuschnigg made some apparently minor concessions to save Austria, then, a fortnight later, he gave a defiant speech affirming Austria's independence. He strode along the Ringstraße at the head of huge, cheering crowds. All was going well.

3rd to 8th March

Next the army mobilized: artillery, barbed wire and concrete blocks on road junctions, machine-guns on city streets. Schuschnigg opened negotiations with his one-time enemies, the workers. A million of them, across the country, declared their willingness to defend Austria against German attack. In theatres and cinemas every mention of Austrian independence was greeted by spontaneous ovation. He'd caught the popular mood.

Numerous reservists joined us in Korneuburg barracks, even those from 1915 were called up. Next came the order: 'All troops confined to barracks.'

Next, General Jansa was forced to resign by Minister of the Interior Seyss-Inquart, an Austrian Nazi. His appointment, ordered by Berlin, had been one of Schuschnigg's 'minor concessions.'

9th to 10th March

Now came the raw politics, a real roller-coaster ride. In Innsbruck, surrounded by our national colours in great banks of red, white and red flowers, Schuschnigg unexpectedly announced a plebiscite in four days time. 'For a free and independent Austria', he proclaimed, 'with equal treatment for all. I stand and fall by this confirmation of the Austrian people! Red-white-red until we're dead.' His speech was cheered to the echo, Fatherland Front supporters greeted Schuschnigg's train at Westbahnhof, shouting the slogan. The Nazis, outnumbered, slunk off the streets, their swastikas swamped by patriotic flags and badges.

The next day the Nazis issued secret orders to their Soldatenring. They were not to vote in the plebiscite but were to hoist swastika flags in barracks, disobey any orders to fire and allow the Nazi's *Sturmabteilung*, that's their party's stormtroopers, the SA, free passage through any barriers. All this we detected and passed to Franz.

Friday 11th March

The atmosphere in Vienna was electric. Schuschnigg's plebiscite was popular. His propaganda planes circled over the Innere Stadt, scattering leaflets like snow across the streets, election lorries careered around, full of young men and women with placards reading, 'Yes! With Schuschnigg for a free Austria', cheered on by pedestrians. For once Socialists, Monarchists, the Fatherland Front, the Catholics and Communists were united, and this new coalition thought it controlled the streets.

The Nazis still held their rallies, but away from the streets. The rhythmic throbbing of *Deren Sprechchöre* – their chants, senseless reiteration of howling, blind, shrieking frenzy, was like some ju-ju ceremony aiming to destroy the brain's ability to reason - seemed audible across the city, but always in the background, offstage, a menacing noise.

One minute the government was defiantly backing its plebiscite, the police were on 'our' side (even though, as it turned out, many had swastikas armbands hidden in their pockets), the army was preparing to defend the country... and the next?

The next, in an instant, all that was gone...

Out of the blue the Chancellor broadcast. Hitler, he said, had demanded the plebiscite be postponed, that he resign and hand government over to Seyss-Inquart. If he disobeyed, Germany would invade Austria.

'Rather than shed German blood', Schuschnigg announced, 'I have yielded to force. The army is to withdraw without resistance.'

He ended his speech, 'I take my leave of the Austrian people with this heartfelt wish: *Gott schütze Österreich,* God protect Austria.' The Austrian national anthem was played, for the last time.

Minutes later he was a prisoner of youths in white stockings and close-cropped hair who'd invaded the Chancellery. Our new masters.

Outside, the line of police gave way. With a yell of triumph, a demonic, brown-coated mob of Storm Troopers, Hitler Youth and teenagers brandishing flaming torches and wildly shrieking 'Heil Hitler!', 'Death to Jews!', 'Hang Schuschnigg!', swept through Vienna's streets, overwhelming everything in its path. With faces distorted by hatred and bitterness, and that unceasing, rhythmic chanting. It was like a flood of sewage, or as if the gates of hell had opened and the foulest, most unclean spirits had been let loose.

And me? What was I doing in all this? Up in Korneuburg we were doing everything – 'On the trucks!', 'Off the trucks!', 'Do this! Do that!', the usual frantic activity of an army preparing for battle – and nothing. For, when it came to it, we remained confined to barracks, we weren't allowed to go to war.

Saturday 12th March, Anschluß

At dawn, and for the following three days and nights, hundreds of German aircraft filled Vienna's skies, circling endlessly over every district, including Korneuburg. It was devastating, the noise paralyzing, the unspoken message: 'Resistance is useless.'

Then came the noise of the Wehrmacht's guns and tanks grinding around the Ringstraße. Huge crowds sang out as each weapon thundered by, *'Wir danken unserem Führer!'* Time after time, gun after gun, tank after tank, 'We thank our Führer!' and that ludicrous salute. It was mass hysteria, utter madness.

Within moments swastikas hung from every window. German uniforms filled the hotels. All night long streets were filled with torchlight processions of teenagers, boys and girls. Uniformed young men charged about in stolen vehicles, smashing their way into homes, dragging people away. Jews, men, women, children, all were hauled from their homes, made to crawl, were beaten, and worse. There were shots in the night. None were investigated. Under orders from their new masters the police stayed inside their stations.

Two days later, the Führer entered his country of birth, progressing from Linz along roads lined by excited crowds. Cardinal Innitzer ordered every church tower be bedecked in swastikas and ring its bells as Hitler passed. He arrived in Vienna in his six-wheeled, open-topped, built-to-impress Mercedes-Benz. He was stiff and upright, his arm jerking from time to time like some asinine puppet. Outside the Hotel Imperial – swathed in swastikas, in black, white and red – hundreds of thousands of adoring Viennese waved and cheered, bursting into frenzies of chanting, *'Sieg heil! Sieg heil!* Hail to victory! Hail to Victory!', or 'Hitler! Hitler! Hitler!' His speech from the first-floor balcony was rapturously received by crowds, their faces shining in ecstasy.

He stayed just twenty-four hours. The next day he flew back to Munich.

March to April

If the Wehrmacht's speed was rapid, the Gestapo's was stunning. Almost overnight they imprisoned or brutally killed 69,000... 69,000! Can you even imagine such a number? Anyone who threatened the new regime, anti-Nazis, Jews, Socialists, Communists, Monarchists, active Catholics, anyone, simply disappeared from view.

Even Major Fey was dealt with by the Gestapo. I reminded Frieda of Major Fey's proclamation in 1934, '"I'll turn the Blue Danube red with Socialist blood"; now listen to this, from the newspaper: "Three metal cylinders were carried from his apartment containing his body, his wife's and their son's. He lost his nerve, murdered them and his fierce dog, then he killed himself."'

Frieda said, 'They say he shot himself twenty-three times. But how could he shoot a dog?'

'You are mistaken', I said, '"The dog, it says, also committed suicide."'

All soldiers - overnight we became German nationals and members of the Wehrmacht - had to take an oath to the new leader: 'I swear by God this sacred oath that I will give absolute obedience to the Führer of the Reich and people, Adolf Hitler, the Supreme Commander of the Wehrmacht, and will be ready, at all times, as a brave soldier, to lay down my life to this oath.'

Franz ordered us to do this. 'Brünn says all illegals must. You're no use to us in prison.' So, I swore the oath.

That same day the Minister of Defence was dismissed, his predecessor murdered, 67 officers were sacked and 30 who'd refused to take the oath were punished severely, some died later in Dachau. I know, it was amongst the intelligence I passed to Franz.

We were marched to the Quartermaster's to be kitted out with German uniforms. Except, wonder of wonders, the Germans were not so efficient after all. They hadn't enough Wehrmacht tunics and trousers, so we marched out only with new cap badges and belt buckles. We were happy to keep our old uniforms, but we kept it to ourselves.

That evening, walking home on leave, I saw on a ladder a workman with a swastika armband hoisting up a street sign, 'Adolf Hitler Platz.' The discarded sign, 'Dollfuß Platz', lay forlornly on the pavement.

At home Papa was chuckling to himself. 'Yesterday', he said, 'my old friend Stefan was on Westbahnhof's platform when the security people turned up in force to expel an English journalist called Gedye. The Gestapo, Kriminalpolizei, uniforms, they were all on the platform, plus a crowd of this man's friends, foreign journalists who'd gone to see him off. The Germans pushed him into a carriage and the train started. But - you'll like this - Stefan swears that as the carriage pulled out, he saw the man's dog at the window with its paw raised in the Nazi salute!'

Mama said sharply 'You mustn't repeat such stories, we'll all be arrested, and if you cared about your friend Stefan, you'd keep quiet.'

My father winked at me. I smiled and said nothing, but inside I was laughing.

Back in barracks, Leo asked, 'Have you seen Part Two orders? No civvies out of barracks, we can only walk out in uniform.' He grimaced, 'Nobody trusts us.'

Hitler's new plebiscite was heralded across the country by fireworks, bonfires on mountain tops, and searchlights. 2 PB was sent with huge anti-aircraft searchlights from Korneuburg to Stephansplatz to build 'a cathedral of light' over Stephansdom's great spire. German officers marched about all afternoon with maps and theodolites, while we manoeuvred the searchlights into position across the Innere Stadt to create a cone of light with their beams.

The next morning, 9th April, just as we switched off the searchlights, every church bell across Vienna started ringing, ordered once again by Cardinal Innitzer. The sound left me feeling sick inside.

10th April

It was all window-dressing for the farce that followed at the polling stations. For days posters had been on trees, lamp posts and buildings across the city screaming '*Das Ganze Volk Sagt am Zehntes April Ja!*' that means, The Whole People Say Yes on 10th April! A grim-faced Führer stared menacingly from every hoarding. The voting paper read: 'Do you agree with the reunification of Austria with the German Reich that was enacted on 13 March, and do you vote for the party of our leader Adolf Hitler?'...

ADOLF HITLER?

and, unlike the Nazis, I exaggerate not.

People could vote in secret in booths but were 'expected' to vote across open tables – woe betide anyone who didn't. 'Why bother with booths?' they were asked, 'of course you are for *Anschluß,* Connection. It's a rubber stamp. Who's going to throw the Germans out?'

It all worked as planned. That evening Vienna reported to Berlin a 99.73% vote in favour. That night I was on sentry and had the keys to the orderly room. There I found out how the 500 men in the battalion had actually voted. Just seven had cast their votes against the Anschluß, most of them officers. Within days they were out of the army and under surveillance. All this went back to Franz.

But that same night someone climbed Stephansdom's spire and attached a red flag bearing the word 'Nein.' At dawn every steeplejack in the city was dragged out of bed by German soldiers and eventually one of them scaled the spire and cut down the highly offensive flag – offensive to Berlin, that is. Every man, woman and child in Vienna had seen it and was discussing the unknown hero's epic climb. '*Ein neuer Starhemberg, A* new Starhemberg', he was nicknamed, after Vienna's 17th century hero. In our barrack-room someone joked, 'It's rumoured he once worked in the circus, and his nickname's *Die Akrobat.* You used to be an acrobat, didn't you, Studeny?'

Across the barrack room Franz Studeny visibly paled. 'Don't joke about such things', he croaked. 'After the February war I went to jail. That's not my way, not now, everyone knows this. Anyway, I was on guard last night, here in barracks. Why, Peppi, you were with me. Tell them.'

I admitted we'd be on the gate together.

'Just don't say such things. You could put me in the Metropol, and for no reason.' That word sent a shiver through everyone of us. Gestapo headquarters, the old hotel had already gained a notorious reputation. Conversation turned to other things.

Two rumours ran around the city. In Innervillgraten in East Tyrol, it was whispered, cut off by heavy snow, 95% of the villagers turned out for Schuschnigg's original plebiscite and voted yes to 'a free and German, independent and social, Christian and united Austria.' And 90% of Austrian priests at a theological college in the Italian port of Gaeta had rejected the Anschluß in Hitler's second plebiscite. The Nazis ignored the first and ridiculed the second, calling it '*Die Schande von Gaeta.*' So, in Vienna people talked openly of 'the Shame of Gaeta', it was the only safe way of conveying doubts about the plebiscite.

I've never been a regular church-goer; at the festivals, yes, or in particularly difficult times. Perhaps that's what led me, one Sunday in April, to attend mass in St Stephan's.

Fixed in my memory is its cool, dim interior, and the uniformed SS officer who received Communion alongside me. I saw him make the sign of the cross.

But if I could scarcely believe that - an Austrian SS officer in church, at Mass - what followed I can barely repeat... minutes later we all left the cathedral, out onto Stephansplatz. There were some gypsies in the square and this officer just went across to them, threw three of them against the cathedral wall, drew his pistol and shot them dead.

Across Stephansplatz two watching policemen did nothing, a priest hurried by. Were they unmoved? What were they thinking? Utter disbelief, disgust, fear? The same as me, I suppose, total, mind-numbing shock and craven cowardice.

And, like them, I did nothing, just walked quickly away. I was so revolted that in a side street I vomited violently into a doorway. But whether from disgust at the evil I'd witnessed or at my own inaction... I still don't know...

Mary: A silence fell between us. I was struggling to take it in.

Josef: She put her arms around me, 'Oh, Josef, how utterly terrible it must have been!'

May

By mid-May - I remember it for the scent of lilac, Vienna always smells of lilac in May - I was reporting to Franz a shift of opinion against our conquerors: 'After Anschluß officers and SNCO's greeted one another with "Heil Hitler", as ordered. They've reverted to Grüß Gott. The rest of us irritate our conquerors by using "our" words instead of theirs, so *Erdapfel* for potatoes, not *Kartoffeln*, and *Paradiesapfel* for tomatoes, not *Tomaten*. The German officers who have replaced our own can only scowl at our sins.'

I told how one of the two Nazis privates in our barrack room, Ernst Gombotz, had tried to 'order' us all to say Heil Hitler instead of Grüß Gott. Everyone told him to 'Put a sock in it', 'Oh shut up, *Männchen* - little man.' He persisted, '*Der Reichsstatthalter* - The Reich Governor, has ordered all citizens...' until a boot accurately hurled from a corner of the room shut him up.

June

I told Franz we'd obtained duplicate keys for the regimental armoury. Eventually an order came from Brünn, 'steal some weapons.' So, at two o'clock one morning, with the three of us on guard together, we broke in and stole three pistols and two machine-guns. I was stashing the pistols when, unexpectedly, Corporal Wenzel came round the corner. He was my section commander and off-duty, but I was holding two pistols, hardly the weapons of a patrolling sentry. What would he do? One shout from him and the rest of the guard would have turned out, my future very bleak.

'Bramminger', he said, 'I always suspected you were a secret Social Democrat and I can sympathise with that, but your way isn't mine. This', he gestured at the armoury, 'is your way. Mine is to do my job, say "Grüß Gott" when I should be saying "Sieg Heil" but to keep my head down. Now I'll stagger off to my bed, blind drunk as I am...'

'But *Korp*, you're stone cold sober.'

'Bramminger', he said, 'sometimes you're not so bright. "I'm blind drunk" means I cannot see what's in front of me, so I'll wake up in the morning with a hangover, not remembering what I saw tonight.'

'Got it, *Korporal*.'

'On your way. And', over his shoulder as he staggered away, 'the best of luck to you.'

I was glad, two days later, when we walked up the Bisamberg with five weapons in our rucksacks. It's three kilometres south of Korneuburg, but it felt like thirty, because if we'd been stopped... well, we'd have had no explanation. I was highly relieved when, near the summit, Franz's contact stepped out from behind an oak tree.

Wednesday 6th July

Suddenly my double life collapsed around me. The Chief Clerk called me in. 'Complaints had been received about you for illegal activity against the new regime', he said, 'you're to report to Army HQ in central Vienna at 0800 on Monday 11th.'

I immediately applied for weekend compassionate leave, but my company was on guard duty so I couldn't get a message out to Franz for an emergency meeting. I had to sit it out for three days.

Saturday 9th to Tuesday 12th July

Mid-afternoon that Saturday, the moment my duty ended, I picked up my rucksack and hitched a lift in the regimental ration lorry to the meat market at Sankt Marx. I asked the driver to drop me off on the Rennweg; for both our sakes I didn't want him to know my real destination. A short walk along Fasangasse took me to Café Meteor, Franz's favourite haunt. He wasn't there so I left a message for him, 'I've a stamp to sell, an 1890 crown red. Are you interested?' It was 17.30 when I arrived home at Quarinhof. As I approached that familiar front door, normally such a comforting sight, I no longer felt safe. I'd never known such a bitter mix of anger and regret, of unpleasant memories fighting with happy ones, but from somewhere came the courage to put my key in the lock, turn it and walk in.

Ignoring Mama's cries, 'You come home in your dirty army boots. You treat it like an hotel...', ignoring Papa as he struggled out of his chair, ignoring even the enticing smell from the kitchen of parsley and buttered new potatoes – I didn't dare speak; I'd have erupted in anger, or burst into tears – I silently walked into the bedroom, closing the door behind me.

A tap on the door and my father entered, closing it behind him, his finger to his lips. With Mama out of sight and hearing, it seemed, he could speak. 'So, the time has come, you must leave us? Mama...' he seemed lost for words, but he gathered himself together, 'she cannot see clearly. Remember us, as once we were.' Odd, it was said as a question. He turned and quietly went out the door.

I quickly changed into civvies, snatched an album from my stamp collection, packed my uniform into the rucksack, strapped my greatcoat across the top, and turned to go. I steeled myself. I must go. Something inside was telling me, urgently, my life could depend on leaving home and family immediately. Opening the door, I strode across that small room. Papa stood gazing through the window, his back to me. I brushed past Mama, trying to keep her words out of my ears... 'They've been told, they know you're involved with the underground. And all your "comrades", those so-called friends of yours', she said it so scornfully, 'We've reported you as a traitor. They'll be seeing you next week.'

Mama using <u>that</u> word, 'They', had penetrated my defences. My mind reeled. Had I been betrayed by my own mother to the Gestapo? My heart was urging me to look back, to think of my parents, of how they must be feeling. Into my head came the words, 'Honour thy father and thy mother', but it was neither head nor heart that answered, it was the pit of my stomach, 'Not now, not now', it said. I didn't argue, to stay alive I had to go. I strode through that front door, closing it firmly behind me...

Mary: 'It must have felt like closing the door on your life.'

Josef: I thought to myself, 'So she understands. Thank God.'

If I hadn't raced down that oh-so-familiar staircase I think my resolve would have failed me.

I headed back northwards in a tram. I needed to suppress my emotions, to review things. The code message I'd left in the Meteor was fine: the *num-*

ber gave Franz the time of the meeting, *red* said emergency and *crown* the second meeting place on our list. I had some money to survive on and a safe address for two nights. But had Franz received my message? Was he available at short notice? Only time would tell. That journey was an agony of anguished memories and, I'll be honest, sheer terror. Finally, at 18.09 in the Alpengarten, across from Swiss Gardens, I saw the most reassuring sight, Franz, sitting calmly on a bench.

He listened to my story. How two illegal comrades had escaped recently. Wilhelm Benko had been building bridges over the *Donaukanal* - Danube Canal, when he was ordered to return immediately. Warned that he was to be arrested he'd somehow got into the barracks unobserved, grabbed his documents and escaped. A week later the other lad, Gustav Schmidt, also fled just before he was to be arrested. Everyone in the battalion was talking about it. A headquarters' clerk told me that units waited forty-eight hours before reporting absences so, on Monday, I'd just be AWOL, not a deserter, but how long would I go undetected?

Franz nodded, 'Go on.'

'The Gestapo are on the alert and systematically investigating our battalion. On 6th July I got the order to report to Army HQ in Vienna at 08.00 on the 11th, this coming Monday. With accusations of political activity against me I'd be with the Gestapo within the hour. Today is my first chance to get away from barracks.'

I didn't say my own mother had reported me. Some secrets are too deep.

Franz said, 'The Gestapo tortured Haas for days on end in their Chamber of Mirrors in the Metropol. No-one walks free from there. We must get you out of Austria, Josef, and fast.'

Soon we were squeezed into the projection room of a nearby cinema with its projectionist, Herr Kucera, Franz's contact with Czechoslovak intelligence. He explained, 'Monday will be the first opportunity for my courier to pass Herr Emmerich's letter to your Social Democrats' office in Brno, in order that Prague authorities will be expecting your arrival in Czechoslovakia. That will help when you're over the frontier, but you must stay out of harm's way until then or Czechoslovak border guards might hand you straight over to the SS's *VGAD, die Verstärkter Grenzaufsichtsdienst* - Reinforced Border Control Service. But get to a Czechoslovak police station after Monday night and you'll be passed to the right people.'

Franz turned to me. 'I'll meet you on Monday evening with forged passes and brief you on the route. Can you stay hidden until then?'

'I dare not go home again. When the Chief Clerk - it's whispered he was once a Social Democrat - gave me the order I said I'd go home for the weekend. He gave me the strangest look and said, "I wouldn't advise it." Then he stood up abruptly and walked past me out of the room, knocking a file off his desk, which landed at my feet. I bent down to pick it up, it was my own file! Inside was the letter to our Security Officer from Army HQ, passing on the accusation of political activity. Chiefy granted me compassionate leave this weekend to visit my ailing grandmother in Traunfeld, north-east of Korneuburg. That's what he wrote down, it'll be the first place they look.'

Franz gave me strict orders to stay put until Monday evening and I slept in the flat of Herr Ziegel, a contact of Frieda's husband, Herr Kendrick. Ziegel was a stamp collector, and, thank God, no one came calling. I packed into the bottom of my rucksack my bayonet, two things I'd taken for Czechoslovak intelligence, what money I had, then, on top of them my dirty underwear. Next in went my reserve, the stamp album I'd rescued from home. Also, like any good Austrian, I had a pouch of personal documents - birth and school certificates, trade qualifications, etc - extracted from my orderly room file when I was on guard duty. All went into the rucksack.

On Monday evening I turned into the Hauptallee. Broad, lined with chestnuts, it runs straight as a die through the Prater, not ideal for a secret meeting you might think, but I'd glanced behind while bending down to re-tie my bootlaces, no shadow. I had to concentrate. These were my last hours in Vienna and I'd be meeting Franz for possibly the last time. At 21.00, in the growing twilight, I turned off through the trees to the edge of the Heustadlwasser.

Franz stood at the water's edge.

He briefed me as we walked. 'Most escapees go eastwards into Czechoslovakia by rail or through the woods and marshes along the border. Your grandparents live in Traunfeld, north-east of Vienna, so "They" will expect you to go from there. For people under immediate threat we have a special escape line, set up by our man in Prague. His underground railway has smuggled 100 people over the border near Znaim and, while They know of it, They don't know its routes. At short notice I couldn't organise a frontier guide for you, but I'll tell you what I know. A word of warning, however: tell no-one, and I mean no-one, about your route. Not now, not inside Czechoslovakia. They have people inside our organisation and have tried to kill or kidnap refugees even there, so beware.'

I asked, 'What is the border? A fence? Posts?'

'Stone posts, square, white, sixty centimetres tall, Ö on our side, Č on the Czechoslovak, always visible one post from the other. Rumour, probably a Gestapo fairy tale put about to unsettle us, says the VGAD are erecting a false frontier inside the real one.'

'Take a minimum of luggage...' Franz nodded at the rucksack I lifted up, 'that's fine. But if you're wearing that', he gestured at my clothing, 'I hope you have a convincing story for travelling to Retz.'

'I think it stands up.'

'Well, recently a man travelled via Retz at night, so he dressed all in black. But as he walked through the town he was followed by children – a regular Pied Piper – hailing him as a priest because of his black clothes. His "camouflage" made him more rather than less conspicuous, so let's hope that...' he gestured again, 'proves *ein Doppel-Bluff* – a double bluff.'

He continued, 'The Gestapo watch all Prague trains. For 90 years the immigrants' front door to Vienna has been watched. But you're taking the side exit, stage left, so to speak, so while their attention is focused on trains heading north-east into Czechoslovakia you'll be on a train heading north-west into rural Austria. Now, about the route at the border...'

'Only tell me routes a kilometre from it. I'll go via Retz, but no need for me to tell you how I'll get to the border from there, that way...'

'...that way, if they arrest me, I can't tell them what I don't know. I wish all my pupils had a head for security.' He carried on, 'From Retz to the border you can go north, middle or east. North is short but highly dangerous; middle is longer, still dangerous; east is longest but least dangerous ...'

'I'll tell you a useful trick for buying tickets. And...', he paused for effect, 'you can pick up one of those pistols you stole.' Then Franz suggested a farewell coffee at the Café Diglas in Wollzeile.

I was astonished. 'That's where the Monarchists met. Do we want to be seen there?'

'We'd rather not be seen anywhere, but half the staff of my favourite café, the Meteor, are paid by the police, the other half by the Gestapo. In the Diglas nobody has any idea who I am, or you. It's called hiding in plain sight.'

After that final coffee in the Diglas, and a final '*Wir sehen uns wieder* – We'll meet again', I set off for the lamppost where Franz had secreted that pistol and two loaded magazines. 'It's behind the inspection cover', he'd explained.

Into the rucksack they went, pistol and magazines. Then off to the station through dimly lit streets. In my mind each shadow hid a watcher but I used every trick I'd ever learnt to evade followers, pacing myself to arrive at the station with just enough time to buy a ticket but none to hang around waiting.

Nordbahnhof is all turrets, mock battlements, frescoes and sculptures, ornate as any fairy-tale castle. I went straight to the ticket office window and put down a Reichsmark. '*Eine Rückfahrkarte für die 2330 nach Hofern, bitte* – One return for the 2330 to Hofern, please.' The ticket seller looked up at me and smiled, 'You're quite the German warrior, young Josef.'

'Not by choice.' It slipped out. 'What an idiot', I thought to myself, 'now's not the moment for taking risks.'

But, from the look on his face, my foolish response seemed to have heartened the man. 'You probably don't remember me', he said, 'Walter Leutken, I worked for years with your father at Südbahnhof and I remember you, as a youngster. He used to smuggle you onto his engine. How is he now, *Genosse*?'

I breathed a sigh of relief. He'd called me comrade, an enormous risk, he must still be a Social Democrat at heart.

'I remember you well, Herr Leutken, and those trips...', I smiled at the memory. 'Papa's well enough, on a pension, better off than most. And you say "Genosse"... certainly. So please don't tell my parents you've seen me. They'll only want to know who I'm going to see.'

I wanted him to think I was off to see a girlfriend.

Ticket in hand I walked across the concourse. Passengers pouring off the train from Prague were being controlled by two SS officers and three Gestapo. They lunged at a woman traveller, who screamed and struggled violently as she was bundled away. With peoples' eyes on that commotion I slipped past to Platform 3 and joined a short queue for the ticket collector. Moments later my own ticket was punched and I was walking down a nearly deserted platform, no one taking the slightest interest in me. Franz had been right. 'They' had orders to watch the Prague trains, Retz didn't interest them.

I'd crossed the first hurdle.

.....

From the end of the platform I looked at the lights around *Die Reisenrad* – the Great Wheel, and across Vienna to the red light atop Stephansdom's steeple. 'How long before I see you two again?' I asked myself, then got into the middle carriage. The train was nearly empty, it smelt of axle grease.

The guard's whistle, 'Vienna's parting sound', I thought. We were off, over the Danube, past the Bisamberg transmitter's red lights. Two minutes later the train passed through Korneuburg station. I made out the barracks and, as the lights of the guardroom came into view, went to duck below the window before remembering, 'They don't even know I'm deserting, not yet.'

As the train trundled into the moonlit countryside I tried to relax, but couldn't stop turning over and over in my mind the risks, the what-ifs... 'The ticket inspector will be coming round. No. No. Not here, and, anyway, most railwaymen are Social Democrats, or once were. Remember Herr Leutken.' Then, 'What about roving VGAD checks? No, not yet, stop worrying!' I'd endlessly rehearsed my story: I was visiting Ernestine, the old girl friend, at her address in Retz. 'I'm in the clear, I've nothing incriminating on me...' all of sudden a warning sounded in my head like a klaxon. 'What about those two documents, and the pistol?' Suddenly I was fully alert. 'How stupid am I? That manual's only restricted, I can say I'm taking it to learn on leave. But the one with "SECRET" on every page, would never be bedtime reading. And the pistol... !' I broke into a cold sweat. Abruptly I stood up, and stuffed my knapsack under the seat opposite. I sat down with my heart pounding.

The train passed through a station without stopping, a dimly lit platform sign flashed past, 'Spillern', then the train was slowing for Stockerau. The door opened and a farmer and his son sat down diagonally across from me. A whistle sent us on our way, the train pulling to the right as it headed north, out of the Danube valley.

The smell in the carriage reminded me of school, the same cheap floor polish. I sat thinking of friends, Leo, still in barracks, of Franz and Ernestine. I tried to think about Mama, to answer the question 'Why?' Why had she – I just knew it was her, not Papa – reported me to the Gestapo? Did she truly believe in Nazism? Had her devotion to the Habsburgs, rudely shattered in 1918, warped into this new creed? Was it the same with my sister? And if her, why not me? My brain refused to grapple... it wandered. What of the future? What awaited me? Where? What would I be doing? Who would I meet? Would I fall in love again? Maybe I'd fall at the next hurdle and be taken back to Vienna, spotted by some eagle-eyed border guard. To face what? God only knew.

I gave up trying to think and, somewhere deep inside, said a prayer, putting everything into God's hands. One by one my thoughts and fears fell away and I felt calm again. Across the compartment the father and son were dozing, heads slumped. I kept repeating to myself, 'I mustn't fall asleep, I mustn't fall asleep.' I'd memorised the sequence of stations and checked them off one by one.

Spillern, Stockerau, Sierndorf, yes. Hollabrunn was next. Soon we'd pulled into its station. That November training exercise when Captain Unger had talked of blowing up its platform came to mind.

I'd bought a ticket to Hofern station, <u>beyond</u> Retz – Franz's trick. Actually, I'd be getting off before either of those at Guntersdorf. It was further from the border, a border-crosser's least likely dropping-off point.

I heard a carriage door opening. Suddenly two VGAD men – they must have boarded at Hollabrunn – were standing in front of me, the younger one demanding officiously, '*Ticket! Border-Pass und Reiseerlaubnis!* Ticket! Border pass and travel permit!'

'He has the look and zeal of a true Nazi', I thought, as I handed over my ticket.

'*Dieses Ticket ist für Hofern. Sie sind auf dem falschen Zug! Dieser Zug geht nur bis Znaim. Sie müssen sofort aussteigen!*' This ticket is for Hofern. You are on the wrong train! This train goes only to Znaim. You must get off at Retz! His tone was sneering – how those Party men hated soldiers! But their only real interest was in border-crossers so off they strode to the next carriage. I got up – the father and son were already asleep again – pulled out my rucksack and sat down. Franz's wrong-ticket-trick had worked! That young Nazi's 'triumph' over a soldier in uniform meant he'd not even glanced at my ID.

Eventually, far off down the train, a door slammed, a guard's whistle, the train pulled away.

It rumbled through an empty landscape before slowing for Guntersdorf. The man and his son, now wide awake, got up to leave. I followed. I recalled the town's motto, '*Leben Sie eine gute Zeit in Guntersdorf, alles mit der Zeit.* He who lives in Guntersdorf has a good time, all the time.' The shortest possible time was all I wanted...

Along the station's unmanned platform ran a long white signboard, lit by dim lights and festooned with hops and vines, announcing...

AUSLANDSDEUTSCHE UND AUSLANDSÖSTERREICHER!
DAS FREIE DEUTSCHE ÖSTERREICH GRÜSST EUCH!

GERMAN AND AUSTRIAN EXPATRIATES ABROAD!
FREE GERMAN AUSTRIA GREETS YOU!

My heart fell. The last sign I'd see in my beloved Austria and it had to be this, this hollow fiction, this lie, wreathed in alluring garlands. I shook myself and strode off the platform.

I'd crossed the second hurdle.

.....

The station lay outside the town, giving me a chance to think.

Franz had said: 'Border guards have fingers in both pots. They take bribes from the refugees then a bounty from the government on handing them in, so I recommend the long route to the east, it's patrolled less often. But it's a long way, only consider it if you've plenty of time and there's no moon. Watch yourself close to the frontier, though, that's where any patrols concentrate.' Well, I had little choice, it was well past midnight and tonight was a full moon. I just had to get a move on.

Guntersdorf was deserted, not even a stray dog, but as I approached the town centre a horse and cart was slowly heading north-west along the same road I was on. A man was slumped in the seat in a drunken stupor, his reins dragging in the dust, his horse plodding its familiar route home. Reluctantly I followed, thirty metres behind.

In the town I recognized the great mass of Schloß Guntersdorf, then, silhouetted against a dark, dark sky, the church tower and steeple. Eventually the cart turned north – again, the very road I had planned to use – then, at a distinctive roadside white shrine, the cart turned half-left into an avenue of *linden,* lime trees. Their sweet smell brought memories flooding back. Of course, I'd seen that schloß, steeple and shrine before, the company's trucks had taken this very same route last December.

For five minutes I walked behind that cart. It was slow work, but I didn't want to draw attention to myself. At the end of the avenue of limes the cart suddenly lurched off the lane towards a grey huddle of buildings and barns in the moonlit countryside. Immediately a lantern flared, there was a cacophony of dogs barking, a woman screaming, shouting angrily. I'd been discovered!

Instinctively I jumped across the ditch beside the lane and ran eastwards for my life into the fields, my heart racing. But, as I ran, I made out her shouts more clearly. It was my friend in the cart getting a furious 'welcome' from his wife. I laughed at myself and got back on the lane, setting off briskly northwards, into open countryside.

Soon I was walking along a hedgerow where, at first, silence seemed to reign.

Then I started hearing noises. First the sound of my own footfalls, then a horse snorting nearby – for a fleeting moment I made out its shape before it merged back into the landscape – nearby a toad croaked, behind me a dog yapped, now a whinny... that horse again.

I spoke sternly to myself. 'Why worry? All that training in the Schutzbund and the army, you know what it is to patrol at night – "Take risks early, take care late" – you know this. You're ten kilometres from the frontier. Keep going, stop two kilometres short, assess the situation, it may cloud over and most of your problems will disappear along with the full moon.' That training sergeant's words rang in my head, 'You're infantrymen; but you're better than infantry-men, you're ENGINEERS!' That raised my spirits. I carried on alongside a wheat field to a hedgerow, a broken line of black against grey.

Apart from the frontier the most difficult part might be the tarmac road from Pernersdorf to Hadres, with small villages strung along it like beads on a string. Once I was over that and up on the railway line, I'd be fine, I knew the spot exactly from our training day. I must hit that embankment between Pfaffendorf and Peigarten.

Just as I was thinking this the wheat field ended and there was the tarmac road, the very same roadside verge our vehicles had pulled onto – 'Off the trucks!', even now I could hear the sergeants' voices. What had looked like a distant horizon resolved itself into the embankment and I ran across the road and wormed into the bushes beyond. I listened, nothing. Easing the rucksack off my shoulders I pulled out the pistol, loaded the magazine, released the safety catch and, holding it in front of me, set off as quietly as the undergrowth allowed. A few metres on... the railway embankment, then up Sergeant Gloeckner's wooden sleepers – but this was no time for jokes, this was serious. Get this wrong and I probably faced execution in Dachau – with that grim thought in mind, I set off eastwards in the ditch beside the railway line.

I'd crossed the third hurdle.

.....

I was making good progress until, way ahead, a torch flashed and there came the clink of metal on metal; railway linesmen replacing sleepers. I scrambled back down the embankment and found myself up against a wall of vegetation, wooden stakes and wires strung between them... of course, a vineyard.

In Vienna I'd sold my watch, but I suspected it was past two, closer to three, so I needed to hurry up. But, to stay alert as I walked, I asked myself, 'Who walks at night?' Thieves and prostitutes, then a more cheering thought: 'Soldiers too, and I'm a better soldier than any border guard. Wild animals, of course...', at that very moment an owl hooted nearby, more a blood-curdling screech – I almost jumped out of my skin.

I recalled moonlight walks in happier days, by night through the Wienerwald, clearing my head. 'Stay focussed on the border', I reminded myself, 'just five kilometres away.' That Training Sergeant screamed at me again, 'Darkness is the infantryman's best friend. Are you scared of the dark? Are you? By the time I've finished with you you'll be more scared of me than of the darkest night!' Just then, from that moonlit landscape off to the west came a sound I'd know since childhood, a train. 'That's comforting', I thought, 'The last train to Vienna, from Unterretzbach.'

The railway ran west of the main Prague road to the frontier. The moon had gone in but in the wide, grey panorama of countryside to my right I'd seen a darker line, trees bordering the Prague road perhaps? As I debated this headlights appeared, moving slowly northwards along that line, disappearing behind some buildings, a kilometre away. That must be Kleinhaugsdorf, the only village on the border.

Minutes later I was in the ditch beside that highway. I was so relieved I said a quick prayer of thanks, unusually for me. Despite the darkness I could make out a wall of trees beyond the silvery grey of the road. For half a minute I lay still, listening, peered left and right into that darkness... no signs of life, so I dashed across and through a break in those trees.

I remembered Franz's instructions: 'There's a hollow lane east of Kleinhaugsdorf, it leads north to the border.' Hollow lane? What did he mean? – as if on cue it opened at my feet, I almost fell into it – '900 metres along it', he'd said, 'you'll come to the corner of a wood. 190 metres from there is the frontier, marked with those white stones, about thirty metres apart, you can't miss them.'

I set off along it, more cautiously than ever, finding every patch of shadow I could, pausing, listening, scanning ahead for the slightest noise or movement. That short stretch took me twenty minutes. I'd counted my paces and knew I was 100 metres or so from the frontier when the hairs on the back of my neck stood up.

I froze.

Out of the blackness ten metres ahead came a whispered, '*Hier, haben einen Licht.* Here, have a light.' A match flared and, as someone cupped his hands around a burning match, two cigarettes glowed. I made out two men in uniform, rifles slung over their shoulders. Then, as one of them threw away the still burning match he must have spotted me in its flaring light. '*Scheiße!*' and immediately the cigarette spun off into the pitch blackness surrounding us. But in that last flicker of light I saw the man grabbing his rifle off his shoulder. I spun round and ran. The words '*Zickzack!*' – you say Zigzag – raced into my head and my feet followed instinctively.

I heard the first two shots almost immediately, twenty metres behind me. I was running so hard I scarcely noticed the next two. I ran for fifty metres, plunging eastwards off the track I'd been on and fought my way through a wall of vines. I stumbled over roots, with leaves and branches whipping across my face. I forced myself to stop and listen. Were they chasing me? Way off a torch swung wildly through the trees and across the sky, accompanied by threatening, abusive shouts. I paid no attention, they'd given up after a few metres. The moon had reappeared, but they had no chance of picking up my tracks.

I had to go with the grain of the land, I couldn't fight row after row of wire and vines. It would be slow and noisy, and I'd reach the frontier after daybreak, but these rows ran south to north and I mustn't go north, towards the border, those two might be there. I turned south.

I smiled to myself, 'I'm on the run for my life, but they're deeper in the deep and murky than me. The whole village will have heard those shots and their NCO will ask questions. How will they account for the missing rounds? They're probably arguing right now about what story to tell their sergeant when he catches up with them at dawn.'

Cheering up I brought to mind memories of climbing the Kahlenberg one *Silvester,* that's what we call New Year's Eve, with Frieda. Through vineyards, laden with bottles of wine and delicious food. The steep climb, uproarious comments, giggles of laughter, torches flickering and failing, and the crowd of revellers at the top, no idea who was who, the anonymity part of the fun. If only then was now...

For a while I ran through the vines, then slowed to a brisk walk across a field of wheat. I thought, 'Franz said the short, middle and long routes were all patrolled, "*immer, häufig, gelegentlich,* always, often, occasionally", it's just my misfortune I met the *gelegent,* the occasional patrol. But, by God, I had got to within 100 metres of the frontier!' In my elation I stumbled into a ditch. I felt myself all over, patting my clothing and the rucksack on my back. Nothing broken. I was still holding the pistol, in fact clenching it so tightly that my hand hurt. I relaxed my grip and tried to settle myself down.

Onto a farm track running towards the border once again. Then, hugging the hedgerow, a bird suddenly burst from its nest on the ground at my feet, squawking and flapping away. I ran for thirty metres or more, my pulse racing, I thought I was having a heart attack.

There was a streak of pink in the sky, dawn at last. It must be close to five.

Next I came to a forestry block. Dotted amongst the trees were buildings, slightly shabby, signposts and – such a military touch – painted kerb stones. Franz's remark flashed into my head, 'There's a little used army camp; skirt it to the south.'

Suddenly, in the dim light, two soldiers were walking towards me. I went to ground. One was wearing a purple top, yes, it came back to me, the 1st Dragoons, Imperial purple was still their regimental colour. They continued towards me and I was strongly tempted to break cover and run. But they seemed unaware of me, carrying a large pail between them. What was going on?

I lay in the long grass until they'd passed, then crossed the track and into a strip of woods. I heard twigs cracking beneath my feet and, hearing shouts of '*Aufhören!* Stop!' I thought the two men had seen me and I froze, but the expected words, '*oder wir schießen,* or we fire' never came, instead I heard a great baying sound.

Now they were bending down, fiddling with a padlocked gate. They were oblivious of me – they hadn't heard the breaking twigs or my pounding heart. I went on to a tall fence and a lean-to building up against it. I clambered onto a window sill, then a gutter, across some slates. From its ridge I was looking down into a compound, across to another tall fence, a forestry track beyond. Then I noticed what was in that compound, kennels. A row of cages with twenty or more dogs bounding furiously about, leaping against the wire sides and, as I broke that roofline, baying ferociously.

Suddenly my brain cleared... of course, they must be the regiment's hounds, that large pail their breakfast. They were baying for it, not for me, the men had been shouting at them to shut them up, not at me, and two and twenty pairs of eyes and – it flashed across my mind – twenty sets of teeth, were focussed on that pail, 'Better them than the Gestapo.' I gently let myself down into the compound and edged towards the next fence.

It was standard army issue, three metres high, chain-link with barbed wire along the top, but more of an obstacle to the eye than to any determined escaper – and I was certainly determined. The pins at the bottom had rusted through and in an instant I'd pulled up a length, rolled through the gap and scrambled into the ditch beyond.

Urgency and the growing light pushed me on. Soon clear of the woods and into a gloriously scented wildflower meadow, I was once again a hundred metres from the border and the sun was in the sky. These compelling thoughts made me start to run when, suddenly, the ground opened beneath my feet and I fell...

When I came to, I realised I'd dropped a metre and was lying in a rocky hollow on the edge of a quarry, shaken, dazed, but nothing broken. I remembered Franz saying, 'There's a quarry, not enormous, but the best checkpoint in an otherwise flat landscape. The frontier runs along its northern edge.' Below me another rock face of five-metres ended in the quarry floor. With the thought of that border ahead – and those hounds behind – I decided across was safer than around. Working my way down that rock face to the quarry floor, I was clearly visible to anyone standing on the rim. I raced across, half-expecting a shout, the crack and thump of a shot. None came.

Climbing the opposite face, I dislodged some scree, the noise seemingly echoing across the countryside, but two handholds later I was over the rim and there – the most glorious sight I had ever seen! – a white stone post, just ten metres away. I ran past it and carried on running until my breath gave out, I wanted to get as far as possible from the frontier. Franz had dismissed the rumour of a false border but here, on the ground, the danger seemed all too real. Was I still inside Austria?

Puzzling over this I ran through another vineyard. I put my hand out to steady myself and brushed against something hard and prickly, definitely no bunch of grapes. 'A cucumber! I must be in Czechoslovakia, near Znaim, it's famous for them. I have crossed the frontier. I know I'm free, and all because of a cucumber!' I was so elated that, for a few seconds, I danced a small polka. I named it, '*Die Gurkhen Polka*, the Cucumber Polka.'

I was over the fourth hurdle.

.....

I paused and found myself reciting that nursery rhyme Mama had so often read to me:

Und stürb', waiß nit wann	*And die, I know not when*
Müß fahren, waiß nit wohin	*I must travel, yet know not where*
Mich wundert, das ich so fröhlich bin	*I'm astonished I am so happy*
Leb', waiß nit wie lang	*I shall live, I know not how long*

I laughed out loud. 'Fine Socialist you turn out to be, leaving your country with a poem by a Habsburg Emperor on your lips!'

As I looked back southwards sunlight was rolling across the landscape and, suddenly, my heart wanted to break. In that early light my own country looked so appealing. Set amongst gently rolling hills were the farms and villages I'd worked my way past by night, their far-off red roofs and white walls looking so inviting. 'I'll miss you', I thought.

Suddenly reason cut through the sentimentality. 'Your oh-so-gentle countrymen shot at you, and you've narrowly missed the Gestapo's not-so-gemütlich questioning. Inviting? *Nein!*'

I turned my back on my country and walked on.

The next thirty minutes, heading into Czechoslovakia, passed in a dream. Franz had said, 'The police in Chvalovice know the form, they're honest, several of our people have passed through their hands.' I'd soon find out how honest for myself. On, past untrimmed hedges, low-roofed houses and – as I entered the village – a church bell chiming six-fifteen. A shiver of emotion went through me, I needed to sit down and relax. There was a sign, '*Alt Hotel-Restaurace-Vinotéka,* the Old Hotel-Restaurant-Wine Shop', with lights in the window, so in I went.

I was so elated that I didn't properly take in the odd look on the faces of the man and boy behind the counter. The man whispered something to the boy, who hurried away, then he turned to face me. Fumbling in my pocket for money I said, '*Ein Schnaps und ein Kaffee, bitte* – A schnapps and a coffee, please', but saw stony blankness on the man's face. I scrabbled for the Czech words, '*Kořalku a kávu, prosím.*' The man lifted his eyebrows, '*Pálenka a kávy.*' Soon I was sitting in the corner with an apricot brandy and a coffee. I downed the first in two or three gulps, then sipped slowly at the coffee, watching the light growing through the window. Relaxing, I allowed my eyes to close, trying to think through the night's events.

Suddenly I was jerked awake by a rising commotion in the bar. A furious crowd of men and women stood around me in a semi-circle, glaring at me, more were pushing in from the street. The atmosphere was utterly hostile. All at once they began shouting questions at me, accusing me, gesticulating, swearing and hurling obscenities in Czech and German. Something was holding this mob back, despite being inexorably pushed forward as more and more people piled in behind. My brain raced, these villagers – surely the whole village had turned out – clearly hated me. With a sudden awful clarity, I knew that at any moment they'd set on me, I'd be lucky to get out alive. Then I noticed my pistol in front of me. I'd been carrying it cross-country ever since that railway embankment and must have laid it on the table as I sat down, only that was holding them back.

I had seconds before one of them sprang at me, then they'd be on me like a pack of hounds. I glanced across at the counter... the man had left the flap open when he'd brought out my drinks. In a flash, I was up and through the gap. As I turned to slam the flap down behind me, I caught sight of the mob, grotesquely immobile, taken by surprise. The next moment I was out of the bar and into a small kitchen. It must have been the adrenalin, but something was nagging at me, 'The door! The door!' I whipped around and slammed the door to the bar shut behind me. I remembered to turn the key – thank God it was in the lock – and pocketed it. It can only have taken a second or two for me to dash through that tiny kitchen, but its cooking smells are still in my memory. A girl and an older woman were standing there, frozen in horror. I pushed them aside and leapt out of the back door. Behind me the noise of the mob had reached a crescendo, howls and sounds of fury as they fought to get through the locked door.

I was in a yard stacked with beer kegs, a horse and cart tied up. Instinctively I turned left, northwards. Through an open gateway I found myself immediately on a road. Twenty metres to my left a mass of people were still pushing and shoving to get in the hotel's front door, so intent on getting in that not one of them noticed me – their quarry – racing across the road. Next I was in a garden behind a church and, without looking back, went over a fence, ignoring a furiously barking dog, then over the next fence faster than I'd managed on any assault course. Another track, more back gardens, the noise of pursuit behind, but way behind! Another dog's frenzied barking, but now the path I was on had brought me back to the village high street, a crossroads ahead. There – again, 'Thank God!' – a door with a blue sign, '*Policie.*' I'd never wanted to see inside a police station but that door looked like the entrance to heaven. I bolted across the road, up two steps and into a hallway. A surprised police sergeant was standing behind a desk, his left hand holding a telephone handset, his right reaching for his gun.

I collapsed to the ground at his feet.

The next thing I was looking up at the sergeant and a policeman, both covering me with revolvers. '*Jak vám mohu pomoci, pane?* How can I help you, sir?' asked the sergeant.

I'd crossed what I hoped was the final hurdle.

They pulled me to my feet, deftly relieving me of my pistol as they did so. They were so polite, I was so elated, it all seemed like a dream. Then, out of the corner of my eye, I caught sight of myself in a mirror on the wall. An unshaven man in uniform stared back at me. In uniform! I'd been in uniform all along! I'd been in the wretched thing so long I'd forgotten I was wearing it. Just as suddenly it hit me, those villagers probably thought I was part of a Nazi invasion. No wonder they'd been so full of hatred; laced with fear it was a potent mixture.

But now I was safe. In sheer relief, and before the sergeant could stop me, I reached up to my epaulettes, forcibly tore them off my uniform and threw them to the ground. All of a sudden, my legs gave way from under me and I crumpled onto the stone floor, out cold.

Chapter 3

From Chalovice to Prague, by way of Znojmo

Tuesday 12th July 1938

Josef: They took a brief statement and at 0800 I was taken by car to Znaim's police station, where I was interrogated.

'Did you shoot back, and when did you dispose of your rifle?' The shouted question in Czech was so crass he should have seen the astonishment in my eyes. He shouted again, 'Answer me, Bramminger! Answer the question.'

'You think they'd trust us to take weapons on leave? The rifles are in the armoury, chained up.' I wanted to add, 'Any fool knows that.' Then I realised, he was no soldier, just a policeman, he no idea about how armies worked, let alone in a Nazi dictatorship. I tried to explain I'd had no rifle, I'd stolen the pistol from our armoury, but he wasn't listening to any answers, he liked the sound of his own voice.

There were two of them and an interpreter. The policeman was a plodder, his interrogation arrogant, ponderous, abusive, he did all the talking, no, the shouting. The other one was military intelligence, I'm sure. He just kept quiet, watching all the while. I told them all I knew about the army, about my battalion's organisation, weapons, bridging equipment and storage depots.

Then the quiet one – I think he had little time for the policeman – asked, 'Do you need money for the two documents?' I said no, I still had 35 Marks. They fingerprinted and photographed me, drove me to the police station in Brünn and put me in a cell.

Wednesday 13th July

In the afternoon an officer took me by express train to Prague, drove me to the police prison in *Bartolomějská ulice,* that's Bartholomew Street, and put me in a cell.

Prague Police Arrest Sheet: Headquarters, Perštýně 9. 18:00 STRICTLY CONFIDENTIAL Case No: 302567. Josef Bramminger, Reichs military deserter, soldier of Pioneer Battalion 2, Korneuburg. Stated he deserted from his unit because he is a person of Social Democratic opinions and did not agree with the present regime in Austria. Deserted from his unit wearing uniform and side arm. Initially interrogated by the intelligence officer of III Force and the local intelligence branch then taken to Police HQ in Prague.

DOB: 15 February 1916, Austria.
Father: Brammenger, Josef, retired employee of Austrian State Railways.
Address: Vienna X, Kvárinovo Square 9.
Nationality: German.
Engagement: butcher, smoked products.
Education: Five years school, three years state school.
Religion: Roman Catholic.
Single/Married: single.
Finances and position: no money, unemployed.
Military service: soldier, German army – performed military service satisfactorily.

Searched by: p a Wimmer in presence of p a Dolejší.
Money: Three Czech Crowns, 20 Reichsmarks, 60 pfenigs.
Personal belongings: Lighter, cigarette case, pencil, shaving brush, comb, razor, pocket knife.
Signature for personal items listed above: Josef Bramminger
Identity documents: baptism certificate No 01070045, state school and higher studies school reports.
Status: solitary confinement.
Inprisoned in security department: 13 Jul at 18:30. Cell 12.
Searched by: Klatovský.
If accused confessed: I confess I crossed the frontier without a passport.
Date and details of findings: 15 Jul, found guilty of offence.
Sentenced: at prison by police headquarters, Prague, to 7 days.
Started: 16. VII at 16:30. 5 days served.
Term in police prison done: Josef Bramminger released after he served his term. 20 July at 18:20.

Thursday 14th July

Josef: Next morning at 11 they took me to the 4th floor to Doctor Hora, first name Josef, a short man who spoke very good German. He sentenced me to ten days in the police prison for crossing the border illegally. Then they took me into the quiet room behind his office, where I spoke with him and another man.

Both asked again about my work in the underground and if my illegal friends in the Army would collaborate with Czechoslovak intelligence by providing information. I said I'd give their details but couldn't say if they'd co-operate. In my cell they gave me pen and paper to write down all my knowledge of the German army. I'd be called for the next day, they said.

Dr Hora – my cell overlooked the courtyard – came into the police station at 1050 hrs in a yellow Tatra, number 7777.

Friday 15^th^to Monday 25th July

The next day I took my notes to the doctor, and he went through them. On his desk were other papers and he read out excerpts from the Brno police report: 'States he is from 2nd Railway Engineer Battalion at Korneuburg. He surrendered at Chvalovice carrying a Steyr-Hahn 9mm M12 pistol which he claimed to have stolen from the unit armoury, plus the bayonet from a Steyr Mannlicher 88 rifle, manufactured in 1888 but his battalion is still equipped with them, he says. His uniform is Austrian field trousers and tunic with engineer tabs, but cap badge and belt buckle are Wehrmacht pattern, issued after the Anschluß.'

He shuffled through my written report. 'You wrote, "The guards who shot at me were VGAD, under SS control." How can you be certain?'

I told him. The light of the man's match had shown up his collar tab, a lightning flash on a circle, confirming what Franz Emmerich had said. 'I know my uniforms', I said, quite sharply, 'I know my job.' That certainly caught his attention. Also, was there a glimmer of recognition when I mentioned Franz's name? Or did I imagine it?

He read on: 'From Klein Haugsdorf I got to the first village inside Czechoslovakia and went into the first inn I found. I was so elated at having crossed the border and still being alive I wanted a drink to mark the occasion – at that time in the morning a coffee would have done but I ordered a schnapps as well. I completely forgot I was in uniform.'

'The bravura of youth!' the doctor murmured, 'And its foolishness', looking at me. His eyes went back to reading my report, 'Within minutes it seemed all the residents of the village came into the inn to see me. They were furious, shouting abuse at me. I think they wanted to kill me. I escaped to the police station and handed myself in. They were very friendly towards me. I felt so relieved that my first reaction was to tear the epaulettes from my uniform.'

Dr Hora looked up. 'I have another report: "He reached Chvalovice police station in a state of near total nervous collapse."' Looking straight at me he continued, 'What you do not know is that the hotel owner's son had run to the police station and the sergeant was telephoning Znojmo as you came in. For thirty minutes the lines to Prague were red hot. It was all we could do to prevent a rumour leaking to Prague's foreign correspondents of a German invasion. You stirred up quite a hornets' nest.'

'Certainly I fainted', I replied, 'I'd been going cross-country all night, shot at by the border guards, and then those villagers...' I remember pausing, in my mind's eye reliving that dreadful moment, 'they'd have torn me apart if I hadn't broken out through the kitchen. I ran a hundred metres till I saw the Policie sign, and still some were chasing me. It was the worst moment of my life. I was panting for breath and shaking all over. Nervous collapse? Probably!'

He continued, 'I was taken to the police station in Znaim and was seen by two men, a policeman and an intelligence officer. I told them everything I knew about the German Army and handed over the two classified documents.'

'Tell me about those.'

'One's the technical manual of a German engineer battalion's bridging equipment, it's only RESTRICTED, the other's the order of battle of the Wehrmacht along the Danube; that's SECRET.'

He shrugged, 'The manual may be useful, but the orbat makes particularly interesting reading.'

Another question. 'Why did you cross the border in uniform? Surely it's easier to pass unnoticed as a civilian.'

I told him. After Schmidt and Benko escaped from our battalion the Germans no longer trusted us and put out an order across Vienna District banning soldiers from wearing civilian clothes when leaving barracks, to stop us deserting.

He asked about the state of officers' and other ranks' morale in the battalion, and how civilians regarded their new masters. He already knew the answers, I'm certain, but think he was really probing the extent I'd been involved with the underground. He also quizzed me about what parts of Austria and nearby countries that I knew at all well.

'So, you have an eye for detail, and a memory for it also', he said, putting the papers down.

'Here's what I intend doing. For the next ten days you'll stay in this building. By day you'll be trained in intelligence, at night they'll lock you in your cell. When your sentence is up, you'll be released and put in an hotel, to assist me by establishing contacts with former colleagues. There may be other things you'll be doing for us, perhaps more interesting, more vital, do you see?'

They told me that if ever I had to account for the next ten days I was to say, 'I spent Saturday 16th until the 25th in the police cells as a punishment for illegally crossing the border.' But, actually, I was being trained by a Czech, Sergeant-Major Čeněk, plus a civilian who never volunteered his name.

Čeněk was no typical Sergeant-Major. He could bark and bite with the best of them, but it was a thin veneer, hiding the thinking man beneath. 'Bramminger', he said, 'I'll teach you some basics, security, observation, memory training and the like. Do well and the Doctor may let you out of here. You may even get to learn some of the tougher stuff, crawling through mud, knives, false beards and grenades, that sort of thing. Do badly and...' his words trailed off, he waved his hand at the windows, which had steel bars even in the classrooms and corridors. What this wordless threat entailed I had no intention of finding out, I was too keen to get to grips with the shadowy world that beckoned.

'From now on you'll have two lives, your ordinary life seen by your family' – I winced at that – 'friends and the world, and your second life in the secret world, let's call it your "extraordinary" one. You'll be tempted to think the secret world is the "real" one. Never submit to that temptation, it leads to madness. Keep your feet planted in the ordinary.'

His favourite saying was, 'Secrecy, secrecy, secrecy, and the greatest of these is secrecy.' In the middle of a lesson he'd bark, 'What may your life depend on?' or 'Above all, WHAT?' The answer, every time, was secrecy. I told him that every day since the February War we'd practised secrecy, no, we'd 'lived' it. In the Schutzbund it helped us stay alive and free. He paid no attention. He had a lesson to teach me and he was going to ram it home regardless.

He trained me in codes, code-names, secret inks, lock-picking, photographing documents and how to dispose of papers. I'd learned my lesson... this time I didn't let on I'd been taught much of this before.

After three days he moved on to observation. 'Stay alert', he said. 'See everything. When you go into a room notice everything and everyone. Who's there? Who's talking to whom? Who represents a threat? Where are the exits?'

He let that sink in, then on he went. 'But were those in the right order?'

I didn't answer quickly enough, because he answered himself... 'No! Look for exits first, threats second, and for what you came to look for last of all. What good's the best intelligence in the world if you don't survive to pass it on?'

He taught me to observe without being observed. 'Never be caught looking. Agents survive in our world by developing a sixth sense. Those who don't...'

I remember that moment. It was the first time he'd talked of 'our world' as if I was part of it. I appreciated that.

He taught me something I'd never been taught in Vienna, upside down reading. Print and typing were easy enough, but I admit struggling with wrong-way-up handwriting.

Next day he moved on. 'Our world needs an excellent memory. Details from telephone directories, long numbers, map references and suchlike. Imagine two scenes: you're observing rail movements in enemy territory. It's a death sentence to be caught with anything on paper, store the information in your head. Second scene: you're on a park bench debriefing a source who's as nervous as a rabbit. If he sees you scribbling down all he's saying he'll clam up or have a heart attack. So, what to do?'

'I'm going to teach you seven systems... the Memory Trick, the Method of Loci, the Major System, Kim's Game, the Mnemonic Peg, Rhyming and Substitute Words.'

'Plus Repetition, of course, it's the simplest. You need to remember a place name you've just seen? Say it to yourself three times. Or, when you first hear a person's name, say it three times in your head then immediately repeat it back to them, use it in your conversation, "Good to meet you, František. What an interesting name." People love the sound of their own name.'

'The first important system is the Memory Trick', he continued, 'storing numbers in your head as pictures. An example: visualize the number one as a lighthouse, standing by itself; for two, a pair of spectacles; three a stool with three legs; four a window – it has four sides, four corners; five, your hand with its five fingers, and so on. The more bizarre your pictures the better, you'll recall them more easily.'

'Next you make up the picture story. So, from a lighthouse a hand waves three times at a tank, helping you memorise that you've seen fifteen tanks in a convoy. A stool being thrown through a window reminds you it was the "34th Regiment" you saw on a soldier's epaulettes. Use your imagination. You'll get the hang of it.'

And on it went.

Monday 25th July

Finally an official came to my cell, gave me a razor to shave myself and 100 Czech koruna to buy a suit, shirt and tie to smarten myself up. He took me for lunch at the Metropol on Wenceslas Square – so different, I thought, to Vienna's Metropol, staffed by the Gestapo, but I wasn't sure Czechoslovak military intelligence had a sense of humour, so I kept stumm.

In Czechoslovakia, it seems, lunch is the main meal of the day so there was no stint... *knedlo, zelo, vepřové,* beef soup, then roast pork with sauerkraut and hot dumplings. They rarely waste time on vegetables, then a dessert that made me feel completely at home, *jablečný štrůdl,* apple strudel. All washed down with beer.

Then he took me across town to the Hotel Merkur, by Denis Station, where the Doctor had arranged a room for me for a fortnight. I was given some pocket money and the official told me to wait for instructions. He warned me not to drink or talk with other people, nor tell anyone about these matters.

27th July

Two days later I met the Doctor on *Karlův most,* it's Charles Bridge in English, over the River Moldau, the Vltava, as they call it in Czech, the medieval one with all those statues, some say it's the loveliest bridge in Europe. It's certainly eerie when the mist's rising from the river, but then it's easy to spot if someone's shadowing you. He introduced me to two new contacts. 'This one', a short, slim man with curly hair and dark glasses (I never saw him without them), 'is the Engineer. He is your controller. This one', a muscular man with red hair and an English moustache, 'is his Interpreter. You can trust both of them; you'll be doing a lot of business with them in future.'

The Interpreter I came to know as Adam – I doubt it was his real name – but the other one never gave me a name; he was always *pan inženýr* or *Herr Ingenieur.* He got down to business straightaway, asking me the names of friends still over the border, then told me we'd meet the following day under the Astronomical Clock.

I wrote down for him all the contacts I had in the Bundesheer – I find it hard to call it the Wehrmacht. He gave me a pre-written letter and told me to write my own copies of it. They'd be sent off once we'd worked out my contacts' addresses.

I met the Engineer six times, but I mostly saw the Interpreter. Some of the letters were posted in Czechoslovakia, some in Austria by a courier. I'd be asked to help test their authenticity once they'd received replies.

After two weeks in the Merkur they rented lodgings for me with Mrs Anna Valášková in Královská Street. The Interpreter told me, 'We've fixed you up with a "job" as cover. If you run into old friends, it'll explain how you can afford to rent a room. You'll be a butcher's assistant in the Hotel Alkron off Wenceslas Square. It's not a real job, just report in every morning but spend your day training under Čeněk; the *sous chef* knows to turn a blind eye when you slip out the back. Anyway, you've got no work permit so it would be an illegal "job", that way other refugees will understand when you refuse to talk about it.' Adam paid me 200 krone weekly.

During that fortnight at the Merkur I kept the lowest profile and fortunately didn't bump into anyone who recognised me. But, once that 'job' started in the Alkron - it's the ritziest hotel in town, stylish, Art-Deco, all chandeliers and Italian marble, very glamorous - I had my story ready. Also, towards the end of July, I reported to Paul, the secretary of the Austrian Social Democratic Party in Exile. He granted me a small monthly subsistence grant, which helped.

Gestapo report, in Prague: 17 II 1942. **SECRET**. Josef Bramminger, last resident in Prag XII, Römische Road 14. As reported to the police 15 VIII 38-25 X 38 lived in Prag X, Koenigstraße 51/11, in lodgings with Anna Valasek, claiming he was a refugee and deserter (he still owes her 65 Tschechisch Krone). Same was living with a citizen of the German Reich whose name Valasek no longer remembered. Both were unemployed and supported by the refugee committee. From time to time he was visited by another national of the German Reich, but no Czechs. Valasek had not mastered the German language so did not know what they were saying or what was agreed. *Behalten Sie dies in unserem Registrierungssystem* - Retain this on the registry.

August and September 1938

Josef: The Engineer gave precise instructions for my in-Prague training. They didn't want us traced, so, from the Alkron's staff entrance, I walked, took a bus, and walked again to a rendezvous where I mounted a covered truck that drove around collecting us students. I was one of nine men and women, but we didn't socialise, the emphasis was on total security. Four came from Czechoslovakia's provinces, there was another Austrian (but not from Vienna; they'd checked we didn't know one another), two were Hungarian, one German. Each of us had a cover name and I never knew their real ones, or saw them again after our training. Other than the German, that is.

Čeněk started by calling me 'Penzinger.' Having no connection with Vienna's 14th District I asked, 'I come from Favoriten, not Penzing. Why've you called me Penzinger?' 'Glad you asked', he replied, 'shows you're paying attention. Any cover name that hints at its owner's identity is unsafe. From your accent and Wienerisch words anyone can tell you're Viennese, so no point hiding that, but if someone tries to identify you by hunting around Penzing they'll waste a lot of time. Ask any magician, it's called misdirection.'

So, every day, off we went in our secret truck with secret names to a secret villa in Zlíchov for a fortnight of intensive training, starting with security. They drummed it into us, starting with how to create false identities. Each 'guise' has its own paperwork, bank accounts, life stories, all taught by a gloomy bureaucrat from the Ministry of the Interior who explained to us how a state tracks its citizens' lives. Then – although it seemed to pain him greatly – he showed us how our multiple personalities must dodge and twist their way unseen through that very same maze.

We were taught how to spot followers and how to shake them off: 'Wear something noticeable, something small: glasses, a cap, gloves, better still, a reversible jacket. Give them something to focus on, then, out of sight for a second, it disappears into your pocket, and you disappear with it.' Or, shopping, 'go straight to the back of the shop, it allows you to spot followers as they come in at the front.'

Another day, another instructor, 'Listen rather than speak. Be the least memorable man in the room, go unnoticed. Become grey, remain grey', he said. 'If you feel under threat, disappear into the background.' Hard for the extroverts on the course.

They drove us out of Prague to Liberec, to a country house in a secluded valley, classrooms in the house, dormitories in the stables. For a fortnight, out in the grounds and surrounding forests, the estate's gamekeeper taught us fieldcraft, weapon training, combat skills, escape and evasion. Fitness was key. I'd always thought I was fit, as a youngster with the Red Falcons, climbing mountains, then Vienna's chimneys, as a recruit and soldier at Korneuburg, not to mention escaping through vineyards. But they ran us ragged, toughening us up to a fitness, a sharpness, we never knew we possessed.

When we got back to Prague I still had the cover job at the Alkron but I'd discovered I was really working for the Czechoslovak General Staff's II Department. That was the name of Dr Hora's organisation, military intelligence, although I'm still not sure if that was his real name.

In early September the Austrian Socialist party secretary sent me to Herr Fritz Löwinger, its committee chairman. He knew I'd been in the Schutzbund, but that was all. He didn't know I'd been in its intelligence wing and I wasn't going to tell him. I can't put my finger on why, but I never fully trusted him. Despite the fact that I'd never been involved in the party's politics he immediately made me a member of the committee.

A dreamlike August passed into September; it turned into a nightmare, yes, but it started idyllically. There I was, under clear blue skies in one of the world's most beautiful cities, training for a task I believed in, and, what's more, being paid for it, in a city where most refugees were penniless.

The nightmare started at the end of September, hearing the news from Munich. Through October and November things got worse. It was the bleakest time I'd known.

At that moment I must have smiled, because I saw astonishment in her eyes.

Mary: 'So how do you look so happy?' I asked.

Josef: I paused before replying. 'Then, I was at the gateway to Hell itself, but now... I'm in Paradise.'

Mary: 'Paradise! Here! Josef, darling, that's hard to believe. You'll have to explain yourself.'

Josef: So I told her the rest...

People say Prague is beautiful and, from the earliest days, when I had the chance, I started exploring its streets. Daily I walked from my lodging in the north of the city via Old Town, or through New Town. I put this variation down to an urge to play the tourist, but eventually it dawned that subconsciously I was heeding Franz's warning in Vienna: '"They" have people inside our organisation and have tried to kill or kidnap refugees even in Czechoslovakia, so beware.' Also, one of his earliest lessons: 'Never, ever set a pattern. Always vary your route and behaviour.' Thank God for Franz, I thought.

From the Vltava river old-fashioned streets wound up the hill to the *Malá Strana,* the Lesser Town, from where Prague Castle and St Vitus's Cathedral dominate the city. It's quieter than the Old and New Towns and provided an escape from the refugee hothouse around Wenceslas Square. There refugees sat in the *Městská knihovna,* Prague's Municipal Library, while those that could afford it spent their lives in the cafés, when they weren't queuing for exit papers. Many gravitated to the elegant Café Continental, with its loud political debates, but most probably went for its inexpensive meals rather than its style. The free newspapers on their bamboo holders, reminders of Vienna, may have helped, plus the blind eye they turned to customers spending a whole morning over a single cup of coffee.

One day I saw a familiar face in the queue outside Police Headquarters. 'Hans', I called out, 'Grüß Gott.' We greeted one another warmly.

Hans Amsel had arrived that very day in Prague and was bursting to tell me all about his escape and ask about mine, 'Not here, Hans', I said, kicking his ankle, 'Let's go for a coffee.' I didn't want him broadcasting our secrets across Prague. But I was happy to meet the young woman with him, 'Erika.' He introduced us, 'meet another Hans...', 'No Hans, that was only my underground name. It's really Josef, people call me Peppi. So, he started again: 'Meet Peppi, one of my oldest friends, and one of us', giving her a knowing wink.

We went to the Deminka café and swapped stories. Erika, it turned out, was from Döbling. Like myself, she'd been an illegal. Together they'd escaped through the Bratislava marshes. I kept quiet about where I'd crossed the border and my contact with Czechoslovak intelligence, but told them about the pocket money the trades union was giving me and my illegal job. 'I've been lucky', I said, 'but my best bit of luck, or providence, call it what you will, was those two border guards lighting up on patrol...'

'And getting a job...', Hans interjected. 'OK, I give in', I said. 'I can afford to buy you a coffee.' Hans grinned.

'So, who wants what?'

Friday 9th September, in London

Mary's story: As I went out to lunch the doorman at Christie's said, 'I'd be careful of Trafalgar Square, miss, there's a demonstration on.'

'Thanks George, what's it about?'

'No idea miss; someone mentioned a banner about Czechoslovakia.'

I set off for my usual tea shop regardless, what harm could a demonstration do me?

A huge, good-humoured crowd filled the square, listening in silence to Violet Bonham Carter addressing them from the base of Nelson's Column, dwarfed by bronze lions on either side of her and huge banners stretching around the column. They proclaimed, 'ANGLO-CZECH SOLIDARITY' and 'BRITAIN • FRANCE • RUSSIA CAN STOP WAR.' Over the traffic I heard her voice on loudspeakers: 'We said to Mussolini, "Keep that pledge", and he kept it because he knew that Britain really meant to put her foot down. If Germany seizes the Sudetenland we must act. Why is Parliament not recalled? Why is Mr Chamberlain afraid to face...', the rest of her words were lost in cheering and clapping.

Soon the crowd, led by four young men carrying large flags, a Union Jack, the Stars and Stripes, a French tricolour and a Czechoslovak flag, set off down

Whitehall. A man had a child on his shoulders, a bobby was waving cars and taxis through, a few policemen were on horseback. Amidst this great mass a band marched towards Downing Street, playing its heart out. People came out onto their balconies to see what was going on, smiling and waving in support. It was all very civilised.

Later, drinking my tea, I thought it over. 'She was right about that man Hitler; we must stand up to him. What's really going on over there?' I was determined to find out more about these Czechs so, in the evening, I went round to Roy Foster, the vicar, to see if there were any ways we might help.

Roy surprised me; he had such strong views on it. 'Yes', he said, 'Mr Churchill has been warning of this for months, and been laughed to scorn by the establishment for his pains. Back in March he said to the Commons...' here he shuffled through some newspapers on his desk, then read from one, '"Where will we be in two years, when the German Army will be much larger than the French Army? We cannot leave the Austrian question where it is, a small country brutally struck down by the Nazis, its Government scattered to the winds, the oppression of Nazi party doctrine imposed upon a Catholic population and upon the working classes of Austria and of Vienna." We must do all we can for any of those poor people who escape Nazi clutches.'

I was convinced.

August to September, in Prague

Josef's story: Prague's weather echoed the political mood. July to September – when things looked hopeful – was golden summer, hot, humid and dry. But thereafter, in my memory, it was always clouds, grey and menacing, thin, miserable rain and a cutting wind, the situation worsening every day.

From the frontier regions came tales of deliberate provocation, Hitler determined to prod the country into providing a pretext for invasion. His speeches on the wireless grew more threatening, Czechoslovak customs men were dragged into Germany, a policeman was shot dead, two were beaten to death with axes. The fascist Henleinists staged pitched battles against the police, leaving dead on both sides. Eventually President Beneš declared martial law in the border regions.

I'd given the Engineer the names and details of several soldiers in the underground. I told him how Franz Grossegger might get the copy of the secret signal code from a sergeant-major of 73 Artillery Regiment even though, like all soldiers in sensitive posts, he was under Gestapo surveillance. But he enjoyed a drink, which was how Grossegger – well known for such contacts – had discovered he opposed the Nazis.

I told them about Leo Pröglhöf, a conscript with me at Korneuburg, a reliable Social Democrat and destined for government service when his conscription ended. The Engineer told me to write to him. I mentioned Franz Czerhold, already involved with Schutzbund intelligence, living at Rokytanskigasse 10, but warned them his father had become a Nazi. And the other Franz, Franz Emmerich, but Hora's people already knew about him. They held him in high regard.

What further contact was made I do not know and have not asked.

I did odd jobs for the Department, like scanning football results in German and Austrian newspapers for any military teams, which leagues they were in, where the matches were played. It all helped build an orbat of the Wehrmacht.

Late in August, Adam showed me the reply from a friend of Grossegger, who'd written that I must write only to Grossegger's girlfriend, but we never found her address in Lehrmann's Directory.

One day in the library I saw Eberhard Röllig, the German I'd trained with at Zlíchov. He's a very reserved man, and only now did I learn his real name. He'd been a judge in Prussia until Hitler took over in 1933 when he'd resigned in protest against Nazi laws and fled to Prague.

Wednesday 14th September

Today, over the wireless, came another threatening speech by Herr Hitler. Suddenly the trickle of refugees from the Sudetenland became a flood. People carrying cardboard boxes and bedding, bewildered children trailing alongside, mostly Sudeten German Social Democrats and a few Communists, terrorised out of their homes. They walked, travelled in carts or by train, all ending up on the square outside Masarych Station. A refugee camp sprang up overnight, a chaos of dusty luggage, eiderdowns and household things rescued from wrecked homes.

I walked past this daily on my way to work. Growing up in Vienna I'd seen the unemployed queuing at soup kitchens, and tramps living under the Danube bridges, but I'd never seen so much misery. These poor peasants had no idea of where they'd go or who'd care for them. They just stood there, fearful, utterly silent, holding each others' hands, ill, tired beyond sleep, a heart-breaking sight. Then, thank God, this was transformed into a beacon of hope by the crowds of Czechs who turned out to welcome them, pressing food, sweets, and money into their hands, Quakers and others busy preparing hot meals, offering accommodation and treating the sick.

Thursday 15th September

Our own time as refugees was clearly running out. Czechoslovakia, which only ever offered temporary refuge, was threatening to fall apart. In the cafés around Wenceslas Square suddenly the only talk was of war...

'Hitler's holding a war council in Munich...'

'It could start any day now...'

'Prague will be bombed... They'll be dropping gas on the city...'

Some responded, 'He cannot be so mad as to attack... The whole world is on our side... France, Britain and Russia will not put up with it...'; around the square crowds chanted their support for Beneš and the army.

A foreign newspaperman appeared with sensational news from his office telegraph, 'Chamberlain is flying to meet Hitler at Berchtesgaden.'

At a nearby table an elderly Czech spoke up, 'He has no option but to tell him, and in no uncertain terms, "If you attack Czechoslovakia the rest of the world will come to its defence."' There was a round of applause.

'I wouldn't be so sure', Eberhard Röllig said, quietly but firmly. No-one listened. That same day Adam – II Department having seen the writing on the wall – handed me a form to apply to the police for a passport. It asked, 'Destination?' I didn't know what to write. He said, 'Some émigrés got to Paris, so put down France, plus somewhere further afield, it reassures our authorities that you're serious.' I wanted to write England or the United States, but they weren't offering visas. So, I wrote Mexico.

Friday 16th September

On the 16th Adam saw me again, he gave me 50 Krone and said if he needed me he'd call. Things looked bleak.

Lord Runciman, leading a mission from the British Foreign Office but dancing to the Nazi tune, left Czechoslovakia without fanfare. No tears were shed in Prague. The wife of the British military attaché and families from their Legation also left for London by train. It couldn't have been clearer, my time in Czechoslovakia must soon be over.

Wednesday 21st September

Adam called me into Bartholomew Street. 'Mobilization is likely', he told me,

'We've prepared for this since 1933, we have a modern army of one and a half million men, fortifications on the border under concrete, an air force that can defeat the Luftwaffe, and the best armaments industry in the world, so we can win this. If you decide to volunteer report to Stefanikovych Barracks.' And, as a parting shot, 'Mention my name at the guardroom. They'll make you welcome.'

Friday 23rd September

Beneš issued the mobilisation order that evening. The next moment, it seemed, men were pouring onto the streets from every house and workplace, heading for their assembly points. As if by clockwork every tram came to a halt, disgorged its civilian passengers and took on-board men being called to the colours; commandeered vehicles raced through the streets of Prague carrying reservists, sporting the national colours of red, white and blue on their radiators.

I was in the Deminka café with Hans and Erika when the wireless behind the bar gave out the news. The waiter looked gravely at us and said, 'I must go at once. Goodbye.' Moments later we saw him, a parcel under his arm, hurrying out onto the street to join the flow of men heading northward to Wilson Station, eager to get to battle stations.

I had to join them. I said goodbye to my friends and walked across the river to Stefanik Barracks to volunteer. I mentioned Adam's name and moments later found myself swearing an oath, 'to serve faithfully for the duration of the war.' Hundreds of Germans and Austrians had volunteered and thirty-one of us ended up in the 5th (T G Masaryk) Infantry Regiment, transported in trucks to Motol Barracks on Prague's western edge.

They were an exact replica of Korneuburg, the same architecture, layout, atmosphere, all very Habsburgian, military through and through. That first night they ran us ragged, parades, orders, stores, issues, more parades. It was past midnight before we got into a dormitory. There, through the windows, we saw Prague go dark. Without warning every street light in the city went out, then, block by block, lights in homes were switched off. Soon there were cries of '*Dal, že světlo ven!*' You'll hear the same cry here soon enough: 'Put that light out!'

When at last we fell on our beds we should have slept like logs, but an oh-so-familiar sound kept us awake, the rattling and squealing of tram cars. Prague's tram depot, it turned out, lay alongside the barracks. All night long they ground their way around the tracks and turntables. I might have been back in my bed in Quarinhof.

Among the volunteers was Eberhard, a happy chance for me. He's older than me and rather a dry old stick – like most Germans he never quite knows how to take Viennese frivolity - but I'd come to trust his judgement and enjoy his company. I like to think he regards me as a friend.

Vienna, Prague, suddenly I realised, this was my second experience of a nation preparing for war.

Saturday 24th September

Next morning, they sent us across Prague to a firing range. The city was oddly quiet, taxis - commandeered by the army - nowhere to be seen, only horse-drawn carriages; elderly men digging trenches; every window criss-crossed with sticky tape. Oddest of all were the cheerful, smiling faces, and the women wearing their best clothes. Everybody was taking the prospect of war and bombing in their stride. The feeling in the air was as electric as in Vienna just before the Anschluß, tremendously optimistic.

Back in Motol I was called to the guardroom. My landlady, Anna, had shown up, having generously travelled out to the barracks with a parcel of things she thought I'd need as a solder. The guard was listening on a wireless to another vile speech by Hitler, demanding many of the country's chief industries, its natural frontiers and fortified defences, most main roads and railways. Czechoslovakian army and police must withdraw by 1st October. His ultimatum: 'If these demands are not met and the Sudeten German lands are not handed over', he declaimed, 'in eight days I will march.'

The officer of the day and the guardroom burst into angry speech, but dear, pragmatic Anna, she simply said, 'At least we have eight days to live.'

Eberhard had a newspaper from battalion headquarters, where he'd been appointed interpreter. 'London', he read, 'is digging its own air-raid trenches and drawing gas masks.' We didn't know what to make of that.

That night, worn out by hours of training, I fell asleep before I could work out whether the noise of those trams cheered or saddened me.

Sunday 25th September

Report to the Foreign Office: Czechoslovak forces have mobilised efficiently. By this evening 38 divisions, over a million men, are ready in strong protective screen of fortifications to resist any advance by the German army. Hitler lost the important element of surprise, and the Czechoslovaks, operating on interior lines, with precise and detailed knowledge of the country and its resources, plus short lines of communication to supply depots and arsenals, have the balance of strategic advantage. Colonel Strange, British Military Attaché.

Josef: We volunteers endlessly practiced drill on Motol's parade ground until, at last, the battalion was paraded and told, 'We are deploying to the Sudetenland.'

Were we Austrians and Germans finally going to have a chance to fight back?

I was one of the first to find out; an officer called out my name, 'Bramminger, do you know how to demolish bridges?'

'Yes sir, I'm a combat engineer' – I was so proud to be able to say that.

'Report to B Company's Sergeant-Major.'

All around me other Austrians and Germans were being detailed off, mostly as interpreters. The parade was dismissed, urgency was in the air. I formed up with my kit in front of the Sergeant-Major. He looked down at his field notebook and barked, 'Bramminger? In that truck...', he pointed, 'you'll find Corporal Dusek. He'll show you the equipment. We're off in thirty minutes.'

And we were. It's quite a sight when a battalion deploys to war, all those vehicles, all those men, but it's the urgency, the sense of purpose that sticks with you.

I don't know to this day what they thought of having an Austrian in their midst, but Corporal Dusek seemed a good man. He watched as I looked over the detonators, fuses and explosives we'd be working with. They were identical to the Bundesheer's, so I needed no lessons. He was decent enough to explain our orders: 'Deploy to the edge of the Sudetenland at Andělská Hora, 100 kilometres west of Prague, forty kilometres from the German frontier, prepare bridges for demolition.'

We drove across the flat plains around Prague to the hills and mountains of the Sudetenland. Corporal Dusek started singing, a Czech martial song, then someone in the following truck took it up, then more and more joined in. Soon, it seemed, the whole convoy was singing. And such voices! Loud and proud, brimming over with self-confidence. These Czechoslovak soldiers had no doubts.

The battalion occupied a position astride the main road from Prague to Karlsbad. This army clearly knew its business: to the west the road was already blocked by rows of trees felled across it, all covered by field guns and mortars on the crest above. Through the trees we could make out troops stood-to in entrenchments and camouflaged blockhouses surrounded by barbed wire entanglements. Of the battalion's three companies ours pushed on towards the frontier and stopped at a road block near the village of Hůrky. Three great walls of concrete blocks already straddled the track through the hills.

Eberhard had been attached to our company and, once we'd debussed, we stood awaiting orders. Talking in German between ourselves he pointed along the track, 'Karlsbad must be down there.'

'Oy!' Corporal Dusek shouted angrily, 'Don't use that Nazi name, it's Karlovy Vary. German isn't popular just now, so speak Czech if you want us to stay friends.' Poor old Eberhard, his job as interpreter wasn't going to make him the most popular man in the company over the next few days.

A few minutes later Dusek and I were ordered forward, with one of the company's three infantry platoons, to work on a local bridge.

Once we'd wired up the explosives, we left the bridge demolition guard to it and came back through the road block. Soon after we arrived a car raced up the track from Karlsbad, sorry, Karlovy Vary, and slowed to a crawl to zigzag through the concrete blocks. There it was halted by the sentries. It looked in a bad way, its bodywork dented, windows shattered. Its driver climbed out looking badly shaken. He was an English journalist and only too eager to tell the major commanding the company his story.

Eberhard translated his English into Czech. The man had had quite an experience. On his way to the frontier he'd failed to return the Nazi salutes of some Henleinist storm-troopers on the roadside, so they'd shouted and shaken their fists at him. In Karlovy Vary itself he'd seen Czechoslovak and Jewish shops smashed up and looted, swastika banners on the houses and Henleinists marching about in uniform. On his return the same storm-troopers tried to stop his car, hurling rocks and shouting, '*Halten Sie ihn auf! Halten Sie ihn auf!* Hold him up! Hold him up!' He accelerated and, driving straight at them, scattered them. Somehow he got through unscathed.

Tuesday 27th September

Neville Chamberlain, on the radio: 'How horrible, fantastic, incredible it is that we should be digging trenches and trying on gas-masks here because of a quarrel in a far-away country between people of whom we know nothing.'

Josef: Our battalion prepared for battle in those forward positions. Corporal Dusek and I made several bridges ready for demolition, but we never pressed the plunger. It was a battle that never came. Instead we got the glories of Munich.

Thursday 29th September, in Munich

Agreement concluded at Munich: Germany, the United Kingdom, France and Italy have agreed the following terms and conditions governing the cession to Germany of the Sudeten German territory, and hold themselves responsible for the steps necessary to secure its fulfilment: i.a.

> (1). The evacuation will begin on 1st October.
> (2). The United Kingdom, France and Italy agree that the evacuation of the territory shall be completed by the 10th October, without any existing installations having been destroyed.

Signed:

Adolf Hitler, Neville Chamberlain, Edouard Daladier, Benito Mussolini.

Mary: Yes, I remember it well. That silly man! He flew back to Croydon Airport and fluttered a piece of paper at cheering crowds, looking like some stage magician astounded at the success of his own trick. Outside 10 Downing Street he declared, 'I believe it is peace for our time.' It was sheer craven folly, shame on our country.

Josef: In those lonely positions near the frontier we took it badly. The officers and soldiers had little idea of the blow that had fallen, or how their allies had so cravenly surrendered to Hitler's demands. Our Major read out General Krejči's surrender order: 'Soldiers. Under the pressure of world events the Government of the Republic has had to agree to the surrender of areas of our State to the Reich. We are soldiers who must always be ready to suppress our own feelings. Our army has not been beaten, and fully retains its good name.'

Keyed up to fight, confident in our position, our equipment, our colleagues and our cause then, suddenly, it was all taken from us, for nothing. A great brooding silence fell. Men ambled away, stunned. When, eventually, officers and NCO's issued orders few heeded them; soldiers just turned their heads away or sat unmoved. A few got their hands on alcohol and drank themselves into a stupor.

People say the whole country broke into tears of shame and anger when they heard of their nation's surrender. For days afterwards the British in Prague found it unwise to speak English on the streets.

Saturday 1st October

So, instead of fighting Nazis, I found myself retreating before them. Part of a huge, undefeated army evacuating its territory in great columns of tanks, armoured cars, siege artillery and motorised infantry. We drove towards Prague along roads clogged with yet more wretched refugees. There was no singing in our trucks; somehow that sullen silence was louder than any singing.

Tuesday 4th October

Czechoslovak Army records: Prague. 6410. I certify that Mr Josef BRAM-

MINGER, of German volunteer service, served with 5 TGM from 24 Sep to 4 Oct. Company Commander.

Josef: I was discharged from the army. We Austrians were angry, our chance to fight back had been snatched away. We could only imagine how the Czechoslovaks felt.

As soon as I was released, I took the tram to Bartholomew Street to ask Adam for instructions.

'We're ordering you to leave Czechoslovakia', he said. 'The Germans already influence some ministries, and when Beneš goes they'll have people in the Interior Ministry, maybe even this Department. I've seen your name on the list the Gestapo have demanded be handed over... your life will soon be at risk in Prague.'

'However', he brightened up a little, 'your name's near the top of our list to be sent to safety. It may take weeks; the Quakers and international trades unions are doing the donkey work, but the system is controlled by the Comité Centrale, where our Department has an unseen hand. William Gillies from the British Labour Party, staying in the Hotel Steiner, is the man you need. Mention Dr Hora to him.'

I hurried down to Voršilská Street and joined a long queue at the Comité Centrale's office... someone had already registered my name, I was already on a list, Dr Hora's doing, Adam told me later. What exact list this was I didn't know, but I was over the first barrier.

Wednesday 5th October

The Germans had insisted the Head of State must go, so Beneš had to resign. He was immediately replaced by a Government of National Defence with little sympathy with Socialists or refugees. Its priority was the security of the emasculated Czechoslovakia, and it was terrified of offending Herr Hitler. 'If the Germans ask us to dismiss everyone with blue eyes, we'd have to do it', one official said.

This was soon evident. In the Hotel Esplanade portraits of Masaryk and Beneš were replaced with hunting prints, so as not to affront the large Gestapo contingent who'd taken rooms. Its agents made their presence felt in the Alkron, brazenly photographing any refugee who dared visit the refugee organisers. In the Café Continental whispered conversations replaced the refugees' loud political debates.

Prague bulged at the seams with every type of refugee: Jewish, Czech, Slovak,

Sudeten German, Austrian, Hungarian, liberals and Socialists of every nationality, and not all Prague's citizens were happy at this. Suddenly we felt crowded, confined and vulnerable.

For refugees, October was the month of queues. For visas you had to be on a list – or you would be invisible to any bureaucrat and his rubber-stamp. To get on a list you had to queue: at Police HQ to register as a foreigner; at the Ministry of the Interior to register an address; at embassies and legations to apply for visas: Holland, Sweden or France offered faint hope, Canada – that great melting pot of nationalities – New Zealand or South American offered less, the United States and Britain none at all. Grim tales circulated of anti-Nazi Sudeteners being pushed across into German territory. Escape was now a matter of life or death.

In this no-man's-land nerves got frayed, the endless routine of waiting in libraries and cafés, daily scanning the lists on a committee's notice boards – all to little avail – allowed back into hostels or church halls at night. A lucky few saw their names on a list, but the promised trains never materialised. Frustration grew, desperation set in, occasionally tempers flared.

In those long, dark days came a rare piece of good news. Priority was to be given to refugees in the most immediate danger, Germans and Austrians – 'Old Reich refugees', they called us – with a record of opposition to the Nazis, whose repatriation was being demanded by the Germans. A comforting rumour, but little evidence that it was true.

Friday 7th October

Hans heard some really uplifting news from Vienna. In Austria's first public demonstration against the Nazis, 10,000 Catholic youngsters met in Stephansdom for the Feast of the Rosary and heard an astonishing, impassioned sermon preached by Cardinal Innitzer. He declaimed, 'There is just one Führer: Jesus Christ. Guard your belief and stand firm!' Outside on Stephansplatz the youngsters started to shout, 'Innitzer command, we will obey', mimicking and mocking the Nazi's *Führerprinzip,* the Leader Principle, and thereby enraging the Hitler Youth. Fighting broke out, but only Catholic youth leaders were arrested by Vienna's police and taken to the Hotel Metropol. The next day the police made no attempt to intervene when the Hitler Youth stormed the Archbishop's Palace, breaking, burning or stealing everything they found, and shouting 'Kill Innitzer', 'Give us the black dog, we will tear him apart.'

This was the man who, seven months earlier, had written 'Heil Hitler!' alongside his endorsement of the Anschluß and ordered church bells to peal. Then the Vatican, outraged, had issued a clarification: 'The solemn declaration of the Austrian bishops was an approval of something that was not and is not compatible with God's law.' Now the Nazis had turned on him. A 'holy man' said some. 'Weak', said others.

Tuesday 11th October

Johann Hirsch: 24 Harley Road, London.

Dear Mr Gillies,

Unfortunately I must appeal on a highly urgent matter. A most alarming letter from our Paris Matteotti Committee tells the tragic situation of Austrian Socialist émigrés in Czechoslovakia, ordered by the post-Beneš Czech government, kow-towing to German demands, to quit the country within a fortnight. Failing this they would be taken to the German frontier and handed to the Nazi authorities. This would not mean just a concentration camp, if that wasn't bad enough, they would simply be lynched by the Nazis on hand-over. If they are to be saved it must be decided within the fortnight.

It is a small number, 30-50. Feverish efforts are being made in Paris to bring some to Scandinavia and France, and 21 to Great Britain, or the rescue plan cannot succeed. The British Labour movement can save them by impressing upon the Home Office to waive the usual formalities in this emergency case and grant British visas within the short time allotted by the Czech authorities.
Yours fraternally...

LIST OF 21 AUSTRIAN SOCIALIST REFUGEES IN CZECHOSLOVAKIA

1. Fritz Loevinger, born 1901; teacher and technician; willing and able to undertake any work, domestic service, car driving, etc. Intends to go to Australia or New Zealand. Mrs Ayrton Gould and Miss Nike, Friends Service Council; Praha 5, Sanytrova 18 are acquainted with his case.
2. Ing Sigmund Schwartz. Radio engineer (expert); was preparing his emigration to Palestine while in Prague; c/o Anna Hagenbuechli, Praha 12, Barthouva 20.
3. Josef Bramminger, 1916; c/o Pilsova, Praha III, Rymska 14/II.
4. (Name removed - transfer to Scandinavia being arranged).
5. (Ditto).
6. Hans Wagner, 1917; c/o Friedmann, Praha XII, Belohradska 34/I.
7. Leopold Bettesch, 1898; Praha II, Dlouha 43, c/o Strelak.
8. Dr Josef Redei, 1880; Brno, Liliova 13.
9. Auguste Mayer, 1890. Same address.

10. (Ditto 4, above).
11. (Ditto).
12. Karl Stoeckner, 1910; Praha II, Tynska ul.5/III.
13. Katharina Varga, 1910; Brno, Hvezdova 4a.
14. Hilde Valina, 1913; c/o Oestrerreische Fluchtlingsstelle, Praha II, Petraka 25.
15. Salomon Riesenberg, 1914; c/o Pinskerova, Praha I, Michalska 21.
16. Emil Mayer, 1893; c/o Persinova, Praha 1, Staroemstako Nam.26/II.
17. Johann Fuerst, 1905; Praha I, Husova 9/I.
18. Gusti Rachmann, 1915; c/o Oestrerreische Fluchtlingsstelle, Praha II, Dlouha 15.
19. Julius Spielmann, 1889; Praha I, Husova 9/I.
20. Johann Schiff. Praha XIII, Madriska T.
21. Josef Haas, 1900; Praha 1, Husova 9/I.

Thursday 13th October

British Committee for Refugees from Czechoslovakia, Prague, to BCRC head office, London: Dr Warriner has arrived, living in Hotel Alkron. Our office here is starting to function, liaising with Quakers and the Comité Centrale. Please urgently procure visas for twelve cases, six Social Democrat, six Communist, who must be got out with secrecy and quickly, who would undoubtedly be delivered and executed if their whereabouts was known.

Letter from BCRC Prague to BCRC London: To Sir Walter Layton. Father, I have also typed up, on an English typewriter, Dr Warriner's letter (attached, below) – she has no access to other typewriters – making it a lot easier to read...

Please excцse tyрiпЂ, I am пot mцch Ђood at the best oГ times bцt this BцlЂaяiaп machiпe has ceяtaiп pecцliaяities.

Yoц asked шhat PяaЂцe is like? Oпe oГ the most beaцtiГцl cities I kпoш, bцt tшo шoяlds, oця шoяk шith the яeГцЂees aпd, iп the otheя. the baпds aяe playiпЂ. Sцicides iп the midst oГ opeяa aпd Ђood яestaцяaпts.

Please excuse typing, I am not much good at the best of times but this Bulgarian machine has certain peculiarities.

You ask what Prague is like? One of the most beautiful cities I know, but two worlds, our work with the refugees and, in the other, the bands are playing. Suicides in the midst of opera and good restaurants.

Aпd its haяd, sometimes оця sепse оГ compassioп jцst dяies цр, ше сап't take апу тояе, theп some Ђood ally оГГеяs уоц a place to stay апd Гeeds уоц Ovaltiпe all піЂht апd ше pick цр аЂаіп.

And it's hard, sometimes our sense of compassion just dries up, we can't take any more, then some good ally offers you a place to stay and feeds you Ovaltine all night and we pick up again.

Theяe's по Ђеятап spokeп іГ уоц сап help it. Ше, the Bяitish aid шояkeяs, all Гeel Ђцilty at the Мцпich AЂяеетепt aпd шапt to covея цр the ЂB plate оп оця сая as the Bяitish аяе so badly thoцЂht оГ.

There's no German spoken if you can help it. We, the British aid workers, all feel guilty at the Munich Agreement and want to cover up the GB plates on our car as the British are so badly thought of.

Оця оГГice is оп Vояšilská stяeet, шheяe most otheя яesсцеяs шояk, шheяe the tяaiпs that шill take яеГцЂееs асяoss the boядея to Polaпd аяе ояЂaпized. The oпly шay oцt is the back dooя to Polaпd, althoцЂh jцst пош the maiп liпe via Мояavska Ostяava is пot яцппіпЂ. Ше'яе пot eveп sцяе that the Poles шоп't be hostile, yet the яеГцЂееs simply саппоt tяavel асяoss Ђеятапу.

Our office is on Voriliska Street, where most other rescuers work, where the trains that will take refugees across the border to Poland are organised. The only way out is the back door to Poland, although just now the main line to Moravska Ostrava is not running. We're not even sure that the Poles won't be hostile, yet the refugees simply cannot travel across Germany.

Sunday 16th October

Josef: I never discovered who pulled what strings, but in the BCRC Dr Warriner was the one who got things done. She was a striking brunette who looked stern but had the greatest sense of humour. She was a brilliant improviser – and she needed to be as she was under Gestapo surveillance from the day she arrived, not least from heel-clicking fellow guests in the Alkron and their silent listeners-in who sat at adjacent tables during her meals. It's rumoured she stole a handful of a general's visiting cards from his office which got her into places otherwise barred to her, and when the Polish consul was being awkward about railway routes, she bribed him with rare postage stamps which she'd discovered he collected.

There was also a Quaker lady, Miss Rowntree, Tessa we called her, who also had a sense of humour. I heard her comment, 'I've just gone and bought 1,000 pairs of gents underclothes. Not many girls can say that, now can they?'

Also in Prague were two journalists who'd been in Vienna before the Anschluß and could be relied on, Gedye and Fodor.

Tuesday 18th

Lord Mayor's Appeal, London: **DISTRESS IN PRAGUE. 40,000 REFUGEES UNDER CANVAS.** Sir Harry Twyford asks you to consider the men, women and children streaming into Prague. Tens of thousands are sleeping by the sides of roads blocked with refugee traffic. The bitter winter is imminent. The heartfelt sympathy of the British public goes out to the refugees in Czechoslovakia - democratic Germans, Czechs, Jews... Help must be sent immediately, help from the thankful men and women whose country has been spared the catastrophe of war. British relief is being organised at once. Money is needed. The situation is desperate. Make your gift NOW, it can save untold suffering - the suffering of innocent, bewildered people. Send your contribution to the Lord Mayor's Fund for Czech Refugees, Mansion House, London, EC4.

Josef: But on the streets of Prague everyone poured scorn on it; they called it 'Conscience money.'

Sir Walter Layton, BCRC to his secretary, his daughter: A friend in the Cabinet Office tells me that Chamberlain fears Twyford opening his Fund may have a bad effect on public opinion in Germany. Don't minute that, my dear, our committee might think our Government had taken leave of its senses.

Foreign Office, London, to Sir Walter Layton: Dear Sir Walter, I confirm our Legation has been authorized to grant one hundred visas to German and Austrian refugees now in Czechoslovakia for admission to this country for three months on the understanding that private organisations accept responsibility for their maintenance here during their stay.

Saturday 22nd October

Sir Walter Layton, to the Foreign Office: Dear Sir Orme, Thank you for the welcome information that the Legation has been authorized to grant 100 visas. I am arranging sufficient funds to provide for them for the three months covered by their visas.

Saturday 29th October

William Gillies to the BCRC: I enclose the list of Austrian refugees in Czechoslovakia. I am assured that all these men are known to the Gestapo... The list contains the names... inter alia, Bramminger.

Josef: I was in the BCRC's office when Dr Warriner came back from the British Legation and described to Mr Gillies how a British official had talked about us Austro-Germans. She was so angry I heard her through the door. 'I couldn't believe my ears. Despite my having just told him that they are in danger of being extradited to the Gestapo he said, "These men are Germans so, in the spirit of the Munich Agreement, they must go back to Germany." Why are they so ignorant? That's the official Nazi line he's peddling.'

Mr Gillies muttered, 'They try your patience, these people.'

Is this the famous British art of understatement?

Late October

The waiting continued. I was grateful for Adam's promise to spirit me out as one of the first Austro-Germans, but my faith in him was severely tested by living with such a promise unfulfilled. They must have had their own concerns, of course: who could they trust? Had anyone in their own Department gone over to the enemy? Would they be able to get their own families out when the time came?

I knew, from that overheard conversation in Voršilská Street, that my safety in Prague could disappear in the twinkling of an eye, but there was no possibility of arranging an escape myself. Travel over German-controlled routes was inconceivable. What remained of Czechoslovakia was surrounded on three sides by German territory, certain death to me. South-eastwards was Hungary, no friend to refugees, and growing ever closer to Germany. I was trapped in a country that was daily more and more subject to the Nazis and my only hope lay north-eastwards, through Poland, the railway on which the BCRC hoped to get us out. But while Poland was a sworn enemy of Hitler it was no friend of Czechoslovakia and it would be no haven for escaping refugees.

Tuesday 1st November

BCRC to the Home Office, London: 'I should be glad if you could arrange for British visas to be supplied to the Austrian refugees in the attached list, and extremely urgently, as all are known to and sought by the Gestapo...'

Mary: On the way into work a piece in the Daily Sketch caught my eye:

"'YOU'LL BE SORRY" AN ENGLISHWOMAN IN CZECHOSLOVAKIA. The strongest impression you get of the Czechs is their extraordinary toughness, resilience and nervous stamina. Prague went back to normal very quickly after the crisis, superficially at least. In Prague Wenceslas Square was brilliant again with startling neon signs and the only traces of air-raid precautions were a few wisps of sticky paper on widows. There were crowds at the Automat eating places, where you can eat cheaply standing at marble shelves. I saw a soldier bringing plates of goulash soup for his wife and small boy and a glass of beer for himself, a large map of Czechoslovakia spread out with certain markings on it. He stared at it for a long time, not saying anything, just looking quietly angry.'

'Disillusion reigns. It's hard to say which is stronger, the anti-German or the anti-French and English feeling. Any Czech, once he knows you are English, tells you plainly what he thinks of England, but nearly always with a curious absence of personal animosity. You are always told that England will be sorry for it and will pay for it sooner or later, probably sooner.'

'There is anti-German feeling: in the vast, cold, cavernous Town Hall in Prague, nothing is now written up in anything but Czech, everyone refuses to speak a word of German. One taxi driver refused me as a fare when I asked him in German. One German Social Democrat said the local grocer did not speak German, though he had spoken it fluently a day before.'

'But there are signs of a new pro-German orientation. Austrian refugees in Prague have become nervous and are making plans to move on, if possible, to Switzerland. There are rumours of a Gestapo office already set up in Prague.'

Minutes of St Saviour's Parochial Church Council meeting, Brixton: 'Decided: to raise funds for those Czechoslovakian refugees. The Vicar has heard some might be brought to London. Resolved: to hold a tea-party to welcome them.'

Josef: Adam finally saw me to give me a warning. 'No longer trust any official. Parts of government have bowed to German pressure. And watch your step, last night, at a secret meeting, young Prague fascists were handed tear-gas bombs for personal attacks on refugees. But', he paused and, for the first time in weeks, I saw him smile, 'we have hopes. Last week the BCRC managed to get some endangered Sudetenlanders away by train via Poland, through Gdynia. Next they intend to take you Austro-Germans on that same route to England.'

I suspect a delighted smile crossed my face, 'To England? To London?'

'That's their intention. The visas are taking time, it may be days, weeks...' his voice tailed off.

'Surely not weeks!' I exclaimed.

'No, no, days, I'm certain of it.'

I am bound for London!

I gave up visiting the refugee offices. It was the first place They – that dreadful word again, which now included some Czechs, Nazi underlings – would come looking for me.

All I could do was keep a low profile.

Saturday 5th November

I was issued a temporary Czechoslovakian passport. On the form they'd written, 'Citizenship: Disputable.' I was about to challenge that when it dawned on me, their dispute was not whether I was Austrian or German but – in a very Czech way of thinking – with the legality of the German invasion of my country, so I kept my mouth shut. On the passport itself they described me as 'Stateless?' – their question mark, not mine – one better than 'German', I decided.

Gestapo report, in Prague: 26 IV 1942. **SECRET**. Identified in Czecho-Slovak Intelligence Headquarters files, Prague: Ref 11.435/38, Cipher Zús 37772. To ministerial councillor dr Novák, Interior Ministry. I present that Reichs Austrian military deserter Josef Jan Bramminger, released on 20 Jul at 18:00 because he was used by intelligence officers to serve as a co-worker for the intelligence service of the Ministry of National Defence, passport issued this day.

20 III 1942. **SECRET**. Identified in Czecho-Slovak State Security files – *Státní bezpečnost StB*, Prague: File 427.177/38. Matter: Josef Bramminger, German citizenship. To the Land Office, Prague, department 22/b: I forward the application of Bramminger at this office for an interim Czechoslovak passport for all European countries to leave Czechoslovakia permanently. Living in Prague 8, Karlín, Královská Street 73. Landlady: A Valášková. The applicant came in July 1938 from Austria. Because of the passport law offence he was punished to 7 days imprisonment. There was not found any moral or political objection. Not gainfully employed, supported by the Social Democratic committee for financial relief for German emigrants. Has registered on the register of foreigners; has applied for a residence permit without a passport, code 52/35. Given his intention to depart for foreign countries these applications are left for now. After dispatch files again to StB. Passport issued: 'Stateless? Visa 26795 Prague, 22 Oct 38-22 Jan 39.'

Tuesday 8th November

Josef: I adored *Česky Párky* – Czech hotdogs, you'd call them, served with bread and mustard, like frankfurters but better tasting. I'd have some for lunch at the street stands, reminding me of the stalls outside Stephsdom selling roast chestnuts. Somehow that thought drew me across the river, up the hill to the cathedral, and through its great wooden doors.

Inside a service had just ended, the smell of incense was still in the air. I'd rather forsaken my Catholic faith after Stephansdom but I dipped my finger in the stoup of holy water and made the sign of the cross. I sat down, just to rest, perhaps to reflect, but all of a sudden I found myself praying. All that lay ahead of me must have been weighing on me more than I knew. Would I break free of the enemy? Would I make it to England? What would I find there, I had no answers, and I heard myself, inside, asking, time and again, 'Please God, help us.'

Was it the sanctuary lamps close by and the far-off altar and its guttering candles? Or was this space really sacred, sanctified by prayer and worship? Was God involved? I don't know, I suppose he would have been. But suddenly the strangest feeling came over me, a complete stillness, a wholeness I can't explain.

When I'd gone in, it had been grey and drizzling, but I walked out into a square that was sunlit. When I'd gone in I'd felt fearful and low, but I walked out feeling more like my old self, confident and cheerful, the way I'd felt in Vienna in happier times.

Wednesday 9th November

Herr Gillies sent a message to meet him privately at the Hotel Steiner. Someone warned me, 'He's an obstinate and rude Glaswegian, but he's well-informed and honest.'

'I'm in Prague', he told me, 'to arrange Polish and British visas for you Austro-Germans on BCRC's first transport, but the procedure is slow in the extreme. Now, you've probably seen Miss Rowntree around our offices. Elisabeth, that is, not her cousin Jean, who also works here; in any event, everybody calls her Tessa. My colleague thinks she's a tough girl and suggests she take the first transport. I'm telling you this because Dr Hora's people' – he looked me in the eye and I nodded my understanding – 'have insisted you be on it. But not a word of this...'

My confidence soared. Minutes later I spotted Eberhard, who had his own good news: 'Adam says I will be on the next "specials" train, if yours gets through. I aim to stay in Stockholm and earn my living as a waiter in a bar.'

I chuckled inwardly, my stern-looking Prussian judge could surprise me at times. We said our goodbyes.

Friday 11th November

In early-October, the Engineer moved my lodging across town at short notice, never explaining why - possibly the Department's files were now open to prying eyes - to Mrs Peková's lodgings on Římská Street, which was where the worries really set in. I could trust Eberhard implicitly, and felt sure of Dr Hora, the Engineer and Adam, but the questions just kept coming... if those four knew then who else? What if some official from the Ministry of the Interior arrested me on the street? Could I be handed across the border to the Gestapo without any opportunity to call on 2nd Department's influence? Anyway, how long would that Department stay free of German control?

I decided to keep well away from my usual haunts so, when darkness fell, I slipped away from my lodgings and into the Hotel Alkron's staff dormitory. I didn't get much sleep that night.

Saturday 12th November

Finally a message, 'Your transport leaves tomorrow. A courier will be at the Municipal Library at five. Take no luggage to the library, it must not be obvious you're leaving. Not a word to anyone.'

Another night at the Alkron beckoned.

Sunday 13th November

Early that morning I slipped out of the back of the hotel. I'd have spent the day in the Deminka café but there was a new customer there. When he wasn't buried in a Nazi newspaper, he was taking undue interest in the conversations around him, and on this day of all days, I couldn't take chances. So I walked across the Charles Bridge to sit the morning out on the riverside that I'd discovered on my walks. Under the bridge, the water lapping against an old wooden jetty, and watching old women feeding bread to the ducks gave me some peace of mind, helped by the fact that it had many exits into Malá Strana's warren of streets.

All was well, though, and shortly before five I set out for the library. I didn't want to be late.

Chapter 4

From Prague to Liverpool Street, by way of Esbjerg

Sunday 13th November 1938

Josef: By 4.55, five of us Viennese were in the Municipal Library, trying to look inconspicuous. Someone we recognized from the committee sidled up and whispered, '*Wilsonovo nádraží*, that's Wilson Station, at seven. Bring nothing that identifies you as refugees, only one suitcase. You'll see people you know; do not recognize them, ignore them. You'll be given further instructions.'

Suddenly I was in a hurry. Back in Římská Street it took me three minutes to pack my entire possessions into a small suitcase and my trusty rucksack. I didn't dare tell Mrs Peková I was leaving the country, for her safety as much as mine, so I told her the Alkron had ordered me to move there, paid her what I owed, slipped out the back and walked to Wilson Station.

The main concourse was busy, with armed police and soldiers with bayonets fixed moving through the crowds. We five stayed together, spotting others we'd known in queues and cafés but making no eye contact. Suddenly the man from the library was there, urgently giving instructions in an undertone.

Karel started to ask, 'Why all this secrecy, why...?'

'Your lives, my life, depend on it', he whispered dramatically. 'Even if "They" are not officially in Prague they have men in the police and emigration who do their bidding. Trust no-one. If a whiff of who's on this train gets to them it will never leave the country.'

He moved off to another huddle of travellers.

I looked about me. The station was a flamboyant spectacle, pure Habsburgian ostentation. Sculptures of naked marble figurines competed with green and pale blue paintwork and dashes of red paint on ochre plasterwork. In comparison its stained glass and gilded wrought-iron were almost subdued. It was hard to relate this finery to the dark tale playing out in its midst.

Our luggage – a motley collection that scarcely merited the name – came up for inspection. The rumour was of valuables confiscated or stolen so we were relieved when the official looked, then simply waved us through. Next, passports.

Again, just a cursory inspection; was someone in government looking after us? Out of nowhere Miss Tessa appeared – what a relief! – and we happily handed our passports over to her.

We were fifty-two men and women, apprehensive, tired and nervous, suspicious to the point of hysteria of everyone in that station, official, soldier, civilian, each potentially a spy for the Nazis. Our departure was meant to be a secret, one our lives might depend on but, somehow, a handful of supporters had gathered at the barriers. Most of them were motionless but, with a few waving and more than one weeping, they were not inconspicuous. Two of the Prague committee materialized by our side saying, 'Harden your hearts, turn away, we cannot afford a spectacle.'

They shepherded us to a distant platform where four carriages lay waiting. With no departure board at the barrier and no announcement on the loudspeakers perhaps our exit was still a secret... the line certainly led to Poland: across the platform sat a goods train, stencilled along its wagons the words: 'Praha-Brno-Wrocław-Łódź-Warszawa.' To me they read, 'Poland-England-Freedom!'

As we climbed aboard our escorts whispered, 'Your single carriage is sealed off from the rest, so no stranger can eavesdrop on your conversations.'

We stowed the luggage rack with every kind of thing: parcels; a rolled-up blanket strapped about its middle; a battered brown leather suitcase with well-stitched corners, plastered with labels from many countries; rucksacks; oddly-shaped bundles; a violin case... fifty-two lives condensed. Gone for ever were the things I'd left in Quarinhof and Korneuburg. My worldly possessions were a small brown suitcase, a rucksack, some spare clothes, a few papers, a book or two, the clothes I was wearing.

Which reminded me of just how alone I was. One or two friends I'd made in Prague were with me, yes, but my past was gone and my future looked as dark as the night outside that terminus. The only light in my head was New Zealand, England perhaps. Those, and the hope of fighting back against the Nazis. Deep inside a voice said, 'You are not alone, child', but it's all too easy to ignore that voice. So, my final memory of Prague is of loneliness, alone, in the midst of fifty-one others – fifty-two, of course, Tessa was one of us. 'How wretched we must look', I thought. I wanted to weep...

Mary: 'You know', I said, 'no Englishman would lay his heart bare like that...'

Josef: 'But I'm Austrian, we're not as shy and reserved as your Englishmen...'

Mary: 'And I'm a poor, wretched Mitzi who can't work out if she loves you because of or in spite of that.'

Josef: We both laughed.

A man, somehow familiar, who'd been hovering around our group on the concourse joined us in the carriage. People whispered, 'Interior Ministry', others, 'A spy', so Miss Tessa spoke up. 'The train should leave for Ostrava at nine. At times we will travel close to territory controlled by Germany so please do not draw attention to yourselves. On a happier note, let me introduce someone who'll be travelling with us to Gdynia... Mr Fodor, from the Manchester Guardian, please make him welcome.'

A nerve-wracking delay of four hours then, just before midnight, an engine coupled on and off we set. We sat quietly, lost in our own thoughts. We were heading for a country that, despite its Munich betrayal, had long been a beacon to us. At that very moment I glimpsed another beacon through the window, across the city, the red lamp on Prague's radio mast. Then it disappeared into the darkness, hidden by the steam billowing past the window. Would England also be extinguished, like Austria and the Sudetenland?

Then... I must have fallen asleep.

Monday 14th November

Of those with me on that train a few stand out. At 22 I was the second youngest, some were in their 50's. There were more Germans than Austrians, more Austrians than Czechs, a handful of others. Forty-four men, eight women; trades union leaders, politicians, writers, artists. Our leader was Hubert Zipperlen, a thoroughly decent man, almost saintly, unlike the rest of us he had no politics at all. Just seven of us were Social Democrats, German and Austrian, nearly half were Communists. That made no sense, they'd formed less than 10% of the opposition to Hitler in Vienna, Socialists over 60%, the same in Germany. 'They'll have comrades working for them in Britain', Ernst Klein whispered. But these were dangerous Communists; Karl Bathke, Otto Brichacek, Walter Kresse (as he calls himself, his real name is Bruno Retzlaff-Kresse) and Hans Winterberg, all fully indoctrinated and active Reds. In Prague Winterberg led a group of Soviet-orientated refugees, he'll surface again, I'm sure. And, as Adam had warned me, some were NKVD.

Ernst is a true friend, a Social Democrat, Viennese and, like me – if three years older – from Favoriten. Like me he'd been on the list – the list that probably saved our lives – which Johann Hirsch and the Matteotti Committee passed to the British Labour Party, whose sponsorship ensured we were on this train. Others on that list included Karel Fuerst, Adele Gratzel, and Hilde Valina, all Viennese, all Social Democrats.

We had more immediate problems. Those who'd travelled across Czechoslovakia in happier times told us that Prague to Ostrava then took three to four hours, but now that the Germans had occupied the Sudetenland their territory cut across most Czechoslovak main railway lines. Our train had to zigzag on little-used branch lines through the night across the narrow remnant of Czechoslovakia. Even with those lengthy detours we were alarmed to see one large swastika set out in electric lights across a hillside by the line.

We never discovered the cause of what happened next, somewhere near Svitavy. Our train must have crossed the new German frontier. It was light by then, so most of us were awake and spotted the field-grey German uniforms standing beside the track. Immediately we were in uproar. Miss Tessa addressed us urgently, in a hushed but forceful voice, 'Behave calmly and quietly! Ignore them! We are crossing occupied territory!'

Worse still: five minutes later our train came to a halt in an empty stretch of countryside, all the more sinister for being deserted. We feared the very worst and in those agonising minutes I'll swear that each of us felt the hangman's noose about our necks. No one approached however and, thank God, the train started again. A babble of voices replaced the hushed silence as we tried to reason through what was happening. Had the secret of our 'closed carriage' leaked out in Prague? Had one of us betrayed the journey for a promise of leniency? Had the Nazis pushed beyond the boundaries agreed at Munich by the British and French and illegally occupied a part of Czechoslovakia? Not that such illegality would save our necks; no-one would be coming to our rescue. Had some official in Prague's Ministry of Transport mis-drawn a line on a railway map? The driver having no control of where the tracks took him might explain that terrifying stop, as he tried to make sense of German uniforms unexpectedly seen at a border that wasn't on his map.

But even that theory held no comfort. For twenty minutes, we rolled through rural stations and level crossings manned by men in hateful Wehrmacht and SS uniforms. Were they playing with us? Would they stop the train at the very next station? Our only defence... 'don't look out of the windows.'

Eventually - sheer bliss - soldiers in Czechoslovak uniforms again, and red, white and blue flags. We were safe, the most perilous forty minutes of our lives were over. People started laughing at how a carriage containing several death sentences and hundreds of years of penal servitude had quietly slipped past the 'oh-so-efficient' Nazis. However, I suspect our laughter was somewhat forced.

That journalist came and sat beside me. 'I think you're the youngest member of this party, Herr ...?' He was angling for my story, one I had no intention of telling. I tried to dodge his question by asking his name in the worst English I knew.

He replied, 'Herr Fodor, Marcel Fodor,' – I had already recalled it, in 1934 he was one of those I'd seen in the Café Louvre – 'but what brings you here, young man? So young, and amongst such important company? What is so special about you?' It was a provocative but intriguing question, one I'd asked myself but found no answer. Certain he wouldn't understand I replied in Wienerisch, '*i hob's gneisst,* I've been very lucky.' He looked about him, glanced down at his notebook then, snapping it shut, replied, also in Wienerisch, '*Gneiss'n,* I understand.' So, that rare thing, a foreign journalist who spoke our private Viennese language. And he'd cottoned on, I sought anonymity. What his profession need are people who crave the limelight, some of the many politicians on board perhaps. Off he went in search of them.

Late that afternoon our train approached the river that formed the frontier with Poland, where road and railway ran together. The road turned to cross the border, a car was zigzagging slowly between huge concrete blocks, just like our road-block at Hůrky. I could imagine, in woods and hedgerows alongside the line, the trenches and fortifications that covered this crossing and, in them, soldiers, stood-to. It was raining, 'good infantry weather.' I felt for them.

Soon the train crossed that river, slowing to a halt. A Polish soldier, rifle slung, climbed into our carriage. Miss Tessa noticed our worried glances. 'It's routine, every carriage has a soldier. I've seen them before, they won't give us trouble.'

As we moved off, she spoke again, 'Soon we'll arrive in Ostrawa or, take your pick, Mahr Ostrava, Mährisch Ostrau, Oderberg, Moravská Ostrava Bohumín or Bohumín. In the times I've been this way, I've heard every variation of its name, Czech, Slovak, Austro-Hungarian, German and Polish, but I've not necessarily got that in the right order, and these days some people get very touchy about the name. However, everything will be alright, their government knows about us. But let's not ruffle any feathers, let's keep ourselves to ourselves. They probably won't take us off the train but, if they do, just keep silent, direct any questions to me.'

Moments later we pulled into the station, where a shiny new sign proclaimed, 'Bohumín.' An official climbed into our carriage, announced that we were now in Poland, spoke briefly to Miss Tessa, and left. Seconds later we were startled by the sounds of a brass band starting up. An official reception? The last thing we needed. There were apprehensive looks in the carriage, was our escape no longer a secret?

'Listen, all of you', Miss Tessa's voice cut through the building tension, 'that band's further down the platform, it's not for us, it will be for someone in the other carriages.' She went to the door, looked out, and immediately turned around, 'It's a sports team that's...', her words lost in a spontaneous round of applause, a buzz of conversation and a gale of laughter, distinctly less manic than that of an hour earlier.

Soon the train was running along a river valley, lakes visible through the trees, as we picked up speed into the peaceful Polish countryside.

At seven that evening we arrived at Katowice, seventy kilometres inside Poland, where an elderly couple stepped into the carriage laden with an urn of hot chocolate, cups and small cakes. Miss Tessa beamed at them and turned to us. 'Quakers', she said, laughing, 'Friends of mine, in every sense.' They wandered up the aisle, proffering cups and cakes, responding to our gratitude with simple smiles and '*Zapraszamy!* You are welcome!' In the face of their simple goodness our suspicions faded away.

All night our train rolled northward through Poland. I went to the window, relishing the smell, that mixture of soot and fresh air. In the darkness I made out snow on the higher ground. Closer in, dotted between stands of silver birch, small villages showed in the moonlight, each with its duck pond and pigs, its Catholic church, its tumbledown houses.

Sergeant-Major Čeněk suddenly came to mind, 'What? Why? What? – What are you looking at? Why are you looking? What will you do with what you've seen?'

The answers came hazily at first, then sharply in focus. Čeněk had drummed into us that every station or junction, every bridge, river crossing or canal might represent a valuable target. I should be noting it all. 'You're seeing it from the ground, that may be useful one day, but visualize it from the air, a pilot's eye view.' As his memory-training kicked in, I felt my brain moving up several gears; I'd not even bothered to notice the station names.

I found Miss Tessa and begged to borrow her timetable. 'Only for a moment. I just want to know where we're going, so I can tick the places off as we come to them. I'll give it back, I promise.'

'Here you are, Josef, but I must have it back.'

'Yes miss', I replied, and hurried off, laughing. I copied the stations down, ticking off the names of those we'd passed already: Katowice, Bytom, Rojca, Tarnowskie Chory... ah, that had just flashed past the window on a dimly-lit station platform... Miasteczko, there it was. Lubliniec, Kluczbork, names I couldn't even pronounce. I steadily wrote notes in a notebook until, with a flourish, I ended with 'Gdynia!' The exclamation mark was celebratory. For the first time since leaving Prague I felt a sense of purpose. I thanked Miss Tessa as I returned it.

Our carriage was 'convertible'; its beds, suspended between the luggage racks, could be lowered. But they were so uncomfortable and, with each six seats producing just two beds, there weren't enough to go around, so we took turns sleeping as best we could, or hung around in the aisle. It was cold and the heaters didn't work, so few got much sleep. By God, it was bitter.

Our travel documents, prominently marked '*Poprzez promocje tylko,* Through travel only', meant the Polish police wouldn't allow us off the train at stations where it stopped. They stamped vigorously on those selling lemon tea and bread, sausages and pickled cucumbers from the platforms, although several silver rings, watches and foodstuffs were surreptitiously traded through open windows. Fortunately at some stations Quakers and the Red Cross were allowed to bring hot chocolate and biscuits to us.

Tuesday 15th November

Half-awake, half-asleep, I looked out of the window. The line was no longer running down the valley of the Vistula but across its flood plain, marshes half-shrouded in mist stretched to the horizon.

I realised we were approaching the 'Polish corridor', the Polish strip of land separating Germany from East Prussia. Around me people were whispering, and I could make out phrases, 'Are "They" in charge there?', 'Will "They" interfere?' The word 'Danzig' emerged from the chatter... suddenly I was wide awake.

Similar questions raced through my head. We all knew, after Munich, of von Ribbentrop's demand that Danzig be incorporated into the Reich, how the Nazis had illegally taken control of this supposedly 'Free City.' Must we cross enemy territory once more? Would we be as lucky this time? What would prevent them from halting the train and dragging us off?

A moment before the carriage had been relaxed, half-asleep; suddenly panic gripped us, I was as terrified as anyone. In a moment we'd cross out of the corridor and into Danzig itself. None of us knew what lay ahead.

Suddenly Miss Tessa was walking down the carriage, waving aside questions that burst around her like some bizarre artillery barrage. 'Gentlemen, ladies, do not worry', speaking in English, 'I've already made this journey and passed through Gdańsk - or Danzig as some might say - without interference. I do recommend, once again, no staring out of the windows as we go through the city, let's give them no excuse.' She said this so calmly and with such assurance that people quietened down immediately. She repeated it in German, with that slight Viennese accent she'd acquired from her time in the city. I enjoyed hearing that, but suspected that beneath her external calm she was as nervous as any of us.

Usually my memory is so good but I have no recollection of that journey through Danzig – perhaps my brain was frozen by fear. It must have been twenty minutes but it could have been as many hours, or seconds. I sat immobile in my seat, not daring to look out. Miss Tessa told us later that after crossing the border we went through the city's railway station, with uniformed men on its platforms, but soon passed into open countryside.

Then, through the mist, a white signboard with black lettering slid past the window, 'Polska | Danzig-Gdańsk', split by a vertical red line, one red line I was happy to cross. We were out of Danzig! Out of Nazi control!

.....

A thrill ran around the carriage. The tension was so intense that when Mrs Schwartz whispered to her husband, cradled in her arms, 'Now *wir sind sicher, sicher,* we are safe, safe', two grown men in the compartment ended up in tears. Others looked away, hiding their emotions.

When the train pulled to a halt men wearing white and red armbands boarded it. In Germany or Austria armbands, and the swastikas that usually went with them, had been a symbol of terror so, when a tall man said to Ernst, 'You must be glad to be out of Germany', Ernst said nothing and we all fell suddenly silent, fearing a trap. Was the train still in German-controlled territory, this a trick to reveal our identity as anti-Nazi refugees? Miss Tessa, sensing the change of atmosphere, got up and walked through the carriage, assuring us in English and German, 'It is true, we are out of Danzig. I know these gentlemen, they really are from the Polish Red Cross.'

Happy now we sat quietly, taking it all in. Freedom and safety were close at hand. Gdynia's main station was strikingly massive and modern, we'd left the Habsburgs behind and joined the 20th century. Miss Tessa appeared with a Polish driver and led us to two coaches that took us to our hotel.

I can recall the first time I saw the sea – the Adriatic – as a child. Papa had taken me on his train to Trieste. But Austria and Czechoslovakia are completely landlocked and, for many of the group, the grey, choppy waters seen from those coaches was their first sight of the sea. Our Polish coach driver called out, 'Huh! That's only the Bay of Puck, the Small Sea we call it. The real sea, the Baltic, is beyond. We call that The Great Sea.'

Moments later we arrived at our hotel, The Corniche.

Wednesday 16th November

Early next morning, after a troubled night in The Corniche, Miss Tessa set off to walk with us to the far end of Gdynia. Trailing behind her, clutching our luggage, we walked alongside an empty sandy beach, stacked with brightly coloured deckchairs and pedalos awaiting winter storage, empty of the Polish families who'd thronged there in the holidays. Our crocodile ground to a halt at the *Polska Riwiera,* the Polish Riviera, a rather grander hotel.

Tessa Rowntree to the BCRC in London:

Dear Miss Layton,

As a place to maintain refugees Gdynia is expensive, inconvenient and dangerous, with difficulties with the police and local people. I'd kept them in The Corniche, but stones were thrown at the windows and I've been forced to move them to The Riviera, a larger, more expensive, hotel, where they'll be safe. Mr Midgley, the British Consul, also stays here. It looks as though I have sufficient Sterling to get them away on a Polish ship this evening. It will be a great relief for them, and me. In Prague there was much tension and panic for those feeling trapped by the Nazi invaders. We were frustrated by our inability to find solutions. Thank God it's nearly over, for 52 of them. I'm going back to see what we can do with the 4,948 still trapped there.

Yours,

Miss Rowntree

Josef: After breakfast, three Viennese friends - Dr Paul Rares, Karel Fuerst and Hilde Valina - and I set out to stretch our legs along the promenade. We might have been walking into a seaside postcard, sea to one side, gardens and cafés the other. Outside each café a grid of tables, like a chess board, was laid out in the chilly autumn air, by now more in hope than expectation. But it looked appealing, even under that overcast November sky. Ernst ran to catch up with us - he'd stopped to buy himself a hat, a fedora - and soon we were talking as we walked. 'We've run away to the northern sunshine but missed the sun!' said Hilde.

'No, no', Paul re-joined, 'We're tourists, not runaways.'

Ernst spoke up, 'Before we set out from Austria on this mystery tour of Europe, the only sea most of us had seen was the Neusiedlersee but I long to see the far side of this one, as far as possible from Herr Schicklgruber and his evil gang.'

Later, we filed into a café. A Polish sailor sat at the bar nursing a beer. Hearing our accents, he came over. 'Mind if I join you? I'm Teodor. I'm on the Baltrova, just back from London.'

That had our attention, the Sudeten refugees had sailed on the Baltrova and we were eager to know more. He sat down and bought us a round. 'I can afford it. I'm getting paid and, anyway, I hear you want to fight those cursed Nazis. That's enough reason to buy anyone a drink.'

'Tell us about the Baltrova.'

'We sailed a fortnight ago, a cargo of grain and fifty passengers, thirty of them friends of yours, Germans from Sudetów...'

'No friends of...' Ernst blurted out, but went silent when Karel kicked him on the ankle; this was no time to parade refugee politics.

But Teodor was into his story. 'All went well till we got to the Kiel Canal' – now he had our full attention – 'Suddenly they were very quiet. I heard someone instruct them to stay off deck and shut the portholes; there were enough swastikas and German uniforms to anger any socialist, like you, I think...' There were nods and murmurs of assent. 'My mates and I are used to it, we just keep our heads down and do our jobs, but imagine it, if those bloody Nazis had stopped us and hauled one of them off just hours from the freedom of the North Sea! And they've done it before now. In October, Klemens told me, a mucker on our sister ship, they took away a much-wanted Socialist; he ended up in Dachau. They had no right, of course, but who argues with Hitler? Not for just one socialist, and a Jew at that. Anyway, on this voyage all went well. We told them, "Just keep your head down till we're past Borkum." It's the last German island and everything after that's Dutch, you can trust the Dutch.'

Paul said quietly, 'But none of us is important enough to warrant a diplomatic incident...'

Teodor replied with a serious tone in his voice, 'But then, who knows...?'

Not one of us dared answer.

Before lunch Miss Tessa assembled us in the Riviera's ballroom. Mr Fodor sat at the back, taking down notes. 'You're all asking what's happening, where will you be going, how you will travel. At last I have some answers. Previously the group from Gydnia to England travelled on a small coaster through the Kiel Canal', there was a sharp intake of breath, the very mention of German territory ratcheting up the tension. 'One was interfered with and the committee in London agrees with my suggestion that you', her gaze swept around the room, 'are too valuable to risk the German authorities flouting international law by stopping a ship in the Canal. It caused some delay, getting permissions, visas, and the extra money, but they've agreed you will travel on a trans-Atlantic Polish liner, the Piłsudski, to Copenhagen, where Danish Quakers will pay for your accommodation. It leaves Gydnia at six this evening, calling at Copenhagen on its way to New York. Then by train to Denmark's west coast, and ferry to the English port of Harwich...'

Her words were swallowed up by applause and a hum of conversation. She'd become accustomed to our infuriating habit of debating every development to the n'th degree and just let us get on with it. She'd given us more than enough to discuss. Some knew of the Piłsudski, one of the most beautiful liners afloat they said, but everything, Copenhagen, Danish Social Democrats, ferries, Harwich and England, had to be dissected, debated and argued over.

That evening, in growing darkness, buses took us to an ultra-modern, glamorous Maritime Railway Terminus. Two huge golden Polish eagles towered over us as we walked twenty yards across the quayside to the ship. She was a glorious sight: a real ocean-going liner, 'M/S Piłsudski' emblazoned on her side. Trim, bedecked with flags, a gangway with polished wooden rails ran down to the quayside, where a handful of armed Polish soldiers stood around in their distinctive *czapki,* caps; optimists saw them as a sign of Polish concern for our safety, pragmatists suggested they were there to ensure we left.

For the first time in my life I'd be stepping off the continent of Europe, my home since birth, the continent I'd grown up on. Was I sorry to be leaving? I don't know. My fellow refugees probably had the same tangled emotions. Most walked up that gangway with a new spring in their step. What had raised their spirits? The ozone? The hope of freedom over the horizon? Or was it the smartly uniformed ship's officer at the top of the gangway welcoming us on board? He must have known we were penniless refugees but still he greeted each of us as a treasured guest, to each one a handshake. His simple act was, for us, a transforming gesture. It allowed us, briefly, to forget that we were refugees leaving everything behind and, for one glorious moment, indulge ourselves in dreams of ocean cruises, palm trees and blue seas.

A white-jacketed steward led us down into the ship, announcing, in German and English, 'Please stay in your cabins, gentlemen, ladies, until your whole group have been allocated.' '*meine Herren,* Gentlemen'... what a step that was on the road back to civilisation, 'Gentlemen'! Imagine it, being addressed as human beings once again!

It was a strangely simple departure from Poland. No identity checks, no passports, all our documents were in Miss Tessa's hands until the moment a ship's officer handed them back to us in our cabins. 'They are determined to get us out of Poland as fast as possible', I thought, 'and with as little fuss.' It was the first time since Prague we'd seen those documents, let alone held them, but it was the last thing we saw of Miss Tessa or Mr Fodor.

On deck scores of flags arched over us, decorating lines that ran from bow to stern. Seeing my enquiring look a seaman said, 'We call it "dressed overall", for when we go transatlantic.' My mind went back to Favoriten, our flags straining in the breeze over factory chimneys, police struggling to bring them down. I chuckled to myself and wanted to explain my laughter to the seaman, but thought better of it. On the deck alongside us a few hearty tourist passengers were playing quoits, quite oblivious to my revolutionary thoughts.

'This is your captain speaking, Commander Stankiewicz...' the loudspeakers announced. The ship was about to sail.

Thursday 17th November

At noon we crowded on deck to witness the Piłsudski entering Copenhagen's harbour, where our 'first class' treatment came to an abrupt end. On Captain's orders our group assembled far away from the other passengers, to be led, clutching our luggage, through the cargo hold to stumble down a gangplank (without handrails!) onto a deserted dockside.

Tessa Rowntree had left us on the quayside at Gdynia saying, 'A courier will meet you in Copenhagen.' On the Piłsudski we'd been all alone. Now, in a bitterly cold, brisk wind we stood waiting for... well, we weren't sure what exactly. Our forlorn huddle stood, slightly fearfully, but with no sign of any courier. Eventually a figure approached, walking briskly, two officials trailing behind at a slower pace. 'He's English', someone said, 'look... that sports jacket.'

He introduced himself, 'Welcome to Copenhagen, my name's Bill Williams. Apologies for being rather late, tied up with paperwork and all that', glancing at the two officials who'd now caught up with him. 'There'll be a minimum of checks, they just want to see the right number of people against our list, then we'll be off to the Hotel Absalon.'

He cheered us up by announcing that leaders of the Danish Social Democrats would welcome us at the hotel. An excellent lunch and welcoming speeches, which praised our courage in fighting the Nazis, raised our spirits still further.

The lunch ended with all singing the Internationale, in Danish, German and Czech, bringing some close to tears.

Friday 18th November

The next thing I remember was being awake; it was past seven. Across the room Ernst and Karel were snoring.

The railway station was just by our hotel and the train didn't leave until midday, so I lay there for a while, thinking. 'Was this the last lap of my journey? Will it end in England, Canada, America, New Zealand? Will I ever see Vienna again? Or my family? Will I ever trust them again? Do I even want to see them?' I couldn't bring myself to find answers.

The very name of the train, *Den englænderen,* The Englishman, should have raised our spirits but our minds seemed to be elsewhere. The fear of Nazism had dominated our lives for so long that it took some getting used to, the idea that we were free of it. In near silence we rolled across the island of Zeeland and on to a ferry that took us over *das Storebælt,* the Great Belt.

Then, at about three in the afternoon, I thought I heard my name being called. I sat up and took notice. An announcement in Danish was coming over the train's loudspeaker, '*Dette tog kører til Esbjerg og stopper ved Kolding, Brørup, Gørding, Bramming og Tjæreborg.*' Ernst – resplendent in his new hat – was translating it for us: '"This train goes to Esbjerg and stops at Kolding..."', he gave up... 'and all those other places...'

I just sat there, stunned. 'Bramming.' Wasn't that where my family came from? As children we'd sat listening to Papa's tale: how, many years ago, four brothers left a village in Denmark and travelled south to look for work. One settled in Hamburg, his children creating a shipping line that still bears the name; the second reached Bavaria; the third put down roots near the Polish border. The last, our ancestor, made it to Vienna. But, so Papa told us, they'd all started out from a village called Bramming. It sounded like a fairy tale but, in German he'd been called '*Der Bramminger,* the man from Bramming', our name, and here I was, minutes away from the very place! 'I've come home', I thought.

The announcement continued, 'Passengers for Esbjerg should remain on the train, passengers for Padborg, Flensburg and Rendsburg change trains at Nyborg...' We sat tight. Soon the train was picking up speed on Denmark's mainland. I fell into a reverie so, two hours later, all I saw of my 'home' was a platform sign flash past the window, 'Bramming.' I looked around to tell Ernst and Hilde... they were both fast asleep.

Soon the line ran down a valley and the sea appeared, just visible on the left. A faint cheer went up around the carriage and we crowded to the windows. The train swung right and, through the opposite windows, the town, the harbour and the sea beyond came fully into view. Esbjerg at last!

From the first door of the first carriage Bill Williams was off the train even before it had stopped. He didn't intend his charges escaping from the platform and into the town. But we knew the routine and formed up in a disorderly crocodile on the platform. Danes and tourists surged past us to the exit.

From the station we walked to the harbour with its forest of masts, the fishing fleet at anchor. The smell was overwhelming, a potent mixture of sea, ozone and fish, mainly fish.

Then another impression, the sounds: behind us the locomotive was panting to itself, like a dog recovering after a long run; from the quays came odd grinding noises, the mechanical creaking of cranes and ships' winches, and, overhead, the screeching of the herring gulls as they wheeled above us.

We came to a halt, as if suddenly and collectively we'd been overwhelmed by the experience, like a party of schoolchildren too travel-tired to get up to any mischief. Mr Williams came hurrying down from the station and the spell was broken. He called out, 'There's our ship', pointing, 'beyond that crane. Come on, on our way, but first give me your passports, and check you've got all your belongings.'

'All our belongings!' Ernst grinned, '"One small suitcase only", those were our orders. What other "belongings" does he think we've picked up along the way?'

'Your new hat?' Hilde said, laughingly.

Then we were all heading through the harbour gates, Bill leading the way.

Inside we prepared ourselves for a long wait, half-expecting rudeness and abuse at the end of it. But those Danish emigration officers surprised us, they were calm, efficient and, miracle of miracles, polite.

Bill stacked our passports alphabetically on their table, handing a carbon copy of his list and a pile of exit visas to a man in uniform.

'Arndt!', called the officer, and Johannes Arndt immediately stepped forward from the queue – we knew the score by now, don't hang around, it only irritates the man. Bill handed over the passport, down came the rubber stamp, once, passport, twice, exit permit, a tick on the list, two lists, the official's and Bill's, then, 'Aschaffenburg!'

'Bathke!', 'Bing!' – Bill leant forward and whispered something – 'Bing, E!' Eduard stepped forward, down came the stamp, in went the tick, 'Bing, H!', 'Doctor Binswanger', 'Professor Bonaforte.' Eventually, 'Bramminger!', and I stepped up to the table. The official peered at the passport, and back to the list, 'This', pointing to the list, 'This says G J. Why does the passport say J J?'

Bill leant forward and said 'Our office in Prague, I think someone typed it from a garbled message. It's the same man, I've been with him from Copenhagen, I'll vouch for him.'

The official paused, then looked up at me. His stony face, his official face, softening to a grimace verging on a smile, down came the stamp. 'Go on' he said, more gently, waving me through. As I turned to go, I saw a note being marked against my name.

Out of the emigration hall and into customs, where 'Anything to declare?' raised a laugh and a chorus of 'Just one small suitcase!' from ten or more voices. The customs man grinned. His eye ran over us and he waved us through.

So, on we went, onto the quayside, past a crane's four gaunt legs, up a short gangplank, stepping down onto the ferry's deck. Then we were inside the ship, being led down a ladder and along a steel corridor by seamen talking in Danish. Parceled off into cabins, four at a time, all obediently filing off as we were told. As soon as the last group had been placed in the dimly lit cabins the seaman who'd led us down into the depths of the ship walked away, choosing not to see the sudden eruption of activity, of figures scurrying between cabins until we'd shuffled ourselves into those groupings that took no account of the official allocation, or any known alphabet. They suited that odd mix of politics, nationalities and personalities that ought to have divided us but, somehow, for now at least, gave us a sense of unity.

Out at sea I stood by the rail. I could still make out the land, a flat coastline at least. Sand dunes at most, no mountains, certainly nothing to remind me of Austria. I suddenly realised how utterly detached I was feeling, with no sense of what I'd left behind, or any destination, as if I'd been cast into a lull, a warp, where fear, hope and emotion were all absent.

Paul Rares's voice broke in on my thoughts: 'Back in Gdynia Teodor told us, "Keep your heads down till you're past Borkum"', he pointed, 'and there's Borkum, a seaman's just told me. Come and join us Josef.' I looked up and saw that while I'd been daydreaming twenty or so of the group had come out on deck, so I went over to them. Two or three voices began to sing and soon we all joined in. An Austrian folk song then some German choruses. I took one last look at the coastline as it disappeared below the horizon.

We were in the North Sea, and the further we got from the coast the more the ship pitched violently, like the giant roller coaster on Vienna's Prater. Soon large seas, cold and violent, bringing enormous waves breaking over the bows, sent me inside. On deck one could identify where the noises were coming from: the rigging, the spray breaking over the side of the ship, the lifeboats shifting in their fittings. Now, inside, the noises had the nightmarish quality of seeming to come from every direction, and when the ship dived down from the crest of a wave it shuddered from head to stern. Utterly unnerved, I went in to dinner.

Saturday 19th November

Afterwards, in the small cabin, I may have slept, I'm not sure. Certainly moments of wakefulness were punctuated by the sound of people retching. After a restless night a grey dawn crept through the porthole and I inched carefully out of my bunk and up to the promenade deck. Ernst was there already: 'They say fresh air's the best cure for sea-sickness, so here I am, ready for breakfast – if I can keep it down!'

It was cold, the sky was still dark and threatening and the wind lashed at us as we staggered to the rail. Quite unbelievably, in the midst of those towering seas, a lone fisherman in a small boat was gazing up at us through the spray, his boat so small that I stood at the rail transfixed. He noticed us and waved, seemingly oblivious to his surroundings.

'We're more than half way to England', Ernst shouted. Cheered by that thought, and by that lone fisherman, we headed back into the lounge.

Inside the heat hit us like a wall. With last night's stale cigarette smoke and the smell of freshly brewed coffee it was a heady mix. When we sat down a steward came round with cups and a jug that steamed invitingly. 'A drink, sir?' he asked.

'Coffee?' I asked.

'Tea', he replied and, without further ado, poured milk into the cup. I raised my hand to stop him, but Ernst pulled it back, 'We're not in Vienna, this must be the famous English tea we've heard about.' Then, to the waiter, '*Dankeschön*, Thank you, thank you for the tea.' He sat back, looking very pleased with himself.

A sea mist enveloped the ship. When it thinned we went on deck again. Suddenly someone pointed out to sea at a warship steaming towards us, seemingly across our bows. The refugees on deck clustered together in huddles, arguing, wildly gesticulating. 'What flag is that?' someone shouted, with fear in his voice.

Rather wearily a sailor pointed to the other ship's stern and called out, 'It's a White Ensign, can't you see the Union Jack on it, it's the Royal Navy.' We gave a muted cheer. I heard the sailor mutter, under his breath, 'and it's not a flag, it's an ensign.'

We'd been so delayed by that storm that we were so glad when finally we sighted the English coastline. As the ship steamed into the harbour at Harwich, in what she later claimed was an outburst of joy, Hilde leant across, grabbed Ernst's new fedora that he was wearing so proudly, and threw it into the sea, shouting, '*Freiheit!* Freedom!'

A ship flying the Red Ensign passed us, heading out into the North Sea, en route, a passing sailor said, for the Hook of Holland. With black hull, white upper decks and bridge, topped by two huge funnels in buff yellow, she really looked the part. One of us Austrians excitedly pointed to the name on the bows... 'Look! *Schauen Sie!*" he shouted, 'Its name, Vienna! SS Vienna.'

I didn't know whether to feel homesick or elated. So far, and yet so near.

'So that's where you lot come from, eh?' chimed in the sailor. 'She looks good, doesn't she? But that Vienna, she's a name to strike fear into strong men's hearts. She's got such a flat bottom that she'll make a breeze on a millpond seem like a typhoon. Want my advice? Always take the top bunk.'

As our ferry inched up to the quayside, a tug nudging her into her berth, along the harbour wall cranes were busy unloading from ships' holds. Preparing to disembark our faces registered every emotion: joy, excitement, despondency, apprehension, fear and utter bewilderment. I'm not sure all of us heard the harsh cries of seagulls overhead and the shouts of the stevedores securing us to the dock with heavy, tarry ropes; minds seemed to be on other things.

I determined to enjoy it, the bustle, the noises, smells and sights. In the distance, beyond some dismal sheds, a train sat at a platform. Could that be the Scandinavian, the famous Boat Train? In my mind that spelt London... and if London then the Houses of Parliament, the BBC, Trafalgar Square, red buses, policemen in strange helmets, myth and fable, but, above all... freedom.

Harwich, it's remained in my memory ever since. Not glamorous, nor exotic, smaller than Gdynia, Copenhagen or Esbjerg, colder, greyer and raining more heavily but, in my mind's eye, the warmest, largest and grandest of all, the high point of my life. I felt enveloped by a sense of welcome, freedom, homeliness. Perhaps I'm confusing that bleak, grey day with the emotions of arriving in London? Or of all that's followed?

By four that Saturday afternoon the SS Jylland had docked at Harwich's Parkestone Quay and, moments later, her passengers – several dozen travellers going about their business and pleasure, plus fifty-two refugees – had started down the gangplank.

I found myself at the back, at the top of the gangway, watching as the queue edged down it and spilt onto the dockside. In Czechoslovakia and Poland Miss Tessa had been our shepherd but here Bill Williams, rushing frantically around the edges of the group, looked more like a sheepdog, I think you say in English. My eyes were drawn to three uniformed officials standing off to one side, calmly surveying us, not saying a word; what were they then, watchdogs? In the background, twenty metres from them, greyest and least noticeable of all, a tall man in civilian clothes was examining us as searchingly as I had ever seen. The man's gaze checked slightly as it swept over me, and some sixth sense told me he'd spotted my scrutiny. He was a professional.

I lowered my eyes back to the crowd, seeing us as if for the first time. 'We come in all shapes and sizes', I thought. 'Every age, from me to the dozen or so greybeards, but no children. Where were they? Abandoned to relatives in Czechoslovakia? Waiting in Prague for another train? Would they escape?' Such despairing thoughts.

By their clothes some of our group were Jewish, but the majority not obviously so. One or two couples, firmly holding on one to another, others in groups, clustering together, fearful even here of being parted, then a handful of individuals, alone like myself – 'all alone in the world', the words flashed across my mind. But another emotion was creeping over me, a sense of well-being, of safety, of being safe; the first time in months, years even, that I'd felt that warm embrace.

The queue re-formed on the quayside, at its head a handful of immaculately dressed men and women, first class passengers. Then others, well enough dressed, business men and tourists. Then came us, wearing what was on our backs; there were few changes of clothing in our luggage, and little or no money to buy more.

At last I started down the gangway.

My first impressions of England? Cold, wet and foggy, no welcoming delegation, only those immigration officers and a dismal shed. But, there again, no undue waiting.

Those immigration officers treated us well, sometimes were even helpful – an unusual experience for us – questioning us when things were unclear. One refugee claimed his papers contained a mistake by the German *Polizei*.

Sensing a problem, Bill, sidled over.

Bill was thinking on his feet. 'They were once famed for their efficiency, but things have gone downhill since Herr Hitler's crew came to power. The police force is overflowing with Party placemen.

The refugee was shaking, the words, *So nah und doch so fern* - so near and yet so far, may have flitted across his mind. Certainly the thought of being returned into the hands of the Nazis had reduced him to a wreck. Perhaps that immigration officer was aware that the stamp in his hand might be the difference between life and death?

He looked Bill straight in the eyes and asked, 'Do I have your assurance that German border control have made a mistake?'

'Absolutely', Bill shot back.

In the back of my mind, to the thought, 'But Quakers never lie...', came an answer, 'Maybe Bill is not a Quaker.'

But that immigration officer must have known that Bill was lying, and Bill must have known that he knew he was lying and, suddenly that rubber stamp in his hand was the focus of this human drama. Down it came with a bang on the man's arrival card. In the tense silence it might have been a rifle shot, the noise was certainly heard all along the queue. '**ADMIT**', it said. All at once the tension disappeared, people breathed again.

Soon it was my turn...

'Port of embarkation: Esbjerg, Denmark.

Passport: Temporary Czech, No 110.

Duration: issued Prague 22.10.1938 to 22.1.1939.

Sponsored by: Labour Party.

Status: C/L - Conditional Landing. Refugee. Leave to land in the UK granted 19/11/38 on condition that holder will not engage in any business, profession or occupation and will emigrate from the UK.'

All fine by me, I'd happily go to Canada, New Zealand..., but finer still when the Immigration Officer stamped '**ADMIT**' across it.

Walking to the station Ernst retold a joke from Prague. 'In heaven the police are British, the mechanics are German, the chefs are French, the lovers are

Italian, and everything is organised by the Swiss. In hell the police are German, the mechanics French, the chefs British, the lovers Swiss, and everything is organised by the Italians.'

'And the Czechs?' Isucher Fischer asked.

'They can't decide if it's a joke!'

Special Branch, Harwich: Report 19 Nov. Arrival of Political refugees from Czechoslovakia. Party of 52 persons under leadership of Mr Hubert ZIPPERLEN. Stated they had come to this country under the auspices of the BCRC, to be met at Liverpool Street by Mr Malcolm, its representative. All the members of the party were anti-Nazi who had fled from Austria and Czechoslovakia. Names given... inter alia. BRAMMINGER, Josef. Born Vienna 15 Feb 1916. Austrian.

Josef: Harwich Parkestone Quay, the platform sign read, while an arrow pointed, 'London-bound trains.' Ernst called out, 'Apart from my fiancée, that sign's the most beautiful thing I've ever seen.'

'The Scandy?' A guard answered Hubert's enquiry, 'Dark blue, Sir, this platform, Number 1. Nothing but the best for the Boat Train. It departs when you ferry passengers are all aboard.'

'Look', Bertha said, 'this is First Class!'

'Why do you say that? They would never do that for refugees.'

'But see, the seats are not wooden, they are upholstered.'

Hubert broke in, 'And why are they sending us to Liverpool? They said we would be housed in London.'

At that moment Bill's head appeared around the door, 'You're going to London, have no fear. It's "Liverpool Street Station", not "Liverpool", I promise. North London.'

The Scandinavian pulled away from the platform at ten past six. Initially the line hugged the coastline, then we were into countryside, field after field, great hedgerows, old churches, mansions, a village with its cottages, then a station, Manningtree. Alongside the line great pylons, new to us, marched for a mile or two, cables strung between, before breaking away to stride away into the distance. At a large town, Colchester, we heard the announcement, 'The train at Platform 1 is the Boat Train for Romford and London...' I caught Ernst's eye, he was grinning, '...Liverpool Street. Mind the doors!' A sharp whistle and we were off again, steam billowing past the windows. There were many small stops, their names sticking in my mind, Hatfield St George, Ingatestone, a road sign to Margaretting...

The train rattled across a junction, jerking me awake. I sat staring out through the window, drinking it all in. I'd swapped the capital of a former empire for the capital of the biggest empire in the world; I didn't know whether to weep or laugh. But, for now, the fields and hedgerows, an occasional village, platform signs with strange sounding names, advertising hoardings, were all, quite literally, foreign to me.

I must have dozed off once more for when next I opened my eyes the train was winding its way through suburbs. Bill Williams put his head around the door of our compartment. 'We'll be in Liverpool Street in five minutes. On the platform do, please, stay together as a group.'

Something about Bill's politeness brought to mind what Miss Tessa had said, days before in Poland, about the officials she'd battled with in Prague, 'Some are Nazi, most are narrow-minded, but every one of them is a bureaucrat first and foremost. And to deal with bureaucrats you must use politeness, always politeness, at times politeness before truth,' she'd laughed at herself, 'although it hurts my Quaker upbringing to say that!'

For some odd reason tears began welling up inside me. I wasn't the only one for whom the tension was too much for, all at once, someone in the compartment burst into tears. In seconds the whole compartment seemed to be sobbing its heart out.

I do love trains, steam trains most of all, and it must have been a real sight, the Boat Train pulling into Liverpool Street. The terminus may be huge but at night it's murky, like a smoky cavern. Imagine it, all that steam, the smell of those engines, whistles blowing, doors slamming, the sheer bustle of the place, wonderful... it must get into your blood if you're the son of an engine-driver.

The train pulled to a halt. In no time we were out on the platform, fussing over our belongings.

Soon that platform was alive with activity – this was the Boat Train, after all – porters standing by piles of expensive suitcases, messenger boys and maids scurrying to and fro. We just waited, huddled together. I'd expected my arrival in London – 'London!' in my head I savoured the word, the long-sought dream, Eldorado and Shangri La rolled into one – to be a moment of elation, but, now, I just felt physically drained and emotionally exhausted. Looking around me I think the rest were just as overwhelmed, seemingly frozen to the spot. Bill disappeared into the crowd to arrange transport. Beside us the train was still disgorging travellers.

An official was fretting around some twins, a boy and a girl, about three years old, refugees who'd arrived on another train. They lacked labels, he was saying - I thought, do labels have the same importance attached to them in England as lists do in Prague? - except these labels were not attached, there was only string around their necks, no labels. Great calamity, what could have happened, was someone stealing labels? A nurse came up, all practicality, 'They'll have eaten them. Come on, we must get these children fed and watered.' The official wilted under this assault and moved off, the nurse, no-nonsense to the last, grabbed two small suitcases that were still unclaimed, put them down alongside the twins and strode off in search of other children.

A press cameraman appeared, wanting to group us refugees for a photograph. Some were wary, publicity the last thing they wanted. Instinctively I went to the back of the group, then sidled away before the camera flashed. Bill returned, and was again darting around, trying to keep his charges together; the BCRC might welcome the publicity yet Bill could see all of us were tired, a few even distressed by that camera. Eventually the journalist had his story and walked away, leaving Bill to regroup us and calm us down.

At the barrier a man with 'Czech Refugees' on his armband was trying to attract Bill's attention. Bill strode across, saying firmly over his shoulder, 'Wait there, everyone!' He soon returned. 'Let me introduce Mr Malcolm, a friend of mine from the BCRC. He tells me transport will soon be here.'

By nine we'd been assembled outside the station, damp, cold and subdued. Out of the fog emerged a huge red bus, a two-storey bus! Was I the only one overawed by that? We'd all seen pictures of them, but the sight of the real thing brought out childish fancies: what if the top falls off? Surely it must topple over on a bend... but there was Mr Malcolm shepherding us aboard and our fears subsided. The more nervous stayed rooted to the bottom floor, but most made a beeline for the stairs. For twenty minutes we drove north-westwards through London's suburbs, into the darkness. 'No hope of seeing Trafalgar Square then', Ernst commented, but we were too overcome to pay attention. Buses yes, no trams - then, yes, 'Look, a tram, also two storeys high!' - small houses so different from any in Vienna, tiny gardens on the street, smoking chimneys...

Forty minutes later we were walking through high, moss-covered old brick walls into a white-painted house, well-scrubbed, an uncarpeted hallway with worn cane furniture and deckchairs. Brightly coloured travel posters on the walls extolling the joys of 'Youth Hostelling' reminded me of walking in the Wienerwald. A middle-aged man introduced himself. 'I am Mr Instone, the warden of the Youth Hostel Association's Highgate Hostel, and I'm glad to welcome you to north London. I suggest you take your things to the dormitories then come downstairs to the hot supper we're preparing.'

Only as I heaved my suitcase onto the bed did it finally dawn that my escape was finally over. My mind went back four months, to the moment I was told to report to army headquarters. It hit me like a wave, I was free, I was alive... in sheer relief I flung my rucksack on the bed.

Sunday 20th November

First thing on Sunday morning some of us surprised passers-by when we appeared before breakfast and plunged into the freezing waters of Highgate Ponds. We emerged, cold but happy, to take in the view of London laid out below us.

Later the whole group, without exception, set off for Highgate Cemetery to visit Karl Marx's grave. There had been much argument amongst the Socialists before this pilgrimage, but Hubert Zipperlen quelled any dissent with an announcement, 'Some of us think of him as a political philosopher of Austrian and German social democracy...', when Isucher Fischer called out, 'And Czech!' 'And Czech, of course', Hubert diplomatically concurred, 'rather than as a hero of Soviet communism, so we will all visit his grave.'

Back at the hostel Bill assembled us for an announcement: 'It's vitally important that everyone register with the police' – the word silenced our chatter. 'That's for tomorrow morning. And, a piece of good news: the vicar of St Saviour's Church in Brixton invites you to an "At Home" tomorrow. He and his congregation are throwing a tea party for you in their church hall at four o'clock, to welcome you to England. It's in south London and you get there by bus, there are directions on the back of their invitation', he pointed to a white card on the table in the hallway.

'"At Home", *das ist sehr großartig!*' said Walter Jahnecke; 'In English, speak English', we chorused, with translations thrown in for good measure... 'So grand!', 'most noble', 'very elegant'; a joker called out 'I think the English would say "Posh, don't you know."'

Ernst muttered to me, 'It's just a tea party, and it will be tea, not coffee. Whether we call it a tea party or *eine Tee-Partei* it will be just as tedious.'

Monday 21st November

At 8.30 we walked half a mile to register at Highgate Police Station. The sergeant at the desk, the first British policeman we'd encountered, was gruff but polite, with none of the hard-faced arrogance we'd known in Vienna. Checking our immigration cards, he listed us in 'Central Register of Aliens, Live Section.'

Another list!

Then we had to debate going to the tea party. Most agreed to set off down the hill at two, and the conductor on the No 214 at Oakeshott Avenue didn't seem in the slightest bit surprised when twenty-nine men and six women invaded his bus and demanded tickets to St Pancras in broken and heavily-accented English.

Two hours later thirty-three of us - two, deep in debate, had missed the next bus at St Pancras - disembarked, under a grey sky and amidst considerable dissension, from a bus in Brixton, two stops before we needed to. We walked south through the drizzle along the Brixton Road, Karel Fuerst practising his English by reading every sign. When we came to a tea shop he began saying over and over, 'J Lyons and Co Ltd', before pausing to read something in its window. He caught up with us, 'What about this?' he asked, reading from a menu he'd picked up, 'It offers coffee under "BEVERAGES", halfway between "Orangeade and Horlicks", but all they show is "COFFEE (Black or White) small cup 2d : large cup 3d." Is this a coffee shop?'

We walked on in stunned silence. Only two types of coffee! Black or white! What sort of country was this?

A debate broke out, how many types of coffee were needed to qualify as a real café? 'Six', 'Nine', 'More than a dozen', the conversation grew faster and more furious until Paul broke in, 'But the real choice, *meine Freunde,* my friends, is this: English coffee', he paused, '... or Nazi coffee. I'll happily drink English coffee, whatever its taste.' That met with scattered applause.

We were ten minutes late when, arguing to the last turn, we finally arrived at the door of St Saviour's church hall in Vicary Street. Argument dissipated into thin air at the sight of an entrance porch bedecked with flags in red, white and blue, Union Jacks and flags of Czechoslovakia... our hosts had certainly gone out of their way to make us welcome. All at once we felt more truly at ease than we'd ever expected to be, and there was the priest at the open door greeting each one of us, smiling, shaking our hands and ushering us inside the hall.

Mary: The first thing I noticed was his politeness. In a sea of darting, suspicious eyes he held my gaze a moment longer, then, in halting English, he thanked me gently for the tea.

Behind the trestle table I carried on pouring out tea then I glanced over at him, thinking to myself, 'He must be the youngest of them. He's about my age. Where does he come from?'

I continued pouring out cups of tea until the rush had died down. I looked around for another jug of milk and, when I turned back, all of a sudden there he was, standing right in front of me, holding out his cup. 'Miss, the tea is...' his confidence suddenly deserted him and out it came in German, '*Der Tee ist sehr gut.*'

I smiled back at him and replied, haltingly – I wasn't very sure of my schoolgirl German – '*Möchten Sie… Möchten Sie noch eine Tasse*? Would you like another cup?'

'*Danke*, no, no... I mean thank you, Miss. You speak German, I think.'

'Only what I learnt as a schoolgirl, it's little and rusty, *wenig und rostig*.'

'But we must speak English, we have been told it is polite, no, it is not polite, to speak German in London.'

'Well, your English is miles better than my German, so perhaps we have to speak English', I replied, laughing. Then, slightly perplexed by the searching look he was giving me, poured him another cup.

Later, as I went around the tables offering biscuits and cakes, I said to him, 'May I ask your name? Mine's Mary, Mary Vida Brown.'

'Josef, my name is Josef. Josef Bramminger.'

I know I smiled. 'Mary and Josef. That has a rather special ring to it, doesn't it?'

Josef: I looked at her for a long time, struggling with my emotions, and for the right words. Then I looked around me. The others at the table were deep in their perpetual debates about Communism or Social Democracy. Perpetual, and noisy, so engrossed that not one of them was interested in my conversation with this English lady. This moment might not come again, I had to ask. Quietly, but utterly determined, I blurted it out, 'Might I see you again?'

Mary: I know I paused for a second or two, a pause as brief as brief could be, but I now suspect that to him it must have seemed like all the time in the world... 'Yes, I think you can, Herr Bramminger. But, oh dear, we haven't yet got a telephone. Would you be free next Saturday, at eleven?' I saw incomprehension in his eyes, even alarm, and hastened to add, 'Eleven o'clock on Saturday morning, that is.' Again I paused, struggling to resurrect my schoolgirl German, '*elf Uhr am Samstagmorgen*, I think it is. We could meet at the Lyons Tea Shop. It's at 506 Brixton Road. That's just north of here, on the main road, the Westminster Bank's next door. Take the No 59 bus, it stops just close by. Golly, will you remember all of that?'

For a moment I may have looked worried, then I smiled at him, 'But of course you will, it's the same bus you came on today!'

Josef: I replied, 'I have remembered it already, how could I forget?' I know I breathed a sigh of relief, the very first important question in all my life that I'd asked in English, and I'd got it right. 'How could I possibly forget?'

So, that's my story, from the day I was born until the day I met you.

.....

Johanna: That's most of the tale Josef and Mary shared in the weeks after they first met. Not all at once, sometimes in dribs and drabs, sometimes when a memory was triggered; much of it told when they were together that first Christmas. Josef often seemed to get lost in the telling, tailing off into wordlessness. He probably needed to unburden some of his secrets, he'd had no one to share them with for months, even years. Perhaps it was simply that he'd fallen in love.

Chapter 5

From Brixton to Birchington, by way of the River Mole

Monday 21st November 1938

Mary: I believe, no, I know, that today I met the one man that I want to spend the rest of my life with. I don't know how I know this; I couldn't explain it to anyone, my family, not even my closest friends. I know it in my heart. But as I write that I don't even 'know' what I mean by my heart... somewhere deep inside.

Certainly not with my head, for it makes no sense, for a dozen jumbled reasons. I scarcely know the man, as things stand he has no prospects, he must be penniless, he speaks only elementary English – that, at least, I can do something about. But, as for the rest I can't explain my feelings, least of all the utter certainty, and that's the oddest thing of all, how I just know I can be sure of him. He is 'true', whatever that means, but, for me it is sufficient, and everything.

For now I must wait and see how things come along, I'm seeing him next Saturday! Six days!

Tuesday 22nd November

Josef: After three days at Highgate the BCRC interviewed me in Bloomsbury.

'Mr Bramminger', said the stony-faced woman across the table, 'With regards to hospitality there's not enough in London, I say this to all refugees. We are sending you to a provincial hostel in Reigate.'

I wanted to tell her about Mary, how she was the best thing that had ever happened in my life, how I needed to be in London to see her. But she must get refugees out of London, my circumstances, my love, wouldn't bother her one bit. I will be sent to Reigate, wherever that is.

Saturday 26th November

Mary: At last Saturday afternoon came around and we met again, in the Lyons near Lambeth Town Hall. I cannot recall what we said, or what we ate and drank. Tea, yes, but the rest's gone, overwhelmed by happiness! When I went to pay, he tried to stop me. 'No', I said, 'don't be silly, this is my treat. At least this time I won't have to pour!' I sensed he was torn between embarrassment and relief. When the Nippy brought back the change I didn't give him a chance to mention it again, just got up and announced, 'Let's go for a walk.'

We walked through Brockwell Park, Dulwich Village, passing Horniman's, south through Sydenham Hill Park, Sydenham Wells Park – so many parks, like pearls on a necklace! – ending up in Crystal Palace, where we wandered around the gardens and statues. The dinosaurs, half-hidden in the foliage, took him by surprise, he marvelled at them as a little child does. As we walked we talked, of this and that and of nothing at all. Sometimes we walked in silence, not awkward silences, contented ones. Somehow, mutually, we skirted the politics and woes of the world. I sensed he wasn't ready to talk of his recent life.

Near the dinosaurs we sat on the grass and ate the picnic I'd prepared. He couldn't have paid for that, even if he'd tried.

I told him about my parents, my father an Anglican priest killed in the Great War, my mother Dorothy, who works at the Bank of England, about my schooldays at St Margaret's, Bushey, 'SMB' to anyone who's been there, a holiday as a child in Cuba and my first job, at Imperial Airways, now as personal assistant to a partner at Christie's the auctioneers, Mr Chance, 'Peter' to everyone, even though his names really are Ivan Oswald. 'Ah', he said, 'This a nickname?' He is learning our strange English ways!

On our way back I took him via Brixton's very own windmill. Then on, past Brixton Hill Court – I already felt confident enough of him to tell him it was where I lived with my mother – 'It is so stylish, so elegant', he said. 'In Wien also my family', he grimaced, 'live in a flat. In a *Gemeindebau*, "municipal housing", I think you say. They were famous in the 1920's, and in 1934', again he grimaced. 'You have read of them, perhaps?'

'Was one called Karl-Marx-Hof?'

His eyes light up. 'Yes. We lived in Quarinhof. Like that, but smaller.'

'Well the Court is fashionable amongst the younger generation, private service flats, rather Art-Deco. It's like some apartment buildings in the United States. My mother and I moved in last year.'

I'd sensed how wrought up he was when he'd mentioned his family, so I added, 'You must come and see it sometime.' He relaxed and took my hand in his as we walked on. It was past seven and fully dark when we arrived back at Acre Lane.

At the bus stop he said, 'They're moving us out of London in four days, to somewhere called Reigate...' His words tailed off as he searched for what to say. I detected hopelessness in his voice.

'Oh! Reigate's only eighteen miles. It's not so far...' I was trying to sound jolly but, inside, I'd gone numb. The very first day I met him I'd known I loved him and now, days later, was he to be snatched from me? How could I see him again? I was panicking, my mind fumbling around, as one fumbles blind for change in a purse. There must be something I could do, for I was sure he couldn't afford the train fare. I must go there.

'Now look here, Mr Bramminger, Josef' – his face brightened at that – 'I shall have to come to Reigate and see how you're getting along. There are easy trains from Victoria.'

He seemed lost for words.

'A week on Sunday? I'll phone your youth hostel and leave a message.'

He paused before he replied, then his smile faded and I feared the worst. But when he spoke he was serious, not dismissive: 'A few days ago and everything was wrong; my life, my family, my country, the whole world, all broken up, wasted. And now', he paused and a faraway look came into his eyes – were scenes from the past few months, from Vienna, from Czechoslovakia, flashing through his mind? – '...and now I have met you and, now, *alles wird gut*.' He stopped, struggling for the English words, I could see him summoning up his courage, then out they came, 'all will be well.' Before I could really take this in the bus had arrived. All of a sudden, he took me in his arms to hug me, then he kissed me, hopped aboard the bus and was gone.

Wednesday 30th November

Josef: I'm in Reigate, in Surrey. Our hostel's a villa, 'The Rock', impressive but shabby. We share rooms, it's crowded, we do the cooking, housework and repairs, but to sixty of us it's home.

I long to be in London, closer to Mary and finding a way to fight back, my two passions. The first makes the second worthwhile.

The Committee gave us 15/- for clothes and 5/- pocket money until 10th December. So we can buy food, nothing lavish. There's a small library of books and we've sworn to speak English to one another. Mary has given me an English dictionary; I turn to it often.

Ernst Hoch and Paul Rares are in The Rock, so part of our 'Vienna clique' survives. Karel was sent to Oxford, we don't know where Jacob, Hilde and Berta went. We have every sort here, Ladislav Hoschl, one-time waiter and painter of advertisements, Vlastimil Forst, baker and chauffeur, Adolf Mizik, radio telegraphist ('20 words per minute', he proudly boasts), a chimney sweep, a lawyer, a medical doctor, a station-master and an officer reservist.

But we're all strangers in a foreign land. For us youngsters, standing on our own two feet at last, confusion is mixed with excitement, but some older ones, who've lost everything, are in despair. The house is poorly insulated and the warden says this winter is one of the coldest ever. We sleep under thin English blankets, not our beloved feather quilts, and must get used to things like light switches that, instead of turning, flick up and down.

British Committee for Refugees from Czechoslovakia
Refugee DO's and DON'T's

DO talk English as much as possible. Bad English is preferable to German. You will learn English more quickly by talking it constantly.

DO make all telephone conversations in English.

DO obey police regulations and all instructions given by officials of the Committee.

DO be quiet and modest. If you do not make yourself noticeable other people will not bother about you.

DON'T talk German in the street. There is Nothing to show a man in the street that you are a refugee and not a Nazi.

DON'T listen to the 1,001 rumours flying about. The only authentic information is given over the wireless and in newspapers.

DON'T go about in groups of more than three.

DON'T discuss politics in public.

Monday 19th December

Mary: On Sunday I went to Reigate to see Josef and had a lovely day. Today, on the bus to work, a headline in the Manchester Guardian caught my eye: **'VICTIMS OF MUNICH – GERMAN REFUGEES – ESCAPE TO ENGLAND.'** I was riveted: '... Most of this very limited quota have already left Czechoslovakia. Their transport out of the country has been beset with every kind of difficulty. The only route was through Poland to Gdynia then by ship to Britain. I accompanied one of these transports from Prague to Gdynia. To travel on a train zigzagging through Czechoslovakia so as to avoid the German frontier, packed with party secretaries, editors and orators – each one assuring me confidentially that he was especially endangered – in their last train journey in Europe to a new life overseas, is not an experience I shall forget. No such politically "explosive" train can have travelled since that *plombierte Zug*, sealed train which took Lenin from Switzerland to Russia under German protection in 1917. During these journeys there have been moments of agonising suspense as, for example, when the carriage we were travelling in was accidentally sent on one of the stretches on the Prague-Bohumin line cut by the German frontier and came to a standstill. Every stranger who casually questioned our party of refugees was regarded as a Nazi spy. Later, with all prey to persecution mania, something like panic broke out lest the train should pass through Danzig or the ship be held up when passing through the Kiel Canal.'

I wonder if Josef knows those people. I must show it to him.

Tuesday 20th December

Five days before Christmas Josef came up to London and it was so intensely cold that he came to the flat. He was strangely silent and, at first, I thought it was because Mother was fussing around. But I was just beginning to understand him and vaguely discerned it wasn't her, or the weather. He had something bottled up inside. I aimed to tease it out of him.

To jolly him along I read out the weather report, '"28 degrees at Kew Gardens... snow showers in Croydon an inch deep with drifting" Ah! This will interest you... "in Prague it was 9 degrees."' That brought a smile to his face.

When Mother was out of the room, I sprang my surprise. 'Darling, what are you doing on Christmas Day? I hope you can spend it here with me. It'll be just us. I've told Mother I'm spending the day with you, come what may, so she's off to stay with the family.'

Josef: She called me darling.

Sunday 25th December, Christmas Day

Mary: Josef arrived at the flat at ten, don't ask me how he got here. I'd been to early communion and was preparing Christmas dinner.

Putting up the tree and decorations I'd wondered if his home in Vienna would have looked very different at Christmas, but he appeared suitably impressed. Over a glass of sherry, I wished him merry Christmas and he replied 'Frohe Weihnachten.' He could see I was busy and let me get on with cooking dinner, even offering to help. What a strange man.

We had to start somewhere so I asked about his name and he told me what his father had said of that village in Denmark. For a moment he stared into the distance, seemingly searching the horizon – in my small living room!

'The Danish train we were escaping on went through a station on the line from Copenhagen to the ferry and a platform sign, "Bramming", flashed past the window. For the first time in eleven months the words "I'm home" came into my head, but now...' and he looked around the room, 'now', he said, 'I really feel I've come home.'

Out loud I laughed, but inside I was lost for words. I was as happy as it's possible to be.

In the pause that followed I recalled that article. I fished the newspaper out and showed it to him.

'Ah, Herr Fodor, so he did write about us.' He read it, looking pleased. 'He writes well. Except we didn't go through the Kiel Canal. That's because Tessa – that's Miss Rowntree, the Quaker lady in Prague – realised the Gestapo would ignore international law and abduct us from the ship in the canal so she arranged we go by liner to Copenhagen. She probably saved our lives.'

'Twice the Gestapo have almost got their hands on me. Someone tried to hand me over to them in Vienna.' He said this slowly, reluctantly, as though the words were being torn from deep inside, then looked away.

Time hung still. When he turned back to me, he seemed to have found strength to continue, 'But already I had made my mind up to escape and they were too late.' I wanted to ask him who could have done this, but sensed so much pain that I took his hand in mine and held it tight, not saying a word.

Later, after the meal, he poured out his story, from his childhood to our meeting in the church hall. It was hard for him, I think. It was certainly hard for me to take in. Politics to us is Conservatives, Liberals and Labour bickering in Parliament, or wilder types sounding off at Speakers Corner; not bullets, torture, concentration camps and death sentences.

When he had to leave, I said 'The bus goes from Lambeth Town Hall...'

Josef sat up, 'Lambeth? Where they dance the Lambeth Walk?'

'Yes, darling, Brixton's in the Borough of Lambeth. *Me and my Girl*, the musical, made the dance famous. Do you want to dance it?'

'Of course. I'll dance with you, yes, but in Prague, whenever Czechs and Germans and Jews were together... and Austrians', he added, ruefully, 'the mistrust was intense. We'd sit there, sunk in despair, eyeing each other suspiciously, but if the band started to play the Lambeth Waltz it was electrifying. Everybody jumped up and danced. It was the only thing that brought us together.'

Wednesday 11th January 1939

MI5 report: We check all refugees to ensure no Nazi agents get in amongst them, but there is much political terrorising among those in the BCRC. They're billeted together in collective 'Groups' at hostels, where the Communist leaders endeavour to control them. Despite the rule that applicants may not undertake political activities those hostels are full of Communist propaganda, while they destroy Social Democrat and other groups' leaflets. This has led to many arguments and at The Rock, in Reigate, housing 70 refugees, police had to be called in to restore order.

The Communists have connections in Prague and London and get their own people out first. In the first transport there were only 7 Social Democrats amongst 52. An intercepted letter from a British-based Communist ordered the recipient to ensure that only 'our comrades' come to London.

Many of the refugees were actively engaged in anti-Nazi activity in Prague or Vienna. Some held high positions in their movements and expect to continue active opposition in exile, preparing for the liberation of their countries; but it's all committee work, their twelve groupings having re-formed from groups which existed in Prague. We are concerned that the politics of some groups represent a security risk.

Friday 3rd February

Josef: Every day I walk from The Rock to Mrs Davies' home on Reigate's western edge. The BCRC told us to write her address in letters, not the hostel's, so in an invasion any paratroops would turn up at her front door, not ours. In theory by then she, and we, would be long gone, but she's a brave lady.

She greeted me, 'A postcard for you from Vienna.'

Seeing Leo's name, I seized on it. One of my best friends at Korneuburg, *Ein Schneidermeister,* a master tailor, he'd been in the Great War, then conscription came around again and he ended up, like me, both private soldier and secret underground member. I'd written to him soon after arriving in Reigate so, as the Gestapo monitor all mail in Austria, he's being very brave, or foolish, replying to me, a deserter.

I read it avidly, 'Leonard Pröglhöf, Vienna 16, Albrechtskreithgasse 3/27. To Mr Josef Bramminger, c/o Mrs Davies Reigate, St Albans Road, Holmdene, near London, England.

1-Wien-101, 28/1.1939.

29/1.1939

> Lieber Peppi, Best wishes! I received your dear letter with thanks and joy, but I've left it a long time before answering. I have so much to do that I end up doing nothing. The 2 cigarettes tasted good. Hopefully you are well. On Tuesday I was found fit for service by the Wehrdienst, but don't have to enlist immediately. Meanwhile I am going to Graz. Also a beautiful greeting from Mrs Kendrick.
>
> Your friend,
>
> Leonard Pröglhöf
>
> Write again!'

I read it again, more slowly. Then, looking up, I realised I was still at Mrs Davies's front door and she was smiling at me. 'It must be important; you haven't even said hello.' My apology came out in German, not English. 'There's no need to say sorry', she said.

Three things had struck me. He'd handwritten 29/1.1939, yet it was postmarked 28.1. Why postdate it? Carelessness? No, it was our security check: any date error tells me he's in the hands of the Gestapo. Also, when I escaped, I'd left two cigarettes for him in my bedside locker. Likewise '2': all quantities up to ten must be in words, if in numbers it would be a warning: 'I'm not a free man.'

The third thing? Mrs Frieda... Frieda Kendrick, the girl I'd grown up with in Favoriten. I'd introduced her to Leo in 1937, by which time she'd met her Englishman, Mr Kendrick, in Vienna. Now they're married and living in England. What was a 'beautiful greeting'? Does she have some secret message for me?

Wednesday 15th March

Today the Germans invaded Czechoslovakia, or what remains of it. In my brain something stirred... back in October the head of Czech intelligence, František Moravec, had discovered the Sudetenland Nazis' password was '15 März.' He reckoned the Germans were arrogant enough to use a top-secret date in advance, so he, at least, wasn't taken by surprise.

Aberdeen Press and Journal, in 1943. Interview with Colonel Kalla, Czechoslovakia's Military Attaché in London. "In the morning the posters at Hyde Park Corner told me that Czechoslovakia had been invaded. At mid-morning a secret telegram arrived from the Minister of Defence at Prague telling me to secure all government monies, remove all important documents and do the best I could to carry on.

Some hours later another telegram arrived, again from the Minister of Defence, this time dictated by the German invaders. It ordered me to hand everything to the German Ambassador to London and proceed immediately to Prague.

I had no intention of handing over the Legation or of returning to German-occupied Prague. But I knew that the Czechs in London would need money so I sent a reply saying if I were to return to Prague I would have to settle my financial obligations here, make arrangements for storing my furniture, letting my house, etc, and that I would need £700. I am still waiting for that money.

I decided to go via Harwich to the Hague, where considerable Czech money was held, and bring it to London. I quickly completed my business there. After lunch with a Czech officer and his wife I dropped off to sleep – not surprising as I hadn't slept the previous two nights. I was roughly awakened by my hostess. She said the Czech Minister at The Hague had acted on the German-inspired instructions from Prague and handed the entire Embassy to the Germans.

As fast as we could the officer and I got on the boat.

When we arrived in London, I asked my companion if he was armed – he was, and so was I. We decided that if necessary we would make a fight for it.

The Legation door was opened by the caretaker, who quickly drew us inside. 'You are too late', he said. The Germans are taking over tonight.

'Over my dead body.' I said grimly, and gave instructions that all doors be barred and defended. Next, I telephoned the police and told them the position. I said I intended to resist any attempt to take over the Legation. I also rang my wife asking her to bring me another revolver and whatever ammunition she could find.

I need not have feared. Whether the sight of a solitary London policeman patrolling his beat or a discreet word from other quarters was responsible I do not know, but the Germans did not attempt to interfere with us.

Josef: I told Mary what I'd heard in Reigate. The Czech head of intelligence has escaped to England with eleven of his top officers, getting out of Prague on a KLM flight hours before the Germans arrived. 'You British love your cricket and have nicknamed them "Moravec's XI", because Colonel Moravec's in charge. They flew into Croydon. That's quite close, isn't it?'

Her face lit up. 'Yes, it's less than five miles away. When I worked at Imperial Airways my boss gave me my first flight, in a Tiger Moth, from Croydon Aerodrome. It was great fun.'

Anyway, Moravec's been set up in a house in Dulwich.

Late March

I could happily spend hours simply looking at her as she moves about the flat, treasuring her every glance, watching her hair, her face, her eyes. I'm enchanted.

It's so good to be with her, away from that hostel, from all that politics and intimidation. An unseen war's being fought in the BCRC for control between the Social Democrats and the Communists, and they seem to be winning. Party members get priority in the best hostels, places in universities always go to them, you must join 'the Party' if you want to study.

My old friend from Vienna, Johann Svitanics – the trades unionist who ran Favoriten's Red Falcons' youth group – is in the thick of it. He escaped to London after 1934 and helped found the London Office of Austrian Socialists. They re-established contact with the British Labour Party and trades unions through William Gillies, Labour's man in Prague – the man who helped me escape. Gillies fully understands the danger the Communists pose and ordered the TUC to accept as trades union members only Austrian workers who've registered through Johann's organisation. I remember him telling me, 'Communism is as dangerous as Nazism. It's not genuine democracy, it's dictatorship wrapped in red instead of black.' They hate him for seeing that so clearly, and not hesitating to say it. Johann's a good friend to me, but because he refuses to register their party members he is hated by the Communists.

Mary: Josef wrote to his parents and a reply came from Vienna in his mother's handwriting. He was miserable when he read it. 'They know of my connection with Franz Emmerich, that he helped me escape. They say he's held in the Hotel Metropol, Gestapo headquarters', his face had the grimmest expression on it. 'They write that they're both convinced Nazis. I'm so ashamed.'

'But didn't all Austrians become convinced Nazis after the Anschluß?'

'I didn't, and Mama had no need to, she already was.'

Taken aback at his own bitterness he said, 'Sorry, I shouldn't have said that of Mama. But for Papa to become one – a Socialist, a railwayman – that shocks me.'

I let it pass. I'd realised by now that I was deeply in love with Josef; life without him would be unbearable, but I sensed that there were things he finds difficult, maybe impossible, to talk about. I noticed how sometimes his hands formed tight fists, his brow became knotted and a great black cloud seemed to envelop him. I'd do my best to change the subject and talk light-heartedly. Until one evening, one terrible evening...

It was a Saturday. Josef had arrived cold, tired and slightly agitated. After I'd given him a cup of tea and some cake, I sat down beside him. His head was bowed and his hands grasped the cup as if his life depended on it. I pretended not to notice and prattled on. Josef sat almost motionless, his eyes rooted to the fire's fading embers. As I stood up to add more coal, he spoke in almost a whisper, but his voice trembled with pent-up emotion, 'It was my own mother who tried to turn me over to the Gestapo. Her own son!' He became still, his shoulders hunched in despair.

I was aghast. How he must have been feeling I can scarcely guess. The horror of it filled my heart and we held each other in silence for what seemed an eternity.

Tuesday 4th April

Today, over tea and cakes, I read out something from The Times. '"Liechtenstein has voted 95% in favour of retaining their independence from Germany." That's a good thing, surely.'

He nodded. 'What's not in the papers is that Liechtenstein's Nazi party attempted a coup against Prince Franz Joseph II von Liechtenstein. They failed, although I never thought I'd be glad to hear that a Prince had survived.' He added, as an afterthought, 'Especially one related to the Habsburgs.'

'Well, darling, that same Franz Joseph once offered me a job as his secretary.'

He was suitably surprised. '*Fürst*... Prince Franz Joseph?'

'It was early last year. He was Mr Chance's client at Christie's, a highly valued client, his family's art collection is one of the greatest in the world...' Josef nodded, 'and Peter Chance had me help with the Prince's account. So, for some months, I saw him often. He took me out to lunch and dinner several times and wound up offering me a job in his palace in Vaduz.'

'So why didn't you accept?'

'I don't know, darling. I couldn't quite get it out of my head that at times he was charming me. It was a tempting offer, and I know he's a devout Catholic, but I felt safest keeping my feet firmly on the ground here in London, so I refused him.'

Sunday 7th May

Josef: The BCRC has moved me from Reigate to their hostel at 17 Wimbledon Park Road in London. But life isn't easy: I have little money as we're not allowed to earn a living; the Communists are always manoeuvring and manipulating; there are always petty squabbles and arguments about politics, psychology and illnesses. I try to shut them out, but the atmosphere is despair and sadness. One poor lady hanged herself, she left her baby screaming in his cot. It was dreadful.

In Prague Hora's advice had been, '*sich immer zurückhalten,* Always keep a low profile. Sitting unnoticed in the background, nose in a book', he'd said, 'is the surest way to hear without being observed. People say things when they're boasting, especially those who, with a nod and a wink, claim to work in intelligence.' His advice? 'Always be the last to speak and say less than you know. People will either think you wise, or simple. Let them, their opinion of you does not matter.'

Mary: After Josef moved to Wimbledon, he came to see me almost daily. Then, one day, looking out of the window, I saw him walking into the flats. Something struck me, he'd come from the south, yet buses from Wimbledon stop north of the flat. So, when he got in I told him, 'It doesn't matter how I found out, but I think you've been walking from Wimbledon. Have you?'

He must be a terrible spy (or I'm an ace interrogator!) because he hesitated. I could see it on his face, he wanted to lie to me but couldn't. 'Yes, I walk', he replied finally. 'But it's not far across Clapham Common.'

A few days later I announced, 'Darling, it's sweet of you, quite romantic actually, but I enjoy our time together so very much and I cannot bear to think of you walking that distance in this weather. So I've had an idea, and it will hurt me deeply if you refuse. I've sold an unimportant trinket which means absolutely nothing to me, to help with your bus fares and when this is all over and we're together, you can, if you like, pay me back but, until then, please accept this as it would give me enormous pleasure.' He fought a rear-guard action all the way but eventually, and reluctantly, he accepted. A minor triumph!

Tuesday 30th May

Josef: Today I could bear it no longer, I had to do something, so I just walked up to Whitehall and into the War Office. I don't know where I found the courage. Such places - even as a teenager in Vienna I'd heard of it - mighty, daunting places, were not for the likes of me to visit.

But it proved so simple, at the reception desk a man just handed me a form. The question, 'Nationality?' gave me a small flicker of pleasure to answer, 'Austrian.' Against 'Purpose of visit?' I wrote, 'To offer my services for intelligence work.' When I handed it back, I hoped for a glimmer of interest or surprise on the man's face but was disappointed. No emotion, just a wooden response, 'Please take a seat, Sir, someone will attend to you.' He waved me across the room.

Thirty minutes later another clerk escorted me along dimly-lit corridors and up some stairs to a door, 'Room 427A.' He showed me into a bare, sparsely furnished office, with an empty chair and a plain desk with ashtray and inkwell. Behind the desk sat a captain in uniform who gestured me to sit down. His manner was remote, there was no introduction, no explanation; rather disinterestedly he just shot questions at me from a piece of paper on the desk, seemingly finding the task tedious. The usual: name, date, place of birth? Parents? School? But when, under the heading 'Military experience?' I spoke of Korneuburg and my training as a railway engineer, his manner changed. He was a Royal Engineer, I could see the grenade badges on his uniform, maybe that's why suddenly there was interest in his voice.

'Tell me your story', he said.

So I told him. About the underground, the Anschluß, the Wehrmacht, my flight to Prague and the training I'd been through there. About volunteering for the Czechoslovak Army, bridge demolition guards, the escape through Poland, and my need to fight back. He was interested, I'm certain, for he began firing off questions and scribbling in a note-book. For a few minutes he sat silently, completing his notes. I tried to ask questions: What could they use me for? How soon might I start? He was polite but non-committal; he gave me no encouragement to continue. The interview had ended.

'Someone will be in contact. It may take a week, a month possibly, it's been busy here.' He gestured, seemingly encompassing the War Office, Whitehall and a nation preparing for war, not just his own small part in it. 'Thank you for your time. We will be in touch.'

Friday 9th June

Ten days later I was summoned back to the War Office. I was immediately taken along corridors to a door marked '55.' Another dowdy office, although this one had a double-lock.

Behind a desk stood a tall civilian. He offered me his hand. 'Mr Bramminger, pleased to meet you, please take a seat. Do call me McKenzie-Smith. We have heard from colleagues in this building that you are anxious to assist this country and I may have found a way.' He didn't define who 'We' were, and it seemed unreasonable to ask. There was something familiar about him.

He asked me to repeat my tale, 'the important parts of it.' So out it came again. When I talked of my military experiences he hurried me on, 'yes, yes, and...?' But when I mentioned the Schutzbund, or Dr Hora and the training I'd received in Prague he encouraged me to talk, probing deeper, asking questions that made me realise that 'McKenzie-Smith' really knew his job. He was especially interested in the escape across Poland. No, that's wrong, not in the escape. 'Tell me about your "*Weggenossen*"', he asked, looking intently at me, 'your "fellow-travellers." Who were they? What were their backgrounds, their allegiances...?' he left the word hanging in the air.

I'd already noticed a list on the desk. He'd made no attempt to shield it from me but I could see he was watching me... I'd automatically started to read it, upside down. Ha! He'd caught me at it! But I'd seen enough to recognise it. It was a list of the fifty-two of us who'd landed at Harwich. Suddenly, I knew where I'd seen him before. 'We have met', I said, 'well not met exactly, but you were there when we landed at Harwich.' The suggestion of a grin creased his face.

I gestured at the list, 'I am certain of the politics of thirty-one of them. Seven Social Democrats, twenty-two Communists, plus two or three nationalists. The rest kept stumm, out of shock or canniness I couldn't say, I'm no psychoanalyst. There were two Czechs, eleven Austrians, two Ukrainians, a Russian and a Pole, thirty-five Germans. But you know that.'

He smiled. 'You are very knowledgeable about this. Were you a train-spotter as a child?'

'No, I collected stamps, although my father was a train driver. But since 1934 I've been trained to observe and recall. The question I ask is, why so many Communists, and so few Social Democrats? In Vienna never more than six per cent voted Communist, sixty per cent ASD. But they had three times as many as us on that train.'

'I also ask that question. Would you be interested in some work?

'If it helps defeat the Nazis, yes, although your Home Office does not allow me to earn a living'

'You've persuaded me. I will be in contact.'

At last, the wheels are in motion. As to McKenzie-Smith's real name, and who 'We' are, those can wait.

Sunday 11th June

Mary: I took Josef along to my church, St Saviour's, Brixton, to meet our vicar, Roy Foster and Stella, his wife. Roy had been a priest with my father before the Great War, and I'm always popping around to the vicarage to pour my woes out to them. Roy is keen on supporting refugees and he hit it off well with Josef. As we came out of St Saviour's I noticed Josef studying the tower. 'Are you interested in architecture?'

'No, no', he replied, grinning, 'just wondering how I'd climb that steeple.'

'Don't you dare!' I said, crossly. 'I'd be really upset if you did, and you wouldn't want to offend the Vicar, or me?'

'No, he's a good man. Don't worry.'

Thursday 15th June

Josef: Called back to the War Office. McKenzie-Smith came straight to the point: 'We need someone inside the Czech refugee organisation to tell us what the "Blacks" and "Reds" are doing. You Viennese understand these things better than us, we English wouldn't be caught dead discussing politics. Are you interested?'

Of course I was.

'The Czechs will be in touch next week', he said, and gave me a password.

MI5's files: Dick White has told Guy Liddell: 'That Czech organisation I'm looking into. That's going fine. I now have two refugees, a German and an Austrian, who should prove useful to us.'

Wednesday 21st June

Josef: This morning I got a note to meet at 2 o'clock, a mile from the Wimbledon hostel. There were two of them, civilians who I'd not seen in Prague, but the password worked. Mary had said, 'It's bound to rain this week, the tennis championship's coming up' and, sure enough, we set off across the Common in a thunderstorm. But rain suited us, we didn't want to be seen together. They threw questions at me, one after another. My whole life, Austria, Prague, my escape, every detail; the Schutzbund, the Austrian army, the Wehrmacht, who I'd worked for in Prague. All afternoon I answered their questions. They told me to produce a handwritten report the next day.

I sat in a café writing it late into the evening, all twenty-six pages. I couldn't write it in the hostel, too many inquisitive eyes. But it's done.

Thursday 22nd June

In the morning I was glad to hand it over, along with Leo's postcard; that really interested them.

Friday 23rd June

Czechoslovak Military Intelligence, Porchester Gate: We attach 26 pages of BRAMMINGER's story from Vienna to Prague and his escape to England, the postcard received from Pröglhöf, and information on Bramminger's contacts (partial extract below); some of those in Vienna could be possible sources.

Soldiers in his platoon of Pioneer Battalion 2 – Railway Engineers. Listed in order of potential as sources/agents:

1. Leopold Pröglhöf. Illegal, active in my cell. Master tailor, lives 3/27 Albreitskreitgasse in Wien XVI. A good illegal whose collaboration I have valued. This Spring was found to be fit for service in the Wehrmacht. Knows several soldiers, but postcard's security codes suggest he is in Gestapo hands.
2. Wilhelm Benko. Illegal, active in my cell. Butcher. Family lives in Wien XIX, sisters Gerta and Ernestine – she lives in Retz. He and Pte Gustav Schmidt escaped to Prague before me.
3. Hans Gerhold. Illegal, but from Oct 38 serving in the Wehrmacht. Born 1917, butcher's assistant. Lives Wien XVII, 10 Lacknergasse, mezzanine. You can get his address from parents by writing to them saying a girl is asking for his new address.
4. Jan Grossegger. Illegal. Came to PB 2 19.1.1938. Baker's assistant, used to work with me underground. A socialist from head to toe. Answered my letter sent from Prague on orders of your 2nd Dept. He had a connection to a SNCO in hvy arty in Kaiserbersdorf. Parents live Wien XVI.
5. Johann Frisch. Illegal, nfd.
6. Wilhelm Podhorsky. Was Social Democrat until 1934 though if later an illegal I don't know. Bricklayer's mate. Family in Wien XX.
7. Franz Kladig. Social Democrat but NK if he is an illegal. Carpenter. Father a pawnbroker in Wien XVII.
8. Josef Hofstetter. Social Democrat until 1934. NK if he is an illegal. Electrical engineer. Parents in Wien XVIII, side street off Wahringerstraße.
9. Johann Helm. Social Democrat until 1934. Baker's assistant. Lives Wien II, acquaintances there and still rents a room. Parents in Lower Austria.
10. Franz Meindl. Social Democrat until 1934. Factory locksmith, parents in An der Mur district, Steiermark.
11. Klement Jankowitz. Social Democrat until 1934. In conversation he very much against Nazis. Carpenter. Joined Austrian Army as volunteer. Parents

in Wien IX. His father also a carpenter.
12. Franz Studeny. After Feb fighting they accused his parents, him and his brother of giving help to the Schutzbund. All were locked up for months. Was employed in circus. Father was caretaker in Wien XXI.
13. Karl Wolf. Politics uncertain. From Steiermark.
14. George Maly. Politics uncertain. Czech, small by height. Was in the Home Guard. In July a charge was brought against him by a German officer in PB 2.
15. Hans Schneider. Politics uncertain.
16. Julian Eider. Is Nazi. From Wien XVII.
17. Ernst Gombotz. Is Nazi. From Steiermark. Highly unpopular in platoon.

Overall impression: During our questioning on 21-22 June nothing suggested Bramminger is a provocateur. He is quiet, a non-aggressive person trying to find a life in London and to improve his position as a refugee.

He registered with British War Office to offer his services to Czechoslovak military intelligence and does not impose any conditions. He suggested we test his information as to its credibility. He does not trust other immigrants residing in the hostel – he will not discuss with them his offer to co-operate with Czechoslovak intelligence. When we parted he promised to be always at our disposal.

Our incomplete London card index does not show Bramminger or Grossegger. Possibly after connecting with Grossegger the results of cooperation were not valuable so he was not used as an agent. More likely he could not be fully exploited as he was acquired just before the Munich agreement.

He was paid 5 šilinků – shillings.

Mary: Christie's is paying for me to attend Anti-Gas Training and I've been enrolled for training in Lambeth's Red Cross detachment, in Lambeth Palace; I don't know what the Archbishop of Canterbury thinks of us! I've made any number of new friends and – slightly bizarre – I love all those bones: femur, fibula, humerus, radius, tibia, acromion. I've even passed the exam. Next week it's splints and bandaging the wounded, then what to do after air-raids. If war comes, we'll be nurses on ambulance trains.

Saturday 1st July

At last it's dawning on people that war is on the way. A government circular arrived: 'All windows, glazed doors or other openings, must be screened in wartime with dark blinds or brown paper on the glass so that no light's visible from outside. Instructions will be issued about dimming lights on vehicles. No street lighting allowed.'

Wednesday 2nd August

Josef: The CRTF (overnight the BCRC has become the Czechoslovak Refugee Trust Fund) requested the Home Office extend my permission to stay in England by six months.

Someone from Czech intelligence warned me to take care. Since 1933 the Gestapo has been assembling an *Emigrant Archiv* of every exile, and their *die ausländische Organisation,* their English network of Nazi party members, local sympathisers and criminals, is still active. I will not tell Mary this.

Mary: Lambeth has awarded me an Anti-Gas Training Certificate. Hurrah!

13th August, Gas Mask Sunday

I think we've turned the corner: since Munich people, ordinary, quite sensible people you'd have thought, scoffed at the very idea that Hitler would attack, ridiculing anyone who warned what was coming. Now - a shameful spectacle - they clamour and fight in the queues to receive their gas masks.

Everybody's busily preparing for war. Sandbags and planks heaped in the streets, anti-aircraft guns in the parks and men digging trenches. It'll be a grisly business. I've discovered Lambeth has a secret stockpile of hundreds of cardboard coffins, and an Air Raid Precautions officer came around the flats to list how many people would be in each one by day and night. 'It helps us', she said, 'look for casualties trapped after a bombing... and any bodies', she added. Now there's a cheery thought.

I've packed up the china and glass, leaving just the basics. Auntie Lily will store it in Melksham. Mother and I spent nights stitching yards of blackout curtains for the flat which Josef helped hang. He said it reminded him of Prague, a year ago.

The end of August

There's an odd feeling of waiting for something to happen. London's always quiet in August, people away on summer holidays, but it's quieter still this year. Some companies are evacuating staff to the country, although Christie's evacuated only the paintings, not us. Few children play on the streets or in the parks, while crocodiles of them, with gas masks and bundles, head for the stations. The LCC slogan is 'No fuss, no tears' - most children think it's just another school outing; mothers being very very brave, hiding their tears.

Friday 1st September

Piccadilly: most buildings sand-bagged and windows shuttered while amongst the pedestrians there are many in uniforms, last-minute trenches being dug. Ever more sandbags are being piled against lampposts to put out incendiaries, our lovely red pillar boxes painted in yellowy-green gas-detector paint, but those oddly beautiful barrage balloons overhead bring a sense of fantasy to it all.

Sunday 3rd September, Declaration of war

I went to the early service. Everyone knew what was in the air and the church was packed. Roy gave a moving address on 'Love never faileth' - so there's some hope - the congregation was unusually attentive. There was no chin-wagging afterwards, not even the customary cup of tea, everyone wanted to get home, to familiar surroundings, the radio on, just in case.

At 1115 hrs Mr Chamberlain started speaking:

> 'This morning the British Ambassador in Berlin handed the German Government a final Note stating that, unless we heard from them by 11 o'clock that they were prepared at once to withdraw their troops from Poland, a state of war would exist between us. I have to tell you now that no such undertaking has been received, and that consequently this country is at war with Germany. ... Now may God bless you all. May He defend the right. It is the evil things that we shall be fighting against - brute force, bad faith, injustice, oppression and persecution - and against them I am certain that the right will prevail.'

'At long last, after all the shilly-shallying, it's out in the open', I thought. 'Now we can get on with it.'

Twenty minutes later the Town Hall's air-raid sirens sounded their dreadful screech. A false alarm, they were just being tested. Perhaps it was a good thing, it got us in the mood, if that's the word, for war.

People seemed to mobilise immediately, with Red Cross and St John's nurses and ambulance drivers in uniform on the buses and trains, off to report to hospitals. I know what I must do tomorrow, report for work, but only to tell Mr Peter that I have to leave, then on to an ambulance train, my place of mobilisation.

Later on, we listened to His Majesty addressing the nation from Buckingham Palace. I hoped, probably the whole nation and the empire hoped, his voice would hold out. Although hoped isn't quite right, many were probably secretly praying. Either way, lo and behold, it worked. He spoke well, with just enough hesitation to remind us of how human he is, but his pace and deliberation fitted the gravity of what he had to say:

> 'In this grave hour, perhaps the most fateful in our history, I send to every household of my peoples, both at home and overseas, this message, spoken with the same depth of feeling for each one of you as if I were able to cross your threshold and speak to you myself.
>
> For the second time in the lives of most of us, we are at war... We have been forced into a conflict... For the sake of all that we ourselves hold dear, and of the world order and peace, it is unthinkable that we should refuse to meet the challenge.
>
> I ask my people to stand calm and firm and united in this time of trial. There may be dark days ahead, and war can no longer be confined to the battlefield, but we can only do the right as we see the right, and reverently commit our cause to God. If one and all we keep resolutely faithful to it, ready for whatever service or sacrifice it may demand, then with God's help, we shall prevail.
>
> May He bless and keep us all.'

Josef, usually so quiet, was the first to speak. 'I hated the Habsburgs and all they represented, but your King, I do not understand every word he said, but I understand why his people love him.'

Wanting to share this day we went up to London and at 10 pm were standing on Westminster Bridge, the city's lights all around us. Suddenly an area went out, then another, and another, district by district, until only one remained. Then it too was gone and we were peering into an intense darkness. I was just happy to be holding his hand as we walked home through that blackness.

Monday 4th September

I got to work very early this morning, as did my boss. I think we both knew what was coming, probably the same as in offices all over the country. We both had something to say and, for such a serious moment, it was the funniest of things. 'Mr Peter...' 'Miss Brown...' our words clashed in mid-air. We both laughed. I managed to say, 'Mr Peter, please go on.'

'Mary, I have to tell you that I have been called up and must leave Christie's today. I'm joining the 58th Middlesex AA Battalion, based in Harrow of all places.' He laughed. 'Typically Army, sending an Etonian to defend Harrow.'

'Well', I replied, 'Mine's less warlike. I'm being called up to a Red Cross ambulance train somewhere, top secret doubtless, they certainly haven't told me. Heaven knows when we'll see each other, or Christie's again.'

So we cleared our desks and off we went, he to his house in Jermyn Street, me to Brixton.

My call-up papers were waiting in the flat, with a letter from cousin Trixie in Herefordshire: 'An hour after war was declared the sirens went off in Ross and the air-raid warden in Peterstow courageously drove round the lanes in his Morris, its windows down and his wife shouting "Take cover!" to the sheep and cattle. We'll be talking about nothing else for days. Such excitement!'

I've just heard that Unity Mitford shot herself in Munich. Poor girl. At SMB we were both ill, bedded down in the San together for a whole term, so I got to know her well and to like her, even though we were politically poles apart.

Josef: I went up to 131 Piccadilly, the Czechoslovak Ministry of National Defence, and signed on to the army in front of Colonel Kalla and Captain Pollak. Kalla – he joked about his hatred of Germans, but he accepts Austrians simply because Mozart was one of us; a music lover, it seems – is clearly involved in military intelligence, Pollak is his deputy.

Tuesday 5th September

Mary: Reported at Streatham station, south of Brixton, to a doctor – 'Doc' he insisted – and a Sister Wallace. We are two SRN's, ten St John Ambulance men and nine other Red Cross Nurses, one being my dear friend Marjorie.

Doc told us: 'We'll be on the Flying Flea.' Our puzzled looks made him laugh, 'Oh, that. It's the nickname for Ambulance Train No 32, because she'll be gadding about here and there. The way I've seen you Red Cross types go at things no flea would dare get on-board! Anyway, it's stabled – as railwaymen insist on calling it – alongside Train No 34 in Streatham Carriage Sidings, just south of here. We'll entrain patients at Victoria, Streatham Common and Penge East for hospitals in Brighton and Hastings. Let's go and have a look at her.'

Naïvely we expected a lovely clean ambulance train. Ha! For starters there was a distinctly odd bouquet in that sidings. Once we'd clambered on board it became obvious that in their previous life the carriages had been ferrying fish around and, by golly, they smelt of it!

Sister Wallace was not put out at all, she had us organised immediately. Overalls and leather knee pads appeared and everything, and I mean everything, was disinfected. Then the men set-to, painting the insides white, while we girls polished the floors with Cardinal Red. Wall-brackets were fixed for stretchers, windows blacked out, and Elsan toilets installed. Before long we were ready for anything, fleas OR Germans!

MI5, memorandum from Dick White: The Czechoslovak Trust Fund. Having exchanged ideas with Col Kalla our views on this appalling organisation closely agree. He is maintaining his own observers in this Fund, whose names he has given me and whose information will come to us. This is a great help. As I told Maj Kendrick, we are extremely pleased with the results of our new liaison with Kalla. He displays the utmost keenness to help in our Central European work, and his great experience of CE mentalities and wide knowledge of German SS methods are likely to prove of real value. DW.

Thursday 14th September

Czechoslovak Trust Fund, Miss E B Montgomery to Home Office: Enemy Aliens. List A. i.a. BRAMMINGER Josef, Austrian. Active in Social-Democrat underground movement in Vienna, but has never shown particular interest in political events. Was a soldier in the Austrian army, deserted to Czechoslovakia after the Anschluß. Since resident in UK has received letters from his sister praising German policy and asking him to return to his mother. He appears to have been impressed by these letters. Nothing more definite is known against him. Does not wish to be repatriated.

Mary: I queried how he could know his story was correct. He replied, 'It's in my diary.'

'You kept a diary? How did you manage to carry a diary across Europe?' I exclaimed.

'No, no', he laughed, 'I want to stay alive. It's up here', he tapped his head. 'If I get a moment of peace, I may write it down, but not while I'm in hostels full of people I cannot trust, denouncing fellow refugees, plotting insurrection and calling it politics. It's terrible.'

'Darling', I said, 'Perhaps I can help. You tell me what's in there', I lent across and stroked his head, 'and I'll take it down, like dictation. It's what I did every day at work.'

'Can I trust you? Could you keep it secret?'

Missing the twinkle in his eyes, I was really offended, 'Trust me? Of course you can, surely you know that by now.'

'But...', then he saw the worry in my face and gave in, '*Nur ein Scherz, nur ein*

Scherz! What is it in English? I'm only joking. Of course I trust you, with my life', and he kissed me.

It turned out it wasn't the only thing he'd got out of Europe: one day I surprised him fiddling with a piece of equipment, something so small it could have fitted in a packet of cigarettes. He showed me: 'It's a spy camera, Sergeant-Major Čeněk issued it to me in Prague, and I've used it a few times since. It's made in Czechoslovakia, they have the finest optical companies in Europe, one of the reasons the Nazis wanted to invade...'

It didn't make sense. I interrupted him. 'But darling, how did you get *that* across Europe? How on earth could you carry that? What about the risk of getting caught with it at a frontier...'

'I never said I carried it. I used those NKVD agents who travelled with us, I hid it in their baggage!'

He was clearly pleased with himself, but I must admit I never saw that camera again. I wonder whose belongings he hid it in after that...'

Saturday 7th October

Today my heart is singing!

One of the oddest things about Brixton is its windmill, built on the summit of our Brixton hill to catch the wind. It stopped grinding flour five years ago but you can still imagine you're in a farmyard. Although we had both talked, self-consciously at first, about how we felt about each other, when Josef asked me today, on bended knee, outside that windmill, to marry him, I felt as if I could fly! Despite all that's going on, in that precious moment it was the thought of a lifetime with my darling Josef and all we could achieve together, and my soul was filled with happiness.

He said he must marry me before any more princes tried to grab my attention. One or two men have proposed to me before now, in more glamorous places than a slightly run down, suburban farmyard, but this was the first time I was ever tempted to accept.

Which I did.

Our wedding date is set for January!

If I live that long, that is, and it's not the Germans I fear but the blackout. Since regulations were imposed on 1st September, street lights went off, cars had dimmed lights, and road accidents doubled overnight. Last night I was nearly run down outside the flat, and I've fallen in more than one ditch as I've tried to creep along, arms outstretched, nerves on tenterhooks. A dangerous place, London!

Josef: I asked her and she said 'Yes.' How could I have doubted for a minute she would say anything else. I am overjoyed.

Monday 6th November

At last, I've been 'called-up.' A signboard on the gate read, 'Beaconsfield House, Birchington-on-Sea, Kent. The 1st Czechoslowakian Home.' By a gravelled driveway a huge white, red and blue flag fluttered in the sea breeze in front of a small country house, but white-painted rocks edging the flower beds at regular intervals - as regular as a pace stick? - were clues to its newly-acquired military status.

Inside a sergeant marched me to the Commandant's office, where Captain Pollak greeted me as if this were our first meeting. He spoke in English, 'Private Bramminger, welcome to the headquarters and training camp of the Free Czechoslovak Army, I am pleased to meet you at last. I understand you've already served in the Army so the oath you took in Prague in 1938 remains valid, there's no need to swear you in. When I've finished with you Sergeant Winter will take you to the orderly room, then your dormitory.' He nodded to the NCO, who left the room and closed the door.

'Now I can speak freely. In this grand mansion we have twenty-six men. Some you'll have known in Prague, one or two you'll have met in the hostels. For our own security we know a considerable amount about each of our volunteers, especially those who've been forced on us by the CRTF.' He was watching me closely and seemed satisfied when I grimaced at that name. He continued, 'Colonel Kalla tells me that you speak no Czech', I nodded, 'at least, so I must tell your fellow soldiers. You understand?'

'Yes, sir.'

I understood. So Pollak also had a foot in that murky world, Kalla's world, Hora's, the world of intelligence, of Czechoslovak military intelligence.

'So, to our real business. For now just keep your head down and soldier on. Sometimes there'll be a task from the Colonel. Speak only German or English, struggle to understand anything in Czech. It won't make you popular with your colleagues but stick with it. It'll open up opportunities. So, ears open and note what's said around you. Once they believe you understand nothing but "yes-no, left-right-left", they'll probably become wonderfully indiscreet. Report to me fortnightly, but if you urgently need to pass information...,' he gave details for emergency meetings.

In the orderly room the Chief Clerk looked me up and down and said, 'Listen carefully, this is your Free Czech Army enlistment form:

Národnost: Austrian
Příjmení (občanské jméno): BRAMMINGER Josef, pan
Aktuální adresa: 17 Wimbledon Park Road, SW18
Osobní dokumenty: Police registration document
Civilní povolání: Normal occupation: butcher, sausage specialist. Current employment: Training for the Army of the Czech Republic
Jak finančně zajištěno: Financial situation, nil
Znalost řeči: English and German
Speciální znalosti: Motorcyclist
Průběh vojenské služby: 10 months pioneer of the Austrian Army, 2 Btn Korneuburg, Vienna. 1 month in platoon 5 TGM, Prague, Army of Czechoslovakia
CRTF Case 105: Sponsored by Labour Party. Registered with BCRC through ASD committee. Now in CRTF's Loewinger Group

Is that correct?'

'Yes sir.'

Sergeant Winters showed me to the dormitory where – a real surprise – I found Eberhard, Eberhard Roëllig. '*Gruß Gott, Eberhard!* It is good to see you.'

'*Guten tag, jugendlich Josef.* Or should I say, Good day, young Josef', he replied, a smile on his usually solemn face.

When I'd settled in Eberhard told his tale. 'I travelled to Stockholm through Gdańsk and earned a living as a waiter in a bar. English humour is hard to understand but that seems to be a very English joke, a judge called to the bar! I attempted to enlist in the Czech Legion assembling in Poland but when the Germans invaded the Legion fled to France, so I wrote to Czechoslovakia's National Council in Paris, asking them to accept my services for their army there. In October a British visa was granted to enter a Czechoslovak military training camp in England. I left my job in Stockholm, boarded a ship and here I am.'

Birchington-on-Sea, on the north coast of Kent. It's a typical seaside resort: postcards, grottoes, ice-creams, a pier and a beach called Minnis Bay – we march there on occasion, to swim. On Remembrance Day we paraded at All Saints' church in the town square and laid up the Czechoslovakian flag on the altar beside the Union Jack.

Friday 17th November

War Office: MI-R report, 1st Czechoslovak House, Birchington-on-Sea. This institution is based in Beaconsfield House, taken on in October by the CRTF. They allocate 2/6d a day to the inmates. It is run like a barracks, with bedding neatly folded and suitcases at the foot of the beds like kit boxes. Facilities and space for training are limited, about an acre of lawns where PT, drill and preliminary weapon training are done, but no outside facilities. They go for walks in the countryside, and train in judging distance and fire orders.

PERSONNEL: In command, Captain Pollak, of the Czech Legation, was an infantry officer in the Czechoslovak Army. The men whom I saw varied greatly in appearance. On the whole a smart looking lot, obviously many former soldiers. They gave the impression of being very keen, living for the day when they could have a chance of getting their own back. Some are restive and feel they would have a better chance of getting to the front if they were in France.

DAILY PROGRAMME: Morning: 7-7.30: PT. Breakfast. Drill or training. Military lecture. English lesson. Lunch. Afternoon: Work in vegetable garden. Drill. Military lecture. 6 pm: Supper. Saturday afternoons and Sundays free.

CONCLUSION: It might be possible to give rudimentary preliminary training to 50-60 men but greater expansion on this site is impossible. But I think it politic to encourage this enterprise before official sanction is given to the formation of a legion, to keep up the morale of Czechs in this country, and some interest being shown will make them feel they are not neglected.

Signed: Lt Col Holland, MI-R.

Sunday 19th November

Josef: During Bren gun training Captain Pollak called me to his office, 'Your tribunal papers have come. Let me explain the Tribunal categories. "A" is Nazi sympathisers: interned immediately. "B" is men of uncertain loyalty: left at liberty but banned from travelling over five miles or owning cameras or maps. "A" covers less than 1% and "B" about 10% of German and Austrian refugees. Category "C" is the vast majority, 90% or so, men the police and Special Branch deem friendly: not subject to internment or restriction. You'll be one of those. Some people refer to them as "Friendly Enemy Aliens." Perhaps this is English humour.'

'Your papers are ready?'

'Yes sir.'

'Add this letter from Colonel Kalla to them. His recommendation will carry weight with the tribunal. At this office tomorrow, smart suit, 0930.'

Monday 20th November

Captain Pollak drove me into Margate. 'I attend the Tribunal as your "Friend." I'll sit next to you but I cannot address the bench, only give you advice.'

Inside the magistrates' court we sat in silence in a waiting room under a forbidding notice, 'MARGATE DISTRICT ENEMY ALIENS TRIBUNAL', avoiding eye contact with three other aliens similarly awaiting their fate. It will be held in secret, no press, no public and, apart from Captain Pollak, I'm on my own.

Rumour has it Tribunals are unpredictable, some sympathetic, some dispassionate, a few harsh and unreasonable. One London chairman regards all domestic servants as unreliable so automatically puts them down as 'B.' The Cardiff tribunal awards only 'A' or 'B', no 'C's at all. In Sutton if you own a car the chairman makes you a 'C', if not then a 'B.' In Reigate – I'm glad I'm no longer there – the chairman announced that it was better to be safe than sorry and put everybody into 'B.' I'd heard no such tales of the Margate tribunal.

There were two of them, a high court judge and a police inspector. My mind ran over past such encounters: the sergeant-major in Korneuburg bawling at me for some petty offence in front of my company commander, whom I'd always thought rather benign; or the hard, searching eyes of the Gestapo men questioning me after Schmidt and Benko's desertion. These two wore serious faces, but more sympathetic, I decided, than hostile. Mind you, I'd been wrong about the company commander in Korneuburg. He'd listened to the evidence in icy silence then awarded me seven days confined to barracks...

'Mr Bramminger', the chairman's words cut through my thoughts. 'Now we have your attention, let me ask you...'

I told them my story, in part at least: life in Vienna, my escape to Prague, the Labour Party sponsoring my journey through Poland. I left out anything related to intelligence, such things aren't for everyone. I ended by saying, 'I have handed you statements in writing from my fiancée's mother, from the Vicar of the Anglican church in Brixton, from the Czechoslovak Refugee Trust Fund...' but here the judge interrupted me, staring at me intently.

'I also have a letter from...' he hesitated, perhaps realising he should not blurt out its provenance. He'd been keeping one letter separate from the sheaf of papers in front of him, and now he looked down at it. He continued, 'a letter. Tell me, Mr Bramminger, have you ever had any connection or dealings with the Gestapo?'

I was knocked sideways, who could possibly accuse me of THAT? Beside me Captain Pollak gasped and put his hand on my arm, a reassuring gesture.

'The only connection I have ever had with that hateful organisation', I couldn't trust myself to speak its name, 'was an order to attend an interrogation by them in July 1938. It was to have taken place on the very day I escaped into Czechoslovakia.'

The judge turned the letter over in his hand and showed it to the man beside him. As he did so I made out the signature at the bottom and was astonished, it was the very same signature as at the end of the rather bland letter – 'We know nothing of this man...' – that the CRTF had given me and which I'd handed over to the Tribunal. It was the signature of Miss E B Montgomery. I made out the letterhead. Again, the same on both letters.

The two men had a whispered discussion. As I waited a cold fury grew inside me, 'How could she accuse me of that?' Miss Montgomery doesn't know me and all I know of her is that she works for the Trust's Chairman in its offices in Windsor.

The words '*Angriff ist die beste Verteidigungo,* Attack is the best form of defence' floated into my mind, and the moment the judge looked up I spoke out. 'Sir, there is another letter amongst those I handed to the Tribunal, one from Colonel Kalla of the Czechoslovakian Air Force, Military Attaché...'

He seemed slightly taken aback, and for a moment I feared I'd spoken out of turn, but then he smiled sympathetically and waved his hand to stop me.

After another whispered conversation with the police inspector he turned back to me. 'Mr Bramminger, you will be treated as a friendly enemy alien. Thank you for your time.' I was so happy, but the judge was still speaking, '...hand your registration book to the clerk as you leave.'

Outside the tribunal Richard Pollak was talking to me, 'You look dazed. Surely you never doubted the outcome?'

'Perhaps. But that letter! I must tell Mary.'

'Yes, yes, but first the clerk.'

Down it came, the rubber stamp. The clerk wrote something then handed it back. 'Carry this at all times', he said, expressionlessly, 'and produce it when required by a Police Officer or anyone in authority.'

I turned it over and read, 'The holder of this Certificate is to be exempted until further order from internment and from the special restrictions applicable to enemy aliens under the Aliens Order, 1920.' And, underneath it, handwritten in blue ink, words I found so oddly reassuring that I read them twice...

... Refugee from Nazi Oppression

Out in the chilly November air we walked to the staff car, where Pollak let himself go. 'That was an outrage, a libel. How dare they tell such lies, people who are paid by the British?' He paused, gathering his thoughts. 'I shall speak to Colonel Kalla about this. He must talk to his contacts in government. Such treachery cannot be allowed.'

He turned to me and a smile broke over his face, 'But "they"' - in Prague and Vienna the word had signified the Gestapo, here he meant a different 'they' (although, come to think of it, Nazis or Communists, there's nothing to choose between them) - 'failed in their aim, to get you classified A or B. Despite their worst efforts you are a friendly enemy alien! You must indeed telephone your fiancée with this excellent news.'

Friday 1st December

Sometimes it seemed the call to arms would never come. While we waited, we trained, although it wasn't real soldiering, no rifle ranges, no field exercises, none of that. We were lectured to, we improved our English and kept ourselves fit. Taking pity on me some of my friends tried teaching me Czech, but, as per Pollak's instructions, I proved abysmally slow and dunderheaded; they eventually gave up.

This Friday I was ordered to London. 'The story is I'm giving you two days leave to plan your wedding with your fiancée', Pollak said, 'See the clerk for a travel warrant.'

Saturday 2nd December

In London I reported to Colonel Kalla in Piccadilly. He wanted to talk about that Tribunal. Apparently, I wasn't the only one the Trust Fund had similarly 'denounced.'

'I spoke to my contact in British intelligence. He talked of "CRTF's poisoned pen letters"', Kalla said, 'Dr Walter Schultze, another refugee, reported something similar. My contact was already uneasy about the Trust Fund and is launching an investigation. We must wait and see what develops.' Then he angrily exclaimed, 'That organisation, always conspiring, always undermining. It calls itself "Czechoslovakian", but most of its staff and refugees are German or

Sudeten, for whom I have no regard.'

Then, in an instant, his anger dissolved. 'At our first meeting I told you that, because of Mozart, I do not consider Austrians as Germans.' He looked straight at me and smiled, 'Tell me, young Josef, do you play the piano?'

'No, sir. Though my fiancée does.'

Sunday 3rd December

Mary: Josef got the weekend off to see Colonel Kalla - his musical friend, I now call him - yesterday in London. Today we took a coach trip to Box Hill, which was as glorious as I remembered it from childhood. Tranquil, beautiful, just what we needed amidst the rush and worry of everyone preparing for war.

From the coach we went across the meadow to where the River Mole flows by, as calmly as ever, and on to the stepping stones. Some workmen were installing concrete dragon's teeth across the meadow and into the river. Josef took a professional interest in those, saying, 'I've never seen round tank traps before...' I was telling him to keep his voice down - people might look askance at someone discussing our defences in a German accent - when one of the men came over and said, 'You can go over the stepping stones Miss, but you'll be the last ones to do so, we're about to take them out. It's an anti-invasion measure.'

I smiled and told him we'd come back over the wooden bridge.

So, we got to walk over those stones, seventeen of them, just as when I was there with Uncle Bernard and Auntie Beatrice, all those summers ago. I'm sure they've grown smaller in the intervening years!

We started to climb the Hill itself, Josef carrying picnic things in that rucksack of his - which he's SO proud of that I sometimes feel slightly jealous! - and rounded a turn in the footpath. Ahead were some chalk cliffs, seventy feet high or more. 'The Whites', their name came into my head as clearly as when Uncle Bernard had said it to me as a child. Suddenly Josef had put down his rucksack and was at the base of the cliffs, scrabbling up the slope of scree. He turned to me and said, 'I won't be long.' Then he was off, climbing up the nearly sheer face.

Before I could say a word he was several feet up. I didn't know if to laugh or cry, to applaud or remonstrate. I wanted to call out, to urge him to be careful, but was terrified of distracting him and making him fall. Up and up he went, a handhold here, a foothold there, astonishingly quickly. As a child I've climbed on top of wardrobes and scrambled into trees, but rocks, not for me. The thought nagged at me, 'Don't climbers need ropes?' but I bit my tongue. He dislodged a small shower of small rocks that pattered down around me, and my heart was pounding like I'd never known before. I couldn't bear to watch but was transfixed by this diminishing figure silhouetted against the white of the chalk. A prayer came into my head, and I prayed it as urgently as I knew how when, all of a sudden, he'd reached the top and disappeared from sight.

I was left sitting on the grass, alone with his rucksack. I tried to marshal my thoughts, what I'd say to him, this man who'd deserted me, no explanation or warning, for what, a cliff! I kicked out at that rucksack, words were battling in my head, angry words, bitter words, when I heard a noise and he was there, standing in front of me, smiling as broadly as ever I'd seen.

'Josef! How...' but my angry words were silenced as his own, joyous and proud, tumbled out. He was so happy that some came out in German, that language he'd sworn never to use. 'I've climbed, seventy feet, *Keine Geräte,* no rope.' He was so full of joy at it that he seized me in his arms and hugged and kissed me. A moment before and I'd have pushed him away, telling him just how upset I'd been, but now I hadn't the heart to. 'Look, I climbed that', looking up at the cliff, 'in shoes! Not climbing boots, shoes! Don't you see? I can still climb, I haven't climbed for so long, but I still can!'

Then those self-same shoes staunched the flow of words. Looking down he saw them, all scuffed with chalk, a lace undone, and suddenly went quiet. Letting go of me he bent down, seized a handful of grass and set about wiping them clean, then retied his laces.

'Come on', he said, sheepishly, 'let's get up there and have our picnic.'

I never got to have my say!

Monday 4th December

MI5 report to Home Office: Commenced investigation of Czechoslovak Trust Fund following information received from Scotland Yard re Communists on its staff. DW.

Friday 15th December

Mary: We'd been told The Flying Flea is going to France to support the BEF but the order to move hasn't come. We gad around, as Doc calls it, all over southern England, evacuating patients from London hospitals to county hospitals, making room for possible air-raid casualties. In between, Sister trains us rigorously on getting wounded on stretchers onto the train - difficult where there's no platform - administering penicillin, morphia and M&B 693 - sulfapyridine, 'Winnie's life saver', as people call it. We splint the odd broken arm or leg.

We use the kitchen stove to brew hot drinks and, with allotments and chickens around our sidings, we make wonderful soups, omelettes, rice puddings, even sausage and mash. Except at weekends we sleep on the train, giving a telephone number if we leave our siding. We've come to adore our lovely train and everything's spick-and-span in case we're called out for evacuations.

Monday 25th December, Christmas Day

There was a real pea-souper of a fog last night. On the radio the King made his first wartime speech. He may still stammer a bit but he spoke so poignantly of the man who stood at the gate of the year: 'Put your hand into the hand of God. That shall be to you better than light, and safer than a known way.'

It couldn't have been more moving.

3rd January 1940

MI5 internal report: Communist cell within the CRTF. Inspection of Sir Henry Bunbury's staff list forwarded to the Home Office shows four known and active members of the CPGB:

Bruce Bedford WARREN, Legal Adviser.
Mrs Yvonne KAPP (in touch with Paul FRIEDLANDER, Comintern's agent in Paris), Assistant to Director.
Miss Margaret MYNATT (aka MEINHARDT and MANDER), Head of Tribunals.
George MUSGROVE (aka MUSGRAVE), Finance.

It seems clear that Sir Henry is skilfully manipulated by these members of his staff.

8 of the 14 staff in the Case, File Index, Statistical, and Tribunals Department at the CRTF's Windsor outstation are Party members. Three British subjects are under suspicion of same:

Miss Erica Blaithwaite MONTGOMERY.
Mrs Maureen KENNING-HAWSELL - PF 48855.
Derrick HOBSON - PF 53521.

These three are all middle-class members permitted by the Party - in order to penetrate otherwise reputable bodies such as the International Peace Campaign, the League of Nations Union and the China Campaign Committee - to keep their party membership a close secret.

Source 'H' reports that in the Card Room at Windsor, where refugee files are kept, there are six Communists, in a position to obtain any information the party considers useful. The Tribunal and Hospitality Departments are staffed by Communists. In Hospitality they are in a position to send a man to any place they like and to punish an opponent by sending him somewhere he dislikes.

WOLFSSOHN considers the Communists, who denounced SANDER and SCHUTZ, are playing similar tricks on Reigate Group to those they played on Windsor Group. He thinks someone should investigate the nest at Reigate, which could be very dangerous unless looked after pretty soon.

Cases have come to our notice of the blackening of political enemies. At least four persons have been interned by the Aliens Tribunals on information placed before them by the CRTF which is not substantiated by our records. We are inclined to think Communist influence responsible.

Recommendation as to action for curtailment of Communist activities inside the CRTF: The dismissal of the Cell of the CPGB from executive positions and the removal of foreign Communists from duties connected with the Filing, Hospitality and Tribunals Departments. Take no action on this report without reference to D G White, B2.

Sunday 7th January

Mary: In the middle of preparing for our wedding I began to feel unwell at the flat. I struggled along to the train, my self-diagnosis being 'it's nothing really', but Sister Wallace is no fool and took me immediately to see Doc. In his no-nonsense way he immediately diagnosed a severe bout of pneumonia and ordered me to lie down. So, protesting for all I was worth, but feeling as weak as a kitten, I found myself lying on one of our very own stretchers.

It's hard to achieve 'bed rest' when your friends and colleagues are fluttering around you every few minutes, but, with ten nurses to one patient I certainly received the best possible treatment. Sister telephoned Mother at the Bank to warn her she'd have a patient to look after when she got home. Then one of our own ambulances was only too happy to be called out to take me there. I wasn't very *compos mentis*, so some of this I only learnt later from Marjorie.

Wednesday 17th January

Guy Liddell's MI5 diary: Dick White's been looking into the affairs of the Czech Committee run by Sir Henry Bunbury. It was a shock to Cooper at the Home Office to learn that both Sir Henry's private secretary and his chief assistant, Mrs Ivon Kapp, are Communists. Bunbury is unaware of the situation.

MI5 files: Source 'M/S' EICHLER contends that Bunbury is a benevolent old gentleman whose one idea is to do good to these poor refugees, but too readily takes people on trust. He gives two sorts of letters to aliens appearing before Tribunals. In one he warmly recommends the applicant for all the privileges of friendly aliens, and in the other merely states that he knows nothing about the man. The first type is given to Communists, because their leaders have explained to Bunbury that they keep their rank and file under party discipline and so vouch for them, whereas the other organisations are more loosely knit. Bunbury swallows this, so Communists always get the best testimonials.

EICHLER and his friends are fed up with Communist intrigues. They believe all Communist refugees act under direct orders from Moscow to harm the other emigrants, to get rid of or discredit anyone who might lodge awkward information against them with the British Government.

To Hoddell, take no action on this report without reference to D G White, B2.

Saturday 20th January

Mary: My wedding day. My postponed wedding day that is!

Josef: I'd been staying up in London for our wedding but when that had to be postponed I was ordered back to Birchington. Poor Mary, she's only slowly recovering, and still she doesn't look well.

Monday 29th January

Mary: Drat that pneumonia. It has forced my resignation from the Red Cross and delayed our wedding – I should have been a married woman for the past nine days! Today I dragged myself to Rootes Motors at Devonshire House to be interviewed for a job by Mr Rootes himself. Felt rotten but managed to stay upright and keep a smile on my face at all the right moments. He's an impressive man, one of the wealthiest men in the country, genial, incisive, and an excellent judge of character... but I would say that, wouldn't I, because after waiting until he'd seen the two other candidates he came to an immediate decision and chose ME! I start next Monday on a job that's at the very heart of the war effort, so three cheers are in order.

As I walked back along Piccadilly (spiritually walking on air, but physically I could have crawled along that pavement) a newspaper poster seemed to shout at me, '**REFUGEE SPIES**.' With horror I read of an MP saying that all refugees were potentially spies. He claimed – just how ridiculous could he be – that along the North Sea coast, by hanging out their washing, of all things, they were signaling enemy aircraft, with the result that our ships joining convoys were being destroyed. He urged the Prime Minister to intern all refugees aged over 14, and to close all areas within 30 miles of the coasts. I wanted to shout at the paper, how could it print such tosh? But others will believe it. Poor Josef. Hopefully the people of Birchington have more sense.

Monday 5th February

Started work as personal assistant to William Rootes. My first job, to join the fire watching rota. Once a week I must sleep on fire watch at Devonshire House in case the Luftwaffe drop incendiaries on the building.

Josef: Kalla sometimes orders me up to London, with Pollak putting out the story that I'm doing translation work at 131 Piccadilly. In reality I report to a building in Porchester Gate, north of Kensington Gardens, where Czech intelligence has its headquarters. An unsigned, anonymous modern office block that gives no clue as to its occupants (we come and go through an inconspicuous back door). Once inside it's just bland offices filled with paperwork, files and directories, rather like Prague's Bartholomew Street, although without the metal bars. They're interested in factories, railways, water-works and power stations, not just in Czechoslovakia but in Hungary, Austria and even Poland. Some research is ordered by Whitehall, but we work to a distinctly Czech agenda.

Something about Eberhard tells me he's back in the game, working like me for Kalla, but we never discuss it, the less you know the safer you are. One day I saw the back of him going through a door at Porchester Gate. What's he working on? I have no idea, and people there have fingers in so many pies that I'm unlikely to find out. Perhaps they need a steady hand or two, and you can't get much steadier than a judge.

Home Office, Statutory Rules: Protected Areas coastal belt to include northern Kent.

Thursday 7th March

Guy Liddell's MI5 diary: Dick White is doing well with his Czech liaison, having already unearthed three Gestapo agents and three Communists who had joined our forces.

Monday 18th March

Czechoslovak National Committee, London: Cj 812/voj. Subject: Josef Bramminger. To: Czechoslovak National Committee, Paris. Ref our Cj 122/1940, this headquarters sent you an application, with his passport, for Bramminger J, an Austrian national who escaped from Austria to Czechoslovakia. As already reported, he volunteered for the Czechoslovak army. Mr Bramminger makes a very good impression, does not speak Czech. Please reply early, enclosing his passport, with any visa granted by the French government, so he can be notified as soon as possible.

Signed: Lt Col Josef Kalla.

Thursday 21st March

MI5 internal report: B.4b. By Dec 39 CRTF's staff had swollen to fifty, forty of whom are communists. Wilhelm SCHOLZ (CRTF refugee; formerly Communist Party secretary in Graz, Austria, married to Frau Hilde SCHOLZ, communist functionary in X District, Vienna – ref SIS report SF75/Austria/7) has been given job of Secretary of the Council of Austrians in Great Britain in Westbourne Terrace, W2. With Eva KOLMER he is ousting all non-communists from the Council and the Austrian Centre Management Committee (B24 report, source MILLER; speak Hoddell), their object being to sabotage the British war effort in factories so that England would be forced to sue for peace, and to work for the revolution that would follow the war. Describes himself as a Revolutionary Socialist but actually he's employed by Moscow.

Friday 29th March

Mary: First air-raid on south-east London last night, five bombs on Lambeth, just north of here, seventeen died.

Tuesday 16th April

Seventy-four more died in raids on Lambeth, Kennington and Stockwell.

Wednesday 17th April

Another air-raid tonight. All too soon it's become a ghastly routine. I hadn't seen Josef for a fortnight when they started and I miss him dreadfully. I have Binkie, my cat, as company and tonight I realised she's also my early warning system. Without fail, before the bombers are overhead and before the sirens go off, she comes right up to me, nudges my face, meows piteously, then sticks by me wherever I go. She must hear their engines' distinctive sound in the distance. That's the moment to scoop her up, plus the bag with water, food, torch and a book that I've prepared, and call to Mother to go down to the shelter. Personally, I head under the staircase with Binkie. I don't believe in shelters, somehow they go against the grain. Stand up to that man, I say – insofar as that's possible, crouched in my hidey-hole under the stairs!

Thursday 9th May

Josef: Last night thirty of my comrades-in-arms went up with wives and children to an hotel in Russell Square. Today Kalla waved them off in coaches to fight in

France, all in good spirits, optimistic.

All except me and Eberhard, that is. The French government hasn't granted us visas so we're stuck in Kent. We've trained together for nine months, why can't we fight alongside them? It's so unjust.

Pollak is spitting with rage at the Communists. In 1934 in Vienna they hid behind Moscow's orders and refused to fight, now Czech party members refuse to join our volunteers because Moscow declares this an imperialistic war. It's so frustrating, they could fight the Nazis but won't, I want to but can't.

Friday 10th May

On the radio: German land and air forces entered Holland, Belgium and Luxembourg at dawn. Aerodromes were assaulted by many airplanes, followed by troops landing. London has announced that Neville Chamberlain has resigned as Prime Minister and that a coalition government has been formed, led by Winston Churchill.

Saturday 11th May

A newspaper headline: '**ACT! ACT! ACT! DO IT NOW!**'

Churchill's first cabinet met to consider the threat of invasion to Great Britain. Driven by the scare stories it decided that all enemy alien males in Protected Areas must be interned, regardless of category, and ordered Chief Constables to arrest them the following day.

Josef: Oh God, let me fight, and let me marry Mary!

Chapter 6

From Kempton Park to Quebec City, by way of Liverpool

Sunday 12th May 1940, Day 1

Josef: Tonight I've started a real diary. Darling, I hope one day you'll read it.

At seven this morning – Mrs Branksome was cooking breakfast – there was a heavy knocking on the door. It was *Pfingstsonntag* – Pentecost, but we didn't receive the Holy Spirit, instead we got the Kent Constabulary, it said so on their helmets.

Eberhard opened the door to a sergeant and a police constable. 'Excuse me, sir', the sergeant said, 'gentlemen', correcting himself, as I appeared. 'Am I speaking to Misters Bramminger and Rollig?'

'Correct.'

'I'm afraid I must ask you to pack a suitcase each and come with us, Home Secretary's orders. It won't be for long, just till we get things sorted out.'

Judges know how to deal with policemen. 'Thank you Sergeant. May I see your authority?', said in such a tone that, for a fleeting second, I pictured Eberhard in a judge's wig and robes. The policemen saw only a man in a dressing gown but I swear they braced up at his words. He capped his mastery of the situation by adding, 'and can we offer you a cup of tea, officers?'

Mrs Branksome appeared from the kitchen and immediately took command. 'In you come officers, let's get you that tea, but...', suddenly she exploded, 'WIPE THOSE BOOTS!' Before they could get a word in, they were seated at the kitchen table with cups of tea and, refusals brushed aside, platefuls of bacon and eggs appeared in front of them. Somehow she got away with it.

The constable joined us upstairs as we packed. Eberhard placed the book he'd been reading on the bedside table, as if it would be there when we return. An optimist.

Ten minutes later they escorted us out of the front door. The sun was shining in a perfect blue sky. 'Never mind Mr Bram', said Mrs Branksome, loyally, 'Never mind, Judge.'

'Never mind.' Even as I write this her phrase rings in my head!

We sat silent in the police car as it drove towards Margate.

More men joined us in the police station. No one questioned us, no policeman answered any question, except one, 'No, it's forbidden to telephone your wife, father, fiancée...' A man in his seventies was the most bewildered of all. He'd been in Dachau two years before and showed us the scars. He seemed to be expecting to be tortured here as well. Most sat in silence, bemused.

Outside, in the yard, sat a motor coach, jauntily painted in cream and red, gold lettering proclaiming 'East Kent Road Car Company', as if for a seaside holiday jaunt.

At 8.50 we climbed aboard and set off, destination unknown.

We passed the magistrates' court. Seven months before, its tribunal had awarded me Category C. Three days ago Eberhard and I had been preparing to go to France to fight the German army. So how, today, are we a threat to our adopted home?

Does Mary know of this? No! How could she? It's Sunday, I'd only been interned for two hours.

What is she doing right now? I pictured her preparing to go 100 yards to St Saviour's – along the Brixton Road; which we'd just crossed the southern end of! – where three months ago we'd have been married, if she hadn't been so ill. If only. Maybe she does know, her job at Rootes seems so close to the centre of things. Perhaps she heard of this internment on Saturday and wasn't allowed to tell me, secrecy and all. But surely she'd have tried to tell me something... my mind wandered.

In the invasion scare signposts and street signs have been swept away, to confuse Nazi paratroopers they said, but they'd missed out shop names: 'Croydon Co-operative Society' couldn't have been clearer. We were heading west across London's southern suburbs. My mood darkened.

From the moment we left Birchington no one gave our destination, always: 'It's secret.' Someone's comment, 'We'll be on the Isle of Man, uncle Max was interned there in 1914', brought out a range of theories. The British and German governments will swap us with British internees taken in France... We'll leave via Southampton... via Bristol... We'll be interned in South Africa... Australia... Canada. Vast internment camps have been built in Wales, across the Midlands, Scotland..., every location known to man.

Up front the driver drove on regardless. Two policemen on the exits sat silent, they wouldn't be drawn.

Eberhard nudged me, 'Josef, wake up, I think we're there.'

We saw ahead a huge structure, a grandstand. Ascot, Sandown Park, Epsom Downs, all were touted and, for one bizarre moment, I imagined someone taking bets. Someone said confidently, 'It's Kempton Park. I was at the races there a fortnight ago.'

We turned through a gateway into a car-park full of coaches and army lorries, where the huge grandstand loomed above us. The coach stopped, a sign read, 'Kempton Park Race Course.' We'd arrived.

A soldier opened the door, 'Off the coach, come along, let's be having you. Don't faff around, GET OFF THE COACH!' The harsh words of the parade ground rained down around us.

We climbed down into a crowd of civilians milling around. Suddenly there was Hans, I hadn't seen him since Prague.

'Hans, it's good to see you, a friendly face!'

'And you, Peppi. Let's stick together.'

'Get a move on. In groups of forty... oy, you, can't you count? I said forty. GET A MOVE ON!'

Eberhard whispered, 'He has no idea... "Can't you count?" That's Karl Koenig he was shouting at, professor of mathematics in Cologne. I'd tell the sergeant but suspect irony isn't his forte.'

Internees stood in endless queues. Someone said it's the holding centre for London and the south. Two-thirds Jewish, half over thirty. There's a former barrister, a fat banker, a sculptor, a scowling turf accountant – can he see the irony? – men from the rag trade, students, chefs, Sigmund Freud's son Martin, professors, numerous scientists. Every sort.

'By the right, quick march!' and off we went, although marching's hardly the word.

'It's better than queuing', a humourist called out.

'SILENCE in the ranks!' roared the sergeant, and a ripple of giggles passed through us. 'Ranks.' The humourist whispered – he'd learnt fast – 'we must be in the army now.' It was the first time the mood has lightened since those abrupt early morning calls.

But we only hurried to wait. Our group soon halted, joining the end of that huge queue.

A sudden roar, 'GENTLEMEN!', as insincere as it was loud, 'No waiting around. Form lines at Registration Desks. Come on now, move yourselves!' The voice of a sergeant-major, seemingly as tall as the grandstand. On his shoulder, 'Grenadier Guards.'

An officer took our money, slowly writing the amounts against names in a ledger. 'Receipt! Why should you need a receipt? It's in the book.' Who were we to argue?

Another queue, a thorough body search. Books, razors, scissors, matches, all taken. People in the queue saw this and soon everybody was trying to hide stamps, writing-paper, a watch, a ring, money – to each the vital thing in their suddenly very small world – in their clothes or luggage. These frantic efforts, comically surreptitious, usually to no avail – where can you, at short notice, hide a book or a bottle of brandy? – had that queue writhing like a snake. Asking questions had the sergeant-major intervening with his metal-tipped stick, abusive shouts the height of his conversational powers: 'Shut up! SHUT UP!'

They confiscated Eberhard's Oxford Book of English Verse as 'unsuitable.'

Into a glass-domed enclosure where people were emptying pockets onto tables. Suddenly I was at the front and my ration card, a lighter, a penknife, Swan Vestas, some small change, were all swept into a large brown envelope, 'OHMS.' Out of another envelope a captain extracted an Alien Certificate, my own, I recognised the stain where Dorothy had spilt coffee on it.

Sergeant-Major Čeněk had said, 'Do three things as an agent and you may survive: know your exit; treat your weapon better than any woman you've ever loved, and' – that having gained our attention – 'read upside down.' I blessed his memory. Standing there it was child's play to read that certificate: '**B6092**. Interned under the general direction of the Secretary of State, 11th May. Alien: BRAMMINGER, Josef Johann, 701978; By: CC – Margate', I heard again Mary's voice, '"Chief Constable", darling.'

Then my photograph and signature. 'Nationality: German', that still hurt. 'Born: 15.2.1916 Vienna. Address: Beaconsfield, Birchington, Kent. UK arrival: 19.11.38.'

Then words I'd read so often,

THE HOLDER OF THIS CERTIFICATE IS EXEMPTED UNTIL FURTHER NOTICE FROM INTERNMENT

I laughed to myself, 'Exempted!' The officer added a stamp:

DETAINED BY DIRECTION OF HOME OFFICE
KEMPTON PARK ALIENS INTERNMENT CAMP

then wrote, '12 May', and his signature: 'Capt I J Henderson, Gren Gds.' Did the words, 'Refugee from Nazi Oppression' count for nothing'?

We waited in the Grill Room, now a store. We signed for an enamel mug, mess tin, knife, fork and spoon. 'How many times have I been issued KFS?' I asked myself. 'And why a knife? Ten minutes ago they confiscated all knives.' I pulled myself up, 'It's the army', no explanation needed, none given.

Everywhere smelt of horses.

More queues in the hot sun. They'd given up marching us, now we shuffled between lines of men with rifles.

'Group... group, HALT!' brought us to a standstill. We filed inside a large room, windows high up on its walls, badly strung with barbed wire. An NCO sat behind a trestle table piled with cotton sacks: 'Each of you makes his own mattress', pointing to bales of straw. So we're spending the night here. Another table, two thin blankets.

On again, dragging bedding and luggage. 'Totalizer Hall' a sign proclaimed, a long, dark room, journey's end. Low down, boarded-up Tote windows, where the public once placed their bets. Higher up, grimy external windows festooned with cobwebs and more barbed wire. Rows of palliasses, no furniture, no hooks, little air, a few bare light bulbs.

A hundred of us are to sleep on these concrete floors. For no reason Dorothy's words came back to me, 'Just because you're born in a stable doesn't mean you're a donkey.'

Around me men dropped palliasses on the floor, making their own spaces, trying to re-establish some sense in a world that had fallen apart. Confused, unshaven, demoralised, without warning we'd been forced out of very ordinary lives into this underworld of barked orders, dust and hunger.

I wrestled my palliasse flat and slumped down. In the police station and the coach we'd largely been silent, too stunned to talk. Now the shock was wearing off and that gloomy room saw the beginnings of conversations. The noise grew, tales of misery set off by unexpected humanity, harsh, bullying policemen, sympathetic neighbours. Older men recalled internment in Alexandra Palace and Douglas in 1914. A few recalled being arrested by the Gestapo. That quietened us down.

Those who'd seen army service, in Germany, Austria, Czechoslovakia or, irony of ironies, the British army, had seen it all before. Those commonplaces of army life, coarse words, shouting, the sense of imminent violence; these NCO's and warrant officers would treat their own soldiers just the same, meaning everything and nothing by it. But for those to whom it was entirely new, men and boys, teachers, academics, musicians, clerks and errand boys, the sudden transformation was devastating.

A warrant officer appeared. To every question the answer: 'I'm the one who does the talking, shut up!'

'SHUT UP!'

Silence descended. The Grenadier Guards are in charge and intend us to know it.

A string of orders: 'Internees will comply with all rules and regulations as deemed necessary for their safety, good order and discipline. They will immediately obey the orders of all officers and guards placed over them. Reveille 0630 hours, breakfast 0800, roll call 0900, sick parade 0915, dinner 1330, tea 1700, roll call 2100, lights out 2215.'

Then a surprise, 'Cooks are needed. Any volunteers?' Two or three hands went up.

'Come along, volunteers to cook put your hand up.' One or two more this time. He began to shout, 'If you want to eat...'

A voice called back, 'People are not understanding, Sergeant-Major. Do you mean chefs?'

'SILENCE IN THE RANKS', he thundered. Then, in a quieter tone, 'Volunteers to be cooks', he paused, 'or chefs, hands up.' Fifteen or more shot up. 'Report to me after this parade.'

Eberhard spoke to me, 'Volunteer, Josef. Army cooks lead a life of their own, unearthly hours, but no guards or fatigues, just think of that, eh?'

'I didn't volunteer for the Czech Free Army to cook, I can't kill Nazis with a soup ladle, can I?'

'Nor did you volunteer to be interned in a stable. Look, Josef, you and I are alike', looking me straight in the eyes, 'we're both entangled in that strange world where nothing's what it seems, Kalla-land, you might say. Yes, we should be there, not here, and probably Kalla's doing his best even now to get us out of this mess, but I'd say a cook is the ideal job for the likes of us - you, that is,

I don't qualify. Your time's your own, to compose letters to the Home Office... or Mary. No one wants to cross a cook, we all hope for a bit extra on our plate in the cookhouse. And no guard duties. Give it some thought is all I say.'

'You make a good case, milord!'

'You are an idiot, Josef. Go on, volunteer.'

The sergeant-major took my name down. But, he said, his regiment having received no warning about the number of internees, there'll be few rations to cook with.

Monday 13th May, Day 2

That first night was bad, I hardly slept. My bed - bed! - a thin palliasse, even thinner blankets - was a long way from the door. The air was foul, a mixture of horses, dust and our sweat. In the middle of the night there was a panic, men stumbling about, trying to get out. I must have got some sleep but woke up bathed in cold sweat, thinking I was in prison in Vienna. For seconds I lay there terrified, although it felt like minutes. Eventually I nodded off.

A kick in the ribs, 'Peppi, Peppi, wake up!' Hans was standing above me in the grey early light, 'It's six o'clock. Let's get out of here.'

I reported for cooking duty but with few rations the best we could do for breakfast was a piece of bread and jam, not even margarine. There was tea, but only the first few got milk or sugar, the rest black tea.

Lunch was tense, a huge queue, people hungry and tired, nerves on edge. We cooked a pretence at stew, with few vegetables and less meat, but when the army cook sergeant took the lid off the pot fighting broke out, some ruthlessly barging in. Most stayed in line, appalled by the spectacle. It took the guard platoon and the cocking of rifles to restore order.

The soldiers won't talk, NCO's and warrant officers shout but won't listen, officers - occasionally a well-dressed, godlike figure materialises, utters a hushed word to an even smarter figure then disappears, ignoring us. The smarter figure, pace-stick in hand, struts about bellowing orders; junior NCO's and guardsmen, bayonets fixed, rush about inflicting the orders on us.

All around me men's faces have odd, vacant looks. I know, it's all I can do to even think, like in a nightmare.

The weather's so hot the sentries have their sleeves rolled up and we sit in the shade of the grandstand. Lorries and rusting metal are strewn across the grass; barricades, it's rumoured, against gliders.

Why won't they allow us to write? We're hardly state secrets.

Guards tell us the commandant, Major Braybrook, admires the Nazis, not us whining internees, all the while pocketing commissions from the black market that he allows to flourish.

Tuesday 14th May, Day 3

Braybrook's gone, replaced by a Major Fache.

On Sunday we were told – one of few things we have been told – 'Internees may not send correspondence.' There was a wave of protest. One of us, quiet, unassuming Dr Schneider, protested so loudly that he was marched in front of the commandant, who tried to silence him by saying, 'But you're civilians, not prisoners of war, the Geneva Convention does not apply.'

'But sir, it does! Articles...'

We knew, and Fache soon discovered, that Schneider, lecturer in jurisprudence at Heidelberg University, had drafted the Convention. So this afternoon a notice appeared: 'The postcard you are permitted to send will be worded as follows, "I am at Kempton Park Internment Camp. I am well. I'll let you know my permanent address soon. Name." No greetings, no "My dear so and so." Postcards will <u>not</u> be posted unless the wording is as above. Major G L M Fache, Commandant.'

Even these, rumour says, will be censored twice and take a fortnight to arrive.

But the army does its best to entertain us: a Black Maria pulled up, its rear doors opened and two guardsmen with rifles stepped out, followed by a little boy in short trousers, then two more guardsmen. It was his sixteenth birthday. How we cheered. Someone called out, 'Britain's a safer place today!' Our humour isn't appreciated.

Wednesday 15th May, Day 4

We've added coffee to the menu. Humourists joke, 'It looks like coffee, it smells like coffee, it tastes like tea.'

They've interned some of Berlin and Vienna's leading scientists, philosophers, musicians and artists, along with lawyers, bankers and street-traders from the City and East End. They're all slowly recovering from the shock. David Lomnitz – we've elected him Room Father – declared, 'Perhaps our Commandant thinks Kempton Park is his country estate. Imagine the sales catalogue, "Set in extensive grounds, with all amenities, accommodation fit for royalty, superb lawns, stables and shooting rights." The appeal of shooting rights, however, rather depends on which end of the gun you find yourself.' He sat down amongst much laughter.

Dearest Mary, Lom cheered me for a moment, but now, about to go to sleep, fear and anguish crowd in. WHY have the English arrested us? What will they do to us? Above all, why are you and I apart?

Thursday 16th May, Day 5

The officers believe we're all Nazi agents, ready to rise up against Britain when invasion occurs. True, a tiny number of us internees - probably 1 or 2% at most - actually are pro-Nazi. 'Hitler will come', they boldly proclaim, 'by August 16th he'll be parading down Whitehall. Then he'll fetch us out of here and put us into power.' No one listens.

The Communists are another matter. Just like Vienna in 1934 they're a small minority, much less than one in ten, against two-thirds Social Democrat. But, disciplined, organised and rigidly following the party line, they're wheedling and twisting their way into positions of influence here, and we're too blind or lazy to oppose them. Again, just like Vienna.

Friday 17th May, Day 6

After five awful days a train steamed into the racecourse station. It's rumoured it'll take hundreds of us north, but who and where... unknown.

For once a rumour's true. At eight they lined us up in the Collecting Ring. My name was on the list, also Hans and Eberhard. What will happen to us? Five days of little food and less information have left us hungry and disgruntled, but we've learnt some camp wisdom... expect nothing, and be surprised if something good happens.

The sergeants counted us, several times - maths isn't their strong point. They finally agreed a total and marched us to the platform, where the Grenadiers handed us over to the Scots Guards, competing over which could bawl loudest, whose chins could jut most menacingly and whose officers appear the more languid and indifferent to the whole affair.

On the train they gave each group a loaf and a slab of cheese, then lent us their bayonets to cut it - having taken any KFS off us in the Collecting Ring. We ended up with a miserable chunk of cheese half the size of our thumb.

We shuffled around London's outskirts then off westwards. Passing through Reading station people waved and gave the thumbs up, probably thinking we were being called up. If only. We tried guessing our destination from station names until a sergeant – bribed by cigarettes – mentioned a camp called Huyton; the name passed along the train in seconds.

Conversation flourished. 'My policeman had a sense of humour', Arpad Greidinger said. 'My landlady asked him who she should apply to if this spy – me, a spy! – didn't pay her the rent that was due. "Adolf Hitler", he said and had me out of the door before she could reply.'

Martin Baecker said, 'I was a waiter at Schmidt's. Schmidt, knowing that in 1914 most of his staff had been interned, claimed he was Swiss, although he's as Swiss as I'm Chinese. His wife's the real boss, with a prominent moustache to prove it.'

We laughed! We all know Schmidt's in Charlotte Street, '*Charlottenstraße*', we call it. The only restaurant in London for decent German food.

The train turned northwards and we dozed off. When it stopped the platform sign read, 'Huyton.' A muted cheer went up.

From the station we were marched through suburban streets, people staring at us from open doors. Some swore blind we were spat at, but I'm not sure. Hans saw a girl go to an ice cream vendor on the pavement, buy a cone, then walk across to our column and give it to an elderly man. Did they hate us? I don't know. Probably they're no different to the crowds in Vienna, praising the Schutzbund as we marched by, next day applauding the Nazis; Palm Sunday's cheers to Good Friday's jeers.

We turned through double gates in a tall barbed wire fence into yet more suburban streets, but with something odd about them. The houses were familiar, brick-built, tiled roofs, but no doors, no glass in the windows, no people.

Hans, Eberhard and I have ended up in one of those bare brick houses, three to a room. After a hundred in the Tote Hall at Huyton that's almost privacy!

Look, Mary, I have a proper address: '132 Parbrook Road, Huyton Aliens Internment Camp, Liverpool'! It's a half-finished council estate, we sleep on concrete, but it's a house of our own – not that I'm allowed to write to you.

Saturday 18th May, Day 7

Despite being a cook I'm hungry. Rations are calculated from the previous week's roll, so, with daily arrivals they're short, quantities are pitifully small, spoonful's not ladleful's. Breakfast is awful: porridge, a mug of bitter tea, a tin of milk between a hundred mugs, two thin slices of bread and a bare taste of margarine and jam. Complain and they say, 'There's a war on.'

Tuesday 21st May, Day 10

An order: 'No letters may be sent until you've been in camp two weeks, only two letters a week, 24 lines each, only on the paper provided.'

In the Camp Office there's a letter from Mary, I've never felt so happy. Hurray! She wrote it on 15th May. She says my musical friend has seen the War Office to apply for my release. And she loves me.

Wednesday 22nd May, Day 11

Home Office Aliens Department, file B.6092 (BRAMMINGER, Josef): To The Home Office.

BRAMMINGER, Josef Johann, Alien Internment Camp, 132 Parbrook Rd, Huyton
Police Cert: 4714
Home Address: Czechoslovak Military Training Camp, Birchington-on-Sea

Sir,

I beg to apply for an early review of my case with the view of my release from internment on the following grounds:

I've come with the first transport of German and Austrian refugees from Czechoslovakia to UK through the British Committee for Refugees from Czechoslovakia. I got permission on Grounds of my anti-nazi activities to escape the danger of being captured by the Nazis. Col Kalla has accepted me because of my duties for the Czechoslovakian Republic, where I served as a volunteer in Prague. In November 1939 in London I volunteered again and Colonel Kalla recruited me and sent me to the Czechoslovakian Military training camp at Birchington-on-Sea, Kent. I've been waiting for French Government permission to join Czechoslovakia's Army in France. I had to send my passport in Mar 1940 to Col Kalla, Czechoslovak Ministry of National Defence at 131 Piccadilly. On 12 of May the Police arrested me at Birchington and sent me here. In the meantime Colonel Kalla has made an application for me at the War Office. I beg you to review my case and provide my release, that I am able to make my duty as Allied soldier, to serve a good cause.

Thanking you in advance,

Yours faithfully,

Josef Bramminger

Josef: When I'm not cooking I wander back and forth along the barbed wire.

There's little else to do.

Sunday 26th May, Day 15

Lunch of unspeakably rotten stuff. Half a potato, six beans and really no meat at all.

The lavatories are terrible, out in the open with everyone sitting in one long row relieving themselves.

Wednesday 29th May, Day 18

Many are near suicide. Even I can feel its icy fingers trying to draw me in.

Saturday 1st June, Day 21

The officers have no clue how to run roll calls. Their procedure changes almost daily, lining us up by houses, then by streets, now in the marquee. They couldn't understand our names so appointed Habicht as Chief Clerk to read them. The count's still wrong.

Wednesday 5th June, Day 25

A new internee tells us how bad things are: the BEF's defeated, its remnants evacuated from a beach called Dunkirk. Rumour and questions sweep the camp. Might Germany actually win this war?

This evening we held a performance on the square with drama, music and acrobatics. The Commandant was visibly shaken when we (his 'Nazi spies'!) stood up and sang God save the King. In his 1914-18 war Germans were clearly the enemy, he finds it hard to think of us as allies. He said to his adjutant, 'I never realized so many Jews were Nazis.'

God bless the British!

Saturday 8th June, Day 28

One officer, Captain Jenkinson, drunk or off his head, started confiscating musical instruments, snatching a clarinet from an astonished internee who was playing it, a flute, a concertina. Finally he seized an umbrella - it was raining heavily. He didn't reappear after that.

Sunday 9th June, Day 29

She still remembers me! My second letter from Mary, written on 24th May. She asks why she's received none from me, but I've sent four. The rumour is letters take well over a fortnight. Or get lost.

This evening we had a sing-along by the barbed wire, off-duty soldiers joining in, one with a harmonica. We took turns to sing, them and us, applauding each other. It was very friendly.

Wednesday 12th June, Day 32

Today's rumours: Italy's declared war on Great Britain and Italians are being interned. Switzerland, Russia and Turkey have entered the war. No one knows what's true. An officer read out an official bulletin, 'Italy has declared war on the Allies. Malta has been bombed. The RAF is flying over Libya.'

We have a real aristocrat amongst us, interned as a student at Cambridge. Count von Lingen he calls himself, but Eberhard whispers he's actually a Prince, grandson of the Kaiser. He keeps his head down.

Thursday 13th June, Day 33

It's a nightmare, the Germans are encircling Paris. What's happening to our Czechoslovak brigade?

2,000 men despatched to the Isle of Man, including Eberhard. We 750 who remain have no idea of our fate. It's said another 5,000 are coming here.

The officers stopped us singing with the guards.

Saturday 15th June, Day 35

Alfred Meindler, a late arrival, says George Orwell complains he can't get a decent meal in London as the chefs from most Italian restaurants have been interned. The officers at Seaton Camp in Devon never eat in their own mess but with the internees. Who can blame them? Some of Vienna's best pastry chefs are interned there.

Sunday 16th June, Day 36

Parbrook Road is close to the barbed wire. Through it we watch life in the world outside, families taking Sunday walks, cyclists, children playing in the street. Total freedom. Sometimes they stare at us and we stare at them, in complete silence. Like in a dream.

There's no piano in camp, just a flute and two violins, so Hans Gál has written a 'Huyton Suite' for those instruments. He's from the Wienerwald so it's cheerful, 'Made up', he says, 'of air, light and sunbeams' to capture these warm summer days, plus a bugle call. Darling you'd love it.

The days seem endless. We all feel utterly desperate. Two men attempted suicide overnight.

Wednesday 19th June, Day 39

Some Italians arrived from a camp called Warth Mills. They told us, 'Its Commandant is your Major Braybrook,' - so that's where they 'sacked' him to! - 'and from the moment he arrived he stole from us. First it was gold, money, typewriters, then he sent us through "Luggage Control" - his name for it - a simple system: officers take wallets, soldiers take suitcases. We stood behind ropes watching the soldiers and NCO's sharing it out, cigarettes, chocolate, pens, paper, books, everything. The officers just looked on.'

Saturday 22nd June, Day 42

A guard muttered, 'The bastards have signed.' What stops the Nazis invading Britain if the French have surrendered? They handed all their interned refugees to the Nazis as part of their Armistice, so will we wake one morning to find guards in grey instead of khaki? But darling, even if I could escape it would mean leaving you.

Thursday 27th June, Day 47

The Trust Fund have sent all Czech refugees 8s, causing a run on the canteen. They call it 'Pocket money.' It's pure gold to us, although it scarcely meets the cost of what's not provided: soap to wash clothes, 8d; shaving soap, 6d; toilet soap; razor blades; sewing and mending materials (taken from us on arrival); haircuts 5d; and there's no toilet paper to be had for love or money, people use the tissue paper apples come wrapped in. As refugees they gave us ten shillings a week, how can a shilling a week now be enough? And where's all that money stolen from us at Kempton Park?

Army doctors vaccinated us all, refusing to say why.

Last night I dreamt I was with Mary.

Sunday 30th June, Day 50

They told 50 of us, 'You're going overseas.' No choice, no consulting the Camp Father, just a list of names, no destination, just 'overseas.' I packed, my mind numb. A train took us to Liverpool Docks. We stood watching men filing up the gangway of a large white ship. Someone called out, 'It's the Arandora Star, wonderful ship, I cruised to Panama on her.'

Internees from the Isle of Man went on board; finally, past midnight, those of us from Huyton embarked. I was half-way up the gangway when word came that the ship was full, the ship's captain refusing to take any more. So, back down to the quayside to wait for orders. Then the strangest thing. The officer said to his sergeant, 'Call the roll' but the sergeant answered back, 'No roll, sir. No one checked who was boarding.' The officer didn't seem to care, just 'Carry on, sergeant', and turned away. That was that, so unlike the army. Eventually a train appeared and by three this morning we were back in Huyton.

Monday 1st July, Day ~~44~~ 51, forgetting ten days, I must be going mad!

Today the catastrophe has come, will an epidemic follow? Mr Linkoln committed suicide in the cloakroom, another man hanged himself.

Another rumour. Internees aged twenty to thirty to leave tomorrow, only 40 lbs of luggage each. That debate again, where will they go? The Isle of Man? Australia, Canada, South Africa? Building defences in Scotland? And what about U-boats?

Mary, why is the world so evil? Have you abandoned me? Perhaps something's happened to you. I don't know what to think.

Tuesday 2nd July, Day 52

201 Prisoner of War unit war diary: Movement order, Aldershot to Liverpool: HQ and three guard companies.

Commanding Officer:	Lt Col W H M Freeston
Adjutant:	Captain E Howell, MC
Intelligence Officer:	Captain J A Milne
Interpreter:	Captain A Ornstein

Josef: The transport goes tomorrow. Few have any money, and none any documents, all our paperwork went ahead on the Arandora Star. With quotas to fill they need volunteers: young, single men, but older, married men are accepted. Some offer money to be on the list, others to be taken off. Half of Huyton must go, what should I do? Until I met you, England was a half-way house to another country, then all my dreams changed course.

We crowded around the camp office for the final list. Captain Cole addressed us but someone interrupted: 'Names, please!', visibly disconcerting Cole. He stammered, 'They're being typed' and ducked back through the door.

He re-emerged clutching sheets of foolscap in shaking hands, handing them to his clerk. 'I'm sorry, I can't read the names, I might make mistakes. Please read them, Habicht.'

Poor Habicht, white in the face and close to collapse, nervously rattled them off to a seething mass of men. They'd said it was voluntary, but there'd been no choice, selection was by street, one street goes, the next stays. Parbrook Close was on the list, so we're going.

Some took it quietly, others had queer, contorted looks on their faces. And me? Even this evening, as I write this, I don't know what to feel.

Once again I pack my belongings with no chance to say goodbye... my eyes fill with tears, I must put my pen down...

This evening men are on their beds. Someone said, 'Our last night in Huyton, it's so exciting! I'm setting the alarm clock for five-thirty, let's go to sleep and, fellows, no stories about girls, please.'

Exciting's not the word. What about those U-boats? I looked across at Hans, he has a faraway look on his face. Off goes the oil lamp.

Wednesday 3rd July, Day 53

War diary: 0500 hrs: Arrived Lime Street Station. 8 officers, 377 OR's plus baggage to Canada Dock.

Josef: As I walked to the marquee it was grey, foggy and raining. Any other day we'd have been sitting quietly at the long tables; today we seemed infected by a fever, on edge, sudden greetings, staccato farewells...

'All those on the List' - I could swear I heard a capital L - 'parade at nine.'

'Luggage on the truck! Come on, get on with it!' They'd said only 40 lbs, but most suitcases were twice that and more - no one checked - over the tailgate they went.

We lined up on the square. It was cold so I put my hands in my greatcoat pockets, what's this? A bar of chocolate! Daniel must have put it there when I wasn't looking. What a friend. Around the square our friends had gathered to see us off. I spotted Daniel and waved, he waved back. Who was the lucky one, him or me? I pondered that, but had no answer. Not sure how I feel, no elation, no foreboding, just emptiness.

Suddenly, the emptiness was gone, Mary was there. I wanted to wave to her too.

An officer and two soldiers passed along the front rank. 'A search! Hide your matches, quick, quick!' I pushed mine through a hole in my pocket. The soldiers went by, there was no search.

The officer called the roll. A clerk scurried to and fro. A decision was made and the sergeant took over, barked orders and we were off. Someone started singing, a moment later we all were, our friends around the square joining in. We looked at one another in surprise, we were singing in English!

So, after six weeks it's goodbye Parbrook Road, goodbye Huyton, off to Liverpool. The camp was emptier by 1,094 men. Overnight two had died, two were ill, two refused to go.

Where to after Liverpool? No one said. Apprehension replaced our cheerful mood. The ugliest idea, Germany. Soon, through the carriage windows, we saw ships' masts and barrage balloons and heard the sound of a ship's foghorn.

War diary: 0900 hrs: Embarked HMT (MTS) Ettrick. 1035 hrs: Ship left for Princes Landing. The CO is told this transport is going to Quebec.

Josef: 10.30, our train stopped at Liverpool Riverside, then just sat there.

At 11.10 the usual army bustle, 'Do this! Do that! Off the train! Get a move on! Line up, on the platform!' Nervous, expectant, we were led onto a quay called 'Princes Landing.' Another sign, 'Cunard White Star Pier.' They go overseas, don't they?

Three great white buildings loomed over us, towers and domes, a jumble of styles, as if three chefs had baked three ornate wedding cakes. A giant clock gave the time, 11.16.

A white liner, 'MTS Ettrick', docked alongside two smaller ships. If we embarked on her it would be Canada or Australia, the others are just ferries. Internees started up her gangway, disappearing into her belly. Definitely Australia or Canada.

A voice hailed me, 'Josef! Josef!' Eberhard Röllig greeted me with outstretched hand, 'Good to see you.' When I took my hand from his a rolled-up paper was in my palm, I quickly secreted it in my pocket. Putting his arm around my shoulder he lowered his voice, two old friends greeting one another, 'Take care Josef, we've enemies amongst us. I volunteered in Douglas as a clerk, and the last thing I typed was that', he nodded towards my pocket, 'I put in too many sheets of carbon...'

I nodded. 'Any idea where we're going, Eberhard?'

'None. No one knew. See you on-board.'

Half-way up the gangway I looked back. Farewell England, farewell darling Mary. I'm so confused. No idea where I'm going, and I'm being parted from you. For how long? Will you still be there if I get back?

'I can't believe it!' Hans exclaimed, 'German soldiers in uniform are coming up the gangway.'

At every level barbed wire, more sentries with bayonets, all shouting, 'Keep moving.' Into the ship's bowels, below the water level, down again, then pushed through a hatch into the lowest deck of a dimly-lit hold.

It was barbed wire all the way. But what barbed wire! I've handled the stuff in four armies but never saw it done this expertly, this closely woven a man couldn't get his head through it.

The hold's like a tropical inferno. A penetrating stench of oil mingled with fish, meat, potatoes and sweat, the only ventilation a single electric fan. No portholes - two-thirds of us are below the waterline. A sentry outside the closed hatch, no way out, if we're torpedoed we'll drown like rats.

War diary: 1530 hrs: 11 German officers and 874 OR prisoners came aboard. Also 1,294 German and 403 Italian aliens.

1730 hrs

Ship sailed. Difficulty in allotting quarters. Far too many prisoners and aliens for quarters available.

Josef: The tables started trembling from the throb of the engines.

The sentries wouldn't allow us to use the toilets and we started to shout. Eventually buckets were passed down but it was difficult even to get to them. The soldiers shouted, 'Piss on the deck!' We only calmed down when the guards allowed us in small groups through the barbed wire to the toilets.

The sentries hate us more than they do the German POW's.

Hans made friends with an English guard, Corporal Bowyers. His sergeant told them they were going to Quebec - it's Canada!

Bowyers said the British military, plus the German officers, live in first-class cabins on deck. The German POW's are in second-class cabins. Below them two holds are filled with us Austrian and German internees, the third hold with Italians, each of three decks, sixty feet by ninety. The officers refuse to come down into our 'rat hole', or even to speak to our leaders.

Twelve of us volunteered as ship's cooks and soon were so busy in the galley we never noticed we'd left port. Only when the saucepans started rocking did we guess we were out in the Irish Sea.

The galley - 'never call it a kitchen', Cook shouted - was reached by a short passage from which the sea was visible. In a break from cooking I walked to the other side of the ship and suddenly found myself amongst German soldiers in uniform. Before I could even think about it a guard seized me and led me back to my part of the ship, 'Don't mix with them, they're German U-boat men and parachutists. Not your sort.'

Nothing makes sense.

When their orderlies came to collect food from the galley, I discovered that those parachutists had been captured in the Netherlands. They bragged to our orderlies they'll be going home soon, when they win the war. They gloated over our fate.

An Indian cook said the Ettrick was built for 1,500, we're catering for 3,000. The German officers eat in the English officers' mess – 'Wardroom!', shouted Cook – their soldiers are allowed on deck; internees aren't.

By eight we'd produced a meal of sorts, the first food men from Douglas had had for thirty hours. An angry squabble turned into a fight before a guard broke it up with his rifle butt.

Someone found blankets at the bottom of the hold. A scramble started, men got trodden on, fights began and many were stolen – we call it 'organised.' Hans organised a few, pushing his way out of the crowd draped in them. Then hammocks were discovered and our leaders, including von Lingen, worked in shorts in that tropical heat, sweating like pigs, throwing them to us through holes in the decks. There were only 400 of them so people fought for those too, the rest sleep on tables.

In my hammock I unfurled the paper Eberhard had passed me. It read, 'Central Camp: Active Nazi sympathisers'; suddenly I was wide awake. I scanned down it, fifteen names, Martin Bockweiller, Otto Epstein... Johannes Wilde. Two Doctors, a Baron, all Nazis... in the hold with us! Are the British blind?

I'm frightened you'll give up on me Mary. If I could be certain that you'll see me later I'd bear anything.

End of a nightmarish day.

Thursday 4th July, Day 54

At 05.30 I went to the galley. Cook shouted, 'Hey, you! Take this ledger to the Purser on the bridge.'

Off I went. A sentry, seeing my cooks' whites, let me pass unchallenged. Then the ship rolled violently and I lost my footing.

Lying there, winded, I looked up and couldn't believe my eyes, a swastika was flying high on the rear mast. I closed my eyes and shook my head, was I imagining it, a swastika, on a British ship? I opened them, but there it was, red, black, white, as arrogant and hateful as ever. Above it flew the Blue Ensign.

'*Das muss runterkommen!* That must come down!' I decided. I looked at the mast. It was perhaps 140 feet tall, half-way up a spar crossed it, that would give me somewhere to rest. Guy-lines, at an angle, anchored it to the ship, but I'd use the two halyards that went straight up the mast. I needed two ropes and a sharp knife.

I returned to the galley and, when Cook's back was turned, crept in and grabbed a knife. Outside I again slipped past the sentry onto the top deck. He had no idea what was in my mind, he only saw a cook.

I found a lifeboat, cut out two ropes dangling from it, wound them round my waist and went back to the mast. I fashioned a harness from the ropes and lashed it to the halyards with a Prusik knot, something I'd learned in the mountains. Commending my soul to God, as they say, I started climbing.

My leg protested and I struggled to recall half-forgotten mountaineering tricks. The first thirty feet were agony, but that knot worked, sliding freely up the halyards and locking firmly in place when I put weight on it. Soon I'd reached the spar then, still apparently unseen, I set off towards those flags.

Both stretched away, taut in the breeze. With my left hand I gripped the halyards, braced my feet against the mast and, with my right hand, stabbed at the edge of the swastika. The knife caught high in the material and I sliced downwards, through the bottom seam. Instantly it whirled upwards, was held for a moment by a few threads at the top, then the wind tore through them and carried it away. I was elated.

An instant later I found my face pressed hard up against the mast, the knife gone from my hand. I'd slipped and instinctively grabbed for the mast with my right arm.

I looked down. Reality dawned. I was high on a mast that was swinging with the ocean's swell, bitterly cold, soaked through by rain, spray and sweat. I clambered gingerly down to the spar. For the first time I noticed the noises all around me, vibrating wires and halyards, the wind plus, suddenly, the sound of shouting. Seventy feet below me a sailor was running towards the mast, peering upwards. I'd been seen.

A knot of men quickly gathered, sailors, a ship's officer and two soldiers who ran to join him, rifles in hand. One brought his rifle to his shoulder to take a shot at me but the officer thrust the barrel to one side. Too late. I heard the unforgettable crack and thump of a rifle shot. I'd intended to get back down on deck, suddenly that looked less appealing.

Looking up I saw only the Blue Ensign. I'd achieved my aim, I'd sit tight.

.....

On the bridge Colonel Freeston was arguing loudly with the Ettrick's Captain, beating the deck with his stick. 'That man', he jabbed upwards, 'has flouted my orders, defied your authority, and torn down a nation's flag that was acting as our protection. I demand he be dealt with severely and the swastika be replaced immediately! If I had my way my soldiers would shoot him off the mast...'

'To which he's attached by a rope. Your proposal is both illegal and impractical, it would leave me with a body dangling from my mast. I would remind you, colonel, that that emblem you refer to is the enemy's. I found it abhorrent that the Admiralty ordered I fly it over my ship and suggest you make no further reference to that aspect of the matter.'

Freeston was incandescent with rage, 'I insist...'

'Insist be damned, colonel! This is my ship and everybody on-board, I repeat, everybody, is under my command, you are merely a passenger. A German-speaking internee will be hoisted up the mast to bring this man down. When he's in custody I'll see him in my cabin and determine his punishment. Those are my orders and my officers will see them carried out.' He turned and strode off his bridge.

.....

Josef: Twenty minutes passed. Below me the crowd grew, gesticulating and shouting. Two more army officers appeared, Milne and Ornstein, the interpreter, I recognized his blonde hair. I made out '*Komm herab!*' – Come down! Then, plaintively, '*Kommen Sie sich, bitte!* – Come on, please!'

Ignoring him I checked the knot holding me to the mast and settled on my perch. I couldn't hold them off, but a word came to mind, 'Boots.' In those far-off days in Vienna we'd night-climbed barefoot, why not now? I took them off and hung them around my neck.

Activity below caught my eye. The two halyards wriggled as two sailors lashed something on. The group was joined by someone in civilian clothes. A sailor fitted ropes around him, then the two halyards went taut and they started hauling him up towards me. From his clothes, neither naval nor military, he must be an internee.

I couldn't make him out because he was looking downwards. I gingerly took the boots from around my neck and flung one then the other, shouting, '*Lassen Sie mich alleine!* – Leave me alone!' The first glanced off the intruder's shoulder, the second struck a glancing blow to his head. He looked up – it was von Lingen!

'Grüß Gott! Is this the Austrian greeting for a fellow internee? Herr Bramminger, I would...', he interrupted himself to say, 'may I call you Herr Bramminger?' Dangling sixty feet above a swaying deck, his head sore, his manners hadn't deserted him for a moment.

'You, an aristocrat and prince, ask how to address me, a Socialist, a working man from Favoriten? I'm honoured! And how would you have me greet you?'

'A much-reduced aristocrat, I fear! Look', he jabbed his hand down at his perilous bosun's chair, 'my throne, this terrifying contraption of rope and wood!' I could not help but laugh.

'Up here...', he went to make a sweeping gesture with his arm, but thought better of it and grasped the ropes more firmly, 'you may greet me as you wish. I hear wits call me "Prince of the Jews." Could we settle on "Herr Friedrich"?'

'Danke', was all I could think to say.

'Now, more seriously, Herr Bramminger, may I ask what brings you up here? Is it a protest about the foul conditions we live in?'

'That, fury at being wrongly interned, living alongside the very men we're dedicating to defeating, who would murder us, every one, given half a chance. And cowardly guards whose officers are afraid to venture below decks. We've never even seen their Commanding Officer. I've known better leaders in all four armies I've served in. But, Herr Friedrich, no, none of those things. It was that evil thing flying over an English ship. That must not be allowed.'

He nodded. 'I understand you better than you think. Their Commanding Officer would not pass muster in the British Household Division, let alone the Panzerkorps. As to that thing', he jerked his head at the mast above us, 'I'm as glad as you it's gone. It's alien to both of us...'

His charm must have been working, for I replied, facetiously, 'I suppose you'd prefer *Der kaiserliche Adler* – the Imperial eagle above you. For me red, white and red is best. But we can agree to differ.'

'At this height I prefer agreement to discord, your Socialist footwear was most accurate. I hope we will not argue further.'

I apologised.

'Think nothing of it. We pampered royal princes must be kept on our toes, it's probably good for the circulation. Perhaps not Captain Milne's brightest idea, to send a prince to reason with a Socialist!'

'I may hate what you represent, but his idea seems to have worked. But maybe up a mast, over the Irish Sea - or the Atlantic Ocean? I'm not sure where we are...'

'There', he pointed, 'to the north, that's the Mull of Kintyre.'

'So, the Irish Sea. Here, I can talk with a man, not a prince, and you've persuaded me, I'll come down. But I'll defend myself against those murderous Nazi thugs if I have to. One reason I volunteered to cook is the many knives in the galley.'

'My dear fellow, I'm none too keen to fall into their hands myself. The wilder ones would kill me if opportunity occurred. And you, a deserter from their precious Wehrmacht...' Seeing my surprise he added, 'Yes, I know you served in the Austrian army during the Anschluß. Before sending me up here they...', he nodded downwards, 'told me. I too was in Vienna then, a conscript lieutenant in the Panzerkorps. Like you, not a willing recruit.'

He gestured downwards and the sailors began hauling him down, I followed.

Close to the deck he said, 'Look, you've survived Huyton, you're strong enough to survive this.' He stepped out of the bosun's chair and, as two naval officers grabbed my arms and frog-marched me off, called after me, 'Auf weidersehn, Herr Bramminger.'

.....

On the bridge the Ettrick's captain spoke with Captain Milne, who went across to von Lingen. 'Confidentially, your royal highness, there's no need to speak of this incident to anyone below decks.' von Lingen nodded his agreement. 'The Admiralty believed, from some ancient maritime tradition, that flying a swastika below the Blue Ensign would indicate to U-boat commanders that German prisoners were on board. Unhappily events, the torpedoing of the Arandora Star, that is, soon proved this false. Even while you were up the mast the Captain received Admiralty orders to turn about and return towards Liverpool to marry up with a Royal Navy escort and take down the swastika, so the whole episode need never have happened. Best not mention it again, nor Bramminger's part in it.'

.....

War diary: 1200 hrs: NTR-Nothing to Report. Calm.

Friday 5th July, Day 55

1600 hrs: Rough weather. Escort no longer visible.

Josef: Minutes after the ship's captain sentenced me to six days' solitary I was in the ship's brig. Built for a dozen I was its first occupant, so it was dry, fresh and clean, far cleaner than the hold, and no snoring! But the shortage of cooks meant, the following morning, that they released me to the galley. By two pm I was back in the hold.

They've not replaced the swastika.

'Josef', Eberhard came forward with his hand out, 'you've been the lucky one.'

'Lucky, in jail?'

'Well, we've been trapped in this squalor', he checked we weren't overheard, 'and I hear you're quite the friend of our royal prince. He took me aside and told me that because of you a swastika no longer flies over us. When our comrades down here hear that you'll be their hero.'

'Ha! I expect Herr Friedrich von Hohenzollern thoroughly washed his hands after our meeting and he'll soon forget me. As to the other, let's hope they never hear', I replied, quietly, 'for what use is being a hero, which I deny, if those Nazi storm-troopers', jabbing my finger upwards, 'find out and catch me by myself. Promise me you won't mention this. My life may depend on it.'

Eberhard looked taken aback, 'You have my word', adding, 'I'll speak privately with the Hold Father, I trust him. He'll keep an eye out for you.'

Later Hans came down the ladder, his face wearing a strangely twisted expression. I asked, 'Hans? What's the matter?'

For a moment he stood there, speechless, then out it came, 'The transport before us was torpedoed!'

That's the Arandora Star, the one I almost sailed on... does Mary know?

The story spread like wildfire, people raced about sharing it, panic was in the air. The soldiers woodenly said nothing. Hearing the commotion officers finally appeared. They denied it.

Our Hold Father set off, arguing his way past barbed wire and through locked doors until he found Captain Milne. 'Is this true?' he asked. Milne didn't say yes, but he wouldn't say no.

So Hans went to find Corporal Bowyers. He knew. Their sergeant had told them as they came on duty, ordering them to deny it.

But it's had some effect. At midday we were allowed on deck for the first time. Two hours only, lying about reading and playing cards, wrapped in blankets in the bitter cold, but we were in fresh air.

Tonight, before lights out, the German prisoners began singing, 'Today Germany belongs to us, tomorrow the whole world', and suchlike. Later the mood became more brutal, 'When Jewish blood drips from our knives, things go twice as well.' Down in our holds we heard them and our blood boiled over. We countered with 'The Siegfried Line', 'Roll out the barrel' and 'Run, rabbit, run.' Before long the whole ship was in uproar, the German threatening us through the steel decking, we responding with songs. A general alarm sounded, posses of guards turned out and threatened to shoot. Everyone quietened down and we went to sleep.

The destroyers have gone, we have no defence against U-boats, all we see is sea and sky.

Mary, in that cell I spent my time thinking of you. Are you safe?

War diary: 1930 hrs: In the open Atlantic. The two escorts have left, ship began zigzagging.

Saturday 6th July, eight weeks

Josef: At seven I woke with a start, doubled up with stomach cramps. Most hammocks around me were empty. The rumblings in my stomach made me jump out of mine and run as fast as I could for the lavatories. It was the worst sight ever. Vomit and excrement choked the toilets, covering the bulkheads, deck, the doors, the handles, everything. Each open porthole was occupied by groaning internees being violently sick. I could scarcely stand upright, the taste in my mouth was foul and I was covered in sweat. I felt the nausea rising and vomited, then stumbled back to my own deck. The atmosphere was as foul as ever, but it didn't compare to those toilets.

Soon even the guards were down with it. Shouting, 'Gangway! Sick man!' Military Police appeared, taking rifles from collapsed soldiers.

Later I crawled my way to the galley, but Cook just laughed at me. 'You sleep. No one eat today!' He was right. Men with diarrhoea and seasickness crowded the sick bay, few appeared at supper.

The cause? Laxative in our food? Food poisoning from tinned food? Our doctors say it's the effect of overcrowding.

It's rumoured German officers planned to take control of the ship, today some were led to the cells in handcuffs. People say Captain Milne's spies are everywhere, he knew all along.

Sunday 7th July, Day 57

Eberhard's wrong, von Lingen isn't my friend. I've seen him once since the mast, he nodded to me, no more. But I respect him; he assumes no airs and graces, he's polite and, now, the hero of the ship... at midday he appeared in his wellingtons amidst the filthy mess to start a great cleaning campaign. 'His' Cambridge students formed a gang and started with sick people who wouldn't get up. They didn't ask, they just moved them, hammocks and all, to one end of the deck, then set to with brushes, mops and disinfectant. Older men sneeringly called these brash youngsters the bucket brigade, but most joined in, even diehard Social Democrats. Not a single Communist, of course. Like Vienna in 1934 they left the dirty work to us. By five the place was relatively clean and tidy.

He shirks no duty, voluntarily doing the filthiest jobs. For two nights he's personally cleaned the lavatories amidst endless queues of dysentery victims. His latest nickname? 'Prince Clean.'

I love you, Mary, more than ever.

Older ones who've left families behind are depressed, some have had breakdowns, putting a strain on everyone.

I've seen whales but no ships or birds, the seagulls left us when we entered the Atlantic.

We now know the Arandora Star was torpedoed off Ireland, 1,500 on board, 700 drowned, despite flying a swastika below her Blue Ensign to show she was carrying German prisoners. Mary, do not worry, I am safe.

War diary: 1800 hrs: Sea rough. By 1100 calm again. Protestant and Roman Catholic services held by internees and PoW's. Prisoners and internees exercise on deck daily, two hours each. 1900 hrs: A few cases of trivial irregularities. Dense fog, ship almost stopped.

Josef: Our second group wedged ourselves tightly in a corner on a lower deck to wait for the first to come down when something happened that I never expected of a Briton. We weren't fast enough for a Scottish sergeant. He screamed at us then lost his head, pulled out a long rubber truncheon and hammered people on the skull as hard as he could.

It was disgusting. He broke the truncheon and tried to grab a rifle and bayonet from a sentry, who very decently refused. We roared in rage, how dare he hit us? He wouldn't do it to the POW's.

But his filthy behaviour, an insult to his Scottish uniform, couldn't spoil our good mood when Huyber began playing his accordion and we sang. That boosted our spirits.

Later an NCO said the sergeant will be disciplined. It is proper they announced this.

Monday 8th July, Day 58

The tension with the few Nazis in our midst came to the boil. They camp in one corner of our hold, we ignore them and they ignore us. They're all German except for one Austrian, Bockweiller. He started to argue with Hans, raising his voice, blustering, threatening future violence. Everybody looked round, astonished by the transformation. I also was surprised. Hans isn't given to politics, if that's the word for it, but he replied, 'After *Anschluß* they held you in utter contempt. What did Germans call Austrian Nazis? *Schlappschanz,* and what's that in English, eh?'

He looked around. Austrians near him were quick with translations. Gerhardt offered 'Spineless weeds', Jacob, 'Quitters.'

Hans carried on, '"Spineless", "weeds", "quitters", all those. But we all know what it really means is "limp ...", but no, we shouldn't use such language in the presence of our holy men', his eyes seeking out the Catholic priests, the pastors and rabbis in the hold. 'And', he continued, mockingly, 'they called you that to your faces, and you could do nothing about it.'

Bockweiller looked around for support from his fellow Nazis, but even his 'friends' were laughing, so he shut up. There was a round of applause.

The days drag by, the tension builds, people are short-tempered.

War diary: 1800 hrs: Sea mist, icy cold wind, speed reduced, NTR.

Wednesday 10th July, Day 60

0900 hrs: Land sighted, probably Cape Race. A fishing vessel three miles off. Visibility worse, ship at half-speed. Lt Clayton, South Staffs, taken ill, stage before a stroke. Off-duty for rest of voyage.

Josef: From my heart, in German, *Ich habe dich aber unendlich lieb*. For your sake, and in case the censors see this: My love for you will never end.

Is this a diary or, I think, the longest love letter ever?

Thursday 11th July, Day 61

War diary: Italian internee, Gazzi, had a fit, nearly biting off his tongue. Ship's surgeon stitched him up.

Josef: On deck a thin dark blue shape was seen, a long way off. LAND! The cry went up, and all craned towards the horizon. Mountains, wrapped in mist, disappeared back into the sea, like a mirage. Then again, green hills, villages, a road, more fairy-tale than mirage. Seagulls overhead. We saw two merchantmen heading to England. There's a buzz of excitement across the ship.

Mary, I come close to tears every time I think of you. We hope we'll be allowed to write when we land.

One of the Huyton boys started to sing, 'You'll get used to it...' - our camp song, written at Huyton by Freddie Grant, born Fritz Grundland - then Huyber started his accordion and we all joined in...

You'll get used to it
You'll get used to it
The first year is the worst year
Then you get used to it
You can scream and you can shout
But they'll never let you out
serves you right you so-and-so
Why aren't you a naturalized Eskimo

By the refrain every Huyton man over three decks was singing his heart out...

Just tell yourself it's marvellous
You'll get to like it more and more
You've got to get used to it!
And when you're used to it
You'll feel just as lousy as you did before

Afterwards people lay there, lost in thought.

Friday 12th July, Day 62

War diary: Internee had another epileptic fit. Died 2100 hrs. Windy, dense fog, ship going slowly.

Josef: By midday we were in the St Lawrence River, coastline on both sides.

We smelt pine and spruce, heard a church bell chiming. A car seemed to race against us.

Two months of internment and not seeing you. Moments of utter misery.

After the blackout the lights of America astonish us.

Saturday 13th July, Day 63

An announcement: 'We land today. On deck by nine.'

On deck, with the river bathed in sunlight, we all felt optimistic. In the distance skyscrapers... Quebec! A ragged cheer went up.

Naval vessels swarmed around to stop us jumping off the ship. We dropped anchor at 'Wolfe's Cove' – everybody looked up at the famous cliffs behind. Many soldiers on the quayside, some in solar topees and kilts.

For hours we stood on deck, the sun burning down, German POW's taunting those who fainted in the heat.

War diary: 1230 hrs: PW and internee baggage starts going ashore. 1500 hrs: All baggage off. PWs go off in batches of 20, searched on quay by Canadian authorities.

Josef: The heat affected everyone including Freeston, CO of the guard battalion. He raged about, waving his stick, screaming, 'You're the scum of the earth! Get back! Get back, you lousy lot.' He kicked a young Jewish boy and beat him with the stick. He ordered the sentries to use their bayonets against us, but they had the sense to do nothing. You'll long be remembered, Colonel Freeston, your behaviour was disgraceful.

Finally, the POW's, in Kriegsmarine and Luftwaffe uniforms, marched off, brushing past us in icy silence.

By six pm we were frantic after nine hours in the sun, some bent double with hunger pains.

At eight we finally went ashore. They herded us through checks and searches, stealing from our hands everything we were carrying, rucksacks, food baskets, down to the last violin; our suitcases to be 'dealt with' separately.

War diary: 2000 hrs: Last internees leave the ship. Escort disembarks.

Josef: They drove us across Quebec City, armed guards, police motorcyclist escorts, sirens wailing. Through heavy traffic, cars with headlights – no blackout – ordinary people going about their business. There were shops, advertising hoardings, bars and night clubs, it felt outlandish. Eventually we stopped at a station, the Gare du Palais.

I'm on dry land, I've survived the Atlantic, I should be rejoicing, but, beloved, all I can think of is you. I cannot talk to you, except, somehow, deep in my heart... I cannot explain this.

Sunday 14th July, Day 64

For twenty-three hours a train, with the piercing, haunting wail of its horn and the 'ding-dong, ding-dong' of its great bell, took us into a wilderness of lakes and forest. Trees, trees, and more trees, until you nod off from sheer repetition.

We slept on the floor but the Red Cross gave us magnificent food boxes, bread, cheese, butter, jam, fruit, sausages and cold meats, more than we could eat.

All station names had been covered up, our armed guards sat tight-lipped, our destination another military secret. Past eleven at night the train finally eased into the siding of a small village. A truck was parked nearby with, painted on it, 'Hardware, Supplies and General Stores, Monteith, Ontario.' Hans laughed, 'Secrecy? The moment we arrive we know where we are!'

It was raining.

They marched us into a triple-wire enclosure with six sentry towers, one large brick building and fifty tents. Into a hut with rough tables and benches. I was so tired I fell sleep with my head on the table.

Monday 15th July, Day 65

At one in the morning they started in on us again. At a table a corporal ordered us to undress completely, then to write our name at the top of a blank form and sign at the bottom. Next, they emptied our clothes out. Some things went into a paper bag, but into their pockets went everything they fancied: combs, pens, watches, packs of cards. They already had our signatures, they just wrote above them the things in the bag and, with a straight face, gave us back our signed receipts.

Almost wistfully I recalled that Arrest Sheet in Prague, 'Signature for personal things taken correctly: Josef Bramminger.' No such niceties here.

An hour later even those receipts were taken off us. It was a disgrace; we may have been naked but they're the ones who should be ashamed.

By four we were in our beds. As he left us a major shouted, 'If you want trouble you can have it, plenty of it, and I won't wish you good night because I don't.'

Soaked through and exhausted, we took no notice.

They got us up two hours later, at six. For nothing. There was a washhouse, but no soap or towels.

Then we were lined up outside in front of a portly medical officer who subjected us to a bizarre inspection, 'For VD', he said. He ordered us to strip completely, and I mean completely. 'Lift it up' he shouted, 'or I'll do it for you', which, using his swagger stick, he proceeded to do anyway. Local women watched us through the fence, with binoculars. Shame on them all. What sort of army is this? What sort of country?

Breakfast didn't appear till noon.

All day our leaders pleaded with Captain Milne – he's now intelligence officer here at Camp Q – for permission to write to relatives. 'No letters until you've been in camp for two weeks', he said, 'and tell your men they're interned here for the rest of the war, there's no prospect of release. This far northern country is a splendid place, 300 miles from Montreal or Toronto, with mosquitoes, snakes and poison ivy all the way.'

Tuesday 16th July, Day 66

Today a new Major appeared: 'I've heard bad reports about you. Don't try any monkey business with me like on your ship, and don't take kindness for weakness because if you play ball, we play ball.'

He didn't give his name; we call him Major Balls.

Last night some guards came in drunk and fired shots all over camp – it was pay day. What a place!

Monday 22nd July, Day 72

At last, we've been given paper and envelopes, but with 'PRISONER OF WAR MAIL' printed across them. We protested. The Commandant finally conceded we could write 'CIVILIAN INTERNEE MAIL' over it.

I use my last tiny piece of soap to shave, to wash myself, my clothes, and my teeth.

Thunderstorm.

Last night an internee was shot dead. He was in the hospital hut after a nervous breakdown, and was killed climbing out of the window.

Saturday 27th July, Day 77

Camp Q standing orders: Revally 6 a.m. Lights out 10 p.m. Roll-call at revally, bedtime and as necessary.

Josef: When I approached the barbed-wire a guard cocked his rifle and shouted, 'Stand six feet back from the wire.'

At night the ghostly howling of the trans-Canada trains keeps us awake.

Wednesday 31st July, Day 81

Mary, I cannot bear it much longer. I dreamt we were together; there was the greatest stillness, joy everywhere. Then I woke up. The pain was almost unbearable.

The Ottawa censor sent those letters back. Canada believes what it's been told, that we're dangerous fifth columnists so we must not cross out 'PRISONER OF WAR.' As a protest our Camp Father told us all to use the same words, e.g. ... 'To: Miss Mary Brown, 32 Brixton Hill Court, London SW2. CIVILIAN INTERNEE JOSEF BRAMMINGER HAS ARRIVED SAFELY AT CAMP "Q", INTERNMENT OPERATIONS, CANADA AND IS WELL. Name: Josef Bramminger. Rank: Civilian.' Just that. With three weeks to pass Canada's censors, three across the Atlantic, two for Liverpool's censors, Mary might receive it in October. I despair.

Thursday 1st August, Day 82

Camp Sergeant-Major Mackintosh is a Scottish pocket-dictator. He's an angry, anti-Semitic, loud bully who hates us all. He shouts and bellows, which is his job, but he's also spellbindingly stupid. He overheard one internee talking about Einstein and butted in, 'Einstein? Einstein? Which group is he in?' We all collapsed into laughter! He had absolutely no idea.

They've announced internees may be brought back to England 'whose release can be properly authorized.' But no-one knows what that means.

Monday 5th August, Day 86

This evening a small concert. They played our tune, Mary, which made me feel so sad. Thunderstorm. In the middle of the lightning and noise I lie here thinking of you.

Wednesday 7th August, Day 88

Rumours of a huge air-raid on London.

It's autumn, I can smell the damp earth and leaves. A hen wandered in under the wire. Karel had us roaring with laughter catching it, and even more when it escaped. Happy for the hen. If only I could get through that wire.

Tonight the Northern Lights, the greatest spectacle I've ever seen. Bright green streaks from east to west, a curtain of light shot through with streaks of purple, orange and red. Mary, if only I'd been watching it with you. Perhaps we were, one of the scientists says we're on the same latitude.

Saturday 17th August, Day 98

Played skat. Mary, will it be weeks, months, years? Are you still alive amidst those bombs? We held *ein Bunte Abend* - a social evening, with stage and curtains erected, Colonel Campbell was invited and Huyton's song filled the camp. We enthusiastically joined in the Canadian and British anthems, leaving Campbell nonplussed. He's convinced we're pro-Nazi.

At 04.00 the electricity failed. Shouting, shooting, torches, a roll call in torrential rain.

Friday 23rd August, Day 104

Look! I could not even be bothered to note our 100th day. It's rumoured the Government found 100,000 letters stuck in the Liverpool censor's office.

Nights are cold. They issued an extra blanket and a pullover.

Saturday 24th August, Day 105

Canteen's opened at last and we can buy some essentials, the first since June.

Monday 26th August

Report by E H Coleman, Under-Secretary of State, Ottawa: The internees are aggrieved because few letters had reached them, though they feel sure their wives and kinsfolk in England are writing to them. There is feeling about internees being obliged to write on paper headed 'PRISONER OF WAR.' Category B and C internees object strongly that it gives a misleading impression as to their status and sympathies. Their fear is that in any interchange of prisoners between Germany and GB they, if classified as POWs, might be subject to exchange, and Germany is the last place any of them wish to see again. I propose they be supplied with paper marked 'CIVILIAN INTERNEE MAIL.'

Wednesday 28th August, Day 109

Josef: No letter. Oh darling, when will I hear from you? Why has Colonel Kalla done nothing? I have no hope of release. I'll be here until the war ends.

Sunday 1st September, Day 113

Fourteen letters I've sent Mary, I've received just two from her, but only in Huyton. I know she loves me, I know it, but still doubt nags at me. Why doesn't she write? I must receive a letter from you soon, I cannot stand the waiting much longer. Hans said, 'It's those bloody U-boats.' And even bloodier censors.

Tuesday 3rd September

Mary's 10th letter, posted 8 July, received today: To Huyton. Dearest, darling Josef, I got your first letter today, you wrote it on 8th June. I have sent you a postcard and nine letters... You must not even think any nonsense of me ever forgetting you, I never shall. I think of you day and night. In every free moment I am visiting people and offices seeking your release... Keep your spirits up, my life and hope is centred in you. I love you, Mary.

Wednesday 4th September, Day 116

Mary's 9th letter, posted 5 July: To Huyton. Darling, many thanks for your card... Did you receive the eight letters I have sent to Kempton and Huyton? I've made a parcel of some pullovers – in the middle of summer! Am I going mad?... Write as often as you can. I love you very much and kiss you, Mary.

Mary's 12th letter, posted 10 July: To Huyton. Darling Josef, I have read and re-read your one letter so many times. Please, darling, don't let things get you down, I shall stick to you whatever... even if for now we are apart... I have little to say about myself, things go on as normal. I miss you so terribly. Mary

Josef: One letter yesterday, two today, my first three letters all in two days, but out of sequence. It's rumoured we'll be forced into uniform. Things are very difficult.

They've posted notices in German. 'Anyone in this "*Konzentrationslager*" – as they call it – who goes within six feet of the wire can be shot without warning.'

Thursday 5th September, Day 117

Camp Q Routine Orders (LAC R112, RG24, Volume 41324): Censorship. Following will be rejected: Letters to organisations outside the British Empire, US Consulates, etc... Containing objectionable matter: complaints regarding living conditions; adverse criticism of HM institutions or individuals; irrelevant, obscure, ambiguous or sarcastic phrases; needless dots, figures or marks whatsoever.

Josef: Our final humiliation, we must give up our civilian clothes, our last link with home. We must dress as clowns in POW uniform: blue trousers with a red stripe down the right leg and blue jackets with a huge red circle on the back so they can shoot us more easily. So we can't make civilian clothes from them they've cut out the cloth beneath the circles and the stripes.

At first Mary's letters cheered me up but now I'm worried. They were written eight weeks ago, what has happened since? I live in terror of the answer. All those bombs, and Devonshire House is in the centre of London.

Mary, I can scarcely bear this, fenced-in, a 100-yard fenced-in square of nothingness. I cannot concentrate. Some mornings I feel so exhausted I don't think I'll make it through the day. And every day is rumour after rumour after rumour...

Saturday 7th September, Day 119

In the stores Colour-Sergeant 'Nobby' Clark stood arms akimbo behind the counter as his storeman handed out those uniforms. 'We call 'em bull's-eyes', he said, looking very pleased with himself, 'for target practice, sweeties for us to enjoy.'

Johann Evens shouted from the queue, 'The enjoyment will be all ours, when we meet the guard who pulled the trigger.' That wiped the grin from Clark's face. He made himself scarce.

I have no privacy, can they not see that? In the hut, everywhere in the camp, they're talking, discussing, quarrelling, no where's quiet. Even my sleep's wrecked by their snoring, when I wake in the middle of the night it's hell on earth. I'm thinking, 'I'm useless here, I should be out there, fighting back. I will never get out.' Night after night, and never an answer. Have they forgotten us in England?

Thursday 12th September, Day 124

Official Report by Ernest L Maag, Swiss Consul to the International Committee of the Red Cross, (LAC RG117-A-3, 2219 11977): Visited Camp Q, Monteith. 501 prisoners, 332 of them Jews. Most refuse to meet with me, regarding me as a German government representative, which might lead to their being repatriated to Germany. Standard army rations, 5lbs 3oz per man per day. The prisoners are satisfied with their food, both quantity and quality. They do not like having to dress in prison clothes.

Josef: Somehow, I hold on to a conviction you are unhurt, otherwise I could not stand life. I've had to give up the blue shirt you bought me in Piccadilly. This depresses me more than I can say.

Friday 13th September, Day 125

Really cold, hoar frost.

Monday 16th September, Day 128

I feel hopeless. Hans is more than usually cheerful, that weighs me down. He doesn't understand. And others in the hut irritate me, during the day I get as far away from them as I can, but can go only as far as the wire. I worry that your mother will try to turn you against me and I'm powerless to prevent it.

Maybe Mary never wrote those letters, I cannot find them now, someone has taken them. It's the sort of thing Röllig would do. 'It's only for your own good', he'd say. I know his ways. I will search his bed space when he's out of the hut. I can't hear Mary's voice any more. Has she also given up on me?

I feel sad, hopeless, utter despair.

Friday 20th September, Day 132

He keeps looking at me strangely, asking me what I am doing. I mustn't tell him, I'm sure he's in with them. And they've put something in our food, I know they have, there's a strange taste to everything. It will be on Milne's orders, I've seen him in the kitchens. Why else would he be there?

Saturday 21st September, Day 133

We hear of terrible air-raids. Last night a violent storm, but it's only thunder, for you it's bombs. I feel helpless. If only we could face the dangers together.

Tuesday 24th September, Day 136

London must be terrible, and Brixton's under the bombers' flight path. No letter. Disheartened. A lot colder.

Wednesday 25th September, Day 137

It snowed for the first time. The guards worked furiously clearing it from the barbed wire, scared we'll tunnel through the snowdrifts and escape through the wire. Not a bad idea, but I mustn't talk of it. I'm sure there are spies all across the camp.

The RCMP came to the camp and fingerprinted and photographed us. Are we criminals?

Friday 27th September, Day 139

Postcard from Mary. It took eight weeks, the censor is rotten. Mary, are you still alive, after all those raids?

Our shoes and boots are worn out.

Tuesday 1st October, Day 143

Mail arrived, but the censor had put black lines through almost every line. Last night I saw Montreal and it isn't so far away. I think Mary may be there.

Wednesday 2nd October, Day 144

Ottawa had ordered lists of Aryans and Jews to divide the camp into two parts, some will stay, most will go. There's an uproar about us being separated on this basis, but our fury won't make the slightest difference.

Today I stood close by the perimeter wire, thinking about it. It's the barbed wire that'll slow me down, all three rows of the hateful stuff, plus those watchtowers. Hans spends too much time with those Viennese psychiatrists in the other hut. He says I'm suffering from internitis, 'Barbed Wire Psychosis', he calls it. He can't see that I have to get out of this place.

Thursday 3rd October, Day 145

Freezing. No letters.

The hen was a sign, I see it clearly now. I've made my mind up. I'd ask Hans to create a disturbance, to distract the sentries, but he'd pass it on to Röllig who'd only try to stop me, or tell them. I'll go after dusk, when the boys are playing football, the moment a goal's scored, the sentries always watch that.

Friday 4th October

Jews are going to 'N' Camp in Quebec, Gentiles to 'S' Camp in Montreal. Slept badly. Letters, none. A ship's been sunk, the Benares, with children on board. My letters also, I think.

I've never felt this low.

Saturday 5th October

I've worked it out. Sunset's at 6.58, we have to be in the huts by 7.30 when they switch the searchlights and perimeter on. But it's already getting dark before that. When there's a goal, that's when I'll go.

I stood quite still, looking out over that flat, snow-covered landscape, outwardly calm, but inwardly my mind tumbled over and over. Here I was, 3,000 miles from home - 'my home'! Is Mary's home my home? Is that flat still there? Is she still there? The last letter from Mary was written in early August. It is my lowest point yet. I am so miserable, I feel despair crawling over me, enveloping me, I didn't care what happens to me.

But then the cloud lifted, I could breathe again. I was on my way, I was sure of that. I heard the football crowd roar and I must have started for the wire. At any moment a sentry could have shot me, but then you were there, standing just behind me, looking at me. I saw you - I must have turned - in my mind's eye or in my heart I saw you, and heard you. 'Josef', you said, so urgently, so forcefully, 'you're coming home to me, but not that way, NOT through the fence!' - suddenly I could look you in the face - 'To the love we share. You know it; all shall be well, don't let go...'

Now, now I know you're waiting for me and want me to wait here for you, to be strong for you and for the life we're going to have together.

Today started as the worst of days but, by God, it has ended as the best. Whatever was going on, something held me back and I've decided to stick it out. I feel as if I've never been closer to you.

Chapter 7

From Brixton to Whitehall, by way of Devonshire House

Sunday 12th May, Whitsun, 1940

Mary: Today's Pentecost and Roy preached on the Holy Spirit from Romans 8, 28, that bit about 'all things working together for good to them that love God.' After a sleepless night of worrying about bombs that took some believing.

Monday 13th May

I woke late, feeling strangely out of sorts. After a breakfast so hurried I didn't even turn on the wireless, I rushed downstairs to catch the bus.

In the seat ahead of me a passenger was reading his newspaper. Over his shoulder my eye caught the words '**ENEMY ALIENS**.' Immediately I was wide awake. I read on, 'The Home Secretary has made an Order for the internment of all male enemy...' then, oh so casually, he turned the page. I could have screamed. I wanted to tap his shoulder and ask to borrow his paper, but knew I couldn't. I waited impatiently as we worked our way through Kennington, over Westminster Bridge, eventually arriving at Piccadilly Circus. I ran to the newsstand and immediately was immersed in the story. What would it mean for Josef? But how could it involve him? He's category C, he's in the army, of course they won't intern him.

I was so absorbed in it that before I knew it I was at Devonshire House. George, the doorman, held the door open for me. 'I'm sorry to hear the news, Miss Brown, I hope your fiancé will be alright.' Rudely I scarcely stopped to acknowledge him and just rushed up to the office. 'How on earth does George know? It's buried on the inside pages...'

Miss Drury, Mr William's personal assistant, came over, 'Miss Brown, I'm so sorry to hear about this internment...'

I cut across her well-intentioned words, 'But I probably know less about it than you' – 'not to mention the doorman', I thought to myself – 'only what's in the newspaper. The authorities haven't told me anything, I don't even know if Josef is one of those poor men. But I would be so grateful if I might make a call during my break.'

'Of course you must. I can see you won't be concentrating on your work until this is settled. Get everything ready for Mr William before he arrives, but then please use the telephone to make enquiries, I will authorise that.'

I rang Mrs Branksome. She said Josef and Eberhard Röllig had been interned yesterday, taken away by two Kent policemen, but beyond that she knew nothing. The Kent police's only answer was, 'Contact the Home Office.' After a lengthy wait its phone was answered by a harassed-sounding man who would only say that all German males in Protected Areas had been interned, regardless of category. As to whether Josef was amongst them he simply could not or would not tell me. 'No, madam, Defence Regulations forbid me from giving further information.'

Arriving home this evening my heart soared, there was a letter from Josef. But, of course, it was postmarked Saturday, before that dreadful Sunday. It was full of his usual endearments, but one sentence puzzled me: 'I applied to join the Pioneer Corps, in case the French will not allow me into France with my Czech friends.' What did this mean, would it affect his internment? 'Yet more questions to ask tomorrow', I thought to myself.

On the radio by my bed Vera Lynn was singing,

We'll meet again,
Don't know where, don't know when,
But I know we'll meet again,
Some sunny day,
Keep smiling through…

I fell asleep hoping.

Tuesday 14th May

Today I went early to work but walked straight past Devonshire House to 131 Piccadilly, the Czechoslovak headquarters Josef had talked of. It was hidden behind a nondescript brass plate and an impenetrable and surly doorman. Finally my story, at its third telling, seemed to penetrate and I was ushered in. At the reception desk an officer in an exotic military uniform apparently understood little English, but at the mention of the name Kalla his manner changed. He took my name and the subject, 'Private Bramminger, interned', then spoke into a telephone. At once a diary materialized and an appointment in my lunch hour was offered.

When I returned at midday the atmosphere had changed dramatically. The doorman was now intelligent and courteous, the man at the desk almost deferential. Then a door burst open and through it strode a man with a shock of white hair and numerous medal ribbons on his blue uniform. His hand was outstretched. 'Colonel Josef Kalla, military attaché, delighted to meet you, Miss Brown. Josef...' that was encouraging, 'has spoken to me of you. Please come in.'

In his office he courteously offered me a chair. Behind his desk two portraits of Masaryk and Beneš stared down, a huge Czechoslovak flag dominated the room. I was taking in my host as he sat down – he reminded me of the composer Liszt, there was something Hungarian about his face – when I noticed a pistol on the desk, close by his hand. Seeing the alarm on my face he laughed. 'Not long ago the Nazis intended to take over these premises by force, as they have my country. We are prepared for them.'

He laughed again. 'But this can go away, I believe we are on the same side', putting the pistol away in a drawer, although I noted he left it ajar. He continued in a more serious tone, 'I have no time for Germans or Sudetenlanders, but Austrians, I forgive them much for Mozart's sake. I believe you play the piano, Miss Brown.'

'Yes, colonel, a little. I love his Piano Sonatas.'

'Then we shall get on well. Now, I believe you are here to seek my help in freeing your fiancé. We are doing all we can. I myself have already spoken to the War Office about him and another man, asking for their release, and I have hopes, although it may take time. I hesitate to criticize our greatest ally, but your War Office does not know – how do you say? – if it is coming or going. No-one could tell me if my men had been interned and, if so, where they were, nor to whom I should speak to seek their release. But we are pressing the matter.'

He paused, giving me a quizzical look. 'May I ask, Miss Brown, how much you know of your fiancé's involvement with us?'

What could I say? Could I trust him? Then the thought of that pistol and its story gave me heart, so I spoke up. 'Well, Colonel, Josef told me how he volunteered for your army in Prague, having done other work for your government after escaping from Austria. Is this, perhaps, what you are referring to?'

'I think we understand one another well enough. You yourself work for a powerful man, some of whose work is, I think, most secret.'

'The very word. I am secretary to Mr Rootes, some of whose affairs require considerable confidentiality. Perhaps this is true of Josef.'

'So, you do understand the position. Private Bramminger is of use to us as a soldier of course, every soldier is, we are a highly democratic army', a wry smile passed across his face, 'but he is most important to me in the work he does wearing a different hat. In that work he reports to me and another officer, whom you must meet.'

He spoke into the intercom on his desk, '*Zeptejte se plukovníku Lukas přijít.*'

Moments later a colonel entered, in army green rather than Kalla's air force blue. 'Let me introduce Colonel Karel Lukas, one of our chief staff officers in England. He deals with your fiancé in these matters.'

The new man greeted me in less perfect English than Kalla's, but his handshake was just as warm. Sitting down he asked in Czech, '*Kolik můžu říct? Je slečna Hnědá spolehlivý?* Kalla nodded.

'Colonel Kalla says to trust you, so let me say something of Josef's work. We find ourselves in London lacking much of the apparatus we had in Prague. Most Czechs living here are loyal and faithful, but many left family members in Czechoslovakia so are open to pressure. Therefore, when we find someone we can trust, we value them highly. Josef does some translation work, but I also use his experience as a soldier in the engineers and his knowledge of Austria's railways. As a young man in Vienna he received training from the Schutzbund in intelligence-gathering, I believe he may have told you of this...' I nodded. 'So, we were pleased to find him once again in our army.'

'And equally displeased', Kalla interjected, 'to discover he had been interned.'

Lukas continued, 'He has an exceptional ability to memorize and recall facts, and there is little we can teach him on the critical subject of security. But I must tell you, not a word of this to anyone. Not your mother, not those you are closest to, at work, an old school friend, no one. There could be times when his life would be in danger if talk gets out of his secret work', adding, as an afterthought, 'and others besides.' He looked so very sad, I thought.

'One thing... when you write to your government you should not mention this work, but you should say that their War Office, Room 427, holds papers about him. Also mention our names', Kalla nodded his agreement, 'and our ranks, it will reinforce our efforts on his behalf.'

Clearly our meeting had concluded. I said to Kalla, 'I have two questions, if I may. Yesterday I received a letter from Josef, saying he had applied to join the Pioneer Corps. Does this affect his situation as an internee?'

Colonel Kalla nodded. 'Our Czech contingent set off for France some days ago.

At that point we had not received your fiancé's passport back from Paris, where our Military Attaché has been trying to obtain a visa for him from his opposite number. The French authorities have been slow deciding if they would allow German or Austrian nationals into their country. But it makes no difference, since, as Colonel Lukas has said, Josef is useful to us. You had another question?'

'Thank you. Yes. You mentioned a second man. Would that be Doctor Röllig?'

'Yes, I can safely say he is the man. They were interned together and we intend they be released together. But your Home Office works at its own pace and we are hampered because we cannot mention this secret work, so I also speak to another department with an interest in your fiancé. They help our cause.'

'Thank you so much. I must be going. Mr Rootes will not forgive me if I am late back.'

'Having met the man, I believe you might say, "Billy's bark is worse than his bite." Au revoir, Miss Brown.'

As I walked back to Devonshire House I thought, 'His bark is bad enough!'

Wednesday 15th May

I am busier than ever. Beaverbrook has become minister of aircraft production with 'Billy' as his deputy, producing a flurry of missives and directives, and I, as Billy's general dogsbody, carry them out! He announced, 'I'll be working twelve hours a day, seven days a week.' He'll expect us to do the same. In working hours it takes my mind off Josef's situation, but with Holland surrendered and German tanks in northern France will anyone in authority concern themselves with the plight of one interned Austrian? As to how he's feeling I can only guess... I can't bear to put my worst fears in writing. Darling Josef, how I miss you.

Saturday 18th May

I took the day off to trail around offices...

The Home Office, 'Try the War Office',

...the War Office, 'The Home Office, Miss Brown, not us',

...the Red Cross, 'Is he a prisoner of war, dearie? No. An internee you say. Not us. Only if he's overseas, otherwise write to the Home Office',

...the Austrian Centre, most gemütlich, but no help. 'He's registered with the Czechs, not us',

...finally the Czechoslovak committee (the CRTF) in Bloomsbury House, Gower Street. What a place! Crammed with every refugee committee under the sun, speaking every Continental language, a true Tower of Babel. They knew little more than me. 'If he was arrested in Kent he's probably in Kempton Park' – a race course, of all places! – 'we think everyone from the south-east went there. The rumour, and that's all it is, is that the race courses and prisons are temporary, and internees will be moved to proper internment camps. But no-one has any lists, not us, not the authorities, nor will they say who's dealing with this, Home Office or War Office, we get passed from one to the other.'

Just like me.

But they tried to be helpful. 'Yes, Miss Brown, we know you're Herr Bramminger's fiancée, and we'll tell you when we have an address for him.'

Parcels? 'Ask the Home Office.'

Visiting? 'Ask the Home Office.'

Appeals procedure? 'Ask the...'

Against a hubbub of voices, tears and pleading, I left the CRTF, more drowning than swimming. So, back to the flat to write two letters to the Home Office, one for Josef, the second for the Home Secretary.

Monday 20th May

Home Office: Letter received. From Miss Mary V Brown, 32 Brixton Hill Court, London SW2. To the Home Secretary, Whitehall, London SW1.

Sir,

JOSEF BRAMMINGER, AUSTRIAN, CATEGORY C

Upon telephoning today, I was informed that the question of enemy aliens living on the coast (Category C) who were interned on Whitsun, is open to appeal from friends.

May I, therefore, appeal on behalf of my fiancé, and hope that his papers will be examined and his case investigated in order that he may be freed from internment?

I make this appeal because he was living on the Kent coast through no fault of his own. Upon the outbreak of war he re-joined the Czech Army at their camp at Birchington. Recently, however, his papers had to go to the French War Office for permission, as an Austrian, to land in France. The Czech Army was willing for him to stay in London until his papers were returned, as there was nothing he could do at Birchington except wait. We have been engaged for some time but have seen little of each other since war broke out, so he wished to stay in London until the matter was settled. My Mother said that he might stay with us and she would be quite prepared to look after him for the Refugee Committee's £1 pw. They, however, refused to allow him to stay in London as they would have to give him the 3/6d weekly London pocket money instead of 2/6d country pocket money. When he said that he would not mind receiving only the 2/6d they still refused permission on the grounds that the British Government wanted aliens out of London.

Much against his will he returned to Birchington to wait his papers' return.

I understand that you yourself have a file regarding him in the Aliens Department, but some of his papers relating to his political work against the Nazis are with the War Office, Room 427, whom he saw recently. Lt Colonel Kalla of the Czech Army Office, 131 Piccadilly, has also been dealing personally with some of his papers.

As these will show, he has worked untiringly against Nazism, and his greatest wish was to be allowed to continue to work against it. If he had been allowed to remain in London with us, pending his papers' arrival, he would still be free, and it does seem so very hard that, through no desire of his own to live in the coastal areas, he has now been interned, whilst in London Category C men are still free. Naturally, him being a political refugee, I am very worried and anxious on his account, as there are so many people willing to work for the Nazis, intentionally and unintentionally, and it would be so terrible for him, having twice escaped the Gestapo, to fall into their hands by any means.

The young lady who spoke to me when I telephoned said that you would be kind enough to give me his address so that I might write to him. I should be so glad to receive that.

If you should wish to question me further or to give you any information which would hasten the examination of this case, I should be pleased to keep any appointment you may wish to make.

I am, Your obedient Servant, Mary V Brown.

Wednesday 22nd May

Home Office: Letter despatched. To Miss Brown.

Dear Madam,

The Home Secretary desires me to acknowledge the receipt of your letter of the

20th May on behalf of Josef Bramminger, and to say that your representation shall have consideration.

As regards communicating with Mr Bramminger, there seems to be some misunderstanding, as for now people in internment are not permitted to communicate with friends or relatives.

Yours faithfully, Private Secretary.

Internal memorandum. To Mr Prestige, Principal, Aliens Department. Sir, you required action re increase in Aliens Department workload in Marsham Street and lengthy delays in individual cases. Request overtime be authorised pending appt of addtl staff, viz: 2 Paper Keepers, 10 Clerical Officers and 5 Officers from Immigration Branch. N C Powell.

Mary: More days passed and nothing. A fortnight since Josef disappeared from view and not a word, from him or the authorities. At Rootes I'm working non-stop, trailing after Mr William visiting Beaverbrook in his palatial offices in Fleet Street, his ministry in Millbank or his chaotic house in St James Park, not to mention around the War Office's warren of corridors.

Then back to Devonshire House to type up my notes, to enter diary appointments, to try and get a moment to relax... wishful thinking! The intercom booms out, 'Miss Brown, bring through that file on Spitfire production', 'the shadow factories', 'armoured cars...', and on it goes, 'Do this! Do that!'

Not a moment to think clearly about Josef. It's little better when I get home. I fall asleep so readily that breakfast is my main meal. I try to write to Josef twice weekly, but few letters come out straight, most end up in the wastepaper bin. They're hard enough to write in the first place, torn with turmoil and tears from somewhere deep inside, but on re-reading they get scrunched up and re-written. Worst of all is the black void I send them into. With no word from him I can't stop the questions coming. Has he received my letters? Is he allowed to write back? Is he in such despair that he can't? Does he even want to?

Sunday 26th May

Waking up today I was bewildered and knew I had to talk to someone. Most of my friends are away in the Forces. Then it was obvious, Stella, she'd make time for me in the Vicarage.

So, over Stella's cup of tea in the vicarage, and behind a door closed firmly on a surprised Roy – 'He drinks far too much tea as it is, poor darling!' – I poured out my woes: 'If only I hadn't been so ill in January we'd be married and he'd be living here, not on the Kent coast. If only that committee hadn't been so obsessed over just one shilling of weekly allowances. How must Josef be feeling? The country he's trying to defend treating him like a traitor. Why doesn't he write to me? Does he still love me?' – it all came rushing out. Stella just sat and listened. When I'd run out of sobs, tears and questions she said, very gently, 'Now drink that tea, darling, it's getting cold, and we'll look at all those one by one.' Which we did, and slowly but surely made some sense of the swirling mass of doubts, fears and guilty feelings in which I'd been drowning. Thank God for a good friend.

But as I went to leave Roy popped out of his study. 'Dearest Mary, you must be going through it, you really must. All I can say is, "Hold on." Daily you are in our prayers, and not just ours. Here, take this,' he pressed a battered book into my hands. 'I've often found it most helpful. Take a read – if you get the chance – and tell me what strikes you about it. There's a particular phrase I think you may find really... well, spot on. Tell me when you think you've found it; I'll be most interested to hear what you say. Good bye!'

Monday 3rd June

Home Office: Internal memorandum. To H H C Prestige. Appeal against internment. HO reply: a 'C' case in a Prot Area. Appeal is broadly on grounds that he was in a PA through no fault of his own. An Austrian brought to the UK under auspices of the Czech Committee, on outbreak of war he 're-joined' the Czech Army and was sent to Birchington-on-Sea to the Czech camp. There has been difficulty in getting a French visa for him, as he is Austrian, and through some dispute within Czech Commee he has been kept at Birchington, whereas he wd have wished to return to London to live with his fiancée (the writer). This was unfortunate for him but doubtless many 'C' cases wd have removed from PA had they anticipated the S/S's action. In present circs there are no grounds for return of this Austrian-cum-Czech. Permanent Secretary has sent the writer an ackn. Action: 1) To PS to see. 2) Again on 29.6.40. S A Cleal.

Tuesday 4th June

Home Office: Minute. I do not think the PS will wish to answer. There is no case for exceptional treatment. Action: Refuse – stock letter 'Y'. J Matthews.

Wednesday 5th June

Mary: Have written to the Home Office, War Office and every other organisation. No progress, their answers unhelpful and frustrating. Only one letter from Josef, no, not even that, a single postcard with the ominous words: 'NOTHING is to be written on this except date, signature and address of sender. Erase words not required. IF ANYTHING ELSE IS ADDED THIS POSTCARD WILL

BE DESTROYED.' All he could tell me was 'I am (~~not~~) well; ~~I am being admitted to Hospital~~; ~~I am being transferred to another camp~~; I have received your card dated: May 19.' It was sent from Aliens Internment Camp, Huyton, Liverpool (I've found it on the map; at least I now know where he is, or was a week ago, perhaps now he's on the Isle of Man?) I feel so helpless, distraught, fuming. Yet I'm free, how must he be feeling? Angry? Bewildered by the injustice of an anti-Nazi man, serving in the army, whose only ambition is to get back at them, being arrested and locked away. And how is he, really? 'I am (~~not~~) well', I ask you! That could mean anything. He'd scarcely have written 'I am unwell', knowing how upset it would make me.

People talk of the Dunkirk miracle, but the secret reports I take in daily to Billy show the invasion threat is very real. Amidst all that why should they - whoever 'they' may be! - pay the slightest heed to my one anti-Nazi Austrian? But if they send me yet another oh-so-well-phrased letter I think I shall scream.

Home Office: Letter despatched. To Miss Brown

Madam,

With reference to your application of the 20th ultimo for the release of Mr Bramminger, I am directed by the Secretary of State to say that, as he announced in Parliament on the 23rd May, he regrets that he cannot review cases of enemy aliens recently interned in pursuance of his General Directions. Your representations on behalf of this alien will however be borne in mind and considered as soon as an opportunity occurs.

I am, Madam, Your obedient Servant.

Thursday 6th June

Mary: This evening, reading that reply I permitted myself a not-so-very-quiet scream. 'It's nothing, Mother', I replied to her enquiring look, 'It's nothing.'

Tonight I began reading Roy's battered book: Julian of Norwich's 'XVI Revelations of Divine Love.' It looked hard going but (skipping the medieval English), it's really the easiest thing. It turns out that Julian's a she not a he, and she's not even Julian, no-one ever knew her real name - lucky her!

Monday 17th June

I may have found what Roy was hinting at, and it fits!!! 'All shall be well, and all shall be well, and all manner of thing shall be well.' Not just with me and Josef, here and now, but for all the world's troubles. AND, perhaps most significant of all, the first words are what Josef said to me at the bus stop down there - I can see it now, from the flat's window. He said, 'alles wird gut.' then translated it: 'all shall be well.' I remember it so well (perhaps because the very next moment he kissed me for the first time!)

Home Office: Memorandum from MI5. Request PPS send over this man's file.

Thursday 27th June

Memorandum from MI5: TO: Home Office Aliens Department. This is a case in which we should be quite prepared to see BRAMMINGER released to continue his training with the Czechs. We know nothing to his detriment and there is no sufficient reason for the internment of a man who is prepared to fight in the Legion. D G White.

Friday 28th June

Home Office: Copy received. To The War Office, Whitehall, SW1.

Sir,

With regard to Josef BRAMMINGER, interned. I understand that all interned aliens are to be sent overseas for the remainder of the war. If this is so, would you be disposed to allow me to see Mr Bramminger before he is sent away?

We had hoped to get married in January, but unfortunately I was ill and he had to return to the Czech Army Camp at Birchington-on-Sea, and there was interned on May 12th. I understood from the Home Office that all cases of Category C aliens would be re-examined so I did not worry anyone in this matter, but as he is now to be sent away without examination, I should be so very grateful if you would permit me to see him before he is sent off. As he is unable now to fight in either the Czech or British Army I do think it might make it very much easier for him if I could just be allowed to see him.

I am so sorry to trouble you in what must seem so very small and unimportant a matter to you, but the time is so short and things are done so quickly that I felt that unless I actually wrote to ask permission he might be sent away and it would then be impossible to do anything in the matter.

I am, Your obedient Servant,

Mary V F Brown (Miss).

Saturday 29th June

Home Office: Internal memorandum. In view of MI5's report by Dick White. ?/ Immediate release. J Bird.

Tuesday 2nd July

Home Office: Internal memorandum. Since MI5 are satisfied it seems better that this man resume his military training than remain in internment. ? (1) Send usual release lr to Director of Prisoners of War (DPW). (2) Inform MI5. (3) Lay By. N C Powell.

Wednesday 3rd July

.....

The SS Ettrick departed Liverpool. The Home Office, the War Office, MI5 and Mary knew nothing of this.

.....

Thursday 4th July

Home Office: Internal memorandum. In the present wartime conditions & having regard to the policy of general internment of enemy aliens, I do not think it would be right to release this man. Lay By. J Matthews.

Mary: On the way to work I bought a newspaper, more to distract myself from my worries than for the news. A moment later I wished I hadn't. Its headline screamed, '**ARANDORA STAR SUNK BY U-BOAT. 1,500 ENEMY ALIENS ON BOARD**.' The Arandora Star! The Dream Ship, sunk! Everyone knows her from newspaper pictures and posters, cruising the brilliant blue waters of the West Indies or the Mediterranean in her dazzling white paint, now in the grey waters of the Irish Sea. I read on, 'The Germans and Italians were being taken to an internment camp in Canada.'

That morning, the bus ride, the dash along Piccadilly, the lift to the first floor, even my work, went by as if in thick fog. Sir William called for me just once, thank goodness, and I dully took down the letter he dictated. No fooling him, though. He gave me a quizzical stare and asked, 'Are you all right, Miss Brown?' I replied somehow and went back to my desk, typing the letter like an automaton, holding back the tears.

In the lunch break I pulled myself together and telephoned Blue Star Line. Amidst what must have been a storm of enquiries their receptionist was so composed that I felt myself calm down. I was put through to a man who had a partial list of survivors but knew nothing of those who'd drowned. 'No, Miss, there is no J Bramminger amongst the survivors listed, a G Brammer, yes, no Bramminger.' He simply did not know if he was on the list of those lost, it had not been compiled, no-one in England had a complete passenger list.

.....

In the Travellers Club, off Pall Mall, D G White and Harold Prestige were talking things over, a regular meeting to ensure things didn't get out of kilter between White's MI5 and Prestige's Aliens Department. White, nodding towards their scribbled agenda, said, 'Kalla's been to see me about getting these two internees back. In fact, off the record, I'll admit both have been rather useful to us as well. See what you can do', his tone more directive than request.

'Certainly, Dick. Following your note two of the brighter men in my department, Bird and Powell, reviewed their cases and recommended release. Their immediate senior, an older man, rather set in his ways, rejected their advice and put the files into lay-by. I'll chase it up.'

.....

Mary: I heard the typists chattering away. 'She was such a lovely ship, people dancing the night away. I hear most West End restaurants lost their chefs and managers. Maggi, across the road at the Ritz. Bennini at the Hungaria, such a jolly man, Sovrani, all drowned they say.'

I'm in torment, was Josef amongst them?

This evening, in the flat, the wireless described 'great hulking brutes of Nazis sweeping the poor Italians aside in the rush for lifeboats.' I was gripped by fear, but then the announcer added, 'only Nazis and Fascists were on the ship.' I was so relieved. 'Josef <u>must</u> be safe, he's probably still in Britain, somewhere.'

Friday 5th July

Daily Sketch: The 1,000 Germans on the Arandora Star included anti-Nazi civilians and Nazi prisoners, the former included Category C internees.

Mary: Who to believe, BBC or newspaper? Josef, I don't know if you are alive or dead. I believe, I must believe, <u>you are alive</u>.

Then Colonel Lukas rang me in the office, slightly mysterious, suggesting lunch at Ye Grapes, in Shepherd Market, half-way between Rootes and the Czech mission. He steered me to a dark corner, into a wood-panelled inglenook surrounded by old rifles, horns and animal heads. He's a real charmer, raising my spirits by saying that more than once he'd sat there with Josef, although the realist in me suspects he chose it less from sentiment, more so as not to be overheard.

Over lunch he said, 'Colonel Kalla's given Röellig's name to MI5, saying his case matches your fiancé's, and that we', jabbing his thumb in the direction of Piccadilly, 'want them both back.'

Another late night looms, another letter to my 'beloved' Aliens Department but, first, a letter to Josef.

Mary, 9th letter: To 50186 Josef Bramminger, c/o 132 Parbrook Road, AIC Huyton.

My darling,

Many thanks for your card... perhaps you're not allowed to write long letters. Have you received my seven to Huyton? Or the parcel with some pullovers - in the middle of summer, am I going mad?... How are you? I expect you've come across many friends from Vienna... How are your teeth and those dreadful ulcers?... All the time I am thinking of you, my other half...

I love you very much.

Monday 8th July

Daily Sketch: It is now stated that there is no truth in reports that Class C internees, were on board the Arandora Star.

Mary, 10th letter: To AIC Huyton.

Darling Josef,

I got your first letter today!

You must not even think any nonsense of my forgetting you, I never shall, and think of you day and night. In every free moment I am seeking your release... I speak to you every day, as though you are here with me. There is something between us that will last always, of that I am certain... we will be together again and everything will be alright.

Your letter is THE most wonderful thing. I feel warm enough inside to make toast. I now realise just how miserable I've been since you were taken from me.

I love you.

Tuesday 9th July

Home Office: Internal memorandum. To H H C Prestige. Sir, I have spoken to Kalla at the Czech Legation. They know of this man and have no objection on personal grounds to Bramminger resuming his training but are currently precluded from enlisting any but Czech citizens pending a decision by British Govt that they can take foreigners. In the circs nothing can be done about Bramminger. Possibly MI5 - Hoddell - could enlighten us with regard to the prospects? N C Powell.

Internal memorandum. We should consider releases to join Allied Armies which are still fighting for us (See Sir A Maxwell's minute, 34/9408). Mr Powell, pl ascertain first where he would report to the Czech authorities. H H C Prestige.

Internal memorandum. Miss Brown asks permission to visit him in camp before he is sent to Canada.

Hansard: Mr Cross, the Minister for Shipping: 'I am informed by the War Office that all Germans on board the SS Arandora Star were Nazi sympathisers. None came to this country as refugees, were categories B or C, or were recognised as friendly aliens.'

Wednesday 10th July

Hansard: Colonel Josiah Wedgwood, MP (Newcastle-under-Lyme, Liberal): 'We see in the newspapers stories from survivors that the Nazis sympathisers pinned up a swastika flag in one of the wardrooms and forced the non-Nazis to salute it. What sort of discipline is there on board a British-flagged ship which allows that sort of thing?'

Mary, 12th letter: To AIC Huyton.

Darling Josef,

I have read and re-read your one letter so many times... I miss you so terribly.

Saturday 13th July

Home Office: Internal memorandum. To Mr Powell. Yes, pl ask MI5 but pick up first R.15636, ROELLIG's file, a German who is also being accepted for the Czech Army. Kalla advised Miss Brown of the similarity. We should have known first! H H C Prestige.

Mary, 13th letter: To AIC Huyton.

Darling Josef,

I have sent you two cards, ten letters and a parcel, have you received them? I received only one card and a letter from you. Peppi, you can imagine how this worries me.

I have written to the Home Office for your release, and our musical friend also works for it. But it may take some time...

What else shall I write? Without you every day is empty. What keeps me going is the hope that we will be together again. No, I have that wrong. It is not just hope, it is certainty, even if that certainty is sometimes hard to bear, for I cannot explain it to anyone else. Perhaps you know it also. I've just re-read Romans 4, 18, how 'Against hope, Abraham in hope believed.' That's me.

You will try to keep your spirits up, please, for me?

I love you very much.

Thursday 18th July

Home Office: Internal memorandum. Appeal for release.

Action:

1) Ask DPW to inform B his appeal is under consideration. Add that the question of his being allowed to re-join the Cz-Sl Forces is being considered, and in the meantime he shd not be sent out of the country.

2) Again in a week with R.15636. N C Powell.

.....

Richard: The War Office, Admiralty and Home Office were besieged by relatives and friends of internees, frantic for news of the Arandora Star. Some were wrongly told their relatives were safe while others, as wrongly, that theirs had drowned. Unaccountably no carbon copy had been kept of the list of who was to sail on the Arandora Star and the three ships due to sail after her. That single list was put on board the Arandora Star and went down with her. It was to be many months before the government could re-create it.

.....

Friday 19th July

Home Office: Letter received. To the Home Secretary.
re: Josef BRAMMINGER

Dear Sir,

With regard to the above, and to my previous letter, which you were so kind as to say you would bear in mind when examining the cases of Enemy Aliens for release from internment, I saw in last night's paper that individual cases will be examined whose papers show sufficient proof of anti-Nazi work.

May I, therefore, hope that you will be examining the papers of the above, which, as I previously mentioned are partly in War Office Room 427 and partly with the Czech Army Office?

I would not trouble you again in this matter, as I know how busy all Government offices have been, and I wondered whether, in view of new arrangements, etc, it might be necessary to re-state or re-endorse any application for release.

I am, Your obedient Servant, Mary V Brown.

Saturday 20th July

Mary, 16th letter: To Director of Prisoners of War, for Mr Bramminger.

Dearest Josef,

You wrote to me on 2nd Jul from Huyton. I sent you a parcel of the things you asked for. Today it came back: "Return to sender. Left for overseas on 3rd Jul." ... I cannot make that fit with the Arandora Star, so I hope you are alive, but no one will tell me, darling, where you are. Australia? Canada? Did you arrive safely? They have taken my Josef away, and I don't know where they have put him!

Monday 22nd July

Mary: I met Marjorie over coffee and she said when the wind's in the wrong direction they can still smell the fish. The Flying Flea isn't now going to France but she's as scrubbed and ready as ever.

Then I sprang the vital question. 'Does Jim ever work in The Citadel? You know, that ivy-covered concrete lump behind Admiralty Arch.' She gave me an odd look. 'How do you know of that?' she asked. 'It's very hush-hush.'

'Darling, it is to most people, but I often take papers there for Mr Rootes. It's just I need to ask Jim something and thought I might bump into him there.'

'Why not invite him to coffee in the Lyons at Piccadilly Circus?' She wrote on the napkin, 'Here's his number.'

'You are a dear. But does his Sir Dudley ever let him out of the Admiralty?'

'Occasionally! He may be Admiral of the Fleet, but he seems to think enough of my Jim to let him off the leash for coffee with me. It's never often enough, given we have a wedding to plan...'

'So would I, if I ever get the chance', I said, in a small voice.

'Oh Mary, I'm so sorry! That was thoughtless of me. Tell me what you can about Josef, where he is, how he's coping, what...' I had few answers but was just happy to have a friend to talk to.

A few days later I was in the Lyons Tea Shop facing Jim Hunnicutt, imposing in his naval uniform. 'So what's this mystery?' he asked, with that broad smile I like so much. 'Marjorie told me you have a question and I'll tell you anything I can. Except the recipe for Plymouth gin, of course, that's top secret.'

'Oh stop it!' I laughed, 'It's much simpler than that. Have you ever met Colonel Kalla, the Czech attaché?'

'Yes, Sir Dudley saw him at a reception only last week, they know each other well.'

'Thank you. Would you trust him?'

'Implicitly. He may be doyen of the diplomatic corps but he doesn't mince his words. They say that before the war he was no appeaser, unlike some, and he hates the Nazis with a passion. But he enjoys a joke and is easy going. He's a man of many talents, a flying ace of real distinction, a more than competent pianist they say. He's a real delight, just your sort of man. Why do you ask?'

'Well', I looked down at my cup, 'I needed to know how much weight I can put on Kalla, he's the main force in a behind-the-scenes effort to get Josef released, in league with a department on our own side – perhaps you understand who I mean, Jim.' I saw him nod almost imperceptibly.

My spirits had been lifted. 'Now, about this wedding. When is it? And where? Should I start immediately saving my clothing coupons or must I come in my usual rags?'

'Darling Mary, you and your "rags!" You're one of the two most glamorous women I know. We're planning on early December. The rest is very hush-hush, like the gin.'

Home Office: Letter despatched. To Director of Prisoners of War, SW1.

Sir,

Re Josef Bramminger, interned.

I am directed by the Secretary of State to request that this man be informed that his appeal is under consideration and the question of allowing the alien to re-join the Czecho-Slovak Forces is being studied. In the mean-time he should not be sent out of the country.

I am, Sir, Your obedient Servant.

Friday 26th July

Mary, 19th letter: To AIC Huyton.

Dearest Josef,

I've had the loveliest dream. I was strolling along Brighton's seafront, it was warm, blue skies, everyone in colourful summer clothes. All of a sudden, the seafront was empty, except for someone coming towards me. I was thinking, 'is that...' when yes, it was you. I ran to you, my own Peppi, and we were in each others arms. Such happiness, complete and utter bliss. Then I woke up, and burst into tears... But I do not give up hope...

Tuesday 30th July

Hansard: Mr Anthony Eden: 'The selection of internees to be transferred in the 'Arandora Star' was ordered by my Department from those in category A. There were on board 473 Germans and Austrians. It has been verified that all of these came within category A.'

Friday 2nd August

Home Office: Internal memorandum. The circs are much the same as Roellig's case (R.15636) and release on similar conditions might now be authorised subject to any further obsns by MI5.

Action:

1) Send to MI5, B Dept, for obsns.

2) Index, with R.15636.

Home Office: Letter received. From Miss Brown. Note the phrase I have underlined in blue. N C Powell.

Dear Sir,

May I appeal on behalf of J Bramminger for consideration of his case and examination of his papers in accordance with the recent White Paper?

He himself is at present unable to make an appeal, having been deported – I do not know where and cannot find out, but imagine it must be Canada – and I know that just previous to his having been interned he had not been well, having had much trouble with his teeth and a septic leg.

I understand that the Czech Army Office have applied for his release, and that the War Office has some of his papers relating to his work against Nazism. I do hope it will be possible to examine his case, especially Category 5 since he had permission of Chief Constable to be in a Protected Area, or possibly Categories 19 and 22, as he has opposed the Nazi regime and showed himself friendly towards this country. 11 or 12 may apply, owing to his having been living in the Czech Army Camp, which was sponsored by the War Office, and having served in the Czech Army, and also because his papers were under consideration by the Pioneer Corps. I must admit I find it rather muddling!

I have attached his details.

Yours faithfully, Mary V Brown

Attached:

<u>Name</u>: JOSEF BRAMMINGER
<u>Nationality</u>: Austrian.
<u>Profession</u>: Meat curer and preserver.
<u>Date left Austria/Entered Czechoslovakia</u>: May 1938. After examination and investigation by the Czech Secret Police was accepted in Czech Army. Did much work on behalf of the Social Democrat party, and was a keen Trade Unionist.
<u>On outbreak of war</u>: Volunteered and was accepted by Czech Army. At the time of internment he was awaiting return of his papers from France.
<u>Address from which interned</u>: Czech Army Training Camp, Birchington.
<u>Address to which would return on release</u>: Czech Army, wherever it might then be stationed.
<u>If not allowed on release to go to Czech Army Camp if in a PA</u>: He would be able to stay: c/o Mrs DMK Brown, 32 Brixton Hill Court, London SW2, or at one of the Czech Hostels in London.

.....

Mary's remark, 'it must be Canada', had been underlined in blue pencil by the civil servant reading it. Not something you often see in a Home Office file.

.....

Tuesday 6th August

Hansard: Colonel Josiah Wedgwood, MP (Newcastle-under-Lyme, Liberal): 'Are we to understand that there were no C Category Germans on the "Arandora Star"? How does the right hon Gentleman account for some of these being known to have been saved? Did the War Office really not know who were on board?'

Mr Anthony Eden, Secretary of State: 'What I said was that these were all category A.'

Colonel Wedgwood: 'Surely the right hon Gentleman must know by now – he has the names of those who were saved – that they were not all category A but categories B and C?'

Mr Eden: 'I have gone into the question carefully, and that is the assurance that I was given. In view of what the right honourable and gallant Gentleman says, I will go into it again.'

Mary: This evening I talked to Roy: 'I'm nearly out of my mind with worry about Josef. Did he drown on the Arandora Star? Was he saved? Was he even on it? The Daily Sketch stated there were some category C's, but Mr Eden stated all were A's and none were B's or C's, yet Colonel Wedgwood insists that some of those who have been saved were category C anti-Nazis. It doesn't add up.'

Thursday 8th August

Roy asked me over. He said to me, 'A friend of a friend, an army man who was in the guard company at Huyton...'

I cut across him, surprising myself by the sharp tone of my voice. 'Was Josef on the Arandora Star?'

'Dearest Mary, I cannot be certain. He knew Josef was one of a party from Huyton that was sent to board her but', he hesitated, 'at the last moment many of them were turned back. The Admiralty, the War Office and the Home Office never kept proper lists and Whitehall is burning the midnight oil to produce one, but it still won't be accurate. Apparently some internees paid others to go in their place.'

'But Josef had no money', I said, 'no real money, for that, and, anyway, we were, we are, still planning to get married...' Here I faltered, thinking of how my illness had postponed our wedding. 'If only...', then I got a hold of myself. 'So what exactly do you know, dear Roy?'

'Well, he's no longer in Huyton, but if he's in another camp in the Isle of Man, Canada or Australia, I cannot say. I'm so sorry.'

'No need to apologise, you've done your best, thank you, darling. I shall just have to continue bombarding the Home Office. How they must hate me, all those letters.'

'Whitehall cowers beneath its desks, fearing more missives from Miss Brown!'

I laughed. 'You may be right! I never knew how much vitriol I had inside me, although I try to disguise it under great layers of protocol and politeness, "I remain, Your very obedient servant", all that palaver. I'm not secretary to London's most abrasive man for nothing!'

Later I saw Johann Svitanics, Josef's best friend. He was released from internment yesterday, one of the first. He knows Josef left Huyton on 3 July so he cannot have been on the Arandora Star, as she had sailed two days earlier! Thank you Lord. Johann has re-joined his Austrian Trades Union organisation in central London. Now I have some hope.

Wednesday 14th August

Mary, 25th letter: To 50186 Josef Bramminger, c/o Internment Operations, Canada.

My sweet love, *Meine Liebling*,

You see, now you have me writing in German. Finally I have an address in Canada to write to so I hope you get this, perhaps even those letters I have written before now...

On radio someone just now was reading from a sonnet: 'Love', Shakespeare wrote, 'is an ever-fixed mark.' Four words sum the sonnet up, 'I love you still', or five, '*Ich liebe dich immer noch*.'

Home Office: Note from MI5. 'BRAMMINGER is undoubtedly an Austrian national, though holding a Czech interim passport. His claim to serve in the Czech Army is based on previous service with that organisation. D G White.'

Wednesday 28th August

Home Office: Internal memorandum. According to Mary V Brown's letter 2/8 internee has been sent to Canada. Secretary of State letter 22/7 to DPW gave instructions for internee not to be deported. Perhaps it would be well to find out where he is!

Action:

1) Ask B3 (Internment Camps) to inform this department of whereabouts of internee. Refer them to S/S letter.

2) Lay By.

Home Office: Internal memorandum. Aliens Department to B3. I am to request you to be good enough to inform this Department of the whereabouts of Josef BRAMMINGER. This is in reference to S/S letter 22.7.40.

Saturday 7th September

Mary: The first bombs on central London. At teatime people were walking in the autumn sunshine around Green Park when the sirens started off, eastwards, over the City. Some went to find a shelter, but many paid no heed, they'd heard those sirens before but the bombers had always flown high overhead.

But this time it was real. From the office window I made out the aeroplanes, high-up. Then puffs of white smoke of anti-aircraft shells burst amongst them and I heard the big guns firing from Green Park. That started people rushing for the shelters. People fear those ugly, jagged bits of red-hot shell fragments clattering down on them more than the bombs.

Monday 9th September

From the bus it's clear that central London has been badly hit. We crawled past rubble across the approaches to Westminster Bridge, by St Thomas's. Six nurses died there on Saturday night. Across the Thames, Parliament and Big Ben remain untouched.

Wednesday 11th September

Mr Churchill spoke on the wireless, 'Little does Herr Hitler know the spirit of the British nation, or the tough fibre of Londoners.' Our Miss Drury, who lives in Battersea, saw him walking though the bombed-out houses there, complete with homburg, greatcoat and a great retinue of hangers-on – 'Just like our Mr Rootes!' she joked. She's very brave to laugh; her house was one of those that had just been destroyed.

Thursday 12th September

Bombs now fall by day and night. In the middle of a bright autumnal morning we hear the noise of an aircraft engine, then the screech of a bomb and the dull 'crump' that follows.

Friday 13th September

Now Buckingham Palace has been attacked and the Queen said, 'I'm glad we've been bombed. It makes me feel we can look the East End in the face.' Beat that, Mr Hitler.

Friday 20th September

Some humour at last. Peter Chance sent me a press-cutting from Australia, writing, 'You must be getting a bit of a walloping in London so this might cheer you up.' It did!

'"The height of self sacrifice for war funds proposed" At the recent sale of Red Cross gifts at Christie's, in which treasures of jewellery and priceless objets d'art were put up by Mr Terence McKenna, a partner in the auctioneers, and who has the reputation of being one of the handsomest men in England, a woman asked if those present might have the honour of bidding for Mr McKenna, "for the Red Cross." While Mr McKenna, whose fan mail rivals that of some film stars, was endeavouring to meet the suggestion with tact, another Red Cross worker suggested that Lord Willingdon, who has attended the sales each day, should also be put up. Lady Willingdon, vice-chairman of the Red Cross committee, said emphatically, "If Lord Willingdon is put up, I shall buy him back."'

Saturday 28th September

Home Office: Internal memorandum. B3 fwd infn.

Action:

1) Ask High Comm for Canada to arrange for the return to the UK of this man, if he so desires.

2) Inform Miss Brown that arrangements are being made for the alien's return.

3) Lay By. W E Higham.

Monday 30th September

Mary: Now every night there's a raid, not always south of the river but often central London.

Thursday 3rd October

Home Office: Internal memorandum. BRAMMINGER, J, return to UK. Promulgate as Special Case. Send following letter: 'To The High Commissioner for Canada, Canada House, Trafalgar Square, EC2.

Sir,

I am directed by the Secretary of State to say that he would be glad if arrangements could be made for Josef Bramminger, 701978, at present interned in Canada, to be returned to the United Kingdom.

I am, Sir, Your obedient Servant.

Friday 4th October

Home Office: Letter despatched. To Miss Brown.

Madam,

With reference to your letter of the 2nd Aug regarding Josef BRAMMINGER, I am directed by the Secretary of State to inform you that arrangements are being made for his return to this country from Canada, if he so desires.

I am, Madam, Your obedient Servant.

Mary: There, in the post-box, was a letter in Josef's handwriting. My spirits soared. This was no time for a letter opener and I roughly tore it open, what a wonderful noise that makes! Then my spirits plummeted, it was dated 3rd August. Josef wrote it two whole months ago.

Saturday 5th October

Mary, 26th letter: To Internment Operations, Canada.

Dearest Josef,

Wonderful news, this morning I learnt that "arrangements are being made for your return to this country." I hope you know this already, as it may be two months before you hear it from me... Will post this after lunch.

I love you.

Mary: Tonight, I was up late in the flat when the strangest thing happened. I was ironing, lost in thought, or prayer, call it what you will. All at once I was standing in a wide open, sandy space. As the picture in my mind's eye became clearer it seemed I was facing a huge wire fence, somehow I knew it was barbed wire.

And Josef was there, just ahead of me.

I knew, in that way you can with people you're close to, that he'd been looking fixedly at the fence, and he was so miserable that he was thinking of escaping. Then I knew, even more surely, that he was thinking of climbing it, there and then.

Somehow, surely it was my imagination, because I couldn't really see him, on his back was a target, so clear, a red circle. The guard, up there in the tower, wouldn't miss it.

'Oh! Josef! Stop!' I called out, as urgently and forcefully as I knew how. 'You're coming home to me, but not that way, NOT through the fence!'

'But Mary', and I knew he'd turned to me, although I couldn't see him properly through my tears, 'I am so unhappy, so confused, everything is wrong, I have to be with you, nothing else makes sense. I must...'

'You WILL be released, and soon. Colonel Lukas told me and now the Home Office says so, I've just written to tell you. Hold on to that, darling, and...', suddenly I was looking him in the face, 'and to the love we share. You know it; all shall be well, don't let go...'

Then the image faded and I was back in the flat, standing at the ironing board as I had been all along. Or was it the burning smell of the blouse I'd been ironing that had brought me back to the land of the living?

Oh bother, blow, dash and spit!

Monday 7th October

For a month they've bombed London daily, initially by day and night, then only at night because they were losing so many aeroplanes in the daytime. It's getting us down.

Monday 14th October

What a loss! St James's on Piccadilly, the beautiful Wren church I walk past every day, gone. And poor Mr Murray, the verger, and his wife Edith died, trapped beneath the Rectory. Incendiaries set the roof ablaze and it collapsed into the church, along with that dear little steeple. All the pews, plasterwork and those wonderful Doric and Corinthian columns, vanished. It was still smoking this morning as I went past. When will this all end?

Friday 18th October

Home Office:

Action:

1) Write applicant, I am directed by S/S to say that if he chooses to return from Canada the question of his release from internment will be dealt with immediately.

2) Lay By. D Blackman.

Saturday 19th October

Mary: 'But Roy', I said, 'they told me he'll be coming back, but only "if he so desires, when the question of his release will be dealt with." What does THAT mean?'

'It means, dear Mary... now listen, you've told me yourself about the phrase that Julian of Norwich heard, "All shall be well and all shall be well, and all manner of thing shall be well." Endure a little longer. What you need is a soupçon more faith. Can you manage that? For Josef?'

'I thought you were a priest, not a chef! I'll try, but it's not easy.'

Friday 1st November

What a Friday that was! Billy ordered a board meeting for seven so all morning I frantically worked on the agenda, motor business notes, military production notes, shadow factory notes, then on getting the room ready.

At midday three of us, an engineer, the aero-engine designer and me - chosen, I think, because I'd had my hair done yesterday - were sent up to the roof for the company photographer to take publicity pictures. It was all flood lights, tripods and cables, while we stared meaningfully at large charts of factory layouts and engineering drawings, all mocked up for the occasion. It was very surreal, spot-lights in broad daylight and me trying to look as if the inside of an aero-factory meant something to me. Then out of the blue the sirens began to wail.

I just had time to think, 'Binkie will have been under the bed five minutes ago', then we were rushing downstairs. Only I stopped after one flight and rushed back up, remembering I was on Fire Watch. I had to stand on that roof, watching and watching, but all the bombs were south of us, towards Victoria, so fortunately we had no fires to report, no incendiaries to smother with sand buckets. The all-clear sounded - that loveliest of sounds - so we re-stowed our buckets of sand, brooms and fire-blankets and it was back to making the boardroom ready. Sally came in with a cup of tea and some news, 'They bombed Buckingham Palace again' - it must have been one of the bombs I saw from the roof - 'but it only broke some windows, so no harm done.'

I went back to Billy's boardroom on the first floor. It is, no, it was, dominated by a highly polished and solidly-built oak table, surrounded by twelve gilt chairs, all rather grand. The board assembled and I sat at the table beside Billy, busy writing shorthand. It went on for over two hours. I remember him smiling, just once, when he came to the war production numbers. 'They told me daily Spitfire production has increased by 100%. What they didn't tell me was the increase was from zero the day before to one. It took Miss Brown to spot that trick...' that was where he turned to me and smiled, 'a trick they will <u>not</u> be playing again, I may say.' I didn't minute that.

'Have that on my desk in the morning', he growled at me as he left, and off they all went. Soon I heard through the windows their limousines leaving, down below in Stratton Street, and the noises from the Coq d'Or restaurant across the road. Funny, that. I distinctly heard those noises, but I must have been so busy checking my notes that I never heard any air-raid siren.

I remember looking up at the clock, it read five to ten. Then there was the most almighty noise and explosion. I cannot properly describe it. A blinding flash, everything went black, the building rocked, great heat, a blast that seemed to suck the air out of me, choking smoke and dust, and everything crashed about my head. My skin felt as if it was burning. Silly thing, I thought 'this will wreck my hairdo', then a great silence, except that I could hear everything and nothing all at once, a ringing in my ears that seemed to go on for ever, a whistling and shouting, as though a fisherwoman was screeching at me. I can still hear her.

Mostly I remember the all-pervading, acrid smell.

I haven't a clue how I arrived on the ground floor, somehow staggering downstairs – the wardens and police and ambulance men probably thought I was rolling drunk, a survivor, perhaps, of some party in the Coq d'Or! A first-aid party from Dick Sheppard's people at St Martin-in-the-Fields – how lovely they were – dusted me down and gave me a cup of tea. I needed it! I was shocked, but no bones broken. A warden told me I was lucky to survive, given just how wrecked the boardroom was. That massive boardroom table split in two over me, but it saved my legs from being crushed under the debris of the ceiling and walls. I was helped outside. Stratton Street was covered two feet deep in broken glass, the windows from all seven floors having crashed onto it. Poor old Devonshire House!

Billy Rootes soon turned up from his suite at Claridge's, the usual bundle of energy. He insisted on his chauffeur driving me home in his limousine – it was past midnight. He simply ushered me into his car and sent me off. With debris across the streets in the West End and south of the river the drive took nearly two hours so I arrived at the flats in the early hours and nobody saw my triumphal arrival in a chauffeur-driven Humber Pullman! Probably no bad thing, since I must have looked a real mess.

Before I departed Billy had said, magnanimously, 'And you must take tomorrow off, my dear.'

Normally I would have let this sort of thing pass, but it was past midnight and maybe the effects of the shock had begun to wear off, so I was brave enough to respond, 'But tomorrow is Sunday, Mr William.'

He laughed, a rare thing (a smile AND a laugh, all in one day!) 'Of course, of course. Just wanted to see you still had your wits about you, Miss Brown, d'you see? I'll see you again next week, although possibly not in those offices', he boomed, throwing a rueful glance at the hole in the wall above his head.

Air Raid Precautions patrol report: At 21:55 a 50 kg bomb struck the wall of the first floor of Devonshire House on Stratton Street, tore a hole about 15ft by 10ft in the structure and passed on through the boardroom and offices of Rootes Motors. Wrecked them and continued through the floor, finishing in the ground floor car showroom.

Minor damage was pitting of walls of Stratton House opposite Devonshire House and usual blast effects to Coq d'Or restaurant. Fallen heavy masonry obstructs Stratton Street.

FAP case handled by Pacifist Union Patrol, Dick Sheppard Club. The only services called for was one ambulance at 23:21 and casualty taken out of 1 Stratton Street removed to St George's Hospital at 23:50. After the bomb fell and still (08:00) there's been an overpowering smell of ammonia, particularly noticeable in the showroom where the final debris lies.

Monday 4th November

Mary: I'm so happy to have Binkie for company and to be in my own flat (Mother will remain in the old one for a week or so). 'Please do not disturb' on the door worked a treat, although I'd probably have slept through if someone battered the door down. I went to work today, to find Mr William had moved his personal staff across to Claridge's while the offices are rebuilt.

When he saw me he exclaimed, 'But I told you to take the day off!'

'I did, Mr William. I took Sunday off.'

'But I meant today, of course. Do you understand nothing? Anyway, here you are. Where are those minutes you were preparing at the board meeting?'

So Billy, at least, is suffering no ill effects from the bomb! Unlike Rootes' rather grand Minutes Book. Leather-bound and many years old, it disintegrated in the explosion, so all he got were my rather sketchy recollections!

What is it about Billy Rootes? He's a great leader, assertive, enormous drive, so resilient. Yet he's fastidious to a fault, it's like an obsession. Everything, and I mean everything, must be efficient, tidy, immaculate, in its place... 'I will not have sloppy housekeeping!' His clothing, his hair, his office, his desk, all perfect. So when the Germans utterly wrecked the offices he ought to have had tens of dozens of kittens but, two days later, there he was in his suite at Claridge's, as cool as ever. Perhaps it's simply because nothing <u>there</u> is ever out of place, everything runs like clockwork and all things are to the highest standard imaginable (and they make sure all 'his' waiters are clean-shaven, that's vital, he can't abide beards). Claridge's is his idea of paradise.

I've decided not to put every raid in my diary. After experiencing 'my' bomb I agree wholeheartedly with Mr Churchill's slogan, 'Business as usual.'

The weekend, 9th to 10th November

That said I was glad to take a weekend away to Herefordshire. Londoners' motto may be, 'We can take it', but here's one close to saying, 'I can't!'

Uncle Bernard collected me from Weston-under-Penyard's railway station and soon we were in the sitting room at Woodleigh, their 'House under the hill', Beatrice and the maid fussing around with trays laden with tea, scones and cake in a profusion London hasn't known for months. I hadn't seen them for a long time so conversation flowed easily: 'We're so happy you could visit us, your cousin Trixie is looking forward to seeing you. She and her parents are coming for lunch tomorrow. Rationing's so tight, there's so little petrol we can hardly travel, how is your mother, poor Dorothy?'

All was sweetness and light until Josef's name was mentioned. Immediately the air seemed to freeze over. I tried to explain, how he was on 'our side', a friendly enemy alien, his only ambition to fight the Nazis – 'and to marry me', I almost added, but decided it wasn't the right moment.

'How could you, Mary, he's a German...'

'An Austrian, auntie, Josef's an Austrian.'

But she wouldn't have it. 'They're all enemies. They must be, otherwise why would the Government have interned him? You cannot marry a German, we won't have it. I'm sure Bernard and I would want nothing more to do with you if you dare marry this foreigner.'

I was shaken by her outburst. Since childhood Auntie Bea has been held up as the family's epitome of politeness, why is she suddenly so rude and hostile? I noticed that Bernard stayed on the side-lines. Perhaps he doesn't altogether agree with her.

Just at that moment, as I tried to pull my wits together and find a polite answer, the most absurd thing happened. I'd been hearing, miles away, over May Hill, an aircraft flying towards us, a British bomber from the sound of its engines. But then cattle in a nearby field started lowing loudly and something in this combination of noises set off a panic in the room, Beatrice seemingly beside herself. 'It's a raid, an air-raid! We must go into the shelter! Hurry, hurry!'

An air raid, a shelter? Here in rural Herefordshire, a hundred miles and more from the blitz! Surely not. But I was scooped up in the mad rush out of the back door and into the garden – beautiful as always – then hustled a yard or two on, into the corrugated-iron garden shed. Deeper in, the outer door closed behind us, we went through another in the dark, then Bernard was lighting an oil lamp. The four of us had squeezed into a space, barely four feet by eight. As I sat down on a rough wooden bench running along one side I saw that Bernard, at least, had kept his wits about him, he'd brought with him the tea-tray, cups, cream and a plateful of scones.

'This shed's built into the hillside, just below the field gate', he explained, 'I had the gardener pile two feet of soil on the roof, to make a shelter. I'm sure it is nothing compared to what you must have in London, but we felt we should do our bit for the war. What do you think of it?'

I mumbled some anodyne reply, and in the oil lamp's long shadows they didn't notice my shoulders heaving with silent, near hysterical laughter. Then the moment passed and thirty minutes of slightly stilted conversation followed, conducted, oddly enough, in whispers, as if German parachutists were prowling the gardens overhead. Finally Bernard announced it safe to venture out. Thankfully Josef was mentioned no more and we resumed our disrupted Saturday afternoon.

That evening, in the guest bedroom, I wrote up this diary. Rather than dwell on Beatrice's prejudice and hatred – for someone she's never even met – I turned my mind back to that ludicrous teatime scene and found I was shaking with laughter. 'This won't do, Mary', I said to myself, 'it really won't, it's no laughing matter. Poor B and B, they really don't understand you, and they certainly have <u>no</u> idea about the blitz!'

Deep inside a slightly snide voice said, 'But they won't be coming to your wedding, will they?'

Oddly enough that rather cheered me up. Some part of me, at least, clearly believes that Josef will be coming home, safe, and that he still loves me. How encouraging.

But it chimed in again, in an even snider tone, 'And that very same day they'll be cutting you out of their will.'

'Amen to that, I say', I replied firmly, 'it's only money, after all.' That silenced the voice completely.

Tuesday 12th November

Home Office: Letter received. From Miss Brown.

Dear Sir,

re: <u>Josef BRAMMINGER, B.6092/3</u>

With reference to your letter of the 25th October, stating that if Mr Bramminger chooses to return from Canada to this country the question of his release from internment will be dealt with immediately. I wonder if it would be possible for me to be informed of his arrival in England?

Knowing the delay in my letters reaching him and his reaching me, I am afraid either that something may have happened to him as I have not heard for so long, or that, should he be now in England, or arrive soon, and not having heard from me for so long a time, and knowing that London is being bombed, he may worry in case anything has happened to me. It is very difficult when you do not hear from a person and cannot get in touch with them. I do hope that I am not giving you too much trouble.

Yours faithfully...

Friday 15th November

Mary: The most terrible thing, the Luftwaffe have blitzed Coventry, dropping over 50 land mines, 1,400 high explosive and 30,000 incendiary bombs; much loss of life, many of Rootes' factories and his people's homes destroyed. So, first thing this morning Billy drove up there, taking me and his regular retinue with him. Beaverbrook, in the back of the limousine with Billy, dreamed up the Coventry Reconstruction Committee and asked him to head it. Billy accepted and hasn't stood still for a minute since (not that he'd ever stood still for two minutes before), working more furiously than ever. By midday he was standing on an upturned wooden crate addressing the workforce at his Humber works. 'Many of you know I was an apprentice in this city and I will not let it down. I ask your help to clear up the mess the enemy have made, and promise there will be work for you all. The RAF needs every aero-engine and the Army needs every vehicle this city can produce and, together, we're not going to let them down.'

Monday 18th November

What a weekend that was, every minute crammed with work. Finally back to Brixton. This evening I was invited round to the Vicarage. In the living room Roy was reading the paper, and its headline, **'INTERNEES IN CANADA, MR ALEXANDER PATERSON SENT TO REPORT'**, shouted across the room at me.

'Vicar', I said, trying to keep the excitement out of my voice, 'might I read that paper when you've finished with it?'

'Of course, my dear. Is there something in it of interest?' Seeing my impatience, he grinned, 'Of course you must see this', handing the paper over. 'I've been waiting to show it to you. Sit yourself down and read, while I ask Stella if we can have some tea.'

It was a short paragraph, 'Mr Alexander Paterson, the British Director of Prisons, arrived in Canada yesterday to consult with the Canadian government on the future of the German internees there. He will spend two months compiling his report. Reuters.'

'Another two months. Oh dear! And then the Home Office will think about it. It could be months more before... and we're in the middle of the battle of the Atlantic, all those submarines...'

In came Stella, kind and smiling as ever, 'Have some tea, darling, and a biscuit. Roy knows Alec Paterson personally and holds him in very high esteem. He's high up in the Home Office but he's also a wonderfully Christian man; wounded in the Great War, MC, twice recommended for the VC, a founder member of Toc H to boot. Your father would have admired him greatly...'

'He's quite extraordinary', Roy said. 'Sorry to interrupt, darling, but he really is. I've met him during my visits to Brixton Prison, next door, and took to him immediately. He's worked in the slums, he's improved borstals and prisons beyond recognition, all with showmanship, determination and compassion. Ministers and senior civil servants, being so accustomed to yes-men, find him quite unnerving. He's just the man for this job. I am sure Josef will be freed very soon.'

'So, here's to a wonderful wedding, in no time at all', Stella added, smiling and raising her teacup.

Monday 2nd December

Home Office: Internal memorandum. From B3 to B2/ BRAMMINGER, Josef. According to our records this internee sailed on the Ettrick to Canada, where he is in 'Q' Camp.

Saturday 7th December

Mary: A respite at last. Attended Marjorie and Jim's wedding. After months of fighting the Home Office, being bombed by the Luftwaffe, and beaten about the head by Auntie Beatrice (or that's what it felt like), one day of civilised conversation, glamour and good food. Hurrah!

Thursday 12th December

Seven months!

Wednesday 18th December

Home Office: Internal memorandum. B3 query.

Action:

1) Reply Miss Brown/ Ref your enquiries of 12th and 23rd ultimo concerning Mr Bramminger, it is regretted that information regarding movements of internees' ships cannot be disclosed for reasons of security.

2) Lay By.

Mary: Had lunch with cousin Trixie, on a rare visit to London. She invited me back to Herefordshire. 'I'd love to, but I can't', I said, 'I'm sorry, but I must stay in London for Josef. It's important he knows where to find me.' I bit my tongue to stop myself from adding, 'if he comes back.'

'I understand', said Trix, folding her napkin. 'But do come and see us when you're together again.'

I promised.

Trixie: The very mention of his return put a smile on Mary's face.

Mary: Back at the flat. No letters, no telegram.

Tuesday 24th December, Christmas Eve

Three of us from Rootes went down this evening to St Martin-in-the-Fields' crypt to help in their absolutely packed Christmas Canteen. It's massive down there, a bit medieval, it can even feel a bit spooky, despite Dick Shepherd and his merry band being so open-hearted and cheerful. But tonight, with bombed-out Londoners, youngsters, orphans, some office workers about to go on fire-watch, ARP's and off-duty firemen, a half decent-sized tree with more decorations - so rumour has it - than has Harrods's, toys from America for the youngsters and gifts for the homeless it could <u>not</u> have been better. Everyone really enjoyed themselves. Thank God!

Wednesday 25th December, Christmas Day

At the flat Mother, myself and two neighbours sat down to lamb chops (7/-), beans, and mince pies. Turkey (£1) and Christmas cake were too expensive, if you could find them. To each of his staff Mr Rootes had presented a bottle of port, unbelievable luxury, so we drank the usual seasonal toasts in port, then one to 'Our Billy!' On the radio we heard the King's speech and a sermon preached from the ruins of Coventry Cathedral, then all down to the communal shelter where people sang carols. Someone had made tiny presents for us, just knick-knacks, a bath cube, a collar stud, a torch battery – now that had us clapping! Dearest Josef, if only you'd been with us. I hope and pray that, wherever you are, you've had a decent meal, with friends and good cheer. Happy Christmas, darling.

Thursday 26th December, Boxing Day

For most Londoners it's Boxing Day but Billy slept overnight in his office and began today at his desk. I'm one of the handful of staff he insisted report for work. 'If civil defence workers, firemen and medical staff are on duty', he said, 'so will I be. Right, Miss Brown, those Shadow Factory minutes...'

An honour, I'm sure! But my admiration for the great man is sometimes sorely tested.

Monday 30th December

Bitterly cold and snowing on my way to work. On Sunday they bombed London more fiercely than ever. A raging inferno in the City. Everywhere in flames, Aldersgate to Moorgate, Cannon Street to Cheapside... so much for the unofficial Christmas truce! Billy's chauffeur drove me with some papers to the Bank of England and we had to go along the Embankment and then north to avoid it all. Dead were still being pulled from the debris and ambulances were carrying away injured firemen. I must brace myself to write once more to the Home Office, but somehow, after today's scenes, my heart isn't really in it.

Tuesday 31st December, New Year's Eve

At midnight I mustered the courage to drink a slightly unconvincing toast. 'To the New Year. Things can only get better!'

Monday 6th January 1941

Home Office: Internal memorandum. BRAMMINGER, Josef J, last located Q Camp, Canada. A Miss Mary V Brown called here to enquire the whereabouts of this alien. His letters to her suddenly ceased in September last, when apparently he had hopes of release, and she is very anxious about him, fearing that he may have been torpedoed en route to UK.

However, we have traced a BRAMMINGER J on the list of the 45 internees who were, 11th December, to be the first shipped to the UK for release, but said nothing about this to Miss Brown, as we understood that the information is confidential. Could you write to her and put her out of her suspense?

Home Office: Internal memorandum. Alien's whereabouts, request for information.

Action:

1) Reply to Miss Brown that I am dir by S/S to inform her that we have been advised that the alien Bramminger is on his way back to the UK and will probably disembark in two or three weeks. He will then, no doubt, communicate with you.

2) Lay By.

Friday 10th January

Home Office: Late note. SS Thysville, Halifax 30/12/40-L'pool. He is probably on this ship, even though the list shows 'G J Bramminger.' But as it gives the right internee number it is likely him.

Home Office: Late note. Ascertained BRAMMINGER J arriving L'pool on S/S Thysville 11/1/41.

.....

Saturday 11th January

Months had passed, summer had passed through autumn to winter. Days had been hard and dangerous, this one not least. Working hard all day it was past eight before Mary could drag herself away. As she'd walked along Piccadilly the sirens had sounded and, even as she entered the shelter, there'd been an explosion fifty yards behind her, near Devonshire House.

It was past nine before the all-clear sounded. At the exit a warden warned them not to go near Green Park tube. 'The entrances and the front of Devonshire House are wrecked, Piccadilly's blocked', he said. 'Six dead and one serious, she's in St George's.'

On the bus back to Brixton she thought to herself, rather grimly, 'Josef's safer on a ship than he'd be in London.' Then, as an afterthought, 'Look after him, Lord.'

London in early January, held no pleasure for her, long and dreary nights, longer still in the blackout. As soon as she was back in the apparent safety of her flat, she collapsed into an armchair, that near miss having put all her senses on edge. For months she'd wrestled daily with the absence of her love, a refugee from 'a far away country', and with how few letters – always long-delayed – she'd received. What should she make of the Home Office latest reply? Should she be celebrating Josef's impending return, or worrying herself silly about his journey across a submarine-infested ocean? Her longing might have turned into hoping, and praying, but worry overtopped them all.

All evening she sat close to the radio, listening to the Home Service, a self-imposed silence between her and her mother.

At ten, her mother went off to bed but Mary stayed up, the radio on, Debroy Somers' Band playing its familiar jazz tunes. She was turning things over and over in her head, as she had time and time again since May... or was it in her heart? She could never decide which.

'Tomorrow it will be eight months', she thought and was about to turn in when the wireless sounded midnight, and the news started. 'I'll just listen to this then...'

The next moment she was sound sleep.

Chapter 8

From Halifax to London, by way of the Mull of Kintyre

Sunday 6th October 1940, Day 148, 22 weeks

Josef: After yesterday I feel at peace, the first time since May. Peace for me, but not Camp Q: after a fight, Campbell put four internees into custody. Ha, custody! Where does he think we are?

Mary, I have decided. Separation cannot alter our love for one another.

Monday 7th October, Day 149

Eberhard and I were called to the Camp Office and told, 'You'll be returned to England to re-join the Czechoslovak Brigade. When space on a ship becomes available, you'll be taken to Halifax and put on board. Until then you remain subject to Internment Regulations, including wearing uniform.'

At last! It's what Mary told me in that dream – or whatever that was! – two days ago, so it must be true. We're happy, but others seem even happier. We'll be the first internees returned and they see us as harbingers of many more. My back is sore from being slapped!

Nights getting colder. In the early hours we heard the sound of guns firing, as in July. They forced us outside, to shiver at attention in howling winds for a panicky roll-call. Eventually an officer worked out this hadn't been drunken guards firing off their guns, or sentries shooting at escapees, but nails exploding out of the asbestos roofs in the extreme cold. No apology, why should they? They never make mistakes.

Tuesday 8th October, Day 150

Even more cheerful, a letter from Mary.

We're ordered to move out of Camp Q on Thursday.

Wednesday 9th October, Day 151

We, who have nothing, have accumulated so much! Suitcases, satchels, boxes, shelving, paintings framed and packed, luggage piled high in the hut. What we can't take with us or give to the soldiers we're burning.

The prospect of tomorrow's journey has made us light-headed. People laughed and joked long after lights out.

Thursday 10th October, Day 152

Colonel Campbell addressed the final parade: 'I consider you traitors to your own country and I'd have rather had Nazis in this camp, clear-cut enemies, not you refugees, neither fish nor flesh nor good red herring. To me you're sewage.' What does his opinion matter? I'm going home.

A strong wind blew as we shuffled to the train, blowing away all memory of Camp Q.

In Pullman carriages, leather seats, delicious ham sandwiches, apples and ice-cold water for lunch, we felt like ordinary citizens, nodding off to the comforting click-clack of the wheels and that bell's haunting sound.

Ottawa past midnight, at six Montreal, where the train divided, the Jewish contingent going east, we turning south-east. At one-thirty we stopped at a city called Farnham, thirty kilometres from the US border.

Friday 11th October

Major Eric Kippen's recollections (LAC, ISN 380229): 'District Officer Commanding asked me to open an internment camp. "Dangerous prisoners coming over, find a place to put them...", giving me an engineering staff and carte blanche to build it. When I took command, inmates due in two days, it was less than half-finished, only one line of wire, no watchtowers, no huts. Initially they lived in tents while I stayed in Farnham's Montcalm Hotel. I got a shock when they arrived. I was expecting real POW's. I said, "Hell, these aren't prisoners of war. Something's gone wrong with the intelligence, as usual." We've made it far too secure. I never saw a refugee trying to escape, there's no point. So I told them, "I was a prisoner of the Germans in the Great War." I think that helped.'

Camp A, Farnham, war diary (LAC, Can CRG 24 15 397): Snowing. 1330 hrs. Internees arrived, 180 from Camp Q, 139 from Camp L, and 200 from Camp B.

Saturday 12th October, Day 154

Josef: Five months. I slept well. The camp's a building site. von Lingen's re-joined us and this evening we elected him Camp Father.

Major Kippen proved to be the most open and honest officer we came across. He seems almost gentlemanly, so he'll get on with Prince Freddie, as people now call him, though not to his face! He adds glamour to our lives we – excepting the Communists and a few arrogant academics – think he gives us an advantage in battling with most Canadian bureaucrats. They lack common sense or any sense of humour but they are definitely snobs, so the British queen being Freddie's godmother helps.

Thursday 17th October, Day 159

Washroom, showers and latrines are installed, the rest's 'in progress.' No beds, tables or ovens, so we sleep on the floor and eat cold food standing up; but, without Campbell or Mackintosh, we're happy.

When there was grumbling about the conditions Kippen addressed us: 'I understand your protests but I intend to transform these tents and buildings into an outstanding camp with well-heated huts and want your help. I'll provide the materials and you'll be paid, 20 cents a day.' That won them all over.

Monday 21st October, Day 163

It snowed heavily overnight and we froze completely during a long roll-call. Ovens arrived in the kitchens. Hot meals at last.

Tuesday 22nd October, Day 164

They issued gum boots – the guards say there'll be eight to ten feet of snow. Watchtowers now up.

Wednesday 23rd October

The Security Executive, SE85/2. Meeting at Kinnaird House, Pall Mall: Minutes – i.a. Chairman said much information about internees reached the Security Service from Camp Commandants, their Intelligence Officers, MI5 agents in the camps, and censorship of internees' letters.

Josef: In the kitchens I muttered to Len Hutchinson, a 'tame' guard, about having so little pork. 'Surprised at you, Josef', he said, 'not noticing that the number of live pigs never tallies. It's the Quartermaster. He sells one in three downtown, behind Kippen's back, one of several rackets he's pulling. He'll retire a rich man when this war ends.'

Thursday 24th October, Day 166

At last, something to sleep on, two-decker beds have arrived.

And something to think about: this evening Captain Barrass, the Camp intelligence officer, came into the cookhouse and joined the end of the queue. I was serving and he started bantering with me about the food then, looking straight at me, said quietly, 'Tell me, what do you see when you enter the canteen block?'

'A short corridor, sir.'

'What else?'

'Well, a broom cupboard in the corner...'

Barrass cut across me, 'Tomorrow at 10.25 that cupboard will be unlocked. Don't be wearing whites', glancing at my cooks' uniform, 'and make sure you're clean when you get to the canteen.' Without waiting for any sign of assent from me – this was an order, not idle chatter – he continued, 'Go through the door, close it behind you.' All the while I'd been serving food onto the tray he'd been sliding along the counter. Then he went to a table and sat down amongst some internees to eat his supper, joining in their conversation. They're not surprised; everyone knows he's the IO.

Saturday 26th October, Day 168

I finished duty early and changed. At 10.20 I approached the canteen block as two internees came out, talking excitedly about chocolate. I paused, leant casually against the wall, rummaging in my pocket for a cigarette I had no intention of smoking. I was 'clean', as Barrass termed it, and the moment they were gone I was in the corridor, a couple of strides and my hand was on the handle of the cupboard door. Thankfully it turned and I was through, shutting the door behind me, stumbling against a mop in the darkness. A gap appeared beside me and there was Captain Barrass, finger to lips, gesturing me through.

It was a small office, windowless, lit by a single bulb. In the corner Sergeant Jenkins, Barrass's clerk, sat working. A slight click made me turn. Barrass was standing against a large map-board he'd swung back over where the opening had been.

'Sit down Herr Bramminger', Barrass gestured to me, pulling up another chair. 'I apologise for the theatricals', indicating the now hidden cupboard, 'but there's no need to draw attention to such meetings.'

'I know something of your past, so take what I have to say seriously and', giving me a searching look, 'discreetly. Need I say, our discussion is covered by the Official Secrets Act.'

I relaxed, 'Yes sir, I understand.'

Barrass laughed. 'The Act doesn't often bring a smile to someone's face!'

'Well sir, when you've spent five months in the wilderness, it's a relief to find someone knows you're there.'

'No need for sirs in here. But to business. It's come to our attention that the other side and, in this case', he smiled, 'I mean the Gestapo rather than the Home Office, has been enquiring about you.' He had my complete attention.

'Information has reached us that they know you as a Wehrmacht deserter, a traitor to their glorious Reich, no less. They mention two documents you passed to the Czechoslovaks. Does that make sense?'

'I escaped with an order of battle and a technical manual for Czech military intelligence, yes. But how would they know that?'

I was asking myself the question more than him. He continued, 'Well, when the "The Czech Eleven" got out of Prague....' I nodded, 'they brought little with them and couldn't destroy what was left behind, including those two documents. It's taken the Germans two years to identify you, but', he glanced down at a document, 'six weeks ago, as far as we know, they discovered you were in Canada.'

'That's all I know. They certainly don't wish you well, but two things work in our favour. Firstly, their ability to reach into these camps is severely limited, and we soon intend to destroy it entirely. Secondly, they don't yet know which camp you're in...', glancing again at the file he grinned, 'like the Home Office and War Office it seems!'

I sat there, taking this in. Barrass continued, 'Take your time, there's much to digest. As to getting back, and to the Czech army, arrangements are under way, although it's taking time for the Canadians to arrange transport. Recognising that internment has been a mistake was hard enough for the civil servants, reversing it harder. The paperwork, finding space on trans-Atlantic shipping, is a nightmare, and you mustn't stand out as a special case. For your own safety, as much as anything, it suits us that you remain in the background. Not a word about this to anyone, not a smile, not a hint, do you understand?'

'Meanwhile there's a job to be done within this camp, identifying threats, that sort of thing. We believe a handful of active Nazis came into this camp from Camp Q...'

I cut in, 'There are twenty here...'

'Then help me identify them. Give up your cooking duties and join the Postal Section. On Monday I'll call you to my front office and express that as an order. Meanwhile I recommend you take care.'

A gesture from Barrass and Sergeant Jenkins was up from his desk. Barrass swung the map-board aside, the sergeant peered through a spyhole and nodded to Barrass, who gestured me through. 'When I tap twice it'll be safe to step out of the cupboard.'

Later I lay on my bed shutting out the banter of the hut to make sense of all he'd said. I'm going home but, meanwhile, there's a job to do. At last, a chance to fight back.

Monday 28th October, Day 170

I was ordered to report to the Camp's Postal Section - alongside Barrass's secret office - with three others, all Austrians. Barrass appeared through the door and told us we were to help process the mail, four hours daily. I started to object, I was already on cooks' duties, that sort of thing. He shut me up, brusquely. 'You're no longer a cook. Everyone has to do their bit, Bramminger. I don't want to be here any more than you.' He turned on his heel and left. Sergeant Jenkins took over. 'It's easy enough work, you can all write up a list. Who knows how to type?' Two hands went up. 'Good. Report here tomorrow at two. You'll be told what to do.'

Thursday 31st October, Day 173

Camp A war diary: Plowing started. Practice fire alarm. Winter fast approaching.

Josef: All over camp Canadian workmen are digging drains, installing heaters and erecting partition walls. They certainly know how to handle wood, all their work's done with axes, there's scarcely a saw in sight.

A long-delayed triumph. They've distributed writing paper describing us as 'CIVILIAN INTERNEES.' To be honest we'd forgotten what the issue was about. Still, it raised a cheer!

Our job in the Postal Section is about intelligence, not post. Everybody thinks we're doing translation and censorship, but in reality we're helping Sergeant Jenkins' work, which is cleverly done. Into a card index goes all that he and Barrass extract from reading the mail, plus what their camp informants tell them. When we arrived at Farnham the authorities allocated us to tents, ignoring all our friendships and groupings, a 'typical army muck-up' we thought. In reality they did it quite deliberately, to monitor our applications to move between tents, enabling Barrass to spot clusters of dangerous internees. They've all gone into his card index.

We're preparing lists, Nazis, Communists, monarchists, all sorts. Mostly they're easy to identify. Jenkins briefed us about the Nazis. 'The Gestapo have tried to establish themselves in the camps. We've detected incoming messages in cigarette tins sent by the German Red Cross, in books, nutshells, sausages, cigars, all sorts, and outgoing messages using orange juice, urine, curry powder... you name it, they've tried it. Once we identify the traffic, we pick out the plums.'

Then there are the Communists, like Hans Kahle, a famous general in the Spanish Civil War. He runs a cell that openly parades its beliefs in this camp. His members' names have been typed up and despatched to London, another list amongst many.

I think stamp collecting must be in my blood, I just love the incoming letters for the stamps on them. Most are British but some are German, although no Österreich Flugposts, no Schillings, just Deutschmark denominations, anschluß saw to that. But there's the occasional hint of home, like in today's stack of envelopes. I said to Felix, working beside me, 'At last, a Vienna postmark, and that red censor mark, "*Geprüft W* – Checked Vienna."' As we reminisced about the city, I noticed Sergeant Jenkins writing in his notebook.

Friday 1st November, Day 174

Our diet's only variety, salmon or halibut! Played volleyball.

Most of the guards are old soldiers, out to grass. They fall asleep in their watchtowers and if we see the sergeant coming, we throw stones at the towers to wake them up. It makes for useful allies.

Wednesday 6th November

War diary: A representative of the British Home Office will visit the camp soon to ascertain which internees should be released.

Monday 11th November, Armistice Day, Day 184

Josef: It poured all day, the camp's a mud bath.

At eleven a siren rang – the one they'd use if anyone escaped – and we all stood in silence for two minutes.

War diary: During night another great storm, strong winds, rain in torrents. At 2130 hrs all electricity failed, including floodlights, camp in total darkness. All cars and trucks were commandeered and placed around the wire with headlights shining inwards, lighting up approaches to the wire. Every flashlight was brought into play and the situation was kept under control. In the morning the camp looked a wreck, ankle deep in mud.

Tuesday 12th November, Day 185

Josef: Six months ago today I was interned.

Sunday 17th November, Day 190

Most of our Sergeant-Majors have hated us, shouted at us louder than we'd ever heard, showing no interest in us as human beings. But in Farnham we have one who looks and acts fierce but underneath his heart is good. On our very first parade he said, 'Every officer is to be addressed as "Sir", including myself.' Our nickname for him? 'Myself.'

If he finds us loafing around he chases us out of the huts and put us to work, but he calls himself a Christian and lends a sympathetic ear when one of us is really down. Certainly we've never heard him use a swear word. We respect him.

Monday 18th November, Day 191

They've handed out gloves, blue winter trousers and jackets with that appalling red circle, all warmly lined. None too soon. it's really cold.

Another Josef – one of many – Josef Mandel, a merchant seaman from Hamburg, carved a chess set from a block of pine wood, the one thing there's plenty of here. He agreed to teach me to whittle but I'm better at carving meat than wood, so I'm paying him to carve me a wooden chain with a ball and cage, *ein Kugelkäfig*. His price is high, five cigarettes. I love seeing it emerge from that wooden block. Darling, it will be my present to you.

Wednesday 20th November, Day 193

War diary: Much mail and parcels arrived for internees. 18 prisoners believed to be Nazi sent to Camp M.

Josef: A letter from Mary, written nine weeks ago in September. Sends her love, and the cat Binkie's. Binkie's is cupboard love, I suspect.

Tuesday 26th November, Day 199

Canadian winter's well and truly here. It snowed heavily overnight and everything's white. Even the barbed wire looks beautiful... I am astonished to have written that!

It's official, tomorrow the Home Office representative will be here.

Wednesday 27th November, Day 200

War diary: All roll calls will be indoors as weather is too severe.

Josef: thirty-five degrees of frost, eight feet of snow and the sun's shining. Into the camp burst Mr Paterson.

In this bitter cold I watched him arrive, an elderly man, two soldiers struggling in his wake carrying his suitcases, striding vigorously across the parade ground, it reminded me of Bill Williams walking briskly to meet us in Copenhagen. All of us, internees, guards and officers, were wrapped in heavy overcoats, gloves and scarves, he wore just a tweed suit.

A notice appeared: 'Within a few weeks a transport of 200 "C" category people will sail to England, but only people who freely volunteer. They will go into an English camp from where, hopefully, they will be released to go home. Further transports will leave when shipping becomes available. Internees to whom the above conditions apply report to Mr Paterson immediately.'

Instant uproar! Hundreds rushed for interviews; the queue would be long. I feared to look when the camp office issued numbers, but there I was, 'No 2'! We ten, whose return was already announced, headed the queue, I was second behind Karl Bathke. Behind me were von Maltzahn, Eberhard and Kurt Schwabacher... butcher, baron, judge and priest, like some parlour game. Eberhard and I know MI5's hidden hand is at work for us, we can only guess about the other eight.

Soon I was across a table from this extraordinary man, a civil servant looking like a benevolent uncle.

He looked up from some paperwork and smiled. 'Mr Bramminger?'

'Yes, sir.'

'Normally I start by saying, "Your life is more important than my time so please sit down and tell me all about it", but in your case I say two things. Firstly, your friend Mr Svitanics – I know him from the Czechoslovak Trust, where I'm now a trustee – asked me to pass on his greetings. Secondly, before I left Britain, I was handed a list by certain people in Whitehall, whose department I cannot reveal, but can say that Colonel Kalla at the Czech Embassy supports their decision.'

I felt like a drowning man seeing a hand reaching down to him. But he surprised me further. 'What I now tell you is for you alone. Ten of you will be the very first returned to the United Kingdom for immediate release. I do not have to justify to anyone whom I choose nor my reasons for doing so. But...' – he stared me in the eyes – 'actually your release is justified by your anti-Nazi work in Vienna. The public reason, however, is that the Czechoslovak army demands your return. You will, indeed, immediately re-join the Czech army, where our friends in England intend to use your abilities in quite specific ways.'

'Only for your ears, I say. Not to be repeated to even your closest friends, or even hinted at in letters to your fiancée, who already knows that you're to be released. I cannot tell you when since I do not control the bureaucracy or the shipping', he paused, 'although I have hopes you may be on your way before the Christmas celebrations.'

'Thank you, sir, thank you...'

'And wipe that grin off your face before you leave the room.' Paterson stood up, smiled, shook my hand and nodded towards the door.

'Goodbye, Mr Bramminger. Remember, not a word!'

Paterson interviewed over 200 internees, working from nine in the morning to eight at night, treating us all like gentlemen. He's had an extraordinary effect on us, like a heavy shackle removed. This evening snowball fights broke out across the camp.

Home Office, I/GEN 2/12/4. Report to Home Secretary by Alexander Paterson:

Civilian internees sent to Canada. There is a wealth of wire, three banks thick, with machine-guns, passwords and fixed bayonets to discourage the bespectacled professor and the perky school boy...

The Canadian officer tends to be a man of rigid and unimaginative mind, not well-suited to taking care of sensitive and temperamental human beings...

Hotel porters across the world blithely slap labels on tin trunks, but it requires persistence to scrape them off. The Canadian government received these men as dangerous enemy aliens and treats them with greater security and precaution than IRA convicts at Dartmoor. It has not been easy to deface the label...

Their uniform consists of a blue jacket on whose back is emblazoned a huge red circle, and a pair of bright blue trousers seamed by a broad red band, the whole effect derogatory and ridiculous. In most camps this uniform is compulsory, in others mufti is allowed. On this policy, as on others, no one at HQ knows what is happening because no one comes to see...

The return to England. 'My case is rather different from the rest, sir. I don't want to waste your time, but if I could explain...' How many times has the interview started thus. Of course, every man's case is different, and he has spent so many distracted hours worrying that it is idle to hurry him...

The interviews take place in a cell, sitting on wooden forms with a plank table between us. The camp leaders issued tickets numbering beyond 200 so there is a hum of talk, but no disorder or confusion. The leaders know their men and organise with skill. The only shouting is done by the guards in khaki...

Assessing each man's claim to be on a sailing list. Sitting in a cell in a Canadian camp, facing decent fellows on the verge of breakdown, I may have interpreted some of the categories more liberally than a committee in England, but I feared a genuine breakdown if they stayed much longer under the rigid and unimaginative regime in Canada...

Many so far lost their emotional control that I kept them after the interview smoking a cigarette with me to recover their composure and not have to face their comrades in the queue outside with tears on their cheeks...

A Paterson, Director of Prisons.

Josef: Eberhard said. 'Herr Paterson told me, the better brains here are inside the wire." He doesn't think much of Ottawa's military.'

Friday 29th November

Directorate of Internment Operations. (LAC, AA & QMG, MS 2-36-4): Authority to transfer first internees, Camp A to Halifax.

BATHKE, Karl	German
BRAMMINGER, Josef	Stateless
GOLDSCHMIDT, Hans	German
JAMES, Friedrich	British
LIEBETEGGER, Arnulf	Austrian
LOEHNEFINKE, G	German
LUETKENS, Wolfgang	German
MALTZAHN, Norman, Baron von	German
ROELLIG, Dr Eberhard, Judge	Stateless
SCHWABACHER, Kurt, The Revd	German

Sunday 1st December, Day 204

Josef: Very cold, even the guards have frozen feet.

Yesterday a letter from Mary, written on 1st October. Today I wrote, I hope, my last letter to her from Canada. 'For the first time in six months, good news. A high Home Office official came here to sort out C cases to be returned to England. I should soon be back.'

Friday 6th December, Day 209

A change in the weather, the snow's thawing.

Tuesday 10th December, Day 213

HQ Department for Defence. HQS.7236: **SECRET**. Transport Order. To

District Officer Commanding, Montreal. I am directed to inform you that arrangements have been completed with Canadian Pacific for movement of internees and guards. The party from Farnham should entrain on December 17th, arriving Halifax by the 'Ocean Limited' evening December 18th. SPECIAL NOTES - Railway company to supply box meals; News Agents not to travel on this train; toilet doors to be removed from internee cars.

Josef: The Commandant in Monteith and Mr Paterson have both told me I'm being released, but when you've been locked up for so many months you doubt everything. But now they've paid us our 'wages' - I received £3 10s - so the cobbler's repairing my shoes and suitcase. I've even bought a second one.

Thursday 12th December, Day 215

Seven months.

Our (rumoured) departure date is repeatedly delayed.

Several letters have arrived, all addressed to Camp Q. Two from Mary, one to Eberhard from Agnes, three to Helm Bechinger from his beloved Leila, our three fiancées. All written before 3rd November. Mary's had me both smiling and crying. She knows I will be released, I smiled; on 1st November she endured a bomb attack on Devonshire House, I cried. The only treatment she needed was a cup of tea, she says. But still I'm crying, even as I write this.

I could not bear to think more about it, so I asked Helm to tell me about his letters. I'm sure he's bursting to, the story of his love for Leila having been a recurrent theme since Huyton. He read from the first: 'She knows I'm to be released so she's not sending the things I'd asked for, "they might meet you mid-ocean!" she says. Then... "I love you very much Helm, I wish I could put a little piece of my love in this letter and send it to you." But there's a PS, "I have one of my usual colds. Be glad that you're not here with me otherwise you might catch it from me."'

'In the second she says, "Well, maybe I shall get news this week! It is three weeks since I heard from you."'

He read on, nodding to himself, then read again, '"We will get together again. I am sure. It is that thought that makes me bear everything, otherwise I would have nothing to live for." And she hopes I haven't forgotten how to lay eggs!'

Seeing my puzzlement, he grinned, 'I'll explain later', then shuffled the pages to read on from the third letter. 'Her thirty-second to Canada... "My Darling"', he looked embarrassed, 'well you know... "No-one's had letters from Canada for four weeks... it is awfully cruel, my nerves are in a state of constant excitement and tension which won't relax until you are back... Above all I worry about your crossing! I am terribly depressed at times and at others I feel everything will be alright in the end and love will be stronger." Yes, yes, yes.'

His eyes positively shone. I know how he feels, he's a man in love!

Friday 13th December, Day 216

Newspapers full of a huge victory over the Italians in the desert, 40,000 prisoners taken.

Sunday 15th December

War diary: Entrain 100 internees tomorrow for transfer to England: 3 for release on arrival, 44 for review, 53 for enlistment in AMPC.

Monday 16th December, Day 219

Josef: The Commandant wished us all good luck. With the Atlantic to be crossed we need it.

Suddenly the camp's in a frenzy. Innumerable feasts, farewell speeches, dazzling jokes, witty cracks. It's an important night, amongst those leaving are our prince and Hans Kahle, most of the scientists including Max Perutz, Ernst Kellermann, Klaus Fuchs and Tommy Gold, then there's Eberhard and me. Some sang camp songs late into the night, others sit on their beds, dazed, perhaps they're thinking about U-boats. The canteen was crowded with people stocking up on food or presents for those back in Britain.

Tuesday 17th December

Seven o'clock, roll call. The Sergeant-Major marched on and announced, 'All those going to England be in the boiler house with luggage at 0815 hrs. ONLY them. The rest of you, STAY OUT!'

It's the Army... keep you waiting for five months then give you an hour's notice. Frantic excitement, we're all shaving, getting dressed in our own civilian clothes, clothes we haven't seen for months. Last minute packing, giving away what we can't fit in. Hans and Clement rush up with addresses, Hans' wife, Clement's parents. Last handshakes, best wishes.

Amidst laughter and more farewells, we drifted, laden down, towards the boiler house. Where did all this luggage come from? 40 lbs was the limit in Huyton, not that we took any notice, now we have over 100 lbs.

It's odd. Two days ago, when the list went up, 110 men were to be released, Eberhard and I among them. Then a delay of twenty-four hours, everyone on tenterhooks. Today they called out 100 names, our ten names weren't called. My heart fell, at this last moment my release had failed. Why? What was this about? Someone said, 'What of those whose names you didn't call?'

The Sergeant-Major went up to him, threatening, shouting, but Captain Barrass ordered him to stop. He whispered fiercely at the clerk, 'The first list, man, the ten on the first list!'

The clerk, flustered, looked down, leafed through some pages, then began reading again. I heard my name. Relief flooded over me.

We lined up. Major Kippen compared each of us to the camp's photos, we must match his collection. Then they searched the luggage, for once, the first time, taking only what belonged to them, their prison uniform, and even then they missed some. By eleven it was over and we were marched off towards a train.

The rest waved goodbye as we filed out. They began a song about the Sergeant-Major which made Major Kippen and his officers smile, but 'Myself' looked furious. Then Kippen slapped him on the back and he smiled as well. Good-bye, 'Sir!'

Even the guards were smiling.

Our suitcases disappeared into the luggage van and as we stood waiting to board the train there were shouts of '*Auf Wiedersehen*.' At noon, as the train departed, they began waving and singing our song, '*You'll get used to it, the first year is the worst year, then you get used to it, you can scream and you can shout, but they'll never let you out…*' at which they broke down in laughter; us too, it was infectious. I can still hear it, now, as I write this.

Other departures came into my head. By night from Nordbahnhof; from Prague; from Victoria Station for Birchington, and Kempton Park for Huyton. The Gestapo, Prague's police and the Grenadier Guards hadn't waved farewell; Mary did, at Victoria, the last time I saw her.

War diary: 110 internees were marched out of the compound today to the station and entrained. Count F Lingen in charge of them.

Josef: It is Day 220! The train pulled out. A soldier came round with food, enough for three days.

'How long's the journey?' we asked. 'One night', a guard replied, one of two unarmed ones in the carriage. Another sits unmoving at the end with his rifle; they still don't trust us. It was warm, the seats comfortable, the scenery as beautiful as ever. We dozed off.

An hour later the train clattered across a junction and came to a halt in a siding, a huge engine shed in the background. Sudden excitement, 'That's no railway shed, that's barbed wire, it's a camp.' A guard said it was Camp N, Sherbrooke. A stream of men walked onto the platform, dressed like us, well, like us this morning, in those blue uniforms with their damnable circles.

There were shouts of recognition, 'Look, there's Jan Schmidt, there's Huyber, still has his accordion. How did that escape those sticky-fingered hands at Quebec?' For some reason the men clustered along the barbed wire were in fits of laughter. Thank God for that, otherwise what might their thoughts have been, watching us ride off to freedom?

For a night and a morning we travelled through endless forest, no tracks or roads, a few hamlets, wooden buildings, cut off from civilisation. Eventually we stopped at a town called Truro where civilian travellers stood on the platform and schoolgirls distributed apples to us. It's been seven months since people, ordinary people, have been nice to us, it's difficult to explain how good that feels. We're used to being hated and exploited, Kempton Park, Freeston on the Ettrick, those thieves in Quebec and Campbell in Monteith. There have been some decent ones, true, but no warmth, even Kippen was more straightforward than friendly. But here a whole community treated us just like anybody else, smiling, being polite to us... and they <u>must</u> have known we're internees, some of us are still wearing those awful uniforms. Thank God for small mercies.

Mr Paterson's the real exception, I suppose, he gave us back a sense of decency. Barrass says Paterson's an active Christian, despite being a chain-smoking whisky-drinker who has a pink gin for breakfast. We all agree, he's quite a man.

After Truro the snow was gone and we ran through green hills and forests until, about four, we pulled into Halifax. We waited; imagine, like dogs straining to be let loose. Out in the harbour warships and merchantman were visible, looking like a convoy assembling, something we didn't want to miss!

An hour passed. Mr Paterson appeared on the platform; he must have come ahead of us. The call went out for Prince Freddie. He reappeared to tell us we'll be sailing on a Belgian ship that's short of crew. They needed thirty-eight volunteers, cooks, stewards and engineers. We'd be paid. I've only got the little money I've earned in Monteith and Farnham, my money taken at Kempton Park has disappeared, so I stuck my hand up once again to cook, it'll take my mind off seasickness and U-boats. This evening we chosen few were taken off the train and down to the harbour.

'SS Thysville' it said on the bow. Then up a short gangway to be taken to our cabins. The contrast with the Ettrick was, literally, black and white. The Ettrick had been gleaming white, the Thysville is black and dirty. Then I was prodded at bayonet-point into a stinking hold by a foul-mouthed soldier, this time I was shown into a guest cabin with proper beds and a porthole by a deferential Indian steward.

Wednesday 18th December, Day 221

In the morning Mr Paterson assembled us and said, 'Listen, boys, here's the truth of it. You're lucky to be sailing at all. It's only because, back in October, the Admiralty gave Captain Powell command of this ship in the Congo, over the head of its protesting Belgian captain.' He laughed. 'If, in the middle of the night, you listen carefully you'll still hear him protesting, "having drink taken", as they say in the army. He's been confined to his cabin. But don't lose any sleep over him, he has a well-stocked bar in there with him, plus his French mistress.'

He continued, 'The Congolese crew refused to light the boilers because they didn't want to cross the Atlantic, so the Portuguese police threw them in jail. Captain Powell sailed her from Africa to Halifax with a crew of Lascars. Now the Lascars have also taken a dislike to U-boats and refused to sail, so the Canadian police have thrown <u>them</u> in jail. The Belgian doctor, the head cook and some from the engine room are still around, and he's raised a Dutchman as second mate, but he's under orders to take war material to England and hasn't enough crew to get her there.'

'Most of you haven't even sailed a dinghy, but I've persuaded Captain Powell that if it's the only way to get back to England with this convoy, you'll turn your considerable talents to running the ship's engines, stoking boilers, cooking, stewarding and all the rest. I'll hope you'll back me up.'

'We'll find a way, sir', someone said, to a general murmur of assent.

Paterson relaxed. 'I'll tell you as much as I can, as soon as I can, but it'll be hard work, this ship's in an appalling condition. When a convoy assembles - which date remains secret, even from me - you'll sail to England. In a moment I'll ask Captain Powell to say some words, but are there any questions?'

We were stunned. In the short time we'd known him Mr Paterson had earned our trust by his hard work and sheer humanity. For six months we'd been told nothing, this openness was entirely new.

Someone asked if the British government would apologise. Mr Paterson replied ruefully, 'Governments never admit mistakes but, as a sign of friendship, they've provided 200 books and fifty games of chess for the ship. It's not much, but it's more than you could expect from those narrow-minded officials in Ottawa. Their vocabulary is about 200 words and they've got less than five ideas in their heads.' We all laughed.

Then he really surprised us. 'I trust every one of you. You'll have the run of the ship and not be subject to any supervision on board. At my suggestion you'll sail without guards', he said. 'Your escort will be Captain Barrass.'

Captain Powell stepped forward. Red-headed, with blue eyes and a ruddy complexion, he's a striking figure. 'You should know that I don't look on you as refugees or internees, I regard you as human beings and passengers. On board my ship every man on board can expect the same, and that includes Christmas Dinner, when you'll have chicken, Christmas pudding, wine, beer, coffee and all the trimmings, just like every officer, passenger and member of my crew.' He was cheered to the echo.

'I've cobbled together a crew of sixteen nationalities, and I will sail for England, but I need cooks, stokers, look-out men and a quarter-master', he said, 'how about it?'

Moments later we were hard at work preparing his ship for sailing. Later one of Prince Freddie's 'court' (so we jokingly call it; he's blissfully unaware it exists), approached us. Tomorrow's his birthday and, it was hinted, a cake would be welcome. So, overnight, some of our Viennese Konditorei – the pastry chefs in the galley come from the Hotel Sacher – turned out an exquisite Esterhazy Torte.

All day we've discussed what Paterson said. After seven months of guards at every turn no guards... it's difficult to believe.

Thursday 19th December, Day 222

We worked hard, but today we laid down our paint brushes, spanners and ladles to see the 'Royal Torte' escorted ashore with a reverence usually reserved for the Blessed Sacrament. So much for our Socialist pretensions!

Friday 20th December, Day 223

We worked until midnight but were up at five, cleaning the ship, getting ready to sail. She has a permanent list, so it's hard to negotiate the corridors and well-nigh impossible to use saucepans on the stoves in the galley.

Mr Paterson handed us each £5 cash for the trip.

Saturday 21st December, Day 224

Because of broken water pipes the ship's very cold and most cabins have no heating but, for the first time since Birchington, I've had a hot bath, brimming full, a real bath in a real bathroom. I'd forgotten how glorious that is!

An auxiliary cruiser tied up alongside. Around us a convoy's assembling, but nobody knows when it leaves. The Thysville can only do twelve knots so it should take fifteen days. We may land by 9 January.

Sunday 22nd December, Day 225

We've almost finished the ship. I share a good cabin with Helm and a fellow called Alfred. We sleep between white linen sheets on beds with mattresses. True luxury.

The food's good, although not much of it. Daily we prepare breakfast of coffee, grapefruit, porridge, egg and bacon, bread and jam.

I told Helm we were short in the galley, so what was this about him being able to lay eggs. 'Oh, that. One time when I first met Leila I gave her my famous imitation of a chicken laying an egg. I think that's what made her fall in love with me!'

There's a first-class smoking room with tables, comfy chairs and two pianos, where they've put Mr Paterson's gift of books and games such as chess, mah-jong and Dame.

They say we'll be home between 8-11 January, but no signs of departure.

Monday 23rd December, Day 226

Finally, the rest re-joined us. When Prince Freddie came on board by chance I was on deck and bumped into him. We simultaneously glanced up at the mast, then at each other, and burst out laughing.

Captain Powell gave us a welcoming address: we must conform to the ship's discipline, he wouldn't hesitate to enforce it if necessary. There are also two arrogant Belgian ship's officers, two friendly English naval officers and two mystery Englishmen. We all dine together, in shifts, in the dining room. Barrass and the two unidentified civilians sleep in the same cabin.

It's so cold that we've been issued an extra blanket, plus a towel and a second bar of soap (but it doesn't work in the salt water).

From all 2,000 internees in Canada I and Eberhard are two of the first selected for return, on that 'Priority List' of ten, all now aboard the Thysville. I can't understand this: why are so many of them Communists? Why did MI5 and the

Home Office select them? They believe they pose a threat, or Barrass wouldn't have had us typing their names onto the lists for Whitehall, and they know who these fellows are, the likes of Hans Kahle and his cell in Camp A, including that man Klaus Fuchs. He was a cell member and openly gave lectures on Communism. Everybody knew they were Communists. Yet here we are, rubbing shoulders with them on the Thysville. Surely they're not all double-agents.

Tuesday 24th December, Christmas Eve, Day 227

It's so cold. The only warm places are the engine room and the galley (one benefit of being a cook). We all seem infected with the same craving, to go on deck, to go anywhere on the ship, just because we can. I saw Felix standing in a doorway, his hands running over the frame. Minutes later and he was still there, staring at it. 'Look', he said – he'd noticed me watching him – 'Isn't it wonderful, no barbed wire.'

Captain told us to strictly maintain black-out. We have the greatest self-interest in doing so.

I helped prepare Christmas dinner. Captain Powell insisted all internees should sit down together, so a Belgian steward served us. Captain Powell, Barrass, one of the naval officers, and the two Englishmen joined us. We started at seven with salad and egg, then soup with bread and butter. There was fish and mashed potatoes, chicken, apples, Christmas pudding and coffee. It was nine before we finished. What a meal! We used two spoons, three knives and five forks, and, for once, didn't have to wash up!

Next a concert, Canadian radio, the BBC, and 'Joyeux Noel' on a record. The Belgian steward toasted us happy Christmas in the name of his country, to which Captain Barrass replied. It was quite a party.

We hope to sail tomorrow.

Wednesday 25th December, Christmas Day, Day 228

Our 165th day in lovely Canada, but a country we're glad to leave. We're taking on fresh water. Destroyers moved around the harbour.

Thursday 26th December, Boxing Day-Stefanitag, Day 229

Commodore P E Parker commanding, on board MV Penrith Castle: Convoy HX99 Diary. 10:30. Convoy conference held, then embarked with my Naval staff. Weather clear. Convoy, 13 ships, formed up before dark.

Josef: Chilled to the bone. This morning a battleship entered the harbour. Is it ours? But it stayed when we sailed at three. Within two hours, in glorious weather and calm seas, we were off the coast and the convoy was shaking out. There's been lifeboat drill, another contrast with the Ettrick that gives us confidence. Escort aircraft are overhead.

Mary, fifteen days at most and I'll be in your arms.

Friday 27th December, Day 230

There are thirteen ships in the convoy. Aboard are the two naval officers, six civilian passengers, four officers, twenty Marines, Captain Barrass and the two government officials, although no one knows who they are. We're advised to sleep with our clothes to hand.

Every moment we fear U-boats. On deck I picture a torpedo in every wave, on my bunk I expect to hear a torpedo 'knocking at the door' – a sailors' joke. Some take their minds off things by playing high stakes poker, for cigarettes. I'm glad to work in the galley, where I haven't time to worry or be seasick.

One of the naval officers said, 'Don't complain about storms. U-boat commanders hate them, they can't attack in heavy seas.'

Saturday 28th December, Day 231

Mary, now, I think, nothing can keep us apart, not storms nor torpedoes. Darling, I believe we love one another more than we ever have, if that's possible. In a fortnight we'll be in each others arms again, and I can pour out to you my thoughts that I've bottled up for so long, and you can tell me all your hopes and fears.

Sunday 29th December, Day 232

Captain Barrass collared me on deck, when no one was about. 'Report to my cabin in thirty minutes. Keep this to yourself.'

The cabin door was briskly opened by Barrass, 'Come in.' I was surprised to see a second man standing there, off to one side, out of sight of the door, one of those two mystery men. 'Mr Bramminger, good morning. I want you to have a chat with Mr Temple. I'll leave you to it.'

'You'll not be disturbed.'

Temple went across and locked the door. 'Now, we've not met, but', gesturing at a file on a table, 'I feel I know you well. Let me explain. Colonel Kalla has a job of work for you when you get back in the Czech brigade in Warwickshire...'

'Thank you sir', I blurted out, but he continued, 'No need for sir, plain Mr Temple will do, and you may not thank me when you've heard me out.' There was an edge to his voice. 'Sir' might not be required, but he clearly wanted no interruptions. 'As I say, you will enlist in the Czech brigade, where you'll be employed in its anti-tank battery as a cook.' His hand went up to halt the objection he clearly expected. 'Let me continue. We've had a problem in that brigade. In July there was a Communist-inspired mutiny, 500 men had to be removed. We believe we've eliminated the problem but we need a man in there to observe and report back to us. And when I say us I mean my department, although for the sake of inter-allied harmony you will, on paper, be under Kalla's command. I know you've been working as a cook in the camps and you volunteered for it on the ship.'

I cut in, 'But I need to soldier, can't you see? I need to fight the Nazis.'

'That's as may be, but just now the task we have for you could have no better cover than a cook. No one, absolutely no one notices a cook. Soldiers, officers especially, don't register them in the military landscape. No one keeps track of them or notices them, except the cook sergeant, maybe the quartermaster, but to the rest they scarcely exist. Cooks' whites are more invisible than any camouflage. They come and go as they please, and crucially, for our purposes, they get to hear what's being said in the cookhouse and the messes.'

'So, Josef, within two days of landing report to the Czech military office in Piccadilly to enlist. Kalla will give you a full briefing. And three others things. What I have said is not a matter for discussion, it's by way of an order, do you see?' Not waiting for an answer, he continued, 'Secondly, this task will last weeks or months, then I may have something more interesting for you. Stick with it.'

I was slightly numbed by Temple's words but managed to ask, 'And the third thing?'... biting back a 'Sir.'

'Oh, yes. Do you speak Czech?'

'A fair bit. Anyone who grows up in Favoriten does, half the population comes from Czechoslovakia.'

'Well, once again, keep that under your hat. As far as the world's concerned you speak none. "*Ano a Ne*, Yes and No", perhaps, but no more. Remember that.'

He added, 'When you disembark you'll receive a railway ticket, so have no fear, there'll be a chance to meet your fiancée.'

The interview was clearly at an end. 'Please ask Judge Röllig to call on me here, in half an hour', but as I turned to the door, he added, 'By the way, Mr Paterson tells me that you are an excellent cook.'

Later Eberhard caught up with me. 'Herr Temple informed me we'll serve together in the Czech army once again, you as cook and I as clerk. Interesting times ahead, eh? But one thing strikes me. Barrass's title may be "Intelligence Officer", but we shouldn't be deceived. He's not IN intelligence. He may believe he's inside the secret world but he's only an Army officer on its outer fringes. Unlike our Mr Temple, if that's his name, he's the real thing. MI5's my guess.'

Convoy Diary: Bermuda section 4 hours late at R/V. Alaunia went to look for them. Halifax section reduced speed turning Northward after R/V. 16:00. Alaunia re-joined without Bermuda ships. U-boat reported. Rained torrentially during first watch; convoy ran into fog.

Josef: Calm day, not so cold, but no sun and poor visibility, thank God.

A lot of signalling between the escorts and our submarine through the sea mist, an eerie, haunting sight, although oddly comforting. The merchant cruiser sped off early on for several hours. Rumour says a German raider's out in the North Atlantic. All ships endlessly zigzag and the convoy formation changes all the time. We could be in for trouble and must provide look outs; there's no shortage of volunteers.

Mr Paterson was right. The former Belgian captain is drunk most of the time. Today he burst out of his cabin and rampaged furiously around. He's been locked in again. We hear him kicking the door in drunken rage. Mind you his mistress is in there with him! Mr Paterson said she's French, others Malayan. Whichever, she's very pretty but rarely appears and never, ever, speaks a word.

Mary, another twelve days and we shall meet, I hope and pray.

Monday 30th December, Day 233

Convoy Diary: E H Powell (Thysville's Master) having anxious and trying voyage with internee passengers and administrative difficulties, yet his ship does well at signalling and station-keeping. MV Penrith Castle, with my staff on-board has good accommodation, and its officers give me every assistance, but she cannot go at a slower speed on both engines than eight knots. Dense fog and continuous hooting. We drag a rope with a piece of wood producing foam signals to give the course to the ship following.

Josef: Over the radio we heard that on Christmas Day a German cruiser attacked a troop convoy south of us but was driven off by the Royal Navy. A sailor said it was the Admiral Hipper. We see a plume of smoke over the western horizon, a British battleship shadowing us, sailors say.

At dinner Captain Barrass told Prince Freddie a story so crazy that, in the insane world of internment, it made complete sense. The War Office sent too many men from the Isle of Man to board the SS Sobieski, bound for Canada, so, at the last moment, some were put on the SS Dunera, going to Australia, with an internee called Dr Wilde on the manifest. But at Melbourne Wilde didn't disembark. They decided he'd jumped overboard and informed London by radio. His wife had already sailed to join him in Australia, but when she landed she was told he was missing, presumed drowned. Two months later she was told that he was in Canada after all!

The mystery civil servant from the Home Office, who came to the table after Barrass started his tale, tried to shut him up, but the other one, our Mr Temple, from MI5, couldn't stop laughing. He has a sense of humour, the first one hasn't.

Tuesday 31st December, New Year's Eve/Silvester, Day 234

Convoy Diary: Fog. Bermuda ships' whistles heard at intervals. When fog lifted, only 12 in sight. A D Huff re-joined later. Heavy seas, fog lifting, heading NE.

Josef: Fifth day at sea. Fog mid-morning and the ship was shaken by the heavy seas, 'Like a terrier shakes a rat', Prince Freddie said. Ships emerge out of the fog, change direction and disappear again. Mary, I hope you're safe.

All afternoon cooking New Year's Eve dinner. It couldn't have been better nor could we have eaten more, but because of rough sea many vomited during the meal. It didn't prevent them returning to the table.

There was beer, paid for out of canteen profits. Then champagne appeared, a gift from the Cambridge boys. We had dance music then von Lingen and his Cambridge friends sang songs from Berlin. If we were in Vienna tonight we'd have congregated on Stephansplatz. Just before midnight the music would stop and we'd begin counting down, then the chimes would sound out from *Die Pummerin* bell in Old Steff's tower. As midnight passed we'd be dancing and waltzing, '*Glücklich Silvester!*'

We all stayed up. What a year, one I'd prefer to forget but never will. Eberhard and I have been interned for eight months, 234 days. My last thought was of you, darling. As I write this in my cabin, an hour and a half past midnight on New Year's Day (hurrah!) you are much in my mind.

Wednesday 1st January 1941, New Year's Day, Day 235

Convoy Diary: 09:00. Alaunia left convoy to search for missing Bermuda section ships, found five. They were on station by 13:30. Alaunia reported Karabagh and A D Huff 25 miles astern and Teneriffa 15 miles on port beam. Convoy now increased to 19 ships. U-boat has reappeared. Battleship Royal Sovereign is following us at a distance of 15 miles, we are only one group in a much larger convoy.

Josef: Happy New Year! *Glückliches neues Jahr!* Mary, in ten days I'll see you again, the longest ten days of my life. We all worry about torpedoes, but every night I worry about those bombs falling on London. Darling, are you still safe?

Thursday 2nd January, Day 236

A rough night, waves crashing against the hull. The cargo below our cabin was shifting around.

We ploughed through ferocious thirty-foot waves. All portholes are firmly shut but some cabins still flooded. A sailor says we've passed the Gulf Stream, from now on it'll be colder and stormier. In ten days we should land, although no one tells us in which port.

The Captain came round the galley on inspection. 'Where are you from, lad?' he asked. 'Vienna', I said. 'And where are you going in England?'

'Brixton, in south London', I said, 'where my fiancée lives.'

He laughed, 'I know it. I was born in Southwark, less 'an a mile north. I probably know your future mother-in-law!'

People say his salty language could start the ship's engines, but argue whether his accent's Welsh or Liverpudlian. I say he's a Londoner.

In the rough seas the naval lieutenant sits solid as a rock at the dining table while all around him people are sliding away. Eventually he revealed his secret. 'Old navy custom', he said with a grin. 'A piece of toast under a leg of my chair.' We were all impressed.

Clocks advanced one hour. They announced that from Sunday we'll all be 'on alert.'

Mary, you'll get the greatest surprise when you receive a call from me.

Friday 3rd January, Day 237

Roughest night yet, cargo rolling around beneath us, the ship moving about violently. I cannot sleep from the cold and the noise of the creaking ship, doors banging, plates smashing on the floor. They say we're passed the half-way mark. Some sailors laugh at us, 'Rough! Wait and see. It WILL get rough.'

There's breakfast, for those who can stomach it, and coffee, as many mugs as we want, three hot meals daily. Contrasted with our nightmare on the Ettrick this is a fairy tale, then we hit bad seas and feel so rotten there's no time for comparisons. At lunch the ship rolled so much that most plates fell off the tables and were smashed.

Now it's compulsory to wear lifebelts at all times and three light machine-guns have been set up. We volunteered to man them. Rolf Heudenfeld is our best marksman and was on anti-aircraft duty when sailors spotted a squadron of German fighters coming towards the ship. But before Rolf could open fire it turned into a flock of seagulls!

Now our convoy has twenty-two ships with a battleship and submarine as escorts. The smaller ships are moving even more violently than the Thysville.

Sailors estimate we'll arrive on the 12th.

I'm planning the telegram I'll send when we land.

Saturday 4th January

Convoy Diary: Convoy encountered gale from NW. 08:00. Daylight. Only 6 ships in close convoy. 11:00. 20 ships in sight. 16:00. Karabagh and A D Huff caught up and were in station in 58 54N 30 28W, latter with engine room defects. Average convoy speed from Halifax 7.97 knots, rarely more than 8, at which rate no ships appear to have difficulty keeping up.

Josef: The most horrifying night of my life left me miserable and as weak as a child. The ship lurches to port and starboard – I'm writing like a sailor! – while going up and down between the troughs and summits of the waves. The first time I really thought the ship was about to sink. Winds are stronger than ever and waves hammer unendingly against the hull, coming over the lower deck. Most of the other ships are lost to sight under huge waves.

Our Canadian escorts have gone, no sign of British warships. We're still heading north-east, the long way round, further from German submarines, sleeping in our clothes, sailors wearing tin hats.

We set up table cages to stop more crockery slipping off.

Sunday 5th January, Day 239

Convoy Diary: Route alteration received taking convoy further North. Star sights placed the ship 32 miles ahead of where she should have been to reach R/V at programme time, largely due to SW'ly gale, was difficult to waste the necessary time as this ship cannot do less than eight knots. Also, in this weather, large alterations of course are undesirable because the deck cargoes of aeroplanes might easily be damaged. 15:00. Porpoise parted company in 60 20N 25 20W in SW'ly gale.

Josef: Gale blowing, constant snow, sleet and hail, waves sweeping the decks. Eating and cooking impossible. The moaning of the storm is unnerving.

We're 60 degrees north, level with Oslo, 400 miles north-west of Scotland – so the sailors tell us – but still the convoy heads NNE. I feel so dizzy in my cabin that when not cooking I go on deck. The weather may be atrocious but up there it's beautiful, especially when the sun shines.

Captain Powell thinks the Belgian crew are unreliable, they hate the British, he says. Little does he know.

The closer we get the more I think of us. Will we be allowed to be together? When can we get married? Questions flood in and out of my head. I used to dwell on the injustice of it all, and my fear of what has happened to you, but I think I'm over 'barbed wire nerves.' I'm trusting in your love for me more than ever.

Where will we land, Belfast, Glasgow or Liverpool?

Monday 6th January, Day 240

Convoy Diary: 10:00. Found it possible to turn the convoy 100° to port for ninety minutes to waste time. Merchant cruiser and submarine left us. 14:00. Changed course again to SE. Wind moderated in afternoon.

Josef: Heavy seas, rain and low cloud, although milder now and less windy. We had a sleepless night; the sailors tell us this is the most dangerous part of our route. We've changed course to the SE for the first time. A notice went up saying any cameras must be handed in and will be returned on landing. Signs the journey's coming to an end? BBC radio reports incendiary raid on London. Mary, are you safe?

Tuesday 7th January, Day 241

Convoy Diary: Sea calm, convoy heading SE, changing position frequently, no zigzagging. 13:30 GMT. The first RN Local Escort: HMS Shikari, HMS Sardonix, HMS Anemone, HMS Lady Elsa and HMS La Malouine, corvettes, was met 250 miles off Scottish coast in 60 25N 16 00W, 4 hours after programme time. Moonlight tonight. We expect land tomorrow and arrive Fri.

Josef: Boat and fire drill with Barrass and RN officers on duty, armed with pistols, rifles and sub-machine-guns. The escort rushed off and left the convoy behind, no idea why.

Wednesday 8th January, Day 242

Convoy Diary: 08:20. Eastern Star re-joined convoy. 09:20. Sunderland flying boat first seen in 60 20N 10 37W. Aircraft continuously circling during daylight and occasionally at night. Station keeping is satisfactory considering weather conditions and very long nights with totally darkened ships. Ships which got separated from the convoy in fog managed to re-join, very satisfactory.

Visual signalling rather slow in flag work. Morse work satisfactory, W/T no complaints. Message from Alaunia that W/T operator in Olympos was a suspected Nazi. I ordered her to seal her office.

Josef: Slept very well after playing skat and a hot bath, possibly last change of clothes until I'm on solid ground in Brixton. So many cups broken that coffee is served in glasses. Breakfast was Irish stew. We advance clocks by two hours.

Sunny all day, dolphins playing alongside. All the time signalling, flags, lights, and ships hooting furiously at one another. None of us understand it. We saw a French film, 'Final Accord', with Käthe von Nagy.

Destroyers and Sunderlands circle like sheepdogs. We must be nearly home, hurray! Mary, I've been thinking of you all day. Should I surprise you? Would that be fair on you? I don't know what to do. I think I'll try to tell you that I'm back.

Thursday 9th January, Day 243

Convoy Diary: 09:30. The four corvettes noticed a U-boat. One escort vessel dropped three depth charges at 12:30 in 57 05N 9 00W and another at 15:41 in 56 47N 8 29W. 17:00. Still chasing, no obvious success. Sunderlands flew over during night. 18:15. 7 ships left convoy, proceeding to Oban.

Josef: Did lookout duty in the forecastle with Captain Barrass, then with a naval officer. We've taken such a northerly route that the first land we saw was the north-west coast of Scotland, a lighthouse on an island, Skerryvore.

All day we passed along the Scottish coast and by four o'clock could see hills. Unless we speed up it will be Saturday before we reach Liverpool. Barrass knows nothing about preparations for our arrival and we think he's telling the truth. I hope, it's more than hope, that I'll be released and get home (now that's a word to hope for!) on the day we land. Eberhard had his hair cut and shampooed. It cost 2s/6d, double the price in England.

We usually have gramophone records but this evening there was an impromptu sing-song. Barrass played the piano while we and Captain Powell – he has a tremendous voice – sang our hearts out. On the wireless we heard Liverpool was being bombed.

Something has reassured me, Mary. Last night I felt I was coming home. To you, yes, many times yes, I have always felt that, but now also to England. All those months in the camps, from that awful day in May, I wasn't sure I'd ever again think of England as home, but I do. Hurray!

Friday 10th January, Day 244

Convoy Diary: 19:30. In 53 46N 5 8W Ittersum, Yselhaven and Cowrie parted company bound for Swansea under escort of HM Trawler Derby County. 23:20. Whilst heading for anchorage in Moelfre Bay, Anglesey, warning received of enemy aircraft operating south of Isle of Man. Convoy ordered to go on by 'two red light' method 180°. Tonight is full moon.

Josef: We're in the Irish Sea. Captain Powell says Liverpool by midday Saturday. The convoy now has twelve ships, a destroyer and fighters and bombers overhead. Between the Mull of Kintye and Rathlin Island we saw two outbound convoys... it has just occurred to me, the last time I was here I was half up the mast, conversing with a Prussian Prince.

Powell kicked up an enormous fuss over the food his officers are getting, complaining it was poor quality and not much of it. So we, the 'English' cooks, told him the truth: the head cook and the purser, both Belgian, so hate the British that they deliberately destroy food. The purser reports 'Forty eggs used', but only twenty arrive in the kitchen, the rest go overboard. This from our 'noble allies.' Our internee doctors say the Belgian ship's doctor wrongly predicted we'd all be seasick and spitting blood. He invited them all to drink whisky and beer with him, then asked them if they were loyal to Britain. When, without hesitation, they all said yes, he stalked out and refuses to talk to them. Another loyal ally!

Weather cold but sunny.

Tonight the convoy went close to the Irish coast, slowly to get through the minefields, but they still hope to land tomorrow...

Saturday 11th January, England, Day 245

...no, today, I've just seen the clock and it's past midnight. Dear, darling Mary, I wonder all the while about you. When will I get home to you? Will I see you this very day? I feel like a bottle of champagne, full of love and hope instead of bubbles!

Written in my cabin at quarter-past twelve. The next time I pick up this pen I should be on English soil. Good night, my love.

The Ettrick took 10 days for the crossing, the Thysville 17, but we've made it, may God be praised!

Convoy Diary: 10:15. Leading ship of the 10 still in convoy, Penrith Castle, Aelybryn, Eastern Star, Daytonian, West Ekonk, Olympos, Thysville, Abraham Lincoln, Blankaholm and Rokos Vergottis passed buoy at outer end of swept channel. 12:15. Convoy dispersed. DIARY ENDS.

Josef: Sailing cautiously up the Mersey, standing by the rail with Eberhard, there was little for us to see in the darkness of the black out... a few shaded lights glow from the docked ships, but scarcely any light onshore. The first indication of life in the mist-drenched blackness was the baleful sound of air-raid sirens. We're well and truly back in Britain.

Most of the 300 returnees on the Thysville came on deck, watching night turn into a grey winter morning, misty and chilly. We passed lightships and ships with barrage balloons, ships waiting to dock and sunken ships, while the grey of the Irish Sea changed to the yellow waters of the Mersey. Eberhard broke into my thoughts, 'The purser says the convoy carried cargo worth £20 million, and for each of us the government gave White Star £25 for this journey. We're expensive commodities.'

A pilot came on board and the ship began to pick its way through the mass of shipping.

I went down to my cabin to collect my things. All was oddly still. Gone were the ship's constant rolling and pitching in the Atlantic's waves and that unending throb of the engines. That noise had soothed me, but at times those waves came close to unnerving me.

At three, as the ship made fast to the very same pier we'd sailed from six months ago, the sirens sounded the 'all clear.' We all swapped smiles. A happy omen?

Lined up on the quayside seemed to be a company of British soldiers. They turned out to be fifty officers of all three services and as many Home Office officials with bulging briefcases and just ten soldiers with fixed bayonets.

A puzzled lieutenant, who'd clearly expected to take over from our escort, shouted up, 'Where's the military guard?' From the deck a smiling Captain Barrass replied, 'I am the guard.' Captain Powell called the officer on board. His orders were to escort the internees back to Huyton, but Powell cut up rough. 'Not like that you're not! They are going to be released. These lads have worked hard and don't deserve such indignity. Sheath your bayonets.' The bayonets were removed.

By 3.30 the officers and officials were settled in the dining room drinking tea. Briefcases were opened and paperwork set out. We ten 'releasees' came first. Behind us argument raged between the officials. Their orders were contradictory: War Office orders were to take the Pioneers to Bradford, Home Office orders were that everyone go, under guard, to Huyton. Eventually those destined for the Pioneers were ordered off the ship. What would happen to the rest we didn't know nor, I'm ashamed to admit, care, but it sounded as if they'd be staying on the ship. Eberhard and I escaped as soon as we could from that hot-tempered saloon and went on our way rejoicing.

We found ourselves about to step off the Thysville. Captain Powell was standing at the top of the gangway, shaking hands with each of us and handing envelopes to those who'd worked on his ship. 'Josef, here you are, son, you've earned it. Some of the best sausages I've ever tasted. You'll be going along Acre Lane on your way home, won't you, lad? Look in on the Hope and Anchor. Tell them you've sailed with Edwin Powell and you'll get a free pint, or get thrown out, depending on what mood Bill Farmer's in.' He handed me an envelope and pushed me towards the gangway. I didn't tell him that stopping in any pub on my way home was the last thing on my mind.

Down the gangway I went, suitcases in hand, rucksack on my back. On the quayside I looked back at the ship. Tied up there she'd be a prominent target in any air-raid. I pitied those who had to spend another night on her.

Standing off to one side, half-hidden by trolleys and baggage, I noticed Mr Temple. My mind flashed back two years to another man standing in the shadows as we'd streamed down the gangway, at Harwich, Mr 'McKenzie-Smith.' Nothing changes.

At a table a polite army sergeant addressed me as 'Sir.'

Sir!

At the immigration desk I didn't know whether to laugh or cry, my heart was so full of joy, my head of anxious questions. I was free. I was on English soil, I'd be seeing Mary tonight. Then doubts cut in, is she still alive? Does she still want me? Will she see me...

I was forced out of my musing. The man at the desk in front of me demanded to know my nationality, refused to put down Austrian. 'Stateless', he wrote. Then, to drive home his advantage, or so it seemed to me, he added, 'This is only a Conditional Landing.' I nodded, I'd heard that at Harwich. His face wore a bored, deadpan look.

'Address to which proceeding?'

'Czechoslovakian Military Office, 113 Piccadilly.' He looked impressed. 'Object of Visit?' 'To re-join the Czech Army', I replied. At last, a smile. 'Now that's one I don't hear very often, sir. Good for you.' He became positively cordial as he sorted out new documents for me, handing me a registration book, identity card, two ration cards and, finally, a railway ticket to London. 'Now, over there', he gestured to another desk, 'register with Liverpool City Police. Then you're free to go.' He even shook my hand as I moved off.

It was 6.15. Out of the corner of my eye I saw the men who were joining the Pioneers marching away from the ship, towards Riverside, the station we'd come in on eight months before. 'At least they've made it', I thought.

The police sergeant realised Eberhard and I were both going to London so he dealt with us together, 'You have permission to go to London in spite of its status as a special area. But you must both register as aliens on Monday with your nearest police station. Now, don't you forget, that would be a most serious breach of regulations.' I think he was about to make joke about it but decided against it.

'You enjoy the journey, both of you. And, gentlemen' – this English politeness, now we're civilians! – 'you must hurry to catch the London train. One's due to leave in half an hour. It'll leave on time, but don't expect it to keep to the timetable. It should take two and a half hours, but with all this bombing I'd say four is more like it. You'd better get a move on, it leaves at five past seven.'

Eberhard and I picked up our things. Behind us porters were taking luggage back on board. That didn't bode well so we lost no time in getting off the docks. I was thinking, 'Thirty yards to those dockyard gates, once we're through, we'll be free, truly free.' Just then through them came 'our' Pioneers, marching back from Riverside Station towards the ship, guarded by just two soldiers. 'It's all been postponed', someone yelled from the ranks. Another shouted, 'Get out of here quick, before they change their minds about you!' But we could see they were happy; it might mean another night on the ship but freedom, well, the British Army at least, clearly beckoned.

Suddenly there we were, standing outside Liverpool Docks at half-six on a Saturday evening. It struck me, 'I must tell Mary', I blurted out. 'And me Agnes', Eberhard responded.

We collared a man walking past. He wanted to be helpful, we could see that. 'Well, I'm not sure what to advise. All telegram offices will be shut by now, it being past six, and a Saturday an' all. You could try the telephone, but I don't think you'll have the time, seeing as how the train leaves Lime Street in...' he consulted his watch, 'in twenty-five minutes, and it'll take you all of that to get there. Even if you took a taxi, if you could find one this time of a Saturday evening...'

Eberhard cut him off. 'Thank you most kindly. We'll set off, if you'll tell us the way.'

'Up Lord Street', he pointed, 'then Church Street, turn left on Parker Street, you can't miss it. It'll take fifteen minutes...' Thanking him, we set off.

'To think, Eberhard, on the ship I was debating whether I should surprise Mary or warn her that I was home, which was the right thing to do. The choice is out of my hands.'

'And mine', he replied. 'But I live in hope both Mary and Agnes will forgive us.'

'If they're still alive', we might both have added, but we left the thought unsaid.

We'd each left Liverpool with a small suitcase and a bag. Somewhere along the way we'd both acquired an extra, larger, suitcase, more than a man could hurry with. But on a day such as this we'd have happily walked every street in Liverpool to get on a London train. Somehow we struggled into Lime Street Station as the train for Euston was about to depart and – thank God there were no barriers, or ticket collectors – climbed on board as it began to move.

It was packed. As we struggled along the corridor we saw a soldier with 'Czechoslovakia' shoulder flashes on his battledress. I wanted to shake him by the hand, but people behind us were pushing us on and anyway, like any good soldier, he was asleep, so I let him be.

The train was running late, or not running at all. We stopped outside Crewe for nearly an hour and the only news we had was from a guard who struggled along the packed corridors passing on the latest news. In the dark, with blinds drawn and most platform signs removed we had little chance to see for ourselves.

Once we'd found seats, I pulled out pen and paper and began writing, in lighting so dim I could scarcely read my own words. It was largely to stop thinking about what awaits in London. But I've written this diary in far worse conditions than this, in bitter cold, in the rain, in a swaying hammock, and Mary will help me interpret what I've written, I'm sure... if she's there. The realisation hit me, I've had no word from her for weeks. I don't know if she's still in Brixton, has

Brixton Court been hit, is she unhurt, oh God, has she been killed in another air-raid? I couldn't get these thoughts out of my head, they were louder than the train thundering through the night. Perhaps she's given up on me? Perhaps she's met someone else. Why didn't I make the effort to telephone her? If only that immigration officer had been more lively...

The swaying of the carriage jerked me awake, thankfully I'd fallen asleep. Now we were making better time and my gloom lifted. I opened the envelope Captain Powell had handed me. There were my earnings, £17 10s, and a certificate, 'SS Thysville, Volunteer Ship's Cook. 18 December 1940-11 January 1941, 24 days. Conduct: Very Good. Ability: Very Good. Certified, E H Powell, Master, White Star Line.' What a good man! I will drop in for a drink at that pub in Acre Lane, only not tonight, and it will be with Mary, to celebrate a safe homecoming.

For most of the journey Eberhard and I sat lost in our thoughts. Some way north of London the air-raid sirens started to wail and the train slowed to a crawl, but eventually we pulled in to Euston, hearing, over the loudspeakers, the station-master's announcement, 'Air-raid in progress.' It was eleven minutes past eleven.

We hurried to the tube. Eberhard was bound for Mortlake but we'd travel together as far as Embankment. Another announcement, 'Piccadilly Line westwards is closed.' Eberhard asked a guard about it. 'Well, sir, there's been a serious bomb tonight at Bank, so Central Line ain't working beyond St Pauls, and Green Park tube station, you know, under Devonshire House in Piccadilly, that took a nasty hit.'

I said, 'But that was in November. My fiancée wrote to me about that.'

'Oh no, mate, this was another one, tonight, 'bout seven this evening it was, two bombs, six dead, some wounded, poor souls. Just by Green Park station. I know 'cos my mate here at Euston was late in, he lives down that way. It took him an hour and an 'arf longer to get in than usual.'

We hurried down to the tube but my mind was in a flat spin. Two bombs, he'd said, six dead, others wounded. Mary often worked till eight, even later on Saturdays. Was she amongst them? Eberhard was talking to me but I scarcely heard him; he was probably saying goodbye, before he headed off for Mortlake.

To be honest, I remember nothing of that journey until the moment the train slid to a halt and, through the open doors, I saw a familiar platform, nearly there! I can't bear to think what I'll find when I reach the flat, I'm stopping writing.

.....

As Josef emerged from the tube at Clapham North a clock struck midnight. Six months of Canadian food, hard work and sea air made him want to stride out, but two suitcases and a rucksack said otherwise. The blackout was darker than he remembered, but he'd walked this route so many times in daylight he'd have found his way blindfold, and some light from the stars and a few searchlights quartering the sky away to the west helped him pick his way in the darkness. The drone of bombers and, over towards Battersea, the boom of anti-aircraft guns, told him tonight's raid wasn't over. Moments later shell fragments from those same guns rained down on the road and roofs around him. He flinched, but walked on into the darkness. His mood changed from joy to despair, what would he find? He must get to the flat.

Ahead, in the blackness, the road seemed blocked. Out of the shadows a policeman loomed, his hand up, 'Sorry, sir, there are unexploded time-bombs along here. Go to the left, then take any turning right into Acre Lane.'

Josef turned left and hurried on. 'I've come 3,000 miles, one to go. No time-bomb's going to stop me now.'

Chapter 9

From London to Inverlochy, by way of Butlers Marston

Sunday 12th January 1941

Mary: The clock on the mantelpiece chimed half-past midnight and I jerked awake, wide awake. I forced myself to think, to think through the day I'd just endured, an evening working late at Devonshire House, Mr William's cheery dismissal at ten to eight, 'Off you go, have a good weekend.' 'Weekend! What was left of it!' I'd thought. It all came crowding back... those sirens, as I'd started walking, then the all too familiar sound of bombs behind me, two of them, down by Green Park as I'd hurried down the steps into the shelter by Piccadilly Circus. Half an hour later, when the all-clear had sounded, all I'd wanted to do was to get back to the flat.

Then another sound brought me right back to the present. No mistaking it, two knocks on the door. Nobody called during the blitz! Again, a sharp, urgent double knock. As I jumped up, I knew, I just knew who it would be. As I ran to the door my heart was beating faster, the colour must have been rising in my cheeks.

He stood there, looking well and the apprehension on his face vanishing at once into the broadest of smiles. All I could think, as he held me tightly in his arms, was that our love would never die.

Behind them mother came out of her room in her dressing gown, muttering, 'Getting us all up in the middle of the night! Why couldn't he have sent a telegram? Why...'

Suddenly I found I was no gentle Mary, meek and mild. 'Mother!!! Go back to bed and get some of the sleep you so clearly need!' Mother, some resentful remark hovering on her lips, thought better of it. 'And anyway, it's impossible to send a telegram late on Saturday', I added, to her retreating back.

Dorothy disappeared, closing her bedroom door none too quietly behind her. I turned back to Josef and said, 'A cup of tea, darling?'

With thee conversing I forget all time,
All seasons and their change, all please alike.

John Milton

Monday 13th January

We walked arm-in-arm past Devonshire House. George, the doorman, greeting Josef as a long-lost friend – I think Josef enjoyed that – 'Morning miss, good morning sir, haven't seen you for a good long while. All well? Anyway, miss, the great man's offices are open, but after Saturday's bombs smashed those lovely plate glass windows Billy had to have the showrooms boarded up.'

'Thank you, George. Josef must report in down the road. I'll be back shortly.'

As we walked on, I pointed up at the scar in the wall on the side of Devonshire House, telling him the story of 'my' bomb, how I'd been shaken but unharmed, 'like St Paul's Cathedral', I joked.

Josef: Three times I've enlisted in the Czech army, in Prague, at Birchington and now at 131 Piccadilly, this time with Mary by my side.

Lukas told me, 'The briefing will take two hours, you'll be free to spend lunch-time with your fiancée.'

Off Mary went to work and Lukas talked me through the next few months. 'On 15 March you report to the Brigade's training depot at Leamington Spa. Your Prague and Birchington training counts, so you'll just do a fortnight. As Mr Temple told you on the Thysville, following the Cholmondley Castle mutiny we weeded out the left-wing hotheads – the Communists – from the brigade, but report back if you detect any murmurings.'

'But now something new. The clowns in the British Foreign Office want to start an Austrian Legion in the British Army, like our Czechoslovakian brigade, but they stirred up much ill-feeing amongst your compatriots by pushing for von Starhemberg to lead it...'

I started from my chair, 'Starhemberg! A fascist! In 1934 he had Socialist blood on his hands, he...'

'Have no fear, it will not happen,' he said emphatically, but for a week or so it will be useful for us, and MI5, to have your ear to the ground, to detect any rumblings. Dr Roellig will be with you, as battery clerk. So, take your disembar-kation leave, then report to Porchester Gate. MI5 tell us you're a member of the Austrian Centre, so while you're in London drop in on its library and restau-rant. Report what people are saying about this. Later on, the same amongst your fellow Austrians in the brigade. After that, recruit training, then the Anti-Tank Battery. After some weeks your work as a cook will be part-time, more like full-time with us.'

'One other thing: at the depot you are to request transfer to the English Parachute Regiment, it will not come to anything, but Colonel Kalla wants it lodged in your personnel file.'

'By the way, in Warwickshire you'll meet old friends from Vienna.'

14th January

Czechoslovak National Committee, London: Cj 1168/voj. Subject: Josef Bramminger. To: Czechoslovak Depot, Leamington Spa. This headquarters orders this soldier, on completion of his training, be attached to BKVÙP (A/Tk Bty) as Battery Cook. Signed: Lt Col Josef Kalla.

Mary: Back at the flat, a letter from the Home Office, sent yesterday. 'Madam', it read, 'With reference to your letter of 30th ultimo, I am directed by the Secretary of State to inform you that he has been advised that Mr Bramminger is on his way back to the United Kingdom and will probably disembark in a day or two. He will then, no doubt, communicate with you, which will give you the opportunity of conveying to him the information contained in your letter of the 30th ultimo.'

The nightmare of the past year flashed past, but I burst out laughing at the final words... 'I am, Madam, Your obedient Servant.' Those oh-so-meaningless words made me wonder. Had I, like Alice, been living in Wonderland all along?

Josef has given me a present. *Ein Kugelkäfig*, he calls it, a wooden chain with a ball and cage, all from one piece of wood, I love it. I started unpacking his suitcases. 'I've seen this before!', I exclaimed, holding up a blue denim jacket with a red circle on the back. 'Why on earth have you kept it?'

'I'm not sure. I can't make my mind up if I love it or hate it. It's a bit like a regimental uniform, something to wear at parties. But where have you seen it before...'

I'd not been sure how I'd tell him, but this was clearly the moment. 'Back in October, darling, I was standing in this very room, ironing, when I saw you. You were thinking about climbing the wire...'

He interrupted me eagerly, 'It was October the 5th. I heard you. "Josef stop!" you said, "You are coming home to me, but NOT over the fence", and for a moment I saw you, face to face, and suddenly I could face everything once more. I went for a walk, inside the perimeter wire, but I wasn't thinking about the wire anymore, just about you.'

'I tried to tell you, in a letter...'

'The last letter I received from you was written in September... anyway, from that moment on things got better. They told me I was to be released, they transferred us to Camp A, Farnham, further south, warmer, with a Camp Commandant who understood us.'

18th January

Johanna: Days after their return Eberhard and Josef heard of the greatest tragedy of all the many tragic tales that made up internment...

Josef: All of us knew Helm Bechinger. He was popular, a young academic chemist training at Imperial College, but what fascinated us was the love he had for his fiancée, Leila, Leila Mannsfeld. Every time – the all too few times – that he'd received a letter from Leila it just came tumbling out, and the whole camp hung on their story.

Eberhard and I were amongst the happy few, the ten released from the ship the day it docked. Helm was amongst the next most fortunate, so it appeared, he was freed on the 12th, the next day, to make his journey south. But now – I can scarcely bear to write this – we know that when he got to London he was told that Leila was in hospital and, when he finally reached the hospital, he was told that she had died earlier that day, that very same day...

Her last letter to reach him in Canada was written in October. She was well. I remembered the eagerness with which Helm had read it out, us craning forward on our bunks. And it hadn't been the blitz, she was taken seriously ill in January. We cannot imagine how Helm must feel. Eight months of doubt, reassurance, love, qualms, and hope, hope at a fever pinch. She was the focus of his every waking hour, yet she died even as his train was taking him to a reunion that was never to be. For any of the hundred men in Britain who eventually heard this tragedy it was close to unbearable. When I told it to Mary she had to walk out of the room to hide her emotions.

28th January

Returned today from disembarkation leave to work at Porchester Gate, doing much the same intelligence work as before. The nightmarish events and experiences of these last eight months are fading, putting themselves 'in order', some of them even begin to make sense, if an odd sort of sense. But I have no need of our Viennese psychoanalysts. Every day I rediscover Mary is all I need, a listening ear and 'a word in season', as she might put it.

1st February

Mary: Josef was engrossed in his monthly newsletter, *Sozialistische Mitteilungen,* Socialist Releases. News for German Socialists in England. 'What's so interesting, darling?' I asked.

He looked up. 'Here,' he held it up, 'Eberhard Röllig has written our story, they call him "comrade R" but it's him all right. It's all here, Birchington, Huyton, the Ettrick,' his eyes clouded, but he went on, 'Canada, and the Czech army. It's his story, and mine, every detail. How did he manage to get it written and into the *Mitteilungen* so quickly, barely a fortnight since we got back?' He grinned, 'He's a cunning fox! There was me thinking he'd not kept a diary and all that while he probably had the full article in his head. And listen to the ending... "I am still an ardent friend of the Allied cause, but why did they make it so difficult to be their friend and to remain so?" Well said, Your Worship.'

I laughed, 'I worry about you sometimes, a Socialist, hob-nobbing with worshipful judges and princes of the royal blood!'

He looked rueful, but brightened, 'That's not fair and, to prove it, I'm taking you out this evening to the Hope and Anchor on Acre Lane, the ship's Master recommended it.'

'Will your Crown Prince be dining with us? Darling, your democratic foundations are looking increasingly shaky.'

For a moment he was nonplussed, but came back, 'I served him at the Captain's table, yes, but I never SAT with him.' We both laughed.

Josef said, 'I will admit. I find it easier to picture Eberhard in a wig than to think of him as "Comrade R."'

8th February

Free Czech Army. P/File, BRAMMINGER, JJ, Vojin-Pte: Certificate by the President of the Czechoslovakian Government-in-Exile in London, granting the named Austrian citizen permission to join the Czechoslovak army.

Signature: Edvard Beneš

3rd March

Chief Constable of Warwickshire to the Superintendent of Register of Aliens: Bramminger, Josef Yohann, cards placed in the Central Register of Aliens,

Dead Section, the above named alien, nationality Austrian, Identity Book issued at Piccadilly Place, London W, having this day joined the Czechoslovak Army at Leamington Spa as Pte T-178.'

9th March

Free Czech Army, P/File, BRAMMINGER, JJ, Vojin-Pte: The Revd R Foster, Vicar of St Saviour's, to Czechoslovak Military Attaché: 'I certify that to the best of my knowledge and belief there is no impediment against the marriage of Mary Vida Brown with Josef Johann Bramminger. The date of the marriage has been arranged for April 9 1941, at St Saviour's, Brixton Hill.'

15th March

Josef: I've joined the Czech Army (for the 3rd time). Reported to Czechoslovakian Depot at Leamington Spa, where I was photographed, kitted out, medically examined, the usual, including the issue of KFS. A fortnight of recruit training begins.

28th March

Free Czech Army, P/File, BRAMMINGER, JJ, Vojin-Pte: Letter to Commander, Czechoslovak Training Depot, Leamington Spa: K Cj. 7006/18 msgs duv 1941,

Subject: Bramminger, J J, Pte. Application to join Parachute Regiment.

Bramminger, Josef, Pte, trainee Czechoslovak Depot number T-178, has asked how to proceed, as he wants to take part effectively in the fight against the Nazis and to apply to the English paratroopers.

In 1941, an Austrian national, received permission from Ministry of National Defence to serve in Czechoslovak army. Born 15 Feb 1916 in Vienna, German mother tongue, speaks English but not Czech, butcher, engaged, schools 3 years city. Swore Armed Forces oath on 2 Mar 1941 and enlisted at Czechoslovak Depot.

In 1938 served as a soldier in an Engineer Battalion in the Austrian army for 6 months, then 5 months in same after the occupation of Austria, when it was taken into the German army. In 1938 volunteered in the Czech Army and was enlisted in kp t pl Prague, but after Munich was released in October and went in the first transport of refugees to England. After outbreak of war applied to join Czechoslovak army and before it was granted he was interned as a German in England for 2 months and 4 months in Canada. In Jan 1941 was released to England and immediately requested to join the Czechoslovak army and consequently, being passed and his request granted he was summoned before the draft board to the Czechoslovak army depot.

Bramminger is by conviction a Social Democrat, but is not involved in any political party and speaks disparagingly about the Social Democrat party led by Jaksch, against its policy in Czechoslovakia.

Bramminger trained as an engineer in the Austrian army in construction of bridges, railways and demolition. In addition, experienced recruit Infantry training at Birchington-on-Sea depot. As an Austrian he knows well the whole Austrian territory and much of the adjacent territory of neighbouring states such as Italy, Yugoslavia and Hungary.

He requests to be sent where as soon as possible he can actively fight against the Germans and would like to serve in the English para. He has no fear of any danger of combat.

His behaviour during training at training depot has had no complaint or defects. Trainee Bramminger gives the impression of an honest Austrian who hates the Nazi occupiers of his country.

I advised trainee Bramminger to forward his transfer request for attention of the Depot commander.

Company Commander, Czechoslovak Depot
Col del Petr Novak.

31st March

Josef: I received no reply to my application to transfer, and Eberhard and I find ourselves posted to the anti-tank battery, in the Manor House of a very English village named Butlers Marston. 12 guns, 2-pounders, completely mobile. OC is Lieutenant-Colonel Kratky, 2IC is Lieutenant-Colonel Babatka. In any sane army they would be a major and captain, and that's half the brigade's problem, too many senior officers. Many of the soldiers – some died-in-the-wool Reds – came from the International Brigades in the Spanish Civil War, so it's unsurprising they mutinied at Cholmondley Castle; having so many officers just added fuel to the flames.

The Battery's officers sleep in the Manor House. Surrounded by ancient trees its quite dark and forbidding, but its walled gardens and imposing wrought-iron gates make it beautiful. We are in tents and huts in the grounds. I'm the battery cook, working in the cookhouse in the stables alongside the Battery stores. No choice. Kalla said, 'Same as Birchington, speak scarcely any Czech, understand less, then they'll say things in front of you you'd never hear otherwise.' Things could be worse: Eberhard is battery clerk. Imagine it, from High Court judge to typist and messenger boy.

In nearby Kineton there's a NAAFI, run by Lady Willoughby de Broke in an old wooden hall belonging to their Women's Institute. It's a mile and a half from Butlers Marston so we walk there for a drink, and it serves egg and chips almost all day or night. That's where I first met Gabčík, Svoboda, Kubiš and the others.

I was peeling potatoes when a friend I'd made in the Training Depot, Leo Kurtz, found me. He joked, 'Have you heard, B Company's commander received an invitation card from Lady Cholmondley to tea? She wrote requesting, "The pleasure of your company..." So Major Fiedler marched up to the front door with his company. The cook told me it's the only time the butler's been known to raise both eyebrows, for a split second the sight of five officers and 118 men on the drive nearly unnerved him. Lady C had meant him, him alone. But the butler recovered himself and somehow rustled up a hundred odd sticky buns and an urn of tea. Strange language, English!'

'Stranger people.' I added, under my breath, 'but I understand one of them, at least,' but Leo heard and said, 'Ah ha, so you are keen on Miss Brown, after all!'

'Go and play with your pop guns! I've got a meal to cook. Unless you want to peel 200 potatoes.'

War Diary. 22 Liaison HQ, 1st Czechoslovakian Brigade: Location. Barford Hill House, Barford. Task. To conduct relations with War Office. Title. 'The British Mission.' Staff Table. Comd: Col Pollock. GSO2: Maj Fillingham, MC, DLI. LO: Maj Kendrick. IO: Capt Barker, Intelligence Corps. SC: Capt Hart, R Fusiliers. Clerk RASC: Sjt (Int duties) and 3 x civ clerk including one for int duties.

Tuesday 8th April

Mary: Josef's home on wedding leave. Sitting in the flat he laughed, then read from a newspaper with more genuine pleasure in his voice than I'd heard in a long while: 'Alexander Paterson is the man who swept through the Canadian camps like a cleansing breeze.' 'Yes, a cleansing breeze, that was exactly it. The day he appeared six month's nonsense was gone in a moment.'

Wednesday 9th April, a wartime wedding

Invitation: Mrs Dorothy M Brown requests your company at the marriage of her daughter Mary Vida with Josef Johann Bramminger at St Saviour's Church, Lambert Road, Brixton Hill on Wednesday April 9th at 1.30 pm and afterwards at The Church Hall. RSVP.

Service sheet: Psalm 121: I will lift up mine eyes unto the hills. From whence cometh my help? My help cometh even from the Lord, who has made heaven and earth.

Final hymn:

God be in my head
and in my understanding

God be in mine eyes
and in my looking

God be in my mouth
and in my speaking

God be in my heart
and in my thinking

God be at mine end
and at my departing

St Saviour's Register: 'Marriage solemnized between Josef Johann BRAMMINGER, ~~24~~ 25, Bachelor, Hungarian, Salami maker (at time of marriage – Czech Army) and Mary Vida BROWN, 23, Spinster, in the presence of Dorothy M Brown, Roy Foster and Joh Svitanics.'

Mary: I was so glad that Johann could be there, and as his Best Man, some reminder of friends, if not family, in Vienna. But 'Hungarian' indeed! When I got back from the honeymoon, I asked Roy if I should buy his parish clerk a new pair of spectacles. 'Possibly a hearing aid,' he replied, 'the poor man's been in a muddle ever since his home was bombed last December.' I felt rotten.

Josef: As a refugee I've walked past those church doors dozens of times, en route from Wimbledon to visit Mary in Brixton but how could I have known that one day I'd be standing in front of them, in uniform, with her by my side, man and wife?

17th April

Mary: Brixton Hill Court, London SW2

Miss B Woodhouse

Kyrle House

Peterstow

Herefordshire

My dear Trix,

At long last I enclose a photo of the wedding – it is hectic to get things done here, everyone is so rushed and paper, etc, is not easy to obtain so we had to be modest in our photo requirements!!!

You will be glad to hear the wedding went off very well indeed. Two priests took the service, one being Roy Foster, an old friend of my father's. He gave the address, which everyone agreed was one of the loveliest they ever heard. At the end the choir sang, 'And God be in my head and in my understanding.' There were only 78 people as so many could not come, what with war work and travel restrictions, etc. Mother's family are nearly all abroad in Cuba and the Americas, except for my aunt and cousins at Brighton, they came, and naturally there were none of Josef's people. The reception, in the Church Hall, where we first met, went off very well.

For our honeymoon we went by train to Reigate, to a farm cottage beside Kinnersley Manor – half-timbered, stained glass (the Manor House, that is!), wonderful – lent us by a dear friend from SMB. We ended with two nights in Warwickshire, where Josef is stationed in a really lovely, peaceful little village, so very English. What contrasts, one for a refugee from Nazi-occupied Europe and Canadian internment camps, the other an Englishwoman from the blitz.

Josef returned to the Army and, back in Brixton the next night, last night, I had the worst blitz so far. Our flats were on fire, then they came back, dive-bombing. One bomb made a mess of the tram lines just outside our bedroom window – a broken tram cable was writhing and thrashing around like a snake spitting sparks – and five more on the buildings nearby. Within the mile-long road from the top of Brixton Hill they dropped 8 landmines and over 48 delayed action bombs – you may not get many of those in Herefordshire! – which went off all last night and today. We're all glad to still be alive. This morning the traffic was so bad I had to go to the office in a Black Maria!!!! I got there at 12.30. It was very much worse in central London. I've heard that Christie's, you know, where I used to work, was demolished by a direct hit.

Oh, I never told you about the presents. We were so lucky! The office gave us a very lovely dinner service – your sweet cruet looks lovely with it! Billy Rootes gave me a lovely antique silver sauce boat. We had several cheques, a little gold coffee service, some gold and enamel coffee spoons, some very nice modern ones in silver, a grey dressing case in leather cover with pink and pale cream enamelled fittings inside. Lots of tea cloths and luncheon sets, etc, some wooden dishes in walnut and a set of walnut table mats to go with them, a cake stand, a cut glass and silver butter and jam dish, a silver almanac, some silver dinner napkin rings. An acquaintance of Josef's (well, he's a German Prince – he didn't join us, however!) gave us a set of silver coffee spoons that I adore, their backs in the prettiest guilloché enamel in six colours!

My dress was white ring velvet and the bouquet camellias dusted with pale, pale pink, with three pink tulips, a few pieces of deeper japonica and two arum lilies, waxed a deep scarlet sort of pink, so that in the heart of the spray it was a deep scarletty sort of thing, coming out to a pale, pale pink and all the stems bound with white and silver; it was really rather lovely.

I do hope you are all keeping safe and well, and free from raids and so on. I expect, tho', you are well out of the badly raided areas, so you may get some sleep.

Please remember me to your father and mother.

Well, I must stop. There are so many photos to send off!

With much love,

Mary

19th April

Josef: Three days after I re-joined Mr Churchill visited the brigade and watched anti-tank training on our 2-pounders at Moreton Paddox. They brigaded all cooks to prepare dinner for him and, as the only Austrian, I was ordered to make the apple strudel!

22nd April

War Diary. 22 Liaison HQ: Maj Strankmuller, Dep Chief, Czech Intelligence Service, arrived at Bde HQ. They have ordered unit CO's to provide names of men suitable for special duties: they must be brave, patriotic, intelligent, able to keep secrets and to control their emotions under the most stressful conditions. No one with a history of drunkenness or womanising would be considered.

28th April

Mary: My 24th birthday, a day of no air-raids, wonderful! Then, once again, the Home Office goes and ruins everything. A letter from the Secretary of State arrives saying that by marrying Josef, 'You have, in German law, acquired German nationality by marrying an Austrian subject, and so in British law you are deemed, under Section 10(2) of the British Nationality and Status of Aliens Act, 1914, to have lost British nationality.'

But, in their glorious but upside-down world, all is not lost... 'The Secretary of State will be prepared to consider whether you are eligible for the grant of a certificate of naturalization under section 10(6) of the above-mentioned Act.'

He remains, of course, 'Madam, Your obedient Servant.' Oh, the generous lies of Civil Service English.

War Diary. 22 Liaison HQ: Bde HQ despatched list of 36 volunteers to Maj Strankmuller.

.....

Richard: My first encounter with Herbert Lowit was in May 1998, on the telephone. I asked him if he knew Josef Bramminger. His reply – the best words any researcher could hear – was, 'Yes, I remember him well.'

Later, over coffee at the British Library, Herbert told me his story. His family had been part of the anti-Nazi resistance in the Sudetenland and reached England in 1939 in the same operation that had enabled Josef to escape through Poland to England a month or so earlier. He went on:

'I joined the Czechoslovak Independent Brigade on my 18th birthday, 17 April 1941, and was posted to its Anti-Tank-Unit, with the cumbersome name "*Baterie kanónu proti útočné vozbě*", or *BKVÙP* for short, stationed in Butlers Marston. That's where I met him, the battery's chief cook. We'd exchange good natured banter whilst I stood in line with my mess tin. But Joe was 25 and I was much younger so I did not associate much with him, despite the fact that I came from the Sudetenland area of Czechoslovakia, so German was my second language. Few others in the Battery spoke much German, which might have put me close to Josef, but the age difference meant we were not close friends.'

'But I knew that Josef was Austrian and, by his accent, from Vienna. I recall that he didn't speak a word of Czech and seemed unable, or unwilling, to comprehend or memorise the simplest phrase. Since he wouldn't have understood orders given in battle, which were, of course, in Czech or Slovak, Joe wasn't allowed to undertake combat duty. That's why he served as a cook, and an excellent cook he was, he looked after us very well.'

'Working in the cookhouse admirably suited him, and his superiors, because army cooks are a law unto themselves. They keep their own duty hours, are excused roll-calls, military duty, and any kind of guard or orderly duties. And, I must say, Joe looked after our culinary needs splendidly – I for one easily gained more than a stone within weeks. Part of his success lay in the fact that unlike most cooks he didn't flog half our rations on the black market for himself, instead organising a mutually beneficial trade with British units, swapping rations we had in excess, such as tea in exchange for coffee.'

'And he traded our kitchen swill for some of Mr Rudge's produce at College Farm. His son, who delivered our milk, was amazed at us. We used to put some of the milk out on the cookhouse windowsill and let it go sour, producing yogurt (*Joghurt,* as we call it). He'd never seen such a thing. I remember this because for a time I walked out with his sister.'

'There was a soldier called Leo Kurtz who was a close friend of Josef's; he also ended up living in England but, unfortunately, Leo died some years ago.'

'Joe was with the Battery at least until 1943, but for much of that time he would disappear off, we never really knew where to, translation work came into it, that I do know. But then he'd be back and carry on as a cook. Leo might have known more but, as I say, he's no longer with us.'

'I should mention the "British Mission" there. It was permanently attached to the Czechoslovak brigade, staffed by intelligence officers, right through until the time we arrived back in Czechoslovakia.'

.....

Josef: My cooking skills – Mary would be surprised to hear that; she knows little of them! – are being developed at the expense of the men in the battery. It's certainly not haute cuisine. Most is humdrum, vegetables out of tins – except when I can trade our swill for Mr Rudge's fresh fruit and vegetables – and often rice pudding as 'afters', as the English call it. I struggle to use our ration of tea, Czechs and Slovaks just won't drink it, but I've found a wholesaler in Warwick who swaps it for coffee, when the ration truck goes that far afield.

12th May

I was summonsed to the Battery stores where the BQMS handed me a cardboard box. Inside was everything that the Kent police parted me from the day I was interned, so distant, two oceans, a whole continent away – exactly a year ago today, what a coincidence. '*Podepsat zde!* Sign here!' Slightly in shock I signed and staggered outside to open it up and rifle through it. Nothing missing, fountain pen, razor, blades, clothes, every letter, all my papers, even the ring Mary had given me when we'd announced our engagement, a year and half ago.

A shadow loomed over me, Eberhard, carrying a similar box, 'Josef, look what...' his voice tailed off, seeing the opened box at my feet. '*Du auch!* You also!' We both grinned. 'This represents a turning point in our fortunes.' He began sorting through his things. 'Look, my book. The one I left on the bedside table at Alpha House. Mrs Branksome must have handed it in.' 'Thank God for the Czech Army', I said, 'if only the Canadian Army could have been half as honest.'

22nd June

Another day, then the work was rudely interrupted late-morning by news on the radio that Germany had invaded the Soviet Union. A total surprise to all of us, but how will the Communists react?

23rd June

MI5 report: To B24. Source MILLER, Canterbury Hall, Report 16. Germany's invasion of Russia was a great surprise to the Communists in this CRTF hostel. Having received no instructions from Moscow as to the policy to adopt in the face of this new development they continued to believe the Germans were their allies. For now their propaganda amounts more or less to this: 'Churchill has played a false game with the communists and is encouraging the Nazis to fight the Bolsheviks. If the Nazis get the upper hand he will make peace with them. It is for this reason England has not made an alliance with the Bolsheviks, but only promised them assistance.'

Heinz Arndt. Arndt's Story: The Life of an Australian Economist: Within 36 hours, party members had to switch to total support for the war in defence of the USSR, a patriotic fervour that was almost as distasteful as their previous anti-war line. I was only a fellow-travelling supporter, not a party member but it dawned on me I had surrendered my intellectual integrity, not by kow-towing to views I did not believe in but, more corrodingly, by convincing myself that the Party was right. Illumination came from reading Koestler's '*Darkness at Noon*', with its depiction of the self-destruction of the intellectual. That cured me completely.

17th July

War Diary. 22 Liaison HQ: **SECRET**. To HQ IRSB. 8 OR's departed Kineton for Scotland on initial month-long course at STS 25 Mallaig, on west coast near Loch Morar.

.....

That whole thing, the selection, training and, after a long wait, the operation itself, was shrouded in secrecy. A cadre of eight, selected after preliminary training at Compton Verney, including Warrant Officer Jozef Gabčík and Staff-Sergeant Karel Svoboda, was sent off to Scotland. There they were trained by SOE (as we now know it) at Mallaig in the Highlands, a month of combat training, unarmed combat, small arms, making hand-made bombs, survival skills, map-reading, concealment and silent killing. Then two weeks at RAF Ringway in Cheshire for parachute training, where a head injury to Svoboda forced a replacement to be found in Jan Kubiš.

25th July

Mary: Josef was reading the Daily Mail. 'Look', he said, 'our very own Major Braybrook has been sentenced. The bench could be from a West End farce, or Gilbert and Sullivan, perhaps... "Carrington, Flinch and Drew, Maxwell-Fyfe." There's a Lieutenant-General, two Major-Generals, three Colonels, four Majors, and an MP for good measure. The props include a bag of gold sovereigns, two typewriters, and,' he paused, taken aback, '£50-60,000 pounds. Braybrook's defence: "he was holding it pending instructions." That's what he stole from us!'

A moment later he was on to something else: 'Here's an article on "Stamp Fever in Wartime", about how stamps are in great demand. Maybe I could be a stamp dealer after this war is finally over. What do you think?'

'Not a bad idea, darling. Let's think about that.'

16th August

War Diary. 22 Liaison HQ: 4 x English instructors appointed to Brigade. Tuition in English to Czechoslovaks with some knowledge of the language.

Herbert Lowit: I suspected at the time that this English tuition was set up by MI5 for its own purposes. My suspicions were proved right after the war, during my naturalisation application, when the Home Office interviewer quoted from the notes that I myself had written during that training. When 'intelligence' is involved things are rarely what they seem!

25th to 31st August

Free Czech Army. P/File, BRAMMINGER, JJ, Vojin-Pte: Medical record. Year of enlistment, 1938.

- 25 Aug 42: Bde Dispensary.
- 26-31 Aug: Hospitalised to Brigade Infirmary by BKVÙP medic.
- 31 Aug 1942, Returned to BKVÙP. Release note: patient had Polycystitis, Gastritis and Nephritis in April and May, concerning kidneys and liver.

.....

Johanna: Those illnesses, they seemed at odds with the SOE course he later undertook. There was something going on there which I have still not put my finger on.

.....

16th September

Home Office Aliens Department, file B.6092 (BRAMMINGER, Josef): Mrs BRAMMINGER called with, but did not leave, certificates of Birth, Marriage and Registration. Applicant said father and mother British. She was taken at age of 5 years to Cuba where she stayed for 9 months. The only other time she has been out of the United Kingdom was on a two week visit in 1936 for a holiday (France, Switzerland and Germany).

Husband was born in Vienna and educated and brought up there. He joined the Socialist Youth Movement at age 16 and was a member of the Social Democratic Party. Soon after Hitler marched into Austria husband discovered that the Gestapo were after him and managed to slip over the Czecho-Slovak frontier. He was allowed to join the Czech army and after Munich was one of the first fifty to come to the UK, where he wished to stay, feeling convinced that a European war was coming and wanting to take an active part in it. At the outbreak of war he was sent down to a Czech camp at Birchington, but unfortunately was interned and sent to Canada in July 1940. He returned in January 1941 and is now in the 1st Czecho-Slovak Brigade.

His father and mother and two brothers and sisters still live in Vienna. All his family have imbibed Nazi ideas and are opposed to him. In fact, they threatened to give him up to the authorities just before his escape. He is of course ardently Anti-Nazi, and just fretting to attack the spoilers of his country. Applicant herself has never belonged to any political organisation and has no interest in politics whatever. Neither of them has had any trouble with the police. They desire to stay in this country after the war, and applicant's husband hopes to be naturalized as a British subject. She gave the usual assurances.

A nice young English girl with a genuine manner. She took pains to answer my questions carefully, and generally impressed me favourably.

W Bradsmith (B Branch officer sat in).

Mary: I went to an Aliens Department interview. I think it went well. There were two Civil Servants: Mr Bradsmith, and another who never gave his name and sat off to one side, almost silent, 'Just an observer', his only comment.

Josef's down on leave so, this evening, I described that shadowy man to him. 'He was good-looking. He reminded me of David Niven. Perfect English manners, tall, lean, immaculately dressed, blue eyes...' Josef interrupted me, '"McKenzie-Smith", or so he calls himself. He was at Harwich, he interviewed me at the War Office. He's from MI5. Why's he interested in you?'

'In you I think, my darling', I replied, laughing.

27th September

Josef: Heydrich has replaced von Neurath as Acting Reich Protector of Bohemia and Moravia.

18th October

Eberhard tells me Gabcik and Svoboda finished at Tatton Park - where parachute training takes place, that much I know - then were sent by train to London. Later Gabcik and Jan Kubis went to Scotland on another special course - shooting and grenade throwing. All Top Secret, but battery clerks get to see movement orders. I wonder what it's all about.

19th October

Mary: I may have been a German national for the past six months, but Billy Rootes simply ignored this gross breach of security! And now, by the stroke of a pen, I'm British once again: 'Certificate of naturalization granted to Mary Vida Bramminger resident in London who was at birth a British citizen, German by marriage, husband an Enemy Alien formerly Austrian subject of a state that is at war with His Majesty. The Secretary of State is satisfied that it is desirable that the said person be permitted to resume British nationality and that such a certificate may properly be granted and by swearing the Oath of Allegiance to the King at J W Ratcliff, Commissioner for Oaths, 13 St James's Place, London SW1, shall be entitled and subject to obligations of a natural born British subject. Signed, A Maxwell, Under Secretary of State, 13th day of Oct 1941.'

Managed all that in my lunch break, Mr Ratcliff's office being only 350 yards from Rootes and practically next door to Christie's (or the bomb-site, at least, where I once worked).

20th October

War Diary. 22 Liaison HQ, 1st Czechoslovakian Brigade: **SECRET** WO Jozef Gabčík (Slovak) and SSgt Karel Svoboda (Czech) chosen to carry out the operation. Travel warrants issued to STS 27, Brickendonbury Manor, Hertfordshire, to practice explosives handling: booby-traps, fuses and modified atk grenades. Later to move to holding unit under Sustr at STS 2, the Villa Bellasis near Dorking.

Mary: I have felt 'different' for a few weeks now and wondered if I was coming down with flu or something. All of a sudden it dawned on me, I could be pregnant. When my GP confirmed my suspicions, I could not wait to tell Josef that he was going to become a father. Such joy at this difficult time.

Josef: Mary sat me down and, having made sure I was comfortable, announced the most wonderful news, we are having a child. I was immediately concerned for her, jumping up and trying to make her sit down, so many thoughts running through my head. My own new family in my new, adopted, country. As I held her in my arms I felt immense pride and pleasure, although laced, I admit, with quite some trepidation.

10th November

Mary: Dear Trixie, We're moving to a new flat in Linden Court, five miles south of Brixton, near the Crystal Palace, because - oh! it's so exciting to be able to write this - I'm expecting a baby about the ninth of May!

23rd December

Christmas will be no better than last year. Few turkeys and geese outside the poulterers' in Soho and you had to have ordered them a month beforehand to be sure of getting them, although, I don't expect Mary and Josef had turkey in their stable! At least, down in Covent Garden, there are lots of Christmas trees, holly and mistletoe; we'll get by.

No silk stockings, mind you, they've disappeared. When the government occasionally releases stocks, women start queuing when it's still dark. and several thousand pairs sell out within hours. Hastening to add, not to me. I need my sleep if I'm to cope with Mr William in the morning!

Have spent five days with Josef in a cottage in Butlers Marston, now he's home on leave. It's been so restful being there, so quiet and beautiful, even in the winter. On Saturday we walked to the village church - just beyond his cookhouse - the choir was practising, singing their hearts out, which raised my spirits.

1st January 1942

In the newspaper: 'New Year's Honours List: William Rootes has been awarded a KBE for his work as Chairman of the Joint Aero Engine Committee. Knight Commander of the Order of the British Empire.' Did His Majesty say, 'Arise, Sir Billy'? That's certainly how the wits in the office will refer to him, sotto voce at least!

10th February

Josef: After months of cooking I was marched in front of Lieutenant-Colonel Kratky, the battery commander. 'Bramminger, I've been told to tell you this: "You are to go to the Kineton NAAFI tonight, have a drink, then get out unnoticed and report to Woodley House at 8 o'clock. If someone asks where you're going you're to say you're off to see some local woman, or you're meeting a farmer about your swill." Don't ask me what it's about, they won't tell me. And you're to keep this to yourself. Got that?'

An unusual order, but this evening I had my drink then slipped away. Outside I asked a lady walking with a baby in a pram the way to Woodley House, as casually as I could. She exclaimed, 'Oh, the hush-hush place! Yes. Go past the church, on the right-hand side, just beyond the road to Butlers Marston.'

So much for all the secrecy.

When I got to Woodley another mystery unravelled. The door was opened by Harold Kendrick, who I'd never seen in uniform. He greeted me saying, 'Ah, Private Bramminger, call me Major Kendrick.' But he's still Frieda's husband, and a good friend.

'I have important news for you. It was convenient – the hand of Colonel Kalla at work, I believe – that you were posted to the Anti-Tank Battery, as they needed an ear to the ground hereabouts. For your own safety you will remain posted to the battery, but most of the time you'll work for me in the British Mission at Moreton Hall, six miles up the road, or in London, where the work will be a tad more interesting. In a month or so brigade will order your Battery Commander to send you to my headquarters for translation work. Oh yes, your application to join the English parachute regiment passed across my desk. That application, as Kalla intended, plus your translation duties, helps provide cover for your absences from the battery.'

'This is out of the blue, but there are benefits: you'll receive Translator Allowance for each day you're away from the battery. Secondly, when you're in London you can live at home, with your wife. It will not put you face to face with our mutual enemy, but you will be playing a part in our war against them, which I understand is your greatest wish...' he must have seen the smile on my face for he continued – 'other, possibly, than being together with your wife. I need hardly say, not a word of this, the first you will know of it will be in tomorrow's Part 2 Orders.'

12th February

Minutes, 22 Liaison HQ: Lunch in London. Present: General Ingr, Comd Czechoslovak Forces UK, and Colonel Moravec, Chief of Military Intelligence, with M, MX and MYO of IRSB. From the minutes:

'General Ingr and Colonel Moravec stressed strongly the disquiet in Czech circles about activities of Jaksch. Persistent rumours circulate that he wields influence in British government circles, strengthened by reliable reports that he receives financial backing.

The Czech Government considers Jaksch a political danger. General Ingr was confident that less than 1% of the 300 Germans in the Czech brigade were even mild supporters of Jaksch, the other 99% being violently antagonistic to him. General Ingr pointed out that his Government consider it an essential political factor that Sudetenland be considered as Czech territory, as the Czechoslovak state could not exist without it after the war. The majority of Sudetenland's workers are Czech, so it is practical that underground activities be directed from a Czech standpoint, while Jaksch obtained no significant intelligence reports above what is already provided by the Czech Bureau.

M gave assurances that Jaksch wielded no influence of consequence whatsoever with IRSB. In point of fact, all his recruits who had undergone training in IRSB Schools had been returned to the British Army. This greatly relieved Ingr and Moravec.

18th March

Police Records: 18.III.42. **SECRET**. From: Gestapo HQ, Prague 2. To: z Hd d Herrn Chief of Police Board, Dr Vysloužil, oViA, Prague. Subject: Josef Bramminger, 11.4.1916 Vienna, dwelling in Prague X, Konigstraße 51/11. Investigate the above named confidentially and tell me the result.

26th March

Free Czech Army, P/File, BRAMMINGER, JJ, Vojin-Pte: Medical Report. 26 Mar: 4 days bedded down in BKVÙP MI Room, sick. Lumbago, lower back pain.

27th March

The Revd Roy Foster: All Saints Choir School, 7 Margaret St, London W1.

Mrs M Bramminger
11 Linden Court
Anerley Park
London SE 26

Darling Mary,

Thank you for your lovely letter. I am sorry to have been so long in answering but my personal correspondence often has to be left to the school holidays.

Yours was such a dear letter, so lucid and clear. I understand perfectly about Josef and his religion. I don't know if you have decided where the child will be baptized but if you have not already decided Dom Bernard offers to do Baptism himself here at All Saints while of course it would be a great joy to me to be godfather. I know that between now and the time when your treasure is due you will constantly be offering yourself and that treasure to Our Lord, especially uniting yourself to Him in Holy Communion. If you prepare the soil Our Lord will grow a lovely flower in your beautiful garden.

My prayers for you and Josef and the treasure to come,

Ever yours, Roy

p.s. I was sorry to her that Josef is in hospital. Stella and my thoughts and prayers are with you both.

15th April to 7th May

Free Czech Army, P/File, BRAMMINGER, JJ, Vojin-Pte: Medical Report. Pain in the kidney region, admitted to Warwick Hospital, suspected infectious disease. Fever for 5 days, albumin in urine, pain in lower back. Diagnosis not fully determined but ? originated in the foul conditions on an HMT, or patient's treatment in internment? Nephritis or Polycystitis?

6th May

Birth announcement: Announcing the arrival of Johanna Josefine, born to Mr & Mrs J J Bramminger in Queen Charlotte's Hospital, Hammersmith. Sunday 6th May, 1942. 5.10 pm.

.....

Johanna: Not at the time, of course – I'd have been less than a day old! – but it has later occurred to me that not in any announcement, and not known to Mary, at the time that she was giving birth to me Josef was also in hospital, 100 miles apart, in Warwick.

.....

7th May

Free Czech Army, P/File, BRAMMINGER, JJ, Vojin-Pte: Medical Report. Discharged. 14 days home sick leave to 28 May.

9th May

Anti-Tank Battery, Part 2 Orders: BRAMMINGER, JJ, Vojin-Pte. Detached to 22 Liaison HQ on translation duties until further notice, WEF this day.

Josef: I packed my kitbag and was sent on the rations truck to Moreton Hall. As we drove through the peaceful Warwickshire countryside it reminded me of the rations truck I'd taken in Vienna, only this time I wasn't a deserter, I was en route to an official interview with Major Kendrick...

'You'll do a week's translation work here, German to English, but first there's something that's been puzzling me for the past two years. Colonel Kalla allowed me sight of his personal file on you – all very interesting, of course, but what was all that about Freddie, Frieda that is, as you know her, my wife, being mentioned on a postcard from Vienna, back in January 1939?'

'Sir, I remember it well. A good friend of mine, Leo, Leo Pröglhöf, had served with me in the Austrian Army, then the Wehrmacht, but we were also comrades in the underground. On that postcard his last words were, "Also a beautiful greeting from Mrs Kendrick." I didn't know what he meant, it's bothered me ever since. He managed to put two secret signs into the card that told me he was being held by the Gestapo, in Vienna. I have heard nothing more from Leo, or about him, he is probably in Mauthausen, or...' I paused, reluctant to pronounce the word. He nodded, I did not need to say it, he knew the game, and how it so often ended.

'I should have done something. Some things I just keep putting off. Has Frieda, sorry Sir, your wife, has she seen the card?'

'Yes, I showed it to her. She remembered Pröglhöf, she remembers you, and, by the way, sends her greetings – she asked me to say "Grüß Gott, Peppi!" – but the meaning of his words escapes her. She wondered if it was simply a reminder of happier times.'

'*Wollen wir es hoffen,* let us hope so. For Leo's sake I hope I did not miss something vital.'

'Yes indeed. Now, you must sign the Official Secrets Act once again...'

That done he continued, 'I'll explain our place in the intelligence jigsaw puzzle. My job is liaison between the Czechoslovakian brigade and elements of government...' Two of the names he mentioned were only hints but I think he works with the Home Office, Foreign Office, MI5 and MI6.

'But what I will tell you now must not be repeated, it is top secret, d'y see?' then he told me something entirely new to me. 'From this day on you'll be working most of the time with another organisation, both here and in London. If Colonels Kalla or Lukas have work for you, or Mr Temple for that matter, they will contact you through Major Ingle. All you need to know for now is that his organisation is the Inter-Services Research Bureau, ISRB for short.'

He sent me to Compton Verney, two miles west of Kineton, a country house in 120 acres of parkland with its very own lake. A sergeant put me in front of Major Ingle, the man who, on and off is to be my new Commanding Officer. He was in battle fatigues, clearly no 'spit 'n polish merchant', as you might say in English.

'Ah, Bramminger', he started off, 'I see from the file from Kendrick that you've worked for Czech intelligence and Five occasionally. From now you'll be spending most of your time with us, here and in headquarters – in London, that is. We've been given any number of names, some of them pretty damn rude, all you need to know for now is that people think we're called the Inter-Services Research Bureau. Don't ask questions, you'll find out more when you need to. And I see you're Viennese. My name's Major Ingle, Peter, you might have come across my brother Walter, he ran a holidays business in Austria before the war, skiing, that sort of thing.'

'I knew of him, Sir.'

'Good. You'll do selection training here for some weeks, with 29 others from your brigade, one or two of whom you know already, but it doesn't do to ask questions about each other. The less you know the less you can tell, if it comes to that.' Prague swam across my mind; I nodded. 'It will be tough, but it won't be regimental.'

'One other thing, your medical record shows several problems in the past year. Are you up to some tough work?'

'Yes sir. I've been through four armies' training, had four months stuck in Canada's wilderness. I aim to hold my own.'

'Good. As Major Kendrick explained, on occasion you'll be called back to your old job with...' he scanned the letter he was holding, '... your battery, but all they need to know is that you're doing translation work, no more. Sergeant', he shouted, 'Take Private Bramminger to Lieutenant Eckstein.'

We're billeted at Walton Hall - another country house not far from Compton Verney.

16th May

War Diary. 22 Liaison HQ, 1st Czechoslovak Bde: Czech Bde moved from Leamington Spa to Ilminster, Somerset. Coastal and airfield defence duties... ATk Bty from Butlers Marston to Cricket St Thomas, Yeovil.

18th May

Free Czech Army, P/File, BRAMMINGER, JJ, Vojin-Pte: Granted child allowance.

27th May

.....

Richard: Years later it dawned on me, this day, a year and more after planning and training had started, and six months after the team was dropped by parachute from an RAF Halifax that took off from RAF Tempsford on 28th December, Operation Anthropoid was finally implemented on a street corner in Prague. Jozef Gabčík and Jan Kubiš attacked the car carrying Reinhard Heydrich, Acting Reich-Protector of Bohemia and Moravia, with guns and explosives supplied by SOE, severely wounding him. Everyone at SOE was sworn to secrecy. MI6, the Foreign Office and the War Office were never told that SOE had supplied the weapons and explosives - although it was not a secret that would outlast the war.

In the brutal reprisals that followed the SS and Gestapo destroyed the villages of Lidice and Ležáky and murdered most of their inhabitants. More than 5,000 people died in all, including Jozef Gabčík and Jan Kubiš.

One day in the early 1990's, watching the film Operation Daybreak about Heydrich's assassination in Prague, Mary turned to me and said, *'Josef trained with those men.'* Oh, how I kick myself for not asking her more - a feeling every historian must know only too well. A few years later, it was too late, Mary had died. In the 1990's I asked Herbert Lowit about this. He thought about it for a minute or two. 'Those men,' he said - and the cautious way he spoke, almost in a whisper, told me that he still wasn't sure it was yet safe to talk about it - 'they were based at Kineton, Josef will have encountered them there. Some of their training took place in the countryside nearby, on private land, it was very isolated.'

.....

28th May

Josef: After that translation work, then a stint in hospital, I've been discharged to the training cadre. They took 30 of us to Friz Hill House, out in the Warwickshire countryside. The Czech engineers had constructed a practice jumping platform in the top of a tall Scots Pine, where we climbed up metal spikes driven into the trunk to the platform, with a hole cut into it, the size and shape of the hatch in a Whitley bomber. Then we just jumped; with no straw or cushioning landing was hard, but you soon learnt to roll away.

My other task, reporting to Mr Temple on how fellow Austrians were reacting to von Starhemberg leading an Austrian Legion has ended. The prince has been posted to the Belgian Congo.

BKVÙP Records. Register of Married Personnel: Vojin-Pte. Bramminger, Josef. Married to Marie, living in London with her six-months-old child and not working at this time.

4th June

Mary: **'HEYDRICH DEAD'**, newspaper posters proclaimed. He had died on this day, it was said, from wounds inflicted by Czech patriots in the capital of Prague. It was said that the Nazis had declared there would be reprisals against the civilians population. I wonder if those patriots were Josef's friends and colleagues.

5th June

Josef: From what Colonel Kalla showed me today I now know that three months ago the Gestapo in Prague were investigating my stay in the city in 1938. Without a word he handed me a typewritten document:

> '*Police Records:* 8.IV.1942. **SECRET**. From: Police HQ, Prague. To: Gestapo Division III, Prague, for Zl: III 24-7 from 14/III.1942. Subject: Opis s orig.spisu/Description from original file: BRAMMINGER

> Joseph, butcher, born 15.2.1916 Vienna, supposed national of the German Reich, Roman Catholic, last resident in Prague XII, Romische road 14, in lodgings with Anna Valasek/Valášková, claiming he was refugee and deserter. Previously, 30/7/38 to 27/9/38, in Prague X, Konigstraße 51. Bramminger still owes Valasek 65 Krone. On 03/11/1938 reported by Prague police to have moved to England.'

He said, 'They spotted that you weren't just a Wehrmacht deserter but also you had taken two documents to Prague, meaning you committed espionage against the 3rd Reich so now, in their eyes, you are also a spy. But they will dig deeper, and as they now control 2nd Department's records, they will be able to see that you worked for us in Prague, and that you moved to England. Beyond that, however, they probably cannot see.'

Captain Barrass, in Canada, had told me some of this, yet I was surprised that the Gestapo could still be on my heels, four years on. But I was also surprised that Kalla should be concerning himself with my affairs when he must have been worried about his own safety: recent intelligence reports indicated the Nazis intended making an attempt on President Beneš or Kalla as a reprisal for Heinrich, so special efforts are being made to guard both.

7th November

ISRB, whoever they really are, hate giving anything away. I've been shuttled between the British Mission in Somerset, and the Training Cadre with brief stints at the battery since late July with no explanation, just 'wait for orders.' Finally, I've been given leave, a travel warrant to London, orders to report to IRSB (the rumour is that it's just one of several cover names), near Trafalgar Square, and then a course in Scotland. NFD.

9th November

Mary: Johanna and I spent five days with Josef in a cottage in Cricket St Thomas, then home today with him for some leave before he's off on his course. Somerset was so restful.

In his spare moments he pursued Colonel Kalla, keen for official recognition of his part in the intelligence battle. So he was very happy when, after three letters, he eventually extracted this from Kalla's department...

> *Director of 2nd Department, Free Czech Army:* **SECRET**. TO WHOM IT MAY CONCERN. This certifies that Mr J J BRAMMINGER, Pte in 1st Czechoslovak Brigade, deserted from the German Army in Austria on 12th July 1938 to Czechoslovakia, where he reported at once to the

authorities. He subsequently worked for 2nd Intelligence Department of the Czechoslovak General Staff conscientiously and efficiently until general mobilization in September 1938, when he joined the Czechoslovak army as a volunteer. As a result of the Munich decision he was discharged from the Army and his intelligence work, which developed successfully, was interrupted. With the backing of this Department he escaped to Britain.

In 1939 he volunteered again and joined the Czech Army in Britain for military training. In May 1940, as an Austrian refugee, he was interned by the British authorities and sent to Canada. At the intervention of this Department he was sent back to England and on 3 March 1941, at his private home in Brixton, was interviewed by Major Bricht of this Department. He was accepted again into the Czech Army. He hoped he would serve in the intelligence department. When that didn't happen, he applied seven times to his unit for a parachuting course. He was considered suitable in terms of health but was not sent there and instead had to serve as a cook at BKPÚV.

Now he asks permission to seek an active intelligence services job in the British forces. This certification is confirmed by two of our officers, now serving abroad, and is sent to him because it is true.

12th November

Josef: My interview took place in a dingy hotel, the Northumberland, off Trafalgar Square. I was taken to Room 321, bare, plain, on the upper floor, blacked-out, its only fittings three folding chairs and a naked light bulb. A similarly plain room came to mind, in the War Office in 1939, my first encounter with 'McKenzie-Smith.' This time an officer, half-obscured by swirls of cigarette smoke, started to question me then, moments later, a woman burst into the room and, immediately my feet felt on firmer ground. I recognised her. Five years earlier, in pre-war Vienna. I'd seen her entering Franz Emmerich's flat, his 'secret' flat, where he'd just finished giving me some orders – she hadn't seen me. I said nothing, It was the sort of knowledge that might come in useful one day, She introduced herself as Mrs Jefferson. In Vienna she'd been Mrs Coulson, but neither will be her real name, of that I'm certain, any more than McKenzie-Smith is his. So very ISRB-like, I was to discover. Everything layer upon layer, smoke and mirrors. They interviewed me half in German (I caught the occasional word of Wienerisch in her questions), touching on my travels, and my experience of railways. I seemed to 'pass muster', as Mary would say, and was told I'd hear from them, after a course in the Highlands.

16th November

Mary: Churchill ordered cathedral and church bells sounded after victory at El Alamein.

17th November

Josef: Postmarked 7[45] PM GLASGOW

Mrs M Bramminger
11 Linden Court
Anerley Park
London SE26

My dearest Wife,

Am at present waiting for the train at Glasgow and am looking forward to getting to camp.

I very much hope you have arrived home safely and without much trouble, that you and Hanni are both quite well.

I have been very happy through your coming and staying, and it will add to my happy remembrance on all our very happy times and this time it was especially nice to have had you with me.

I send you enclosed souvenir of Scotland, will write again as soon as I can or at camp.

Good bye for now. God Bless you and Hanni.

With all my very best love and kisses for always and always, your loving and devoted husband,

Josef

18th November

The train left Glasgow heading NNW. It took four hours to arrive at a deserted station called Spean Bridge. There, at 0600 hrs, a young lieutenant on the platform cheerfully ordered us off the train. His announcement, 'Gentlemen, before breakfast we shall enjoy a little walk' set the scene for the next grim month, for he then proceeded to march us seven miles down the road to Inverlochy Castle. It was raining so we were soaked to the skin: complain and you get the answer: 'Skin's waterproof.' Arriving at the castle – nothing is what it seems here as this is not the real Inverlochy Castle (that's a medieval ruin two miles down the valley) this is some aristocrat's country house. Castle or not we were allocated to marquees on the lawns. Later that day the instructors – all Czechoslovakian, apart for a handful of British officers and sergeants – were delighted to tell us that had we got off at Inverlochy Halt, the previous stop, we'd have had just 500 yards to march, but they thought we'd enjoy the exercise.

18th November to 18th December

Allied Special Training Centre, Inverlochy Castle, Fort William:

Training Table.

Day 1	Prelim instr on Bren-Rifle-Sten-Tommy Gun, Grenade. Firing Mauser. Morse.
Day 2	Demo Grenade throwing. Fire Bren, Boyes ATk Rifle, Suomi & Belgian automatics. Bathing parade. Kill, butcher, cook & eat lamb. Survival Skills.
Day 3	PT. Use of explosives: Elementary Demolitions; Manufacture of hand-made bomb; Preparing charges of trotyl plastic, gelignite and ammonal; Pencils, booby traps, delays, switches: pressure and expanding.
Day 4	Explosives: Preparing fuses, Bickford, FID, and Cracker; Demolitions; Calculating charges. Unarmed combat. Firing the .38 & Tommy Gun. Night march.
Day 5	PT. Lecture: Organisation, uniforms & armament of local German civil & military administration. Unarmed combat & Silent Killing, Stilettos, Assaults on guards, Disarming, Tying.
Day 6	Explosives: Ambushes employing HE. Fight training of small guerrilla & diversionary groups. Long distance night march, including compass work.
Day 7	PT, Assault Course. Dealing with dogs (poison). Lecture: Police organs: Schutzpolizei, Kriminalpolitizie, Gestapo (incl Methods of Interrogation), Gendarmerie, etc. Abseiling. Elementary Morse.
Day 8	Compass marches on difficult terrain. 1130-1600 hrs, March; climb to 600 m.
Day 9	PT. Lecture: SA, SS (when in police tasks). Endurance test & climbing; Climb Ben Nevis, 4406 feet.
Day 10	Firing Revolver & Tommy Gun. False keys, by-passing locks, breaking into properties. Constructing pontoons. Morse training.

Day 11	Morse. Lecture: German Army organisations, uniforms & armament. Issue Personal Pistols. Industrial sabotage: factories, boilers, reservoirs, buildings.
Day 12.	Work in Camp. Morse. Orientation in Terrain. Camping: Provision from terrain. Night Scheme.
Day 13	Use of explosives. Morse. Pistol Maintenance. Raid Tactics.
Day 14	Demolishing Power & Telephone Lines. Unarmed combat. Lecture: Foreign Maps. Stalk Range Pistol Firing. Morse.
Days 16 & 17	Fieldcraft Exercise. Appreciations, Planning, Reports & Orders. Morse Test.
Day 18	Test on Bren mechanism. Grenade Throwing. Laying an Ambush. Map Reading Night Scheme.
Day 19	PT, Ropework. Digging, Blowing up a Railway Sleeper. Cam & Concealment demo. Practice Concealed Movement & Stalking. Visit Power House of Br Alum Company; Practical demo.
Day 20	Firing Bren, Rifle & .38. March with Compass & Map. Night Scheme, 2100-0115 hrs.
Day 21	Movement through Woods. Fire Bren/Rifle/.38. Use of Explosives. Discussion.
Day 22	Principles of Street Fighting. Bathing Parade. Demo/Characteristics of rifle by CO. Night Raid on Tank Harbour, 2100-0100 hrs.
Day 23	Use of Explosives against Tanks, Anti-Tank bombs. PM. Football v Fort William.
Day 24	Throwing Live Grenades. Stalking Sentry. Bathing Parade. Night Manoeuvre.
Day 25	Railways: Demolition of Railway Lines (Cutting & Mining), Obstructions, Locomotives (incl Hot Axles), Viaducts & Bridges. Morse Final Test.
Day 26	Blowing up Large Iron-Pipe. Movement through Woods by Compass (Haversack Rations). Discussion.
Day 27	Demolitions. Practice Embarkation & Debarkation. (Details to follow).
Day 28	Admin. Final Parade. Interviews.

19th December

Course Report.

SPECIAL TRAINING COURSE	ISRB No 7 (Czechoslovakian Forces)
DATE:	17th Nov 42-18th Dec 42
Number:	T-178
Rank:	Pte
Name:	Bramminger, J

GENERAL REPORT: Medically unsuited to this work

Signed: Lieut-Colonel, Commandant CHM Praed 18 DEC 1942

Josef: It rained for 25 of the 28 days we were there and we were rarely warm, but at least the showers worked, and you can't say that of most army camps.

But that's only half of it! Most nights they roused us out of our bunks at 0230 hrs and took us for another 'refreshing' run. Ben Nevis towers above the castle and wild, steep hills hem it in – most of which we've had to climb. Herds of red deer stood silhouetted on the skylines, stock still until, in an instant, they scattered, to leave a deserted landscape. Every march or exercise was across the most rugged terrain, full of ravines for us to fall into and bogs so adhesive they suck the boots off your feet. Between tramping through rain-sodden pine trees and bracken, with mists rolling down the valleys and icy streams cascading off those summits, we were rarely dry.

None of us will forget the smell of burning peat, sometimes acrid, sometimes sweet, nor the sight of heather and bracken suddenly burning off when one of our explosives flared off in the wrong direction. We found out how to shoot from the hip, to fire five rapid shots from an ordinary rifle as if it was an automatic, and the double tap. All this we learnt the hard way, those who got it wrong were hauled away in an ambulance.

And it was hard, hard work. It never let up. But there were one or two moments of light relief. One was provided by Fairbairn and Sykes, two bespectacled and, to us, ancient ex-policemen from Singapore, teaching unarmed combat. At our very first meeting they clumsily fell down two flights of stairs, tumbling over and over to the bottom, but then, instantly, in the crouch position, .38 in one hand, Commando knife in the other. That impressed us.

One odd thing: mid-course we were visited by the Czech Brigade Commander, accompanied by the usual hangers-on, including two or more ISRB officers. They watched us on the assault course, nothing more. I think they then went off for lunch in the castle. But one of the ISRB officers I immediately recognised as Philby, the one I saw in 1934 in the Wienerwald. He was wearing an old military tunic with no rank. He didn't see me, I would have been just another camouflaged soldier, some way off and, anyway, he's never laid eyes on me before, and certainly not in the Vienna Woods. There are so many types in ISRB: regular soldiers, Socialists, nationalists, Communists, the lot, that him being there didn't seem out of the ordinary. I've put him out of my mind.

20th December

A full time job, at last. But even that's scarcely true. I'm being transferred to the mysterious organisation in Baker Street, but, for administrative purposes, I remain on the Battery roll, but to report in London in the New Year.

Mary: 'Darling, I spotted something in the newspaper while you were away. Look, your friend's in the notices: "Mr John Warder Cadbury, of Moorestown, New Jersey, USA, and Miss Tessa Rowntree, eldest daughter of Mr and Mrs Arnold S Rowntree, of York", that Quaker girl whose bravery enabled you and all those others to escape after the Germans had walked into Vienna and Prague... "were married yesterday at the Friends' Meeting House, Kirkbymoorside."'

Josef: 'It would be an honour to call her a friend, she saved my life, and many others. *Diese Nachricht ist sehr erfreulic...* this news is very pleasing. I wish them a long and happy marriage.'

20th to 23rd December

Free Czech Army. P/File, BRAMMINGER, JJ, Vojin-Pte: Medical record.

- 21 Dec 42: Hospitalised to Brigade Infirmary by BKVÙP medic. Back pain.
- 22 Dec 42: Stomach disorder, hypothermia.
- 23 Dec 42: Released to Czechoslovakian Depot. Sent on leave.

Chapter 10

From Baker Street to Belsen, by way of Blenheim Palace

January 1943

Josef: One day, perhaps, the truth will come out about what they do in ISRB, Inter Services Research Bureau, as the small brass plaque on Baker Street says. Perhaps its real name will become public knowledge. But for now, I record these in my diary for Mary or our child to decipher one day. Perhaps they might then understand some things better.

I was interviewed by 'X', Maj Thornley, Head of Country Section X, partly in word-perfect German, partly in Oxbridge English (Mary's word for it). It covers Germany and Austria.

'We've come across you before, under a different name of course - ours, that is, not yours...', he chuckled - I later discovered he always retained a sense of humour - 'at Birchington-on-Sea. Our predecessors dreamed that show up and financed it in 1939. Anyway, it is useful you know something about Austrian railways. You'll report to Mrs Holmes, she's our expert on Austria, Vienna especially.'

Moments later she joined us. 'Clara', she announced, the Mrs Coulson of 1930's Vienna and the Mrs Jefferson of the Northumberland Hotel, but here this greying, middle-aged widow is code-name X/A.1. I've worked out since that she'd worked for SIS years before the war, in 'Section D', which later merged into ISRB. She knows the continent backwards from motoring holidays there, not to mention living in Austria, Switzerland and Czechoslovakia, especially Vienna. She knew the city inside out, having worked there for British intelligence - MI6, that is. Following the *anschluß* the Gestapo uncovered the organisation she was running, so she had to make a swift exit to avoid capture. She knows all about smuggling lines across frontiers, having transported huge quantities of forged documents, subversive material and 'black' propaganda into Austria and Germany, including letters to Austrian railwaymen, so she knows their strengths and weaknesses.

Above all, to me, in a Department dominated by its work in Germany it's good there's someone who understands Austrians and the Viennese.

I 'caught sight' of her P file: she can drive, ski, swim, shoot, map-read, cycle, run, a regular super-woman, but she's no mountaineer, surprisingly. She's 5 feet 5 tall, but every inch a really tough, determined lady. When I see a steely glint come into her eyes - a look I've seen in Mary's friends from SMB - I know it's time to take cover.

Fortunately the section isn't just about paperwork, plans and leaflets. Its 'Group Lex' - infiltrated from Switzerland - has incinerated a drawing office in a Hamburg plant, destroyed 12 unassembled planes at Bremerhaven, blown up ammunition trains and derailed and burnt-out a train carrying 16 seaplanes and 12 Focke-Wulf's to Kiel. She must have read my mind as I was reading that, since I'd been thinking, 'Shame they weren't in Austria', when she came across to say, 'And in July Lex smashed goods trains, a Gestapo barracks and aircraft factories in *die Wiener Raum* - the Vienna area. I thought that might please you.' It did, the most satisfying thing I'd heard in many months. It controls Group Lex, it turns outs, uses stores infiltrated by rail from Switzerland - air resupply inside the Reich being virtually impossible.

Within a fortnight I had been taken off translating documents and put onto a task much closer to my heart... railways. I think they'd known all along that I had a background and interest in railways and were just testing me out. Soon I found myself working on German and Austrian railway technical issues... lines, equipment, signalling and all the rest, not to mention destroying it, all learnt and practised at Inverlochy.

Mary: I have only the haziest idea of what he does, but, all of a sudden, Josef seems to have found himself. Daily I see how it's 'put a spring in his step.' He spends almost all his time in London (which suits me), the rest... well, where he is sent off to is all hidden in a fog of secrecy.

And it's certainly changed my life... suddenly I'm an inveterate party goer! Josef being based here means he spends his free time in Austrian and Czechoslovak émigré circles. When they're not discussing Freud and art (wittily, gaily and with great gusto) and every kind of politics (often on the verge of fisticuffs), they're throwing a party, and sometimes I get an invitation. So, by day I staunch the flow of captains of industry, civil servants, military figures, flunkeys and lackeys, all 'desiring to be fed with the crumbs which fall from the rich man's table', Billy Rootes's, that is. Then, by night, I find myself in a more colourful *mélange* of refugees, writers, journalists, artists, film directors, poets, politicians and other hangers-on, an odd mixture of conceit and sycophancy. But when I see someone listening rather than talking, like Josef, I immediately wonder what part of the secret world they inhabit.

.....

Richard: I vividly remember Mary recalling something of such refugees in late 1991. We were driving through Herefordshire to the Black Mountains. We'd stopped to view The Skirrid, that extraordinary, split mountain near Orcop, especially memorable because, just at that moment, despite the sunshine that bathed the scene, a triple rainbow was arched over it. The day before Robert Maxwell had mysteriously fallen into the sea from his yacht off the Canaries, and his name was in everyone's thoughts. Mary began talking about how Josef had been involved in émigré circles during the war, and recalled meeting someone at such meetings who was younger than him and not, then at least, of any significance. She was sure he was the man everyone now called Robert Maxwell, although that wasn't his name back then, of that she was certain. I mentioned Du Maurier. She laughed, 'Yes, that's it, cigarettes followed by coffee. It's usually the other way round!'

.....

Mary: All those refugees, goodness, what characters they are, and some real rogues. I don't expect I'll ever quite master who's who and which is which, but Josef thrives on it and has a better eye, or ear, for it than me. It's a bit like living in a Central European village where everyone knows everyone's name and family secrets back to the nth generation. Although it can be more of a minefield than a village.

Most have names, code-names, pseudonyms, and aliases. Rarely are they what they seem. Berta Brichacek comes to mind, a bookbinder from Vienna and married to Otto Brichacek, aka Prhaček. They were with Josef on that ferry to Harwich. In reality both were Communist Party officials – *Parteifunktionärin*; Temple warned Josef, 'They are indoctrinated NKVD agents, trained and highly dangerous, stay well clear.'

By way of contrast is Karl Czernetz. Calls himself Charles, but he uses numerous pseudonyms: including Constantine, Thomas and Fritz Valentin. A photographer from Vienna, but in the underground as a Revolutionary Socialist, and arrested several times in Vienna. Now he's a politician and editor, part of the London Bureau of Austrian Socialists with Oscar Pollak, who has even more pseudonyms and aliases: Austriacus, Paul O, Oscar Paul, Oscar Peter, and Alfred Zay; even, occasionally, if less exotically, 'Mr Smith.' Oscar works hand in glove with Johann Svitanics, so he's good friends with Josef. And I will never forget Hans Hirsch... he's the one who saved Josef's life by putting him on the first list of those needing to be got out of Prague.

This circuit of refugees is also awash with big names: George Weidenfeld, the writer and broadcaster. He never tires of telling how he escaped from Vienna to London in 1938 with just a 16/6d postal order in his pocket. There's Alexander Korda, the film producer and director, and Arthur Koestler, the writer. They all socialise with Billy Rootes.

Some find work with the BBC, some positively thrive on committees (poor fellows), others hint at influential connections in London's murky world of intelligence. But who's to know? Josef has warned me... 'if they hint at it it's probably not true; and if they talk about it, it's almost certainly not.'

And the organisations! They range from the Austrian League, a gullible handful of pro-Habsburg monarchists, a hopeless cause? Perhaps, although people say that Churchill warms to them. But paradoxically, who are the League's greatest supporters in these political games? The Communists – who despise them of course, but happily manipulate them for their own ends.

The Austrian Social Democrats, Josef's party, are far and away the largest numerically. They occupy the centre ground, and call themselves the London Bureau, and they're allied to Jan Svitanics's Group of Austrian Trade Unionists. Their greatest weakness? They still hanker after merger with Germany after the war ends, the socialist Germany that they dream will emerge from the wreckage.

The Communists – the CPGB plus its brood, which includes its newspaper *Zeitspiegel*, the Austrian Centre, Young Austria and the Free Austrian Movement – all are tightly knit, controlled, disciplined, rigidly following Moscow's *diktats*. They also controlled the Czech Refugee Trust Fund, until MI5 cleared them out. Communists use that seductive word, 'democratic', but not as we understand it: their openly declared aim for Germany and Austria is a 'People's Republic', *en route* to the 'dictatorship of the proletariat.' MI5 distrusts every one of them.

Not always easy to remember, in the buzz of a party!

Midday, Tuesday 6th June 1944, D Day

Mary: Sir William assembled us at mid-morning in the Directors Lounge to listen to the radio: 'This is the BBC Home Service and here is a special bulletin, read by John Snagge. "D" Day has come. Early this morning the Allies began the assault on the north-western face of Hitler's European Fortress. The first official news came just after half-past nine when Supreme Headquarters of the Allied Expeditionary Force issued Communiqué Number One. This said: "Under the Command of General Eisenhower, Allied Naval Forces supported by strong Air Forces began landing Allied Armies this morning on the Northern coast of France. ... The tide has turned. The free men of the world are marching together to victory.'

This evening Mother and I somehow, on wartime rations, managed a 2nd birthday party for Johanna.

13th June to 14th July

After two years of peace (ha!), a new terror has begun: V1's. Having endured the Blitz do we have to go through it all again?

'Our' first Doodlebug landed only 250 yards away. Two killed, three houses demolished, 20 severely damaged, 191 damaged; fortunately Linden Court was shielded by the hill, so it only cracked our windows. But we definitely live under their corridor. Penge looks like a continuous bomb site, while Anerley has had hundreds of homes damaged or destroyed. But our flats (and Crystal Palace's dinosaurs!) have escaped so far.

Yesterday I saw one of the dratted things myself, heard the motor cut out, then saw it stall, dive and explode in a column of dust and smoke. A minor blessing: it came down on the same place as a previous one, damaging already-damaged houses.

23rd July

Josef: A rumour spreads like wildfire: a bomb exploded at German field headquarters in Eastern Prussia, Hitler's Wolf's Lair, *Wolfsschanze*. The plotters thought he'd been killed so, in Berlin and Vienna, officials and Nazi leaders were rounded up and key points seized, but soon it came out, he'd survived. The Gestapo reacted ferociously and made their own mass arrests, amongst them, doubtless, some of my friends; I can't bear to think of what's happening to them. The only name in Vienna I've heard for certain is Graf von Marogna, no colleague of mine, of course, but even Counts and Colonels can be brave men.

24th October

Mary: Hurrah! At long last Josef's home on leave. We took Johanna out in her pram to Camberwell. He wanted to see my father's headstone there which, it turned out, had a few days ago been knocked over by a V1 exploding nearby. He noticed, next door to it, a headstone to a sailor with the Victoria Cross. 'Now that must be something, although I suspect that both now have better things to think about than medals and graves.' We both laughed, leaving Johanna sitting there in her pram, so very cute in her white bootees and a bow in her hair, looking puzzled. What she doesn't know is that tomorrow she's being evacuated to the safety – if that's the word for it – of Hull.

November

Section X has been 'promoted', renamed 'AD/X, the German Directorate' and greatly expanded.

10th January 1945

Mary: This evening Josef came home and told me something so astonishing that I found it - I still do, writing this - unbelievable. He was more tense than I had ever seen him, utterly furious, although not with me. He brooded for a while then just launched out, 'You English, you have no idea; in the heart of your secret service is a man who works for the Russians, *und doch sagt er, ich bin derjenige, der im Unrecht ist!'* Then he spoke in English, 'and yet he says I'm the one who is in the wrong!'

I didn't know what to say, so I started from where we were... 'Come on darling, sit down and tell me about it.'

His words came rushing out: 'Today I was in a corridor at, well, you know, Five's headquarters at Blenheim Palace with Mr Temple my contact when walking along it came that man, the one I told you that I'd seen in 1934 in the Vienna Woods, Philby, I knew he was a committed Communist he had to be he was taking orders from one of their senior officers NKVD OGPU or whatever they called themselves then but when I told Temple he ridiculed me. "But he's a Cambridge man, he wouldn't betray his country. Everyone in his service worships him, he's destined for the highest ranks in Six." Then he said, "You really don't understand this country, do you? It's not all plots and counter-plots, treachery and betrayal. This isn't middle Europe or Ruritania you know, old boy."

I interrupted him, 'NKVD, OGPU, I don't understand.'

'Cheka, OGPU, MGB, NKVD, they change their name every few years, soaked in their victims' blood. Soviet State Security.'

I was so confused, trying to calm him down, but it was an evening I shall always remember because, I suppose, for once, I did not believe Josef, or, perhaps 'believe in him' is closer to it. I now bitterly regret saying what came next... 'But Josef, darling, surely no Englishman would betray his country, to the Russians of all people...' He gave me such a look, and for the rest of the evening he wouldn't say a word.

Mid-January

.....

Richard: Anyway, this led him to resign from SOE, he wanted no more to do with British intelligence. Not that you can 'resign', of course. We never knew the full story but, somehow, he managed it without being court-martialled.

But what had he actually done in IRSB, or SOE as we now know it? There are heaps of files on Section X but only two things really have caught the public eye, Ops Periwig and Foxley. Periwig, an entirely fictional German resistance movement with expendable 'Bonzos', reads like something from a pantomime. It came to nothing.

Op Foxley, on the face of it, was altogether more robust: a plan to assassinate Hitler. Josef's 'initiation' into it had been one day in early 1944, finding old files piled high on his desk, with Major Thornley's laconic order, 'Read these, then speak to Mrs Holmes.'

The files, from mid-1941, pre-dated Foxley. They'd tapped into numerous sources: American intelligence, Czech resistance, the French, Poles, Haganah, Fleet Street's finest, academia, science, industry, even MI6 (unknowingly); all had contributed. They identified over thirty plans or attempts, using bombs, explosives, shooting, poisons, poison gas and air attacks; across Poland, France, the Ukraine, the Eastern Front, Austria and Germany; in *bierkellers*, on the streets, against his *Mercedes-Benz Größer 700K*, his personal Focke-Wulf 200 Condor, and his *Führersonderzug*, the Leader's Special Train; involving oh so many, from a madman, through a trainee priest, an SS guard, socialists, communists, Britain's military attaché in Berlin to the Wehrmacht's general staff. The common factor to all this? Hitler survived.

SOE's looked at plans that included bombing his train, poisoning its water supply, a sniper at Berchtesgaden, or a bazooka attack – there were even hints that Josef might be part of them – but they all came to nothing. Despite all his guard forces, personal guards and intelligence, it was Hitler's sheer unpredictability that usually saved him. Josef once told Mary how frustrating it had been. 'The man refused to do what was expected of him – Doctor Hora might have been his tutor – he'd show up unexpectedly; insist on taking a different route; make a twenty-minute speech in fifteen then stride off stage; he'd use his *Führerhauptquartier* cars, rarely Wehrmacht transport. Ambiguity seemed to be his rule: the Poles demolished railway tracks just before – as intelligence told them – his special train was due, only it never turned up; somehow he always missed bombs and bullets by the skin of his teeth.

By late 1944, however, SOE thought they'd assembled every detail about the man, his habits, his bodyguard and that 'legendary' train. In November Op Foxley – by now just a planned sniper attack at Berchtesgaden – was finalised. But what Foxley failed to notice was that, four months earlier, Hitler had left his

Berghof for the last time.

There was another thing Josef had been doing however. After the war Josef told Mary how he'd been involved in an operation using rare and valuable stamps to transfer large sums into occupied Europe to fund SOE's agents and networks. The idea doesn't appear in the many books on SOE or its agent's memoires. Diamonds, yes, Maria Theresa thalers, yes, stamps, no. The closest mention of it is about stamp forgeries being sewn inside jacket linings, or shirt collars.

The idea probably originated in the refugee community. The wealthiest lost everything, but some had managed to get their stamp collections past the border guards, transported openly, or sewn into their clothing. The Nazis were looking for jewellery, art and gold, not stamps.

In 1963, at school, I remember watching that very witty film, Charade, with Audrey Hepburn and Cary Grant. The plot turns on stamps - hidden in plain sight - used to convey a fortune. I'd love to know where Peter Stone and Marc Behm, its writers, got their idea from. It's a faint - if tantalizing - echo of what Josef talked about.

Stamps and wartime intelligence certainly crossed paths. Most famously in the Political Warfare Executive's forgeries used for black propaganda (selling which, post-war, made some dealers minor fortunes). Real stamps also had their uses. One SOE agent in Norway, Sven Sømme, posted his microdots of intelligence reports hidden under red Norwegian stamps, *Offentlik Sak 20 øre* - for anyone who's interested - as memorably shown on the BBC's Antiques Road Show.

Funding agents in occupied territories required huge funds, and smuggled diamonds, usually given as the method, have certain snags. They are very three-dimensional and, even when hidden in, as some politely put it, bodily cavities, they would be immediately spotted by X-Rays or, as the Gestapo and its ilk didn't hesitate to use, intimate and brutal searches.

Many materials were trialled before a compromise was found that did not rustle when hands ran over a courier's clothing yet protected the oh-so-flexible but very high value stamps from water. Rare stamps worth hundreds of pounds in 1944, tens of thousands today - an 1856 Austrian 'Red Mercury' newspaper stamp, for example - would have dropped to shillings if damaged by rain or sweat. Early starters, glassine and tissue paper, rustled. Mulberry silk and balloon silk - tightly woven muslin, not silk at all - were silent but, to be fully waterproofed, had been dipped in paraffin or grease, not ideal. Eventually SOE's 'workshops', at the Thatched Barn in Hertfordshire, found an answer, SOE's skilled seamstresses, dotted across Knightsbridge, did the rest.

Sourcing high value stamps was easy. Across wartime London (and wartime Europe, as it turned out) high grade stamp dealing – by nature, even in peace-time, a secretive profession, found ways to deal clandestinely with whoever wanted stamps. London's trade was a very international affair, with dealers from Czechoslovakia, Austria and Poland. Emanuel Katz, 'Mano' to everyone, who had fled to England from Czechoslovakia in 1938, was known to have links to SOE – post-war, his catalogue offered 'intelligence service stamps and forgeries' – others may have had similar links, such as Papa Beloom, Johnny the Pole, and Trager (dealer by day, croupier by night). Many operated from a building full of stamp dealers in William IV Street. It would not have been hard to source high value stamps. A key trick was to buy a stamp here, another there... never giving away the total value of any one operation.

Maybe the scheme was so successful it still continues...

Knowing so little about Josef's work in SOE from 43 to 45 is tantalizing. Did he travel into occupied Europe? That's not clear. There are hints (hints of hints, to be honest), that he made at least one journey into Ostmark, perhaps via Turkey, possibly from Spain. But, if so, whether that was to do with stamps or assassination planning we will probably never know. And, in 1950, after the family's visit to Großglockner, Josef said something odd: 'I might have gone there during the war', pointing to a road sign to Berchtesgaden. But then he clammed up. When I asked Mary about it, years later, all she said, with resignation in her voice, was 'Secrets!'

And that's about it.

.....

12th January

Josef: Colonel Kalla called me in, sat me down and offered me a whisky, something he'd never done before, probably intending to calm my nerves. Instead it set them jangling. What was coming?

'Now Josef, you've worked for me since 1938, on a path that has not always been straightforward. When you' – he paused and for a moment a faint smile transformed his face – 'ardently supported by your wife's powerful correspondence, tried from Canada to re-join our forces some deskbound lawyers – *právníci na stůl'*, he fairly spat the words out, 'argued that foreigners could not serve in our army. Just a year later, those very same obstructionists were refusing your application to leave it; lawyers! You wanted to be a front-line soldier, I made you serve as a cook. On my order you asked to join the parachute regiment, a request that was ignored. That, at least, was my doing, I did not want any involvement with special work, or intelligence, to appear on your Czech Army file, and that application helped 'muddy the waters', as the English say. And now, my advice to you is...' Once again he paused - there had been several pauses, he wasn't his usual vigorous, decisive self today - 'What I say now you must never repeat, never, do you understand.'

He was suddenly so solemn, intense, that I could only say, 'Yes sir, I understand, I will stay silent.'

'Your resignation from ISRB I do not properly understand, but it suits my purpose. I want, no, I need you out of our Army. When this war ends I fear for my country. It will not be liberated by our Western allies but by our Eastern "friends." President Beneš will prove a broken reed, the Red Army will crush him, plus any others who have experienced Western ideas of freedom and ideas of democracy. Few senior officers will survive the sickle of that terrible harvest on our return. The Reds will seize control long before American forces get near. And you...', he hesitated, then began again, as if on an entirely different matter, 'Every one of your Schutzbündler comrades who escaped in '34 to Moscow were despatched to the Russian gulags. Communists despise Social Democrats more than National Socialists. You, I, we will always be democrats, but the Reds and the Nazis eat from the same trough of oppression.' He paused, then, looking me in the face, began again, 'You would not survive. They will have access to all my department's records, just as the Gestapo have had. They would crush you in a moment.'

Again he paused, gathering himself. 'This is why I am telling you, young man, you must leave us before we reach our homeland, you must join the British Army.'

I am no great drinker, but I drained that glass. His order, framed as advice, came out of the blue, but I should have seen it coming.

24th January

Army Service Record, Bramminger, J J, Pte: SOS Free Czecho-Slovak Army. Enlisted British Army, Pioneer Corp. TOS Interpreters Pool, 21 Army Group, X (I) B) List. Promoted local Lance Corporal.

Josef: With unusual rapidity I was transferred out of the Czech army and into the British Pioneer Corps, posted to Brussels and promoted. But, come to think of it, I'd applied to join the Pioneer Corps in 1940, so a 4,500 mile journey, five years long, is perhaps not so rapid after all!

I'm an interpreter, on the strength of 21st Army Group, on the Brussels interpreter course in, billeted in private houses, near the Belgian Royal Observatory. The course is hopeless. We've learnt precious little about interpreting, although they did teach us to ride the motor-bikes that interpreters are issued with.

I've heard from Eberhard, hanging on in what's been renamed 220 (Austrian) Company, the only unit in the British Army with that honour. After they all went to St Leonards-on-Sea for Commando training Part 2 Orders asked for volunteers for special work. An officer turned up looking for people to join... well, they never said what exactly, 'special work' was the closest, everything being hush-hush, 'Top Secret.' Those who went were under strict orders to say nothing. But the destination on each travel warrant said everything. So, Spean Bridge = Achnacarry = the Commandos, just twelve miles from Inverlochy. Sheffield = Totley = the Parachute Regiment. A London ticket = ISRB. Some were posted to 253 Company PC, but Hans Kohn came back from that with a broken leg = it was another guise for ISRB. Several joined psychological warfare. One sergeant, August Warndorfer, commissioned into the Intelligence Corps, so probably = Six.

Eberhard knew all this, not from any secret paperwork, but those warrants had 'spilled the beans' confirming my theory that intelligence is rarely hush-hush, cloak-and-dagger; it's mainly joined-up thinking plus some plain hard slog.

5th February

After our course we interpreters, down in the tail of 21st Army Group HQ, suddenly received orders to move forward. We'd just been pulled off the road to let armour through when a harassed looking intelligence officer appeared with some POW's. 'Get what you can out of them. We need to know what's ahead, and fast!'

We've had no training in interrogation but this was too easy: a steaming mug of tea and they were ours. They were in shock, not battleshock, but overawed by what they'd seen behind our front line <u>after</u> surrendering. Their side roads, they told us, are empty by day, then, at night a few ramshackle lorries or carts creep out of hiding, well spaced out, terrified of air attack. Here we rule the skies and there's military traffic everywhere, day and night, new trucks in close convoy, soldiers full of confidence, well-fed, endless supplies. One wounded German gushed information: his unit, brigade, locations, equipment, weapons lost to air attack, ammunition shortages, low morale... out it came, no interrogation required. The trigger for this torrential betrayal? A Canadian doctor having casually torn a length of Elastoplast from a huge roll to replace his grubby bandages. 'Against such riches', he said, 'Hitler cannot win.'

19th April

BBC Home Service, Richard Dimbleby: 'I have just returned from the Belsen Concentration Camp, where for two hours I drove slowly about in a jeep with the chief doctor of 2nd Army. ...

I find it hard to describe adequately the horrible things that I have seen and heard, but here, unadorned, are the facts...'

Richard: He talked of seeing 40,000 men, women and children in the camp, many acutely ill or dying of virulent diseases and starvation. He, and those with him, were shocked beyond description. Likening some parts of Belsen to the plague pits of Medieval England he ended his broadcast saying: 'those officers and men who've seen these things, have gone back to the Second Army, moved to an anger such as I have never seen in them before.'

24th April

.....

Richard: Days after Belsen was liberated the establishment table for War Crimes Investigation Teams (WCIT's) was approved.

.....

1st May

Army Service Record, Bramminger, J J, Pte: Granted substantive rank, Lance Corporal.

2nd May

Josef: Hitler's dead. In Berlin. Heard an announcement last night on German radio, but it was a day or two ago that he killed himself.

7th May

The Germans have agreed to Allied demands for unconditional surrender. Tomorrow will be 'Victory in Europe' Day, marking the end of the European war.

Interpreters are being posted to brand new units: T Force, BIOS, CIOS, EPES or FIA(T); all ferreting out secrets, scientific and others; one SAS unit looking for its soldiers who disappeared in enemy territory is so secret it hasn't yet got a name; there are three WCIT's, and Eberhard's joining the International Military Tribunal at Nuremberg. I'm posted to AMGOT, governing Schleswig-Holstein and they've given me that stripe; so, a celebratory schnapps, a letter home and then to bed.

217 Mil Gov Det war diary: Det established as Landkreis Rendsburg in Hotel zum Prinzen, Schloss Platz. Assumed MILGOV responsibility.

Josef: In 1933 Hitler said, 'Give me ten years and you will not recognize Germany.' He's achieved that. Germans call this *Stunde Null* - zero hour, and we rule over a wasteland, like an ants nest we've kicked over. Homeless people scratching around in the ruins, Nazi officials and former soldiers on the run, pitiful refugees and children trailing along on foot, desperate for food, medical treatment and shelter. Normal life has ceased. Little food, doubtful water, no post, no telephones, few shops, banks or offices, no bars, no schools, few policemen - and even those we find hard to trust - the roads are empty except for army vehicles and the occasional doctor's car.

8th May, VE Day

Mary: What a day! Hurrah! Praise the Lord but, please don't pass any more ammunition. Trafalgar Square, The Mall, the Parks, full of endless crowds, joyful, jubilant, civilians, uniforms of every colour, girls kissing soldiers, GI's yelling their heads off and hugging any girl who was handy. I dragged Mother and Hanni up to London, and we were part of that crowd in front of the Palace, by the fountain of the Victoria Memorial.

We cheered ourselves hoarse, every church bell I've ever heard was ringing, people were shinning up lampposts, bus shelters, anything that could be climbed on was. At the Palace everybody called and called, 'We want the King, we want the King' and out they came, the King and Queen were on the balcony, how we cheered! Winnie joined them, we cheered again! It was deafening. Then it was dancing - the only time I've ever gone dancing in the street - but it turned out to be so easy... people shuffled into concentric circles and started a conga, dancing away in opposite directions, well into the night. People say even the two Princesses were in the crowds.

9th May

Josef: Yesterday we paraded on Schlossplatz to hear Churchill proclaim on radio the end of war in Europe. We had the rest of the day off and built a huge bonfire to sit around drinking all the beer, schnapps and wine we could find in the hotel. Hostilities ceased at 23:01 hrs. It hasn't sunk in yet.

Apparently, the surrender was signed by Admiral Dönitz, President of what's left of Germany, the so-called Flensburg Government, 50 miles north on the Danish border. Intelligence thinks many of the most dangerous Nazis are hiding in the area, disguised as ordinary members of the Wehrmacht. At last, real work for us to do.

10th May

War diary: RENDSBURG. Town formally occupied – first British troops entered on the 6th and large American columns passed through heading north.

Sitrep: 20,000 live here but 50% of homes are in ruins. Issues: feeding and housing locals and refugees from the East.

Legal: Summary Courts held. 23 cases involving murder, unlawful possession of weapons, false documents. Sackloads of letters from German civilians accusing neighbours of war crimes.

Medical: Lice and scabies, typhus, scarlet fever, diphtheria, mainly brought in by refugees and ex-Wehrmacht; diminishing but still at high levels. Shortage of bandages and gypsum, many fractures cannot be plastered.

Josef: All the while, I've noticed, another world is being created, highly organised and busy. Like a bee hive, but with stings that can be fatal, the secret world re-creating itself. British, American, Soviet, French even, in all their manifestations, MI5, MI6, ISRB, NKGB, OSS, Deuxième Bureau, and more besides, you name them, they're here, plus four countries' military intelligence. Missions, establishments and units no-one's ever heard of. All liberally spending money, recruiting agents, establishing influence, which, by the way, means finding out people's dirty secrets and keeping them on file; in civvy street you'd call it blackmail!

23rd May

At last, British armour and infantry have entered Flensburg, those last six square miles controlled by Dönitz's comic opera government. Intelligence told us that SS and Nazis on the run were camped out in Flensburg's police headquarters and Himmler and von Ribbentrop were in the town. In fact they, at least, had fled south to the Alps, but our Field Security Section did arrest Hinrich Lohse, Schleswig-Holstein's last Gauleiter, before he escaped to South America by U-boat. But today we caught some much bigger fish...

At 1000 hrs tanks, Bren-gun carriers and lorried infantry of the Herefordshires and the 15th/18th Hussars moved in on Flensburg Bay's submarine base. The German High Command staff were lined up against the walls, hands on heads, under our men's Sten guns. The high-ranking officers had slept late and many were in their underclothes, 'without the moral support of their trousers', as someone put it. We've hauled off the secret documents, wireless sets and personal belongings of 310 officers, including Grand Admiral Dönitz, Admiral von Friedeburg, Generaloberst Jodl and Dr Speer.

We'd arrested them, stripped them, searched them for concealed poisons - or most of them. Friedeburg swallowed a cyanide pill on a visit to the toilet - and we were beginning to process them as POW's when I heard a voice behind me...

'Grüß Gott, Herr Bramminger, we meet again.'

I looked round. As 'McKenzie-Smith', he'd watched our Harwich arrival and interviewed me in Room 55 at the War Office, now he was in a Brigadier's uniform. He asked, 'What are you doing here? AMGOT? Interpreter?'

'Yes sir.'

'Happy in your work?' Noting my momentary hesitation he carried on, 'Anything I can do to help?'

A dozen answers danced inside my head, but all I could say was, 'Well, sir, I'd rather be hunting them down, that's what I'd do best, war crimes work...'

'I'll see what I can do. Now, I've been meaning to tell you this...', he said, 'the day before the Ettrick sailed from Liverpool, I signed a note ordering the Home Office to keep you in the UK. A day too late and it took five months to get Paterson out there to put things right. It will take some time to get you out of this, but more likely five weeks than months.'

'My name's White by the way, D G White, people call me Dick White.'

His attention flicked across the room to where our prisoners stood in haughty silence, awaiting despatch to our interrogation facilities, Dönitz to the well-named Camp Ashcan, Speer to Dustbin.

Tonight, back in Rendsburg, I fell asleep wondering what Dick White meant. Will he really do something? I can only wait and see.

28th May

Max-Otto Richter breezed into our office. He'd sailed with me as an enemy alien in the Ettrick and the Thysville, where no-one believed a word he said, he told the tallest tales of anyone on board. Now he has a cover name, Captain Lynton, and is running a hush-hush interrogation outfit up on the Baltic coast. He recognized me immediately. 'Peppi', he roared, 'I was thinking about you yesterday', and, for once, he was telling the truth... 'a filing cabinet in a bombed-out Gestapo building contained a black list with your name on it.' He passed over the file he was carrying. I'd often wondered what my Gestapo record said and here it was, 'BRAMMINGER, Josef J, born Vienna. High treason. Passed secrets to a foreign power. Fled the Reich.' Had they ever caught me those words would have meant instant execution.

30th May

At last, some hidden hand has been pulling strings. I'm being promoted and transferred to War Crimes, HQ British Army of the Rhine. The Movement Order reads: 'IMMEDIATE. Army Form W-4049. Bramminger, J J, Cpl, to move forthwith to 1 WCIT, Bergen-Belsen.'

I've been thinking about that name of his, Dick White. I asked around, it really is the name he was christened with, his father having a liking for rather feeble jokes. But lucky him, it's something Sergeant-Major Čeněk would have relished: how many pointless hours must Gestapo and KGB minions have spent searching through directories for a non-existent R G White? It's a bit like hiding a book in a library, hiding in plain sight.

Richard: Over the next two years Josef recorded less than usual. His diary entries were intermittent, in a private shorthand that's difficult to decipher at the best of times, a mixture of English and German, laced with Wienerisch. Letters home sometimes provide a clue, but while they tell of his longing to be with Mary and Johanna, about the work itself they're reticent, secretive even. Combining those with what's now in the public record, weaving in the occasional overheard conversation, produces an intermittent, somewhat unsatisfactory sequence, like reading a whodunit where some of the pages are missing. I sometimes wonder if, in the 'missing' pages, something else was going on.

1st June

Josef: We're short-handed: half the officers against establishment; interpreters and clerks borrowed from other units. The pathologist, photographer and two gravediggers are the hardest worked of all of us.

8th June

1 WCIT, Witness Statement: My name is Leon Goldschmidt. On 8 Jun 1945 I went to the Belsen Detention Cells with Captain N Newark, 1 WCIT. There I identified a man whom I knew as ISAAK KÖHN.

I lived in the same Block No 107 as KÖHN at Belsen. He was Capo of the sleeping quarters, extremely brutal in his treatment of Jewish prisoners. I have seen him beating sick and half-starved prisoners with the buckle part of his belt or a wooden board taken from the bed itself. These beatings were so severe that they must have caused numerous deaths.

Before and after morning Appel he would go round the sleeping quarters and beat the sick people who were lying in their bunks unable to get up. He would drag them to the floor and continue to beat them. I often saw them left unconscious on the floor. The hut orderlies would pick up the victims and, if still living, put them back into their bunks or, if dead, remove their bodies.

I particularly remember the case of Rabbi WEIS. One evening in Mar 1945 I heard terrible screams from the washroom. I went there and saw 'ISAAK' savagely kicking him. On seeing me the Rabbi began to say a prayer but collapsed under the blows. 'ISAAK' saw me and shouted, 'Do you want to die the same way?' I ran away as fast as I could. Next morning I saw the body of Rabbi WEIS being carried from the washroom and thrown into the box of the dead.

Signed: L Goldschmidt

Interpreter: I certify that I have translated this summary to the witness in the German language. Signed: J Bramminger, Sgt PC, Interpreter.

Sworn before me at Belsen Camp this 9th day of June 1945. N Newark, Captain RA, Investigating Officer.

Detailed to examine the above by: Lieut-Colonel L J Genn, RA, CO 1 WCIT, BAOR.

21st June

Mary: I'm so worried, Josef hasn't written for three weeks, so unlike him. Agnes told me, from Eberhard, that he's at that grim place called Belsen. I cannot imagine what he's going through, let alone those poor people. I just wish he could share his burden with me.

22nd June

1 WCIT: Atrocities committed at Bergen-Belsen. Interim Report issued.

15th July

Josef: The Team's finished here at Belsen. Most of us are moving out to hunt down war criminals, someone will have to deal with the mess left behind. At long last I can sit down with my diary and a clear head; well, clear'ish. It's beyond me to properly describe this hell on earth. Things were utterly foul when I arrived but they must have been unspeakably worse for those who first discovered it, before we buried the bodies and flamethrowers torched the huts. As for those who lived - although that's the wrong word - through it it's beyond description. Six months in internment drove me close to the brink of insanity, but this... this is worse than anyone's foulest nightmares, many times worse.

Day after day I sat in those bare cells, interpreting as we interrogated suspects and took statements from witnesses, stories of such evil. The Team took over a former Panzer barracks near the concentration camp, but that terrible haze hung everywhere, a smell I shall never forget. It's been the worst time of my life.

I thank God for the Field Ambulances. They really got down to it, reinforced by medical students from London. What happened in this place has shaken my faith, in God, yes, but more so in Man. Without those medics and nurses I would have lost it altogether.

11th Armoured erected a sign at the gates, in English and German, telling the bare facts...

THE SITE OF THE INFAMOUS BELSEN CONCENTRATION CAMP
LIBERATED BY THE BRITISH ON 15 APRIL 1945.
10,000 UNBURIED DEAD WERE FOUND HERE. ANOTHER 13,000 HAVE SINCE DIED.
ALL OF THEM VICTIMS OF THE GERMAN NEW ORDER IN EUROPE, AN EXAMPLE OF NAZI KULTUR.

21st November

At last, we're out of those cramped, oppressive offices in Belsen. I feel cleaner. Now we have free rein across the Allied Zones, with many suspects to hunt down.

Someone gave me a tip, 'You Nazi-hunters often operate in civvies. Get yourself a locally-tailored jacket and trousers, then get Jacobsen's, that local studio, to take photos of you wearing them. You don't want your mug-shot in your civilian ID looking as if it's been taken by an Army photographer.' So I borrowed a suitably Germanic suit and Herr Jacobsen, loudly claiming he had no negatives, no chemicals, no paper, immediately found some when cigarettes were offered.

They sent me on a course. Flown across the North Sea by night to an airfield, by car to a country house in Wiltshire. I never discovered its name, all road signs had been removed and we weren't allowed out of the grounds, no phone calls, nothing. It reminded me of seven years ago, that estate at Liberec, outside Prague. The training was just as rigorous, but here I slept in the house, not the stables. A sergeant trained me on the Army-issue Rolleiflex, a captain taught me the legal niceties of investigations and how to interrogate: best done at night, use a table lamp, never a ceiling light, watch the suspect's face for changes in expression. 'Remember Pavlov's rule', he said, 'not his dogs, his second rule: "an unusual experience creates in a man the need to talk about it." The man in front of you has a compulsion to let something out. You're just pulling the plug.'

Eleven days training, no notes, everything had to be remembered. My memory didn't fail me.

Then back on an aircraft, again at night, over the Channel to Hamburg, on to our new base at Neuengamme. Straight back to work.

And it's hard work. Long hours, travelling all over the British Zone, sometimes driving a jeep with Captain Newark or, better, the Wolseley staff car. Occasionally we have a result, like the three Volkssturm who'd murdered two pilots near Osnabrück. It was very satisfying, eventually, to get them to court...

1 WCIT: 21 Nov 1945. CONFIDENTIAL. BAOR/42711/218/A(PS4).

To: HQ 30 Corps District.

<u>Karl HOFFMANN, Friedrich KOPP, Otto SCHAUBECK</u>.

1. The above-named German nationals, Volkssturm members, are alleged to have been concerned in the murder of two unknown Allied pilots.

2. They will be tried jointly by Military Court under the Royal Warrant (Army Order 81/45) charged with:

COMMITTING A WAR CRIME

in that they

at LENGERICH, Germany, on 24 December, 1944, in violation of the laws and usages of war were concerned in the killing of two unknown Allied pilots, prisoners of war.

3. The following witnesses should be called:

(a) Ferdinand BACHMANN, farmer, LENGERICH, re the apprehension of the pilots.

(b) Otakar TRAUTMANN, formerly police serjeant, Internment Camp ESTERWEGEN. Links the taking of the pilots from BACHMANN and their being handed over to the first accused.
(c) Capt N Newark, RA, 1 WCIT, to produce the accused's statements and give evidence as to how they were obtained.
(d) Sjt J Bramminger, Interpreters Pool, 1 WCIT, present as interpreter at the taking of statements.

4. As it is believed that the victims were RAF pilots, although this does not appear from the evidence, one member of the court should be an RAF officer.

D R S Harris
for Major General, Chief of Staff
HQ BAOR

Josef: It sounds so simple, but we had to drive 190 miles to Lengerich in the Teutoburg Forest, Captain Newark and I armed with War Crimes passes that give us carte blanche to demand assistance from Army and police, a bible, arrest reports, unit stamp, my Rollei, paper and carbon plus, always, our Browning pistols.

It started with a German civilian reporting the murder of two downed Allied pilots on Christmas Eve, probably just another malicious report, a personal vendetta perhaps - so many were - but we had to follow it up.

We booked into Lengerich's Field Security Section then visited the local police station to commandeer some of its men and check its records. Sure enough - Germans record everything meticulously, they can't help themselves - their 1944 day-book for *Heilige Abend* - Christmas Eve, recorded two interments in the cemetery. That's where we found them, two graves, side by side, numbers 18 and 19, Row J. No names, just 'Englischer Flieger', on plain wooden crosses. We photographed them and signalled Neuengamme: we needed the pathologist and his gravediggers.

Next, we traced the crash site and interrogated Bachmann, the local farmer who'd cornered the two pilots near their wrecked Typhoons. Then we drove to Esterwegen, the internment camp near the Dutch border, to interview Trautmann, the police sergeant who'd taken them from Bachmann and handed them to the local Volkssturm leader, Karl Hoffmann. 'He took them away, about six o'clock, he and his sidekicks, Schaubeck and Kopp. You'll find his signature at the station. I saw nothing after that. It was Schaubeck who came in the next morning to tell us the ashes were in the cemetery.'

I wanted to ask more, but the Captain said to come away. 'He's probably telling the truth, or most of it, and, anyway...' I remember him gesturing at the barbed wire and the sentries, 'he's not going anywhere.'

Next day the Lengerich policemen rounded up the two subordinates in separate raids, holding them – at the Captain's insistence – in different parts of the station. That evening I visited our informant, an elderly lady in a first-floor flat directly opposite the Nazi party headquarters. I changed into civvies; we'd decided there was no need to draw attention to her.

I was astonished, not at her story but why she'd volunteered it. This was no malicious tale-bearing, no bargaining for tins of bullied beef or packets of cigarettes, she was telling what she'd seen that Christmas Eve, she insisted, because a wrong needed righting.

From her window she'd seen three men arrive in Hoffmann's car shortly after six – she knew him by sight, he'd been a prominent Nazi official in the town – two pilots were pulled out, and all five went inside. Soon afterwards the lights went on in the first-floor office – Hoffmann's office – and she'd seen shadows on the blinds. She'd heard shouts and screams, then four shots. Hoffmann and his car only left much later that evening, after the blackout.

We interrogated Kopp and Schaubeck separately, neither knew we were holding the other – the British secret service has a formidable reputation here for omniscience and omnipotence, and people think we're part of it. In reality we're more about slogging through street directories and telephone books than cloak-and-dagger, but if the reputation helps, so be it. A few hours standing in front of us, through the night, the only illumination the lamp on Captain Newark's desk – I'd remembered that lesson – and they told us all we needed. Their two stories largely tallied about what had happened that night. But neither of them knew where Hoffmann was now, or so they claimed.

All three were in the party headquarters that afternoon, wishing each other merry Christmas over schnapps. The air-raid sirens went off and the police telephoned through reports of two aircraft brought down by flak. Hoffman drove to the police station, demanding custody of the pilots. They took them to the party headquarters and up to Hoffmann's office. He started screaming at the two men, hitting them in the face with his pistol, screaming at them in the foulest language. Soon he was kicking them in the lower parts of their bodies, screaming, '*Ich hacke dir in die Eier, Sie Englisch Schweinehunde.*' Then, without warning – this was their story – he took his pistol out and shot first one then the other in the head, two shots each. They claimed they were shocked, and quite incapable of preventing Hoffmann. He was their senior, after all, and he was the one brandishing the pistol.

We visited a woman living near Lengerich, the wife of another senior Nazi official. He was in a POW camp, although we had no evidence against him other than his party membership. I asked her if she knew Herr Hoffmann. 'Of course I do, and his wife', she said, smugly.

'His address?'

'He went into hiding', she replied. 'taking the Party funds with him.'

'And his address?'

'I do not know it', she claimed, but I detected a slight hesitation.

We waited two days before visiting her again, now offering her husband's release if she told us the address. After tears and protestations she gave way, 'I am a traitor, but for my husband's sake...', and gave us the address. We were elated.

That evening we parked up in jeeps two streets away from the address while the police visited houses in the neighbourhood, their story 'Checking for spare accommodation for the council.' They hurried back to us. They'd recognised Hoffmann from a photo, calling himself Franz Simon. They drew us a sketch of the house and its interior.

At three in the morning we struck, hammering on the door, but actually entering through a window we smashed with an axe round the back. A woman, his wife, was yelling, he was struggling out of bed, screaming in terror on seeing us. We rammed a torch into his mouth to prevent him biting down on any cyanide pill, then arrested and handcuffed him. As we led him to our car neighbours' lights were coming on and people were shouting, 'Polizei! Polizei!' When they saw our uniforms they slunk indoors.

It took two days before he talked but, from that moment, he wouldn't stop. Cringing and grovelling, he positively fawned on us, it was really embarrassing.

13th December

The Belsen accused are sentenced. 12 to death, 18 jailed, 14 acquitted, one found incapable of standing trial.

1st January 1946

'Happy New Year', '*Guten Rutsch*', '*Frohes neues Jahr*', '*Shaná tová*', '*Bonne année*'... we greeted one another like a mini-United Nations, in English, Wienerisch, German, Hebrew and French.

The best I can manage is a letter to Mary, another to Hanni, a drink in the Mess and off to bed.

Lying there I looked back over ten years' Silvesters: 1936, at home in Favoriten – hello! That's the first time I've used that word about Vienna in ten years. 1937, in Korneuburg's barracks. Then Brixton; Birchington; mid-Atlantic; twice at home in Brixton. 42, at Harwich in the Czech brigade. 43, 44 and 45, home again, in Anerley; and now, 1946, in occupied Germany, three ranks up, a real job to do. Couldn't be happier, except if I were at home with you, Mary. I miss you so.

The London Gazette: State Intelligence. Central Chancery of the Orders of Knighthood. St James's Palace, London SW1. The King has been graciously pleased to give orders for the following appointment to the Most Excellent Order of the British Empire, to be an Officer of the Civil Division: Harold Adrian Russell Philby, employed in a Department of the Foreign Office.

2nd March

Josef: A letter from home. With Mary's love, and two photos: the cosy sitting room in Linden Court, and Johanna, 3½, looking adorable.

8th March

Today Captain Newman announced, 'Remember the Lengerich trial? Yesterday all three were hanged at Hamelin.'

I was promoted to sergeant months ago but now I'm to wear a Staff Sergeant's crown. I'm still on the strength of the Interpreters Pool, but all three War Crime Teams are now grouped with HQ BAOR in Bad Oeynhausen.

8th July

Colonel Nightingale sent Captain Newark and me into the Soviet zone, after a suspected war criminal. 'It won't be easy', he said, 'The Russians still won't let us into Sachenhausen camp, so try your luck at Heckler's birthplace.'

We were amazed when the Russian Mission issued a permit. 'Maybe I wronged them', Captain Newark muttered to me, as he thumbed through it. 'No! My prejudices are right. Look...', pointing at a large red rubber stamp on the back, "**SPEAKS RUSSIAN – ГОВОРИТ ПО РУССКИ.**" They take no chances. That'll have the NKGD taking an interest in me.'

'Well sir, as long as it's you, not me', I said.

He grinned, 'Have you something to hide, Staff?'

'Not that I know of.'

In the Wolseley we crossed into the Russian zone at Lüttow-Valluhn. A grubby red flag flew over a striped barrier pole. Two soldiers clutching rusty Shpagin machine-pistols glared at us. They were the first Russians I'd seen close up. Captain Newark proffered a cigarette. They glanced over their shoulders at the guard hut then shook their heads... an SNCO was standing in the doorway. They inspected our permit. At an almost imperceptible nod from the sergeant the barrier went up and we were waved through.

At Neubrandenburg we asked a civilian the way. He looked terrified. On a street teeming with Russian soldiers he didn't want to be seen talking to us, so obviously British.

We needn't have asked, the Commandatura's massive red flag was visible across the city. We were escorted to an outer office where officers sprawled in armchairs, smoking and bantering amongst themselves. The relaxed atmosphere prevailed even when their commandant walked in. The Russians addressed him as 'Comrade Colonel', to us – strict Pool of Interpreters rules apply! – he was 'Mr Colonel.' Grinning broadly and ignoring our salutes, he thrust out his hand, exclaiming, '*товарищи–Tovarisches*–Comrades!' then led us through to his office and sat us down in more armchairs.

Soon, in German, we were chatting away about his home in Moscow and his family. He showed us a photograph of his wife and children, Captain Newark made some comment in Russian. I saw fear flicker across the Colonel's face. He shouted in Russian, a captain marched in, saluted, and sat down behind us. The Colonel did not introduce him. I followed Newark's eyes to the man's cap. It carried the red band of the NKVD.

That night we stayed in an official guest house, eating and drinking with the colonel, ploughing through many toasts, cognac, vodka, and more vodka. The un-named captain sat with us throughout, listening, not drinking, not saying a word. The other officers simply ignored him.

Next day Captain Newark tested his theory. 'Staff, go down to the *Rathaus*, look up the municipal registers. Then I'll do the same. Let's see if they're interested in both of us.'

So, after breakfast, off I went, walking... no sign of a shadow. On my return Newark set off. A Gaz-67 immediately pulled out from a side turning and crawled after him. In the town hall, he told me, as he asked at the counter for more registers a man in an ill-fitting civilian suit hovered beside him. A Russian-speaking British officer clearly warranted their attention, I didn't.

We accomplished nothing, there was no trace of Heckler. So we set off for home, shadowed all the way, and happy to regain the British Zone.

At headquarters I saw Eberhard, he had a few days local leave following the Nuremberg trials. I was describing my trip into the Russian Zone when he gave me a funny look and said, 'You know the real reason they wouldn't let you visit Sachenhausen? They've filled it with Polish civilians. They can't afford for us to see what's going on there.'

2nd August

Now I'm in Haystack, WCIT's search section, at 24 Lettowvorbeckstraße, or 'Haystack House.' Our task... SEARCH - ARREST - INTERROGATE - PROSECUTE. We're all highly motivated Nazi hunters, but there's one I envy, Captain Walter Freud, Sigmund's grandson. He was one of the few in Section X that ISRB managed to get into Austria, and one of the very few to come out alive.

Former members of the SS make our job easy. They all had blood groups tattooed on their underarm. Many, after capture, burned it with a cigarette, very painful, but rather obvious. Tattoo or scar, you know what you've got.

To not give away our identity we always talk to the Germans with a British accent.

3rd to 10th August

Mary: Josef, home on leave. Daily we discuss what he'll do after demobilization. I got him to see Jim and Nancy about the prospects for stamp dealing, then he went up to Piccadilly to visit the stamp fair in the Panama Club.

Josef: Mary and Johanna saw me off from Penge West, both having made a real effort to dress up for me: Mary really stylish, Hanni looking so *süß,* so sweet. Mary asked why I was wearing medal ribbons but no rank or shoulder-flashes on my army greatcoat. I can't recall what I said... I daren't tell her it was Standing Orders – after intelligence discovered the so-called German 'resistance' had issued 'death sentences' on WCIT personnel.

15th March 1947

In the headquarters I saw DW in the corridor.

'A word with you, Staff', he said. The next thing I was in an office in the Control

Commission building, the door firmly closed.

'Glad to see progress', he said, glancing at the rank on my arm, 'but to business, Josef. Do you recall our first meeting, in the War Office, back in 39?' I nodded. 'You asked how the Communists had packed the Prague escape line with their people. A good question. Kalla tells me you're as wary of them now as then. Is that right?'

'In 1934 I thought them as dangerous as the Nazis, yes sir. My view hasn't changed, although most people remain blind to the danger.'

'Yes, but things are changing. Churchill talked of an "Iron Curtain"; that fellow Orwell writes of Russia waging "Cold War"; and the Americans have launched their Truman Doctrine to contain the Soviet threat. People may have been blind, but eyes are starting to open.'

He talked on, urgently and fluently, of Stalin's power, based on terror, liquidation, and the threat of Siberia, about how the GRU, his military intelligence, is bigger and more dangerous to us even than the MGB, and about Five's work to frustrate them.

'Kalla also mentioned that back in 42 you applied to serve in British intelligence, so I know that you are interested, or were then, at least.'

'I'm saying this because there could be a job for you, with Five. It could be back in London - where I'm working again - or out here, an accompanied posting with wife and daughter, a cover job, officer's rank, that sort of thing. War Crimes work is coming to an end, your demob's due next month... give it some thought is all I ask.'

2nd April

A fortnight later, in the Sergeants' Mess, someone I vaguely knew from CCG bought me a beer and started chatting. Eventually he asked, oh so casually, 'Mr White wondered, have you thought about what you discussed?'

I had. Ten years in uniform - four different uniforms (six, including Schutzbund grey and Canada's 'blue and red'), are enough for me - I'm ready for home. Mary and Hanni fill my thoughts. Them and stamps, the prospect of earning my living excites me. This job needs doing and I'm fortunately good at it, and demob will be a wrench... these last few days have been filled with handover and farewell parties. But I told him, 'Thank him, but please tell him I want to try my hand at selling stamps, and living the quiet life.'

'I'll pass that on. He'll probably say, "That's fine, but if, from time to time, something comes up where you might lend a hand, we'll be in touch."'

'*Danke*', I replied.

Mary: '27 April, I'll be home', Josef writes. Something to cheer about, after three months of the hardest winter ever, snow blizzards, frozen pipes, bitter, bitter cold, little fuel, Johanna and I sleep under heaps of blankets and coats. It's beginning to thaw, but, for five hours every day we still have no electricity.

26th April

Josef: The train to Cuxhaven was jammed with men, demob happy, yes, but that rubber stamp: '**EMBARKED NW Europe**', left us uncommonly quiet.

27th April

Ferry to Hull. Train to 6 Disembarkation Unit, Bedford. Walked - walked, not marched - to a bored looking clerk, who handed me documents, intoning, 'AB-64, AFB-122, AFB-200B, AFH-1157, and AFW-3149 - Pay Book, Conduct Sheet, Statement of Service, Clothing Record, Medical Examination. Sign here...'

... one signature I happily gave, but the Army Form I really wanted was AFX-801, my Soldier's Release Book. Had he produced it with a flourish I'd have applauded but no, he just muttered, 'Next!'

My thoughts wandered, to a quayside at Esbjerg, queuing at a race course, more quaysides: Liverpool, Quebec, Monteith's midnight hut; quaysides again, Halifax and Liverpool. Daily parades, variously hopeful, shambolic, callous, humiliating, tedious. Like this, tedious, but, for once, efficient, and at the end of it...

'Take a seat, Serjeant Bramminger', my reverie was over. 'Ignore most of that bumpf', said the major sitting in front of me. 'But read the AFB-200, your Statement of Service...'

I opened it: 'Army No: 137999815, Josef Johann BRAMMINGER, Serjeant, local Staff-Serjeant...' blah, blah, blah... but the final section was music to my ears: '27 Apr 1945 proceed on Release Leave. Permanent Address: 11 Linden Court, Anerley Road, London SE 20.

Testimonial: Employed with the Control Commission of Germany. Has carried out his work conscientiously. Can be relied on to do his work well without supervision.

Military Conduct: Exemplary.'

I was astonished. How come? 'But, Sir, it says 'Military Conduct, "Exemplary."

I don't know much about military paperwork but why "Exemplary", the highest grade? I thought I'd committed enough offences to be at best "Very Good"?'

The officer looked up in surprise. 'Good question, Sarn't Bramminger. Let's take a look.' He thumbed through the document and spotted an obscure green rubber stamp on the inside cover, 'It looks as if someone's put in a good word for you. An external agency, one we don't talk about, d'yer see?' he asked, looking me straight in the eye.

It dawned on me what he was saying. Someone in Five had 'had a word.' That was something. 'Yes sir. Thank you very much, Sir!' I stood, saluted, turned on my heel and marched out of the room.

Then a warehouse for an ill-fitting suit – a grey pinstripe – raincoat, shoes, shirts, a tie, topped off with a trilby. Another clerk, the railway warrant to London. It was that simple, walk out the far door and I'd be out of the army.

This evening, as I rang the door bell a home-coming six years ago came to mind. Then I'd surprised her, now I was fully expected; then I'd been warmly welcomed by Mary, with Dorothy muttering darkly in the background. This time there was Johanna, grinning from ear to ear.

28th April

Mary: Today's my 30th birthday, and he – my very own Mr Memory – hadn't forgotten. There were presents for me, including the loveliest silver coffee spoons with red garnets from Robbe & Berking of Flensburg – any woman would adore them – and presents for Hanni. Not that <u>they</u> were needed. With Daddy back from the wars she's been in seventh heaven all day long.

But I had a surprise for him. 'Sweetheart', I said, 'I have a treat for us. A wonderful musical opened at the Adelphi on Saturday, *Bless the Bride*. Queen Mary was at the opening night, so was Sir Winston, it's an absolute hit and I've booked two seats for us tonight.'

I'm so excited. All round the flat I've been singing the two songs I've heard on the radio:

In September when the grapes are purple
Marguerite pick the grapes with me
There are silver bells upon her fingers
All the little boys come out to see

Ma belle Marguerite
So beautiful to see

Les mains de ma petite
Marguerite pick the grapes with me.
Ting -a-ling- a-ling- a-ling- a-ling- a-ling-a-ling-ay,
Ting -a-ling- a-ling- a-ling- a-ling- a-ling-a-ling-ay.
Ting -a-ling- a-ling- a-ling- a-ling- a-ling-a-ling-ay,
Ting -a-ling- a-ling- a-ling- a-ling- a-ling-a-ling-ay.

... and my absolute favourite,

This is my lovely day
This is the day I shall remember the day I'm dying
They can't take this away
It will be always mine, the sun and the wine
The sea birds crying
All happiness must pay
And if our ship goes down
She'll go with the flag still flying

Now look at me and say
You will remember too
That this is our lovely day

29th April

They sounded even better in the Art-deco glory of the Adelphi!

Going home on the upper deck of the No 12 I began to tease him, singing, '*This man could never be a spy*', which made him try to hush me up. Then I was on to the second line and wasn't going to stop. Looking around he realised we were alone, so he turned and kissed me instead.

I looked at him and said, 'Mister Bramminger! The things you do to keep a secret! Did they teach you that in Prague?'

Josef: When a girl sings,

'I was never kissed before,
so kiss me once again.'

... what is a man to do?

May to December

Richard: In 2003 I met a stamp dealer and his wife who remembered Joe Bramminger very well. 'We met when I was in my teens, buying and selling to each other. I'd see him at Freddie Beach's Fair, a dealers' fair, on Saturday afternoons at the Panama Club, near Piccadilly Circus. We all went, it was the only one in London, with all these refugees from Europe who'd come over before the war. There were 20 dealers' tables or so.'

'When I knew him, I was in my teens and to me he was an old man - in his thirties - but as I say I used to talk to Joe a lot, he was always Joe, just Joe. I also went to his shop in London Wall.'

'He told me the best percentage of water to put in sausages - he only made best quality sausages himself. The profits in sausages is all about the amount of water you put in, to make it heavier, and also the bread. The more water, the higher the profit!'

Remembering that, he laughed!

'Joe was a very outgoing sort of chap', he said, 'fully conversant in English, with very little accent, if I remember rightly. I recall conversing with him in German, in my *Schule Deutsche*, and in French.'

'Many stamp dealers were émigrés. I knew a lot of them, very intelligent, professional men who'd been wealthy back in their own countries but had lost everything. The only thing that saved them was their stamps.'

16th August

Mary: Josef told me, 'Darling, I thought we might go and see a film in Piccadilly, *The Arlberg Express*. It's about Vienna, stolen jewels and a train like the Orient Express. The lead's Paul Hubschmid and Elfe Gerhardt's the star, she's Austrian. Agnes and Eberhard enjoyed it and Agnes thinks Gerhardt looks a bit like you, which is a good enough reason for me.'

'Is she older or younger than me?'

'Darling, I have no idea, but how could she be as beautiful as you?'

I laughed. 'Josef! What a fibber you are. So now I'm as beautiful as a film star. I don't believe a word you say, but your charm persuades me.'

So we went to see the film and on the bus back to the flat we began to plan our visit to Vienna.

November

With Jim Seagrove's help Josef has purchased the London Wall Stamp Company.

Tuesday 10th January 1948

Josef proudly took me to a debut recital at the Wigmore Hall by The Amadeus String Quartet. 'Sigmund Nissels is one of them. He was interned with his violin at Huyton. He was only 17 but his playing...' he seemed lost in thought... 'was magnificent. It kept us sane.'

It was a great success. Afterwards, waiting to leave, an impressive figure in uniform emerged from the crowd, Colonel Kalla. He exclaimed, 'Mrs Bramminger, what a delight to meet you again! You are looking well. And Mr Bramminger', shaking Josef's hand. We swapped pleasantries then he said, 'Soon I will see you no more, I return to Prague tomorrow.'

Josef looked alarmed. 'Sir, is that safe? Are you sure...' but then was lost for words. How dare he, he told me afterwards, a mere civilian, offer advice to such a man, his one-time commanding officer, experienced in politics and military affairs, doyen of the Diplomatic Corps?

'It is good of you to warn me, young Josef. I know your fears. Having fought against the Russians in the Great War, having seen them in action since, but now...' he looked around him, I wondered what he was searching for, then he looked straight at us again, 'Russia is our big brother, we must live in hope.'

11th January

I have wonderful news for Josef. He's going to be a father again. In eight month's time Hanni will have a baby brother or sister to play with and share our love.

Josef: Another child! I wonder whether it will be a boy or another daughter like my little Hanni. What happiness this news has brought me.

27th August

Birth announcement: Announcing the arrival of David William, born to Mr & Mrs J J Bramminger. Friday 27th August 1948. 2.33 pm.

January 1949

Post Office London Telephone Directory, A-D: Bramminger, Mrs M, 11 Linden ct, Anerley park SE26, **SYD**enham 3886.

25th January

Mary: Since seeing Kalla, Josef has been so busy, his stamp dealing demands his attention, but he's following events in Czechoslovakia closely. He is so concerned: 'They won't be content with Czechoslovakia. Hitler wasn't, why should they be? They already have Poland, Hungary, Yugoslavia, Roumania and Bulgaria, they're fighting for Greece. America's slow to recognise the danger and won't intervene to save democracy in Prague. I'm not sure it will to save Austria, should it come to it.'

And today it looks as if he's right. Beneš, under the threat of a general strike and Red Army intervention, has given in to Gottwald, the Communist Prime Minister. It's a coup, the Communists have complete control.

Philatelic Traders' Society. The PTS Journal: Volume 1, Number 3. New members... Bramminger, J, London Wall Stamps Ltd, 71 London Wall, City of London.

10th February

Mary: Josef has come back from his short visit to Austria. He called it his 'recce', to me it was more like a pilgrimage, making peace with his parents. Some things he finds hard to talk about: all those intelligence secrets he can never share, some inner hurts, but this above all. I know the signs, he goes quiet, turns inward.

But he <u>has</u> talked about his journey on the Arlberg Express. He travelled via Innsbruck, through all four Zones, French, British, American and Soviet, and stayed near his family in Favoriten (not in the family's flat as they have a Russian soldier billeted on them: three children and a grandson makes seven in a space intended for five) I think the pain – more gaping wound, I suspect – of his parents' betrayal, is gone, or lessened at least. I hope so, I've been praying about it long enough! Now he dearly wants me to meet all his family.

4th April

Richard: On this date a NATO Treaty was signed, prompted by the Berlin blockade. A Cold War was under way.

2nd September

Mary: Last night Josef took me to the premiere of *The Third Man*. We loved it. A great thriller, moody, its oh-so-haunting music. It reinforces our resolve to go to Vienna next year. I'm determined to see the Big Wheel (but not the sewers, please), not to mention his family.

17th October

MI6, 54 Broadway, London: **MOST SECRET**
CCE, LONDON
To D G White, B Division, MI5, Leconfield House

Sir,

DEVELOPMENTS IN CZECHOSLOVAKIA

You asked to be kept informed.

A. 25 Feb 48. Communist Coup. President Beneš capitulated to demands of Communist Prime Minister. The Communist-controlled Ministry of Interior immediately started eliminating non-communists from the intelligence apparatus.

B. Mar 48-ongoing. Great purge. 3,000 officers and 250,000 soldiers and civilians sent into internal exile, forced labour camps or prison, including 200 subjected to show trials and executed. Some in unmarked graves.

C. 10 Mar 48. Jan Masaryk. Foreign Minister, found dead at 0520 hrs beneath window of his apartment in Czernin Palace – the 'Fourth Defenestration of Prague.' First on the scene was Dr J Hora, head of StB – State Security. Autopsy signed by Prof František Hájek (who later claimed he didn't go within four feet of the body). Officially suicide, but we and Washington believe it was an MGB-inspired murder, the principal assassin being Maj Gustav 'Franz' Schramm, MGB's liaison officer with StB. He was himself murdered four months later.

D. 19 Mar 48. Gen František Moravec. Head of Czech Mil Int, London, 1939-1945, escaped to USA.

E. 3 Sep 48. Beneš. Resigned as President in June. Died at home, 'of unknown causes.'

F. 24 Nov 48. Brig Josef Kalla. Mil Attaché, London, 1936-1945; MOD, Prague, 1945-1948. After Communist takeover he was retired in Jun 1948 because of associations with the West. Placed under house arrest. Died suddenly in Prague 'of heart failure', autopsy signed by Hájek.

G. 19 May 49. Col Karel Lukas. COS, Czech Free Army, London, 1939-1941; fought at El Alamein, 1942; Mil Attaché, Washington, 1944-1947; returned to Prague, 1947. Dismissed after Communist takeover as 'politically unreliable.' He had brought valuable western goods back from Washington, alcohol, cigarettes, nylon stockings, rare Czech artworks and an American Packard car. On 29 Mar he was arrested by StB at his flat in Prague, taken to Pankrác prison and falsely accused of aiding in the escape to the west in the Packard of his former superior, General Alois Liška. The flat was systematically looted, the car removed and, after his death, flat and car were taken over by a female warden from Pankrác. On 4 May he was interrogated at police HQ on Bartolomějská

Ulice, using the most brutal methods of torture: he was beaten on the head and body with batons and fists, in the stomach and head with a sharp object, then, bound kneeling to a chair, the bones in his feet were broken (standard StB methodology). Back in his cell Lukas received no medical examination. They expected him to die within two days but he lived on for fourteen. His death ascribed to a weak heart. Body not yet found.

H. 21 Jun 49. Gen Heliodor Píka. Chief of Military Mission to USSR, Moscow, 1941-1945; DCOS Czechoslovak Army, 1945-1948. Tried for espionage and high treason, executed. Details under analysis.

I. 7 Oct 49. MGB advisers in HQ StB. Senior Soviet MGB officers Lichachov and Makarov arrived in Prague, head of team of advisers to the Ministry of the Interior and state security organs:

a. Police – Sbor Národní Bezpečnosti (SNB).
b. State security – Státní bezpečnost (StB).
c. Military intelligence – Obranné zpravodajství (OBZ).

They 'make no decisions, only advise', but everybody, terrified of them, does exactly what they say, although the Czechoslovak officer remains accountable, not the adviser. They focus on identifying compromising material from the Nazi occupation or links to US/UK intelligence. They leave no paper trail. Source JK-RVC reports that when one StB officer hesitated to provide information his adviser exploded: 'I didn't come for discussions but to see heads roll. I'll wring 100 necks rather than lose my own.'

Note: Prof F Hájek. Head of Prague Institute of Forensic Medicine. In 1943 the Nazi regime ordered him to inspect the remains of Polish officers murdered by the GUGB at Katyn so, after Feb 1948, he had to collaborate with the Communist regime. Has conducted autopsies of most regime opponents who have died under suspicious circumstances.

Yours sincerely,

Commander John Jeffries, CMG. **MOST SECRET**

19th October

Mary: Today Josef incorporated London Wall Stamps as a limited company.

7th November

In a bleak office in central Prague Major-General Reicin ordered his Deputy to investigate all past intelligence files. 'Any mention of American, British or

French intelligence are to be sent to Moscow.' 'They are especially interested in any work with military intelligence in London, or connections with the traitor Moravec. Start with 1945, work back to 1918, only employ Party members whose loyalty is beyond question. Every page, every document, every file. No short cuts, no mistakes, do you understand?'

His Deputy replied, 'Yes Sir, I fully understand, loyal Party members only.' Then, hesitantly, he asked, 'When you say "They", Sir, who...'

'The MGB, you fool. I expect a report next week on the methods you employ and on which staff members. Every item noted is to be sent to this office, I personally will despatch them on to Moscow.'

Sometime in 1950

Johanna: The story, bizarre even for the world of intelligence, is that in 1950 Philby's ability had so impressed his colleagues in MI6 that Stewart Menzies, its head, and Major-General John Sinclair, his deputy, discussed the possibility of him becoming the next Director-General of MI6. Dick White at MI5, asked to produce a security check on Philby, ordered Arthur Martin and Jane Archer to carry out an investigation into his past. Their evidence wasn't strong enough to convict him of espionage, but it raised considerable doubts, yet the head of SIS simply refused to accept any suggestion of disloyalty.

Did the glittering prospect of 'owning' the Head of MI6, combined with the information that arrived in March from Prague, prompt Moscow to tidy up any 'loose ends'?

But when and why did they decide Josef was a loose end?

1st March

Josef: 'Listen to this in the paper, "Lord Goddard sentenced Dr Klaus Emil Julius Fuchs yesterday to 14 years imprisonment—the maximum sentence—for communicating atomic energy secrets to Russian agents said..." We knew, for certain, that Fuchs was a Communist ten years ago, in the camp in Canada. So did MI5, as it was their card index we filed that information in. Did they lose that on its way back from Blenheim Palace?'

3rd March

Czechoslovak Defence Intelligence, Prague: **SECRET** Referat 45a. Cj 140295/451a-50. Sector BAa-1

Case Bramminger Joseph – offering collaboration with English intelligence. According to written documents supplied by London-based IMO, Bramminger

Joseph, born Vienna 15.II, 1916, last lived Vienna Qnaringplatz, 10 1939 contacted English Ministry of War. Whether his offer was accepted is unclear from document.

Sent for information. 24.II, 1950 / Noted, 1.III, 1950. Dept IV.

ACTIONS:

1. CC: C.j.A-103878/302895-6-50. Attach reports: 14.III, 1942 & 8.IV, 1942, Geheime Staatspolizei, Staatspolizeileitstelle Prag.
2. Despatch to MGB, Moscow.
3. Investigate further.

10th July

Mary: Things are looking up. Josef is so keen to introduce me to his parents so, next month, we're off to Vienna, taking Hanni with us rather than David. When we get back, we plan to buy a house of our own...

British General Insurance Company Ltd, Streatham: To Mr and Mrs J J Bramminger. Cost Comparison for House Purchase through Building Society with repayment under Ordinary and Endowment Assurance Plans. Amount of Loan: £1,000. Period of Repayment: 20 years. Age next birthday of Borrower: 34 years.

.....

Johanna: So, what had become of Mr Philby? What is remarkable is the way in which he side-slipped so many doubts about him and his ultimate loyalty – on both sides. This was evident from the very start in 1940, on being recommended to MI6. Its deputy chief, Valentine Vivian, interviewed his father. He asked, 'Wasn't he a bit of a communist at Cambridge?' St John Philby's answer, 'Oh, that schoolboy nonsense, he's a reformed character now', was all that was needed to completely satisfy Vivian.

That same year a leading NKVD spy in Europe, Walter Krivitsky, defected. Being debriefed by MI5 officers he claimed that one of the NKVD's agents in Britain – whose name Krivitsky did not know – had been a journalist for a British newspaper during Spain's civil war. It was never followed up.

By 1941 Philby had progressed to Section V of MI6, fighting German espionage in the Iberian Peninsula, ultimately as deputy-Section head. Later in the war two MI6 colleagues, Charles Arnold-Baker and Hugh Trevor-Roper voiced suspicions of Philby. Trevor-Roper, knowing of Philby's left-wing past, was astonished to find he had been recruited. Both their doubts were ignored and when, in 1944, MI6 re-activated Section IX, responsible for counter-espionage against the Soviet Union, Philby was appointed its head. He was climbing the ladder in MI6.

Even the Russians, however, were mistrustful. The NKVD ordered a Moscow desk officer, Elena Modrzhinskaya, to investigate him. She concluded that he was a triple agent operating against Moscow and, in 1947, Yuri Modin, his very own case officer in London, believed, initially at least, that Philby was working for British intelligence.

Some Americans harboured doubts. James Angleton, OSS's liaison officer with SIS in London in 1942, and eventually chief of the CIA counter-intelligence, became a close friend. But his suspicions were aroused when Philby failed to pass on information about a British agent in the Rote Kapel spy ring. In 1946 these grew when Philby, having just received the OBE, declared: 'This country could do with a stiff dose of proper Socialism.'

In 1944 Konstantin Volkov, NKVD agent and vice-consul in Istanbul, requested asylum in Britain, offering the names of three Soviet agents inside Britain. Philby, having warned the Soviets, manoeuvred within MI6 to be appointed the officer dealing with Volkov, then he took three weeks to travel to Istanbul. By the time he arrived Volkov had been removed to Moscow and killed. After this debacle John Leigh Reed of the Foreign Office, First Secretary in Istanbul, regarded him with suspicion, thinking him at the very least as bungling and negligent.

In 1945, Igor Gouzenko, a GRU military intelligence communications clerk in Russia's Legation in Ottawa, defected to the Royal Canadian Mounted Police. His evidence led to the arrest of more than 30 Soviet agents in Canada, and others working on the Anglo-Canadian atomic bomb project. Philby was spared because Gouzenko had not worked for the NKVD and so did not know about Soviet espionage in Britain.

In 1946 Philby was promoted to Head of MI6's station in Turkey. He passed to the Russians details of joint CIA/SIS operations to infiltrate émigré commandos into Armenia, Georgia and Albania. That betrayal cost us 300 lives.

In 1949, promoted once again, he became SIS representative in Washington, liaising with American intelligence. His house became a gathering place for key CIA figures - including its Director Walter, Bedell Smith, his deputy Allen Dulles, Frank Wisner, and Angleton (with whom he lunched weekly) - and FBI officers. However, Robert Lamphere of the FBI's Soviet Section, was astonished to hear people speaking of 'this seedy, shabby figure as a future chief of

MI6, in line for a knighthood.' A year later, when Guy Burgess, Philby's fellow Soviet spy, was made a Second Secretary at the embassy, Philby invited him to live in the basement of his home.

Early in the 50's Teddy Kollek - one-time Mossad officer and Mayor of Jerusalem - visiting Angleton in CIA offices in Washington, saw Philby in the corridor. Angleton dismissed Kollek's warning that he had been a committed Communist in Vienna in 1934, but Kollek said, 'Once a Communist, always a Communist.'

Closer to home, since 1945 (and with complete certainty after 1950) Mary had known that Philby was the traitor Josef had talked of. But only in 1979 did she write to 10 Downing Street, setting out the full details. What had prompted this? It was Margaret Thatcher having stood up in Parliament to reveal that Anthony Blunt had been a Soviet spy. Mary received a bland acknowledgement from the Cabinet Office, no more. When, in 2010, a request was made under the Freedom of Information Act to see these two letters, the answer came back, 'No trace.'

Really?

Well, files can go missing, can't they.

Chapter 11

From London to Vienna, by way of the Semmering Pass

Beginning of August, 1950

Mary: When we told her Hanni beamed, 'It's so exciting!'

It started with me telling Josef, 'Miss Drury's advice is, "Get your Aliens Department ID, WO Military Permit, French and Swiss visas, finally the Austrian passport. Only then book tickets. Use Ingles in Bond Street", she said. "they've specialized in Austria since Walter Ingle set them up in 1934"...'

'I know him', Josef interrupted, 'he was in intelligence in Vienna. I'll get the ball rolling.'

Josef: 'It's a difficult time to visit', Major Ingle told me. 'The war in Korea has made the Soviets jumpy. They think we'll counter-attack them through Austria. My advice? Take a dozen passport photos with you, it takes months to obtain any in Vienna and people need so many passes and permits. Well', he laughed, 'Mr Bramminger, you already know that. But...', he was suddenly in deadly earnest, 'inoculation is vital. My advice is, don't take your 2-year old son to Vienna. Your daughter – 8 years old, did you say – yes, but the city's riddled with Typhoid A and B, Polio, Typhus and Diphtheria are rife, it's not just in a public imagination fuelled by that film...'

Back home I announced, 'Three sleeper berths on the Arlberg Express was £50 but the business is doing well, we can afford it. And Joseph will run the shop while we're away, so my mind's at rest.'

Across the room Mary looked up. 'But getting there isn't so simple. Because I'm British we can only enter the Russian Zone at a place called Semmering...'

'Ah, the Semmering Pass, happy memories! As a boy I skied from there to Klagenfurt.'

'Well, we have to leave the Arlberg Express at...', she looked at her notes, 'Bischhofen...'

'Bischhofshofen', I said,

'That's it, Bischhofshofen. Then local trains to Vienna.'

'I'm so looking forward to it.'

Mary: Months of trudging across London, cajoling, biting the lip, smiling nicely, refraining from bitter if witty retorts and, above all, queuing. It may be character building, but it's hard work.

Hanni was reading from my notebook, '"Allied High Commission, Northumberland Avenue; Austrian Consul, Hyde Park Gate; Home Office Aliens Department, Old Bailey"... Mummy, are we're going to court?'

'No, darling, it's just the same address.'

'"Military Permit Office, SW1; French Consulate, W1; Swiss Legation, W1; Thomas Cook Bureau de Change." Why do you have to go to those?' Suddenly her mood changed and she said excitedly, 'It's like a game of Monopoly!'

'Only one's on the Monopoly board.'

'Northumberland Avenue!' she said triumphantly.

'And which station do we leave from?'

'Victoria!', still triumphant; then, less so, 'But that's not on the board. It's not fair!'

I've been battling with the Austrian consul. One day he's gracious, charming and helpful, the next, obstructive and petty, bureaucracy personified. 'That's so Viennese', Josef said, laughing. 'He wants treating as a knight or baron, "*Gnädiger Herr Konsul.*" We're a very formal people, every job its petty title, even Papa was "Herr Bahnlokführer." And every Viennese has two personalities, one day easy-going, benevolent, sociable, gemütlich, the next rude, gossipy, malicious, callous, melancholic...'

'It's a wonder I married you, *Gnädiger Herr Spion*!'

A letter authorised the bearer 'to collect French and Swiss francs to value £10, and travellers cheques for £45 in Austrian Schillings' from Thomas Cook's near Josef's shop in London Wall, much of it behind scaffolding, a bombsite. Will Vienna be the same?

Finally, I spread out my 'winnings' beneath the map of Europe that's dominated the dining room for months. One Austrian passport, one British, military rubber stamps and inter-zone permits galore, a new suitcase for Hanni – which she's so proud of – and three returns, Victoria-Vienna. After months of planning, preparation and packing I <u>need</u> a holiday.

Sunday 6th August

Johanna: I recall scarcely a single thing about this whole holiday, which is really frustrating, because it sounds fascinating (not to mention terrifying). Perhaps that's why most of it is 'hidden from my eyes', some form of self-protection perhaps. There are impressions, yes, but actual memories, none at all. I'm sure a Viennese psychiatrist would have something to say about it, but who can afford one?

Mary: At last, the concourse at Victoria – 'Gateway to the Continent' the sign says. It was packed. Families, day-trippers, porters, trolleys, shoeshine-boys, train-spotters; the latest fashions, glamorous ladies with chic hats, stylish umbrellas and elegant handbags, men in trilbies and fedoras.

Hanni stood fascinated by an illuminated sign arching over Platform 8, '*Golden Arrow-Flèche d'Or*.' 'Not ours, darling, look, the next platform, "London-Paris Express, Folkestone-Calais, all parts of France, Switzerland and Italy." That's us.'

'Why not Vienna?'

'There's no room, it goes to so many places. Anyway, it leaves at 2 o'clock, let's not be late!'

So, down the platform, following the porter's trolley, young Hanni excited and tearful, turning time and again to wave 'last' goodbyes to Grannie. 'There, the brown and cream train, so like a chocolate cake you could almost eat it', I said, to divert her.

Suddenly Josef was asking, 'Rucksacks. Why no rucksacks? Mine's the only one here.'

'Well, it absolutely had to go back to Vienna with you, didn't it, or we'd never have heard the last of it.'

Finding our seats we leant out of the window to wave goodbye. For a few seconds Hanni feigned indifference before bursting into tears and frantically redoubled her waving.

A rush of late passengers, slammed doors, a whistle, and the train was off.

I patted the seat beside me, fussed around in my handbag and asked, feigning ignorance, 'Where's the first stop?'

'It's Folkestone. Mummy, you can't have forgotten already!' Hanni replied proudly, tears forgotten.

'That's it', I said, winking at Josef. Just then the train burst out of the tunnel at Crystal Palace, 'Look', I pointed, 'there's Linden Court and, if you close your eyes for two days the next time you open them you'll see the place where Daddy lived when he was your age.'

Hanni looked at us, wide-eyed, struggling with two quite impossible ideas: keeping her eyes shut for two whole days, and her father having ever been the same age as herself.

In no time it was Folkestone Harbour Station. Onto the platform, a flurry of activity, suitcases and bags, passport control, a pier, a gangway, screeching gulls then... we were on board.

Calais's departure boards showed *Belgrade, Bucarest, Istanbul.* The Arlberg Express's twelve carriages stretched out of sight. I pointed to one, deep blue with gilt lines, a coat of arms, the words, *Compagnie Internationale des Wagons Lits-Voiture Lits-Sleeping Car-Schlafwagen*, and *Calais-Basle-Zürich-Innsbruck-Wien*, 'That's ours.'

A brown-jacketed attendant showed us to our sleeping compartment. Josef remarked, 'The right of the train gives the best scenery in the Alps.'

'Just imagine', I said, 'our home for two days, a very small one, like living in a doll's house.'

Small but luxurious: gleaming brass, pink lampshades, maroon-plush upholstery, mahogany-panelling, a small ladder to the upper bunk, washing basin and mirror behind folding doors, and as warm as toast.

Hanni placed her teddy bear reverently on her pillow. In hospital, under the flying bombs, evacuated to Hull, he'd been with her since she was born. She might be eight years old, but in some ways she's still a baby.

Then the darkness and the swaying of the train lulled us to sleep.

Monday 7th August

6.45, the alarm clock read. I raised the blind to the suburbs of Basle. In the station there was noise and movement and Hanni, awake in an instant, tumbled out of her bunk. 'Another new country!' she cried. Stations had passed unseen in the darkness so Basle was her first experience of continental platform life. She sat there, drinking it all in: a Swiss railwayman with a great leather bag around his knees, little boys in immaculate suits and extraordinary hats, little girls with blonde pigtails, and parents talking in a strange German dialect, quite unlike her father's.

Suddenly it all disappeared under a deluge of water. A man was washing away the grime from the French engine with a leather sponge. 'Only electric engines', Josef chuckled, 'are good enough for Switzerland's spotless landscape.'

A bell sounded, the train moved off for Zürich, while we ate a continental breakfast in the *wagon-restaurant*. Across the aisle sat three passengers we'd first noticed on the ferry, all, by dress and conversation, clearly British. We introduced ourselves: a Miss Wookey - her struggling on board with suitcase and cavernous carpet bag reminded me of my elderly spinster aunt - and a Mr Bailey, 'Charles', he insisted, travelling to Vienna to write articles for Time and Tide. The third man, Mr Heslop, was in his thirties.

Miss Wookey said she'd always slept well on continental trains. She talked of trains in Austria. 'Perhaps we might end up in the same compartment together after Bischofshofen. Things can get slightly fraught', she said.

Mr Heslop said nothing. 'He's a civil servant', I thought.

Then, the border at Buchs, across tiny Liechtenstein and climbing to the Austrian frontier at Feldkirch. Beside the track two arrows showed *'Österreich'* and '*Schweiz*.' Hanni set off down the corridor. I watched, puzzled. She spun round, facing us, held up her hands in triumph and cried out, 'Now I'm in Austria. I got here before you!' before skipping back along the corridor. 'Now I'm back in Switzerland!'

We both laughed. 'Well, Liechtenstein', Josef said. 'where your mother's a friend of the Crown Prince.' This revelation of her mother's connection to royalty left Hanni astounded.

I laughed, shaking my head. '"Was", darling, "was." Your father's only joking, don't believe a word.'

'But a friend of a Prince? Honestly?'

'Well, twelve years ago. He was a client at Christie's. Although he did ask me to be his secretary, here, in his country.'

'Would you have lived in a palace?'

'Yes, but you see...'

'And you said no!' She was struggling with the very idea. 'How could anyone say no to living in a palace?'

I laughed. 'Well, honestly? I fell in love with your father.'

Hanni had no answer to that.

At Feldkirch Swiss Railways handed over to Österreichische Bundesbahnen and the train lurched as the Austrian locomotive coupled on. Hanni raced to sit by the window, she longed to see Austria for the very first time.

I think it was only at Feldkirch, where old-fashioned freight wagons had destinations scrawled in chalk in strange, unreadable lettering, Пловдив, Αθήνα..., that Hanni really felt she was really in a foreign country, asking, 'Mummy, Daddy, Where're those? Josef answered, 'That's Plovdiv, in Bulgaria, and Athens, in Greece. They all come through Austria.'

Johanna: Now, that I do remember, that was the first time I KNEW I was in a foreign country.

Mary: Josef said, 'I've made many train journeys, some longer, some dangerous, sometimes with no idea what I'd find at the other end. This time', he looked at me, 'I'm with my family.' He laughed, 'What could spoil my happiness?'

Soon we were running on a narrow ledge along a great shoulder of mountain that towered above us, streaked with snow between the pines. Then valleys with rich meadows, wooden carts, families loading hay, oxen, dogs and goats; ochre-coloured walls, brightly-coloured chalets, red geraniums overflowing from window boxes; ski-lifts, waterfalls...

Josef shook me awake, 'We're at Langen am Arlberg. You and Hanni can stretch your legs.' Platform stalls sold Nestlé chocolates, Suchard, trays of cakes, coffee, foaming glasses of beer, gleaming trolleys offered Frankfurters and mustard. 'Wait and see', Josef called after us, 'Vienna has the best cakes and chocolate.'

After six miles of tunnel we coasted downhill. A bell rang for lunch. Minestrone soup, veal cutlets and salad, 'At last, *Ein echtes Wiener Schnitzel*', Josef proclaimed, smiling broadly, 'a real Wienerschnitzel.'

At Kitzbühel we seemed to leave the sun behind as we ran alongside the Zeller See. Out of nowhere, as Josef was trying to convince Hanni how beautiful this huge inland lake was, a summer storm broke across it. Suddenly its surface was wild, turbulent, hostile even, the sky overcast, with thunder in the air. Josef just smiled and pointed at a sign in the next station we were passing through, 'Look, *Großglockner-Hochalpenstraße...*'

'What's that, Daddy?'

'The High Alpine Road, it would take us to the *Großglockner*, the highest mountain in Austria.'

'Can we go there?'

'Maybe, *vielleicht, kann sein*. We shall see.'

And, finally, Bischofshofen, where the twenty British passengers decamped from the Arlberg – the Russians won't allow us through the American Zone.

Dark shadows showed that the day had drawn on. On the platform we stood forlornly watching the train disappear towards Salzburg, taking with it those well-heated carriages, 'our home.'

Miss Wookey: I laughed. 'They'll be in Vienna tonight, but better a night in a hotel than standing beside the line miles from anywhere.'

Mary: 'How's that?'

Miss Wookey: 'When Joseph Cotton, the American film star, and his wife travelled from Rome to Vienna to shoot *The Third Man* they got to the Semmering Pass. The Russians threw them out of the sleeping car with just their night-clothes and a bottle of whisky, because they were Americans. Only the British can enter the Russian Zone at Semmering. That took some sorting out!'

Mary: In Bischofshofen's hotel, under heavy eiderdowns, we slept rather well...

Tuesday 8th August

...until five in the morning, when it was a hurried breakfast and a rush to a deserted station. Hanni, too excited to stay indoors, preferred the windswept platform to the waiting room. '*Ich gehen zu Wien, zu Wien, zu Wien*', she kept saying.

'Darling, it's *nach* not *zu*.'

Off she skipped, her face wreathed in smiles, rattling, '*Ich gehen nach Wien, nach Wien, nach Wien*.'

A local train pulled alongside. The guard announced, '*Abreise für Bruck an der Mur!* – Departure for Bruck!' Its five antiquated carriages were less glamorous than the Arlberg Express but they got us off that windy platform.

At 5.55 we set off for six hours crawling slowly up the Schoberpaß, stopping at every wayside halt. Then, at Bruck, on the main Klagenfurt line, we transferred to the second carriage of ten in a luxury train up from Milan, complete with bar and restaurant car. Josef encouraged Hanni, 'First lunch, Semmering by two, where Russian soldiers will board the train, and Vienna by four, just in time for tea and Sachertorte. Look! Alongside us, there's the MEDLOC, changing its engine after coming through the Semmering Pass.'

'Where's Medloc?' Hanni asked.

'The Mediterranean... it's the British Military Train between Vienna and Italy.'

From Bruck onwards we talked and laughed. Herr Föhn, an Austrian in our compartment, produced cards and started playing gin rummy with Miss Wookey. Excitement was in the air, Vienna was just over the horizon and we fell to discussing it. She'd known the city long ago, 'After two world wars everything's changed, only shopkeepers have money now.' Mr Heslop kept himself to himself.

In Mürzzschlag's marshalling yards we felt two significant jolts. 'Those'll be extra engines. We need all three to get us up the pass', Mr Bailey said, 'one pulling in front, the second pushing at the rear.'

Soon all three were hammering away, white steam billowing past the windows.

We saw a jeep, then a British soldier in khaki standing smartly by a sentry box, a red and white barrier across a road, Union Jack fluttering from a flagpole. Fifty yards on and no-man's-land ended in another candy-striped pole, another sentry box, two tattered pink flags. Young Russian soldiers, weapons over their shoulders, lounged beside the road. They took no interest in our train.

The rather bumptious Mr Bailey was still spouting information. 'Semmering's the highest point on the line', he said, 'the engines take a rest here to cool off. It's famous as a health resort and for skiing. After we chucked Rommel out of North Africa in 43 Hitler sent him here to recover. The Soviets fire at anyone who ignores their orders, military or civilian.' I glanced at Miss Wookey. She raised her eyebrows in mock horror. I don't imagine he noticed.

Herr Föhn sighed. 'We're still west of Semmering, two miles inside the British Zone and the regional boundary agreed by the Four Powers. Why did the British ever allow the Russians into their Zone?' No one answered.

The train was braking. Lines of freight wagons in sidings came into view. The station itself crowded in on a platform, a clutter of buildings and a water tower. Immediately behind it pine trees rose steeply up the hillside.

1353 hours

We pulled to a standstill alongside the deserted platform. No one said a word. Apart from the engine, throbbing away quietly to itself, there was an eerie silence. We might have been in a play with stage directions reading: 'A pause', the audience looking on in hushed expectation...

Hanni pointed excitedly at two Russian soldiers advancing along the platform, peering in through each window. 'Look...'

'Darling, you know it's rude to point', I said, pulling back her outstretched hand. Herr Föhn said, 'Best not to stare, you never know how they'll react.'

Miss Wookey: I saw Mary looking around. Young Hanni's attention, attracted by noises from the corridor, was fixed on the door. Josef sat unconcernedly, peering out of the window. Beside him Herr Föhn seemed lost in his thoughts. By the door to the corridor Mr Heslop had a pensive look on his face. To Mary's right I was knitting, as calmly as I could, humming a tune to myself; beyond me Charles Bailey sat by the door, silent for once.

There came the sounds of boots in the corridor, a compartment door slid open, muffled voices, a pause, a door slammed shut, boots. Three times, then the sound of boots again, a massive Russian soldier loomed in the corridor and the compartment door was wrenched open.

A lieutenant stepped in. A small man but an imposing figure in his highly polished jackboots, blue trousers and spotless green tunic with rows of sparkling medals, topped off by a blue-peaked cap with maroon band. The two soldiers who followed him were a complete contrast, unkempt overcoats, their Shpagins covered with rust and dirt, their pallid and unshaven faces looked out from under huge peaked caps.

For a moment the officer scowled at us, then, bawling '*Dokumenti*!', he snatched at Charles Bailey's passport. He leafed through every page, grunted and brusquely handed it back. He seized my papers. The compartment was silent, save for the sound of pages being turned and the metallic clinking of medals. He shifted his attention to Mary's passport. Then, the moment he read her surname, his manner changed and he swung round and glared at Josef. He pulled a notebook from his tunic pocket and began urgently thumbing through it. Suddenly the atmosphere was charged with menace.

He barked explosively, 'Bramminger?'

Before Josef could reply the officer had turned to the soldier directly behind him and shouted at him in Russian.

'Oh dear!', I murmured in Mary's ear, 'they're going to arrest your husband.'

'Over my dead body!' Mary replied. Springing up she thrust herself between Josef and the lieutenant. Pushing his hand away she cried, 'If you take him you take me as well!'

For a moment confusion reigned. The officer tried to push Mary aside, shouting at his two soldiers to manhandle her out of the way but, in that cramped compartment, there was no room to move. One soldier tried to shove past the lieutenant. In the chaos the soldier behind him cocked his weapon. The sound stopped the officer in mid-shout. He whirled round, viciously slashing at the man's hands with his pistol, bellowing, '*Ne strelyayte, Ne strelyayte!* – Don't shoot, don't shoot!' but, before the words were out, a round had gone off into the ceiling.

The explosion of noise was followed by a shocked silence. Everyone froze, the officer as paralysed as the rest. I chose this moment to stand up, slightly unsteadily, I must have appeared oblivious to the drama around me. Muttering, 'Wool, I need more wool', I pulled my carpet bag down from the rack above and, as I struggled with it the bag fell on the floor at the feet of the Russian soldiers and burst open, spilling its contents across the floor. 'Oh, dear me, *Mne ochen' zhal*, I'm so sorry, *O bozhe moya*, let me...' in my embarrassment words came tumbling out in a flurry of English and Russian, then I was down on my hands and knees, scrabbling around on the floor, hastily grabbing blouses, knickers, a paperback novel, skeins of wool, a bottle of gin, all manner of things, busily stuffing them back into the bag. The soldiers, embarrassed but spellbound, tried uneasily to back away from this little old lady fussing around their feet.

The officer also floundered, uncertain what to do. Mary seized her passport from his hand and, brandishing it like the staff of Moses, began beating his chest with it, addressing him with a passion and determination that held him transfixed.

I resumed my seat and, speaking in Russian, began translating Mary's indignant words for the officer. The officer turned to face her. 'She says "If you arrest my husband you must arrest me. If he goes off this train I go with him, and I am a British citizen. And"', Mary gestured, '"what of our eight-year old daughter?"' – the officer turned his eyes to Johanna – '"will you kidnap all three of us? She is also a British citizen. What the dickens"' – I have to say, my translation faltered momentarily – '"do you think you're doing? On what grounds are you attempting to arrest my husband? Your behaviour's inexcusable."'

Suddenly Mary's arm was firmly around Josef's shoulder, but she was still, with her free hand, wielding that passport. Under her impassioned attack the officer recoiled.

Mary: In the corner of the compartment Mr Heslop, silent until this moment, stood up and, drawing a passport from his overcoat very deliberately, began speaking to the Russian in slow, measured German. 'I am attached to the British Embassy in Vienna, here', showing it to the astonished lieutenant, 'is my diplomatic passport.' This softly-spoken Englishman, my unobtrusive civil servant, suddenly had a commanding air. The man meekly took the document from him.

Miss Wookey was now translating Mr Heslop's protest into Russian... 'His Britannic Majesty requires you to allow his subjects to "pass freely without let or hindrance"', and the lieutenant, apparently mesmerised, watched his finger trace the words on the passport. 'The British High Commissioner Sir Harold Caccia will take a personal interest in this case as these British citizens are travelling with me and are under my protection.'

'In any event this train is still in the British Zone of Austria and under the 1st Control Agreement of 1945 your control point at Semmering is illegally operating on British territory. Sir Harold will want to know who has been attempting to arrest people in his Zone. I demand to know your number, rank and name. You should also know that Mrs Bramminger went to school with Winston Churchill's daughter.'

Well, <u>that</u> took me by surprise! Winnie's wife's cousin, yes, she'd been at school with me, his daughter, no. But how on earth did he know about SMB?

I felt detached, as if in a dream, and found myself looking around. The two soldiers were rooted to the spot, Mr Bailey, Herr Föhn, Josef and Johanna sat frozen, although Josef's mind must have been in overdrive. But we were mere extras in this play, on this tiny stage the leading actors, this Russian and my 'quiet man', were battling over my husband's freedom, his life maybe, and I could do nothing to help him...

'Aaaaargh! Stop it! Stop it! Stop it!' Suddenly, in her window seat, Johanna was screaming, shaking and sobbing.

In an instant the scene changed, every eye focused on my poor girl. I found myself back in my seat, my arm around her. Out of the corner of my eye – as if in another world – I noticed Charles Bailey slipping out of the compartment. The soldier by the door went to stop him, but the officer gestured dismissively and said something in Russian.

'"Let him go" he says', Miss Wookey muttered to me. 'Mr Bailey's of no interest to them... or us.'

For several seconds – it felt like a lifetime – the officer stood there, weighing the situation. Then he turned on his heels and started angrily shouting his men out of the compartment. They could not move quickly enough for him and he belaboured their backs with his pistol, yelling, '*Bhe! Bhe!* – Out! Out!' Moments later we heard their boots disappearing along the corridor.

1358 hours

Miss Wookey: The tension in that small compartment had been electric; suddenly all was stillness and silence, as if a thunderstorm had passed by. Then Hanni burst into great sobs, crying out, 'Mummy! Mummy!' Mary flung her arms around her, whispering reassurances.

Mary: Josef and I were struggling to take in what had happened. Johanna simply sat there, white-faced, shivering, bewildered, her arms around me. 'If we can put up with doodlebugs, we can put up with anything, can't we darling?' I said, cuddling her closer. She looked up and, through her drying tears, smiled at me.

The moment the Russians were out of hearing Mr Heslop spoke up, 'Might I have a word with the two of you. Perhaps Miss Wookey could look after your daughter for a moment?'

In the corridor he spoke urgently. 'Herr Bramminger, I'm here at the suggestion of a mutual acquaintance, do you see? Herr Harold Kendrick...' – relief flooded Josef's face – 'so please trust me.' He looked earnestly at us, 'That officer's MVD, NKVD as was. This is deadly serious. They once took an Austrian civil servant from this very train, she's now in Siberia.'

'Not to worry. This train runs non-stop to Vienna and I don't believe they will try to halt it, so for two hours we're safe. At Südbahnhof they'll surely try again to arrest you, but', my heart leapt at that small word, 'if you'll follow my lead, I have a plan to evade their clutches.' We both nodded. 'Meanwhile, perhaps Miss Wookey could rustle up some tea.'

Heslop spoke to a guard who'd materialised in the corridor. 'Herr Conductor, a moment of your time – please, *Herr Schaffner, Einen Moment Ihrer Zeit, bitte.*' They started a whispered conversation.

Back in our seats Heslop announced, 'What an obliging fellow! The last carriage has an empty compartment. We'll take your family and luggage and move down the train. He'll show you where to go.'

Miss Wookey whispered to me, 'It'll turn out fine, Mrs Bramminger. You can rely on Mr Heslop, I happen to know he's the sort of man who's good in a crisis. I'll fetch a flask of tea.' She hurried off towards the restaurant car.

We struggled along the corridor – those eight carriages seemed a very long way! – to the empty compartment, where Mr Heslop was having trouble closing the window blind, the catch seemed not to work. As the train moved off it suddenly sprang open. We saw, as if in a snapshot, the Russian officer on the platform with a telephone to his ear, looking straight at us, his attention clearly caught by the blind springing open. The last we saw was him speaking animatedly into the phone.

'What a pity', I said, 'that he of all people should have seen us.'

'Quite the reverse', Mr Heslop replied, smoothly pulling down the blind, 'I wanted him to know exactly where we are. It makes things much easier when they come looking for you at Südbahnhof.' He winked at me, looking very pleased with himself.

The train gathered speed as it plunged into the Semmering tunnel.

Heslop said to us, 'Let's postpone the whys and wherefores, and concentrate on getting you to your hotel.' Later – Hanni having dozed off – he said, 'A close run thing, that compartment was awfully full.'

I said, half jokingly, 'Oh, that would be my guardian angel and his flaming sword. He can take up lots of space when he wants to!'

He gave me a funny look and turned to Josef, 'You were weighing-up making a break for it...'

Josef replied, looking at me, 'That's true. I thought, it's me they're after. You and Hanni have a better chance if I'm gone. Anyway, if... if they had dragged me off I'd have broken away as we went past the first gap between carriages. They'd have taken seconds to react, the train would've been between us and I'd have been up the hillside, into the trees, heading for the British army checkpoint. They wouldn't have dared follow there.'

'But darling, they'd have been shooting at you. Surely it's not worth the chance of being killed.'

'If they get their hands on me I'd be dead eventually. Anyway, with those rusty weapons? Most of their shots would have misfired.'

I couldn't bear to think of that and, turning to Miss Wookey, said the first thing that came to mind, how lucky it was that she'd upset her bag. 'Call me Rhonna', she insisted. 'Well, all I could see was a terrified young girl watching her mother being manhandled by those brutes and thought, "Little Hanni can't take much more of this", so I did the silliest thing I could think of. Between your magnificent defiance, Mr Heslop's protest and your daughter's screams, it all worked out rather well.'

She smiled. 'And, I know you're dying to ask, I learnt Russian as a nanny in Moscow, before the revolution.'

We were in the longest tunnel so far and we emerged from it high up. In that summer afternoon's bright sunshine we might have been on top of the world.

Then Mr Heslop, speaking to me, but having first caught Hanni's eye, asked, 'How can we tell that that Russian officer was a really clever chap?'

Spotting his smile I replied, 'I don't know, how can we tell?'

'Well, he managed to read my passport upside down!'

Down from the mountains, hairpin after hairpin, to the plain and, about fifteen miles from Vienna, Heslop announced. 'I think we should move up the train.' Smiling at Johanna he continued, gently, 'The nearer the exit the sooner you'll be in your hotel and a comfortable bed!' So we struggled back along that corridor to the very first carriage.

On our right Schönbrunn Palace came into view, glowing in the setting sun. Josef pointed, 'My mother brought us there when we were children...', then the great marshalling yard of Wien Meidling. Josef was pointing excitedly, 'Hanni, look, Grandma and Grandpa's flat, where I lived. Beyond the cemetery, the third block, can you see?'

'I think so, Daddy. Are we staying there?'

'We'll see them in ten minutes, at Südbahnhof, but their flat's in the Russian part of Vienna, we can't go there.' Suddenly he went very quiet.

As we entered the terminal my heart was thumping away like a steam engine. As the train slid to a halt I spotted a Russian officer with a squad of troops on the end of the platform, staring hard towards the last carriage.

Over the noise of the braking train Heslop spoke urgently. 'Someone will fetch the suitcases. Don't wait when I open the door, get out, walk calmly off the platform, down the stairs and across the street outside, that's the British Sector. Our military will protect you there. Stop for nothing, not your family, not an old acquaintance, not a policeman. If someone calls out, ignore them, walk on.'

To Hanni, listening wide-eyed between us, he added, 'It's a race, us against the soldiers. First outside the station is the winner!' He smiled at her and me, 'No fuss, that's the thing.'

And, quietly to Josef, 'If you have to run, run. I'll look after these two.'

As we approached the buffers Heslop opened the door and scanned the platform. He shouted, 'Standish! Standish! Over here, quickly man!' a stocky man in his thirties came running up, then walked alongside the slowing train.

'Grüß Gott, Herr Heslop...'

'Not now! We must get these three into the Swiss Gardens quickly, before the welcoming party', jabbing his finger at the soldiers 200 yards down the platform, 'realise we've sold them a dummy. Get a porter, take these suitcases', he nodded over his shoulder, 'and meet me at the taxis. But if the Reds catch on and start coming after us do whatever's needed to slow them down, a suitcase bursting open perhaps...' Standish nodded and hailed some porters.

The train slowed to a halt. Heslop swung the door open and shouted, 'Go, go!'

The empty platform was suddenly full of passengers pouring off the train, Josef at their head, holding me and Hanni firmly by the hand. Mr Heslop strode briskly alongside, looking over his shoulder.

As I walked I also looked back at that cavernous hall, Josef's favourite childhood haunt. He'd often described the sunshine streaming through its huge wall of glass, the great, red, sign for 'Ankerbrot' bread, the flurries of steam, the smell of stale smoke and goulasch...

... then, all at once, behind us I saw those soldiers forcing their way towards us along the platform and, immediately in front of us, his family, waiting expectantly by the buffers. They spotted him at that same moment and, arms outstretched, screamed with delight, 'Josef! Josef!' Gritting his teeth he hurried on. Heslop shouted forcibly 'Ignore them!' I tightened my grip on Josef's hand.

Miss Wookey: I noticed how bewildered Josef's family looked, then they were running after him. Heslop shouted to them, '*Es gibt kein Problem, Sie sehen uns auf der Arsenalstraße!* – There's no problem, they'll see you on Arsenalstraße!'

Something, possibly the shouts of 'Josef! Josef!', had attracted the Russian officer's attention. He yelled at the soldiers, jabbing towards where Josef was vanishing from sight. Just then three porters started arguing over a customer. Fists flew, and some on the packed platform stopped for the free entertainment. Despite goading shouts and vicious swearing, the soldiers made slow headway, fighting their way off that platform...

... but their quarry was gone.

I saw that the four of them had disappeared down the two flights of stairs and through the great portico onto the street outside. I heard, in the crush of passengers at the top of the stairs, a voice yelling wildly in Russian. Then I could see Heslop's three charges on the pavement; he was shouting, 'Across the street! Across the street!', and waving them over the white-painted kerb stones.'

Mary: Across that painted kerb and we'd won the race, at least that's what I told Johanna! We stopped in the shadows of the trees beyond the taxi rank, and eventually I spotted the Russian officer pacing furiously up and down the far pavement, glaring about him. He'd lost us in the crowd and clearly dared not cross the white line into the British Sector. Around us travellers were greeting family and friends, but when his family appeared all Josef would say was, 'It's been a long journey, especially for little Hanni. Tomorrow, breakfast at the hotel, 8.30. Auf Wiedersehen, auf Wiedersehen.' Then we were off.

Miss Wookey: I spotted Standish paying off the porters and heard him muttering to Mr Heslop. 'Sir, those suitcases, in the taxi?'

'Yes.'

'And you'll sign my claim for the porters?'

'How much?'

'500 Schillings.'

'That's hefty...'

'Not for four, Sir. One for suitcases, three for the fisticuffs, they weren't cheap, and no time to negotiate a rate. Mind you, it slowed them Russki's down and the crowd enjoyed the show. But this you'll want to hear: that was the usual Russian QRF on the platform, corporal and nine men, but they were slow on the uptake because he wasn't their own officer. He was MGB – I spotted him wearing their Distinguished Worker badge, and you don't see that often – so that was no casual effort, it was critical to Red intelligence. He was spitting blood when he lost you and I wouldn't care to be in that corporal's boots. Last I saw the officer was waving his revolver around, threatening the gulag, or worse.'

Heslop grinned. 'I'll send Commander MGB Vienna an apology.'

'Very funny, sir.'

'Flowers perhaps? Oh, and tell Walters, I want two men in civvies, armed, on watch tonight at their hotel, one in, one out. We'll sort out static and mobile rotas tomorrow.' That was Mr Heslop's style through and through, incisive, coolly efficient, but always a sense of humour bubbling away, that's probably why he is so popular with the Viennese.

Mary: The Hotel Wienzeile's baroque façade, covered in scaffolding, somehow reminded me of London Wall. Inside, the receptionist welcomed me with the same Viennese politeness I'd noticed in Josef - the very thing, I think, that had first drawn me to him - and I began to relax.

Mr Heslop appeared beside us - he'd followed us to the hotel - 'Herr Bramminger, tomorrow at half-ten you'll be met in this lobby. Inside, I stress. They'll say, "Johann, it's well past reveille." Reply "So they say." Follow instructions. You'll be away for under two hours, in which time your wife and daughter must not, repeat not, leave the hotel. See you tomorrow.' Then he was gone, through the swing-doors, onto the street outside.

Our room bore the signs of war - or was it liberation? - a row of bullet holes across one wall. Somehow, despite threadbare carpets and faded old velvet curtains, the high-ceiling and heavily carved furniture - so very Viennese, I decided - presented an air of opulence. At that moment, however, all that mattered was hot water, a bath and somewhere to sleep.

The moment we were in bed and Johanna was asleep I turned to Josef and said, 'Darling, there's something I must say. All those years ago, when you told me about Mr Philby' - that got his attention - 'I must have wounded you terribly by not believing you. It was so fantastical, so difficult to believe, an Englishman working for the Russians. Yes, you persuaded me it was true. But after what they did today...' I paused, recalling the enormity of it, 'I'm fully convinced. So, this is me saying, "I'm so sorry."'

Wednesday 9th August

We woke refreshed, Hanni already out of bed, raring to go, overflowing with questions, 'When's breakfast? Where are we going first? The Danube? The Wheel? To visit Grandma and Grandpa?'

'No, darling, they're coming here.'

Later, in the restaurant downstairs, Johanna was pointing, something held her fascinated. 'What is it, darling?' Then I heard it myself and laughed. 'Josef', I asked, 'why is that man hissing? Does he think he's a snake?'

He looked startled, then recovered and said, 'Oh, getting the waiter's attention, that's what we Viennese do.' He chuckled and a grin spread out across his face, 'There, you see, 12 years AWOL, but I still think I'm Viennese.'

'Nothing wrong with that, it's your home, after all.'

Hanni piped up, 'Mummy, what's AWOL?'

'Like playing truant, only more serious!' I replied.

She persisted, 'How much more serious?'

'They don't shoot you for playing truant', her father replied quietly, a faraway look in his eyes.

Eventually he turned back to me. 'On the day I left in 1938, as I stood on that platform everything people think of as "Vienna" went through my head ... cold-painted bronzes, art-deco, coffee shops, potent white wine, Mozart, the Blue Danube, Strauss waltzes, the Boys' Choir, trams, Das Riesenrad, The Wheel, Schönbrunn, *Die Spanische Hofreitschule* – the Spanish Riding School ...' But yesterday, as we left that platform, Vienna was showing the reverse, its ugly face, the politics, the oppression, the violence hovering in the wings. In this next fortnight I'm determined Johanna will only see the good, and not the evil face of my city.'

At 8.30 his family turned up to greetings all round. '*Grüß Gott! Ach so, diese is Mitzi*', his father said, immediately endearing himself to me, '... *und Hanni!*'

Josef: Papa turned and said to me 'I hope you remember us, as once we were'... my mind went back to that flat in Favoriten, in 1938.

Mary: Soon we were sat down over breakfast. I'd expected some rather awkward moments but his parents were clearly trying their hardest, and Johanna was the focus of their attention. For her sake, they insisted, we should call them '*Oma und Opa* – Grandma and Grandpa.'

'*und Tante Liza!* – and Auntie Liza!', added his sister, grinning mischievously.

They were dying to know why we'd so mysteriously rushed past them yesterday and they listened eagerly to Josef's explanation. He spoke in a low voice – we were in the hotel's dining room after all – but I made out '*Russen* – Russians', and '*Ein Missverständnis* – A misunderstanding.' But when he said, '*Sie versuchten mich zu verhaften* – They were trying to arrest me', they suddenly went very quiet.

Josef: After my family left Mary took Johanna to our room while I sat in the lobby. It could have been 1938, me waiting for a contact, reading a newspaper, hopefully unseen, feeling as uneasy as ever. Who will turn up? Back then: Schutzbund? Gestapo? And now: British intelligence? MGB? You never could be certain.

On the dot of ten a young woman sitting in the chair next to me turned and said, 'Johann, it's well past reveille.' 'So they say', I replied, and we were off, in an unmarked car, south to the British headquarters in Schönbrunn. A flash of her pass and the armed sentries waved us through massive wrought-iron gates, then on past Redcaps guarding a side entrance. Drab corridors, barred windows, doors of solid steel. One, marked 'PCO (V)', opened from the inside. Mr Heslop greeted me, ushering me into the office.

He came straight to the point. 'In brief, Herr Bramminger, I and certain people in British intelligence - your friend Harold Kendrick being one, Dick White's another - believe someone inside Six is working for the Russians, and we're acting, unofficially and secretly, to expose him. We know the traitor's identity, but his friends within our two organisations still believe in him, others stifle whatever doubts they have. We have insufficient evidence, as yet, to convince our colleagues, let alone a court.'

'We refer to ourselves as the Cabal. We had a faint indication to suggest that you possess critical evidence, possibly the only thing that ties our traitor directly to the Russians. Semmering and Südbahnhof rather confirm that. The officer on the train was only MVD, Interior Ministry, humdrum stuff, but the one at Südbahnhof was MGB, the real "Secret Policemen." Both wear blue and maroon caps, but the second officer wore a small badge on his tunic - crass stupidity, I'd say - which told Standish he was MGB.'

'Oddly, a year ago in 1949 they could have easily scooped you up on your visit to Vienna, but ignored you, so something has changed since then and, a week ago, Kendrick discovered what. One of our sources in Prague saw your name on a watchlist being sent to MGB Moscow by Reicin, the Major General in Czechosolvak Defence intelligence, *OBZ*. He's a particularly nasty piece of work. He purged their army officer corps and 250,000 civilians after the Communist coup, while your so-very-professional secret policeman in Prague in 1938, Dr Hora, probably helped them make the connection. Hora's risen to Head of *StB, Ustredna Státní bezpečnost* - Czech State Security ... when Foreign Minister Masaryck was found dead beneath his window in Prague in March 48 it was Hora who was first on the scene. He's as wedded now to the Communists as he ever was to democracy in 1938.'

Of all Heslop said *that* was the greatest shock. How naïve of me. Hora saved my life by putting my name on the list that got me out of Prague, he spared me from the Gestapo. Now, to save his own skin, he's had to serve the Communists. The intelligence war isn't fought on sunlit uplands, more often it's down in the sewers.

Through my musing I heard Heslop continuing, '... it wasn't clear that there was a threat to you, only a supposition, and we had insufficient time to prevent your journey. Dick knew I and Miss Wookey were due back in Vienna in a few days and managed to book us last minute seats. Now we need to establish what exactly it is that you know. For your information, our suspect's name is Philby.'

In plain sight, at last!

I replied, 'I trust Herr Kendrick, and you saved my life at Semmering, so I trust you also. This is the story: in February 34, in our civil war, I was sentry at a meeting in the Wienerwald between the head of the Socialists, Otto Bauer, and three Reds: Josef Dycka, a Viennese, Vladimir Alexeyevich Antonov-Ovseyenko, a senior OGPU general', Heslop nodded, 'and the Englishman Philby...' I'll swear Heslop breathed a sigh of relief, '... I overheard the three of them talking. The Ukrainian gave orders to abandon us Socialists to our fate. I remember his words: "we will bury the Social Democrats here, in Vienna", then he added, to your Englishman, "as to your Labour Party, we'll deal with them later."'

'What was their relationship?'

'The Ukrainian was giving orders, Philby and Dycka were taking them.'

'How did you know Philby's name?'

'From my Schutzbund controller, although I had seen him previously, hanging around the western journalists in Café Louvre. I saw him next in 1942 at Inverlochry as an SOE officer and thought nothing of it, SOE was made up of all sorts. But the third time I saw him, in 1945, was in a corridor at Blenheim Palace. I was astonished, I thought. "A Communist, at the heart of British intelligence? Surely this cannot be." When he'd gone by, I grabbed my MI5 contact, the man I was there to see, and said, 'That man's a Communist.' He just laughed, 'Kim! Don't be ridiculous, he couldn't be, he's a Cambridge man, one of Six's best.' I insisted, but he was scornful, 'You Central Europeans, full of your conspiracies. You have no idea how Britain works.'

'What was your contact's name that day?' His voice was insistent.

'Mr Temple.' Heslop's face betrayed nothing at that.

'Did Philby see you, back in 1934?'

'No. I was in the bushes; they never knew I was there. Had they known they would never have spoken.'

Then it was back to the hotel in another unmarked car.

This evening, leaving Hanni in the hotel with Liza, Mary and I had been invited to a British army dance at Schönbrunn. After a dance or two we slipped away to meet Heslop, in a room off one of the Palace's many corridors. He wanted a word with Mary.

Mary: Josef can surprise me. Trapped in a city surrounded by Russians? His answer, a dance in an imperial palace! But, as cover for a meeting with MI6's man in Vienna, it worked. Mr Heslop explained things to me as he had to Josef this morning, and gave us assurances about our safety.

'It wasn't coincidence that Miss Wookey and I were there', he said. 'Kendrick knew I was returning to Vienna and asked I look after you. Now we're working on ensuring a safe return journey and, as for your safety whilst here, I've detailed a couple of chaps to keep an eye on you, armed, but in civvies, so don't think you're being followed. I don't believe the Reds will try anything in the Innere Stadt, although I recommend you keep your eyes on the pavement...'

'Mr Heslop!' I said, 'Or are you Christopher Robin? Will the bears get us if we step on the lines?'

He laughed. 'Well, to stay out of the clutches of <u>these</u> bears don't step over any white lines saying "SOVIETSKIY SEKTOR."'

'Listen. They've used criminal kidnap gangs in Vienna who'd have no compunction about "losing" an Englishwoman and child. But, after Semmering, they're on the back foot. Imagine the headlines: **"BRITISH WIFE AND DAUGHTER ABDUCTED BY RUSSIANS"**, **"ENGLISH GIRL STRANDED BEHIND SOVIET LINES!"** Our Cabal has powerful friends in the press, and it would only draw attention to your husband's story about Philby. But once we prove Philby's a traitor and remove him Josef's problem should be at an end. They'll move on to other business.'

I had a question. 'What you said on the train, about Churchill's daughter. That's all rot, of course, she wasn't at SMB, his wife's cousin was...'

Heslop interrupted, 'Clementine Mitford?'

'Yes. But how do you know this, and why mention Mary Churchill?'

'We do our research. As to Churchill... it's a name he'd recognise. Anything to stop him using that pistol.'

'There is one thing. I want to take Johanna on the Ferris Wheel, she talks about it non-stop. Not Josef, I realise. But is that possible?'

'Excellent. Give the impression that you're not afraid of them, I say.'

That decided me. I am not afraid of them. Well, not for myself; for Johanna and Josef, yes, a bit, but nothing a prayer or two won't sort out.

Josef: Heslop glanced at Mary with a smile, 'You'll be wanting to dance, so back to the ballroom with you,' ushering her out ahead of me. He gestured to me, a finger to his lips, 'These' he said, indicating the pistol, magazines and a box of ammunition that had somehow appeared in his hands, 'will be in your hotel, on the ledge high up in your bathroom. No need to mention it to anyone else.'

Then we parted, us to return to the dance.

Heslop wants me to take him to the Wienerwald, to re-enact that day. He looked uneasy when I told him the location. 'Shame the Russian Sector's so close'; he paused, 'But we'll find a way.'

Thursday 10th August

Mary: I was determined to see Stephansdom. From the day we first met Josef had talked about it like an old friend. It has the disconcerting habit of popping up everywhere, and out of nowhere, just like Herefordshire's May Hill. Inside I adored the light pouring through the pale green glass of some of the windows, illuminating the great brown and white tiles of the floor. Like a gigantic chess-board.

Hanni and Josef wandered off. I sat down. There was the altar, candles flickering, the smell of incense, footsteps echoing on the stone floor. I closed my eyes and, all at once, I found I was praying. I heard my own voice whispering, 'Please God, keep Josef safe', repeating the words time and again. The strangest feeling came over me, a sense of being held, of completeness, of... I suppose 'utterness' covers it.

As we left Johanna said quietly to me, 'No one told me to whisper, but somehow I just knew I should.'

Just outside, to the right of the main doors, Josef quietly pointed to a sign carved into the cathedral's outside wall, 'O5' it read. In an undertone, almost reverently, he told me: it was the cryptic sign of Austria's resistance. 'It's a very Austrian or, more like it, Viennese joke. The letter "O" plus 5, in other words "e", the fifth letter of the alphabet, stood for Österreich, a word the Nazis banned in 1938. In 45 the resistance started to paint it on buildings, bridges, wherever they could get away with it, like our Schutzbund flags before the war.'

Later, in the hotel, Oma said blithely, 'Herr Schmidt, next door, asked after you. He hoped you were enjoying yourselves, seeing the sights, asked where you were off to next...'

Josef suddenly cut her off, 'Is that Karl Schmidt, who was a Communist courier in Favoriten in 1934?'

'Yes, but now he's more important, something on their city committee, isn't he, Josef?' looking at her husband. But Opa, realising how tense his son had become, ignored her. She kept on, 'What is he? You know, Herr Schmidt, what does he call himself?'

It was her son who answered, 'Mama, you cannot trust them. Do not discuss me, or...', his look encompassed us. 'It is <u>not</u> safe.'

His mother, astonished at his seriousness, didn't see his father, from his armchair, nod to Josef. She didn't let up, 'But he means no harm, his mother's a good Catholic. What do I say when he asks again?'

'Nothing, Mother.' Josef paused. With a slight frown on his face he caught my eye and his father's, 'Or tell him we're spending three days in Bratislava seeing Socialist friends', then he added sharply, 'but that's it, Mama, do you see?'

From the armchair his father said, forcefully, 'Pepa. If Herr Schmidt bothers you again with his impertinent questions tell him to speak to me.' His tone brooked no further discussion.

Later I asked, 'Darling, why Bratislava? Would that be safe? And why did you speak so sharply to your mother?'

'It would be even more dangerous than Vienna, so we're staying put, but it might just divert Russian eyes and resources towards Bratislava for a moment. As to Mama, she never had an ounce of political sense; Papa sees things are serious, he'll ensure she keeps *stumm.*'

Friday 11th August

This afternoon the three of us went on trams - red and white, almost like London! - then a bus to Leopoldsberg, the hill that dominates Vienna from the north, 'The last mountain of the Alps', Josef proclaimed proudly. At the bus stop Josef was checking the map. I soon found out why, 'Not that one', he said, 'it goes through the Russian Sector. The next one's safe.'

We went to the last stop, Leopoldsberg. From where we peered at the Danube far below us. Josef pointed north-eastwards towards Korneuburg, 'My barracks, where my escape started from'; on the far side of the river a train was trundling northwards, 'There! The railway I escaped on, maybe even that very same train!' He turned around, 'And that next hill, or mountain, I should say, that's the Kahlenberg, it was "Kahl", meaning bald, bare of trees, so a good look-out post. And down there', pointing down at our feet, or so it seemed, 'is where Herr Beethoven worked on his Eroica Symphony, the one Mummy so often plays. On *Silvester* – New Year's Eve, we'd climb up here with wine and have a party.' He looked as happy as I've seen him in years.

Later, on the way back along the *Hoȟenstraße*, the ridge dividing the American Sector from the Russian zone to the north, he spotted two jeeps, each with two armed MP's, following our bus. Josef grimaced, 'Those two American jeeps are "escorting" us. Mr Heslop arranged it.'

Josef: That afternoon, at Stephansplatz, while Mary and Hanni browsed amongst the market stalls, I recognised a man on the podium in the square; I felt as if I'd been kicked in the stomach. The man beside me told me his name. I clutched at Mary, 'Do you know who that is? That man, on the platform?'

'No, darling?'

'He's Herr Schuster, he's a government minister. He's the one who murdered those three men', pointing at Stephansdom's wall. 'There. You can probably still see the bullet marks.'

I was surprised, Mary's eyes were closed, had she paid no attention? Shaking her arm, I was repeating myself when she said the most extraordinary thing, 'Sorry, I was trying to say a prayer for that poor, wicked, wretched man.'

'A prayer for him, a murderer? Why on earth...?'

She put her hand into mine. 'You've remembered that scene a few times in twelve years', she whispered. 'He has to live with it day and night. Plus the thought of meeting his Maker with that on his conscience.'

'I doubt it. He's a politician.' But, despite my cynicism, I'm glad she was holding my hand.

As we walked away someone was shouting behind us, 'Hallo! Hallo! *Herr Brückemann* – Mr Bridgeman ...'

I turned. A red-headed woman was running towards me, her arms outstretched.

Instantly I was back, sixteen years younger, standing on the Hietzinger Bridge and, once again, she flung her arms around me and kissed me, as impulsively as that first time. Stunned, I could only think of greeting her with the same words, '*Gott sei Dank, der Fluss ist niedrig.*'

'*Ja, kein Hochwasser in diesem Jahr*', she replied. 'What good memories we have. Dear Franz, he said you had the best memory of all of us.'

I felt Mary pulling at my hand and remembered myself, 'But, I must introduce you.' I said to Mary, 'this is', I frowned, 'but who are you? Fraulein Apfel, yes, but I never knew your real name...'

'Frau Helen Haas', she said cheerily. 'Helen Sonntag then, but in 1936 I married Herr Haas, who you have certainly met before.' She turned and grabbed the hand of a man who'd been hovering in the background, looking as bemused as Mary.

But it was Mary who spoke next, 'Frau Haas, Josef may never have known your name but he has told me about you. I mean, how many red-heads fling themselves into his arms and kiss him?' A look of alarm crossed Frau Haas's face, then Mary smiled broadly. 'It's all right, he also told me I was the second woman to kiss him, so of course I forgave him, and you! But as Josef is so lost for words, I must introduce myself, I am Mary Bramminger, and', turning to Hanni, 'this is our daughter, Johanna.'

Hanni, most puzzled of all, had the sense to hold out her hand and whisper, in a very small voice, '*Grüß Gott.*'

'I am so pleased to meet you, Frau Bramminger, and you, young Johanna, who knows so much Austrian. And this is my husband, Herr Karl Haas. He also met your husband on that memorable day.'

Ah! Orange, head of Bauer's security.

'There', I said triumphantly to Mary, 'I told you, I never knew her name!'

Frau Haas laughed, 'We did strange and wonderful things back then, anything to stay out of prison.'

'And what's become of Franz?'

'Dear Franz... Franz Emmerich...' her voice wavered. Suddenly I didn't want her to continue... 'he died in 1942, in Dachau.' Tears welled up in her eyes.

I had to turn away, overcome by a deep sadness. I blurted out, 'In 1938 he risked his life to help me escape.' The memory of our last meeting at the Prater flooded back. His last words, nothing more than '*Wir sehen uns wieder* – We'll meet again', a commonplace... but never fulfilled. Ghosts of the past... my mind wondered... suddenly I felt ashamed. Why have I never once asked what had become of Franz? Or of Leo Pröglhöf for that matter? Deep down I knew why. I'd feared the answer.

'Josef', as if from a distance I heard Mary's voice, 'Josef!' There she was, standing beside me, gripping my hand, 'Where have you been? You seemed far away.'

'*Ich entschuldige mich*', I shook my head, to clear it. 'I mean, I apologize. I was thinking of a long time ago, the last friend I saw in Vienna.' I smiled, 'But now you're here, and my little darling', my hand ruffled Hanni's hair, 'and all's well.'

Johanna looked up at me with her endearing smile; suddenly I felt strong again.

Frau Hass said, 'We must meet again. Tomorrow, I am thinking, at der Demel, 11 o'clock?'

Mary: As we walked away from Stephansplatz I nudged Josef and, ever so quietly, began singing,

> *'I was never kissed before,*
> *so kiss me once again…'*

We burst out laughing.

Johanna tightened her grip on my hand, muttering, 'Mummy, stop it. You're so embarrassing. You both are!'

Saturday 12th August

Josef: We met in der Demel, perhaps Vienna's best café - good enough, Herr Heslop told me later, for the *Stasi* to use it as a front for their secret operations across Vienna - marble table tops, the obligatory glass of water, newspapers on racks. It had kept the atmosphere, the hubbub of customers gossiping, discussing, debating, waiters rushing to and fro, laden with coffees and pastries: *Annatorte*, *Petit Fours*, *Rehrücken*, and so many more. Hanni's eyes were enthralled. I felt at home. Helen and Mary began chatting while Karl and I talked, trading stories about former comrades; who'd died, who'd gone abroad, who was up and who down in the whirligig of Viennese politics. I posed a question that had long puzzled me, 'Karl, that day in 1934. Why did Bauer agree to meet three Communist leaders when we had only two? It made no sense. The Communists in Vienna numbered six thousand, we were half a million, we did all the fighting. If a single Communist fired on the government forces it was against Party orders.'

'I don't know, Josef. I arranged security for the meeting, nothing more. Bauer's dead, his driver, Weintraube, and Kirsche, both died in the sewers. As for the three Reds, Winkler...'

'Ah, that was his name, I could only think of Dycka.'

'Josef Ludwig Dycka, yes, Winkler was his code-name. He was shot in Poland in 1941, by his own side. The Russian also died in Stalin's purges, and the Englishman, I'll bet he's not talking.'

'No, he's keeping very quiet', I thought, but, out loud, 'He wasn't Russian, he was a Ukrainian.'

Suddenly Karl went pale, realising what we'd said. He looked anxiously about him but, with no sign of us having been overheard, he said, more quietly, 'In Vienna "walls have ears." We must never mention this again. You can escape this city but, for us...', he looked across the table at his wife, deep in conversation with Mary, 'we're a city under siege. We drove the Turks away in 1683, but our Red friends...' - hearing the word *rot* - red, his wife looked up, but Karl laughed away her questioning look - he continued, quieter still, 'remain encamped about us, more ruthless than the Grand Vizier, with no sign of folding <u>their</u> tents! I'm only a businessman, I no longer dabble in such things. Let's change the subject.'

'Talking of escape, Josef, have you heard of the British airstrip alongside Schönbrunn's gardens? Or the American's not-so-hush hush strip alongside the Donaukanal. It's said its crosswinds don't suit single-engined planes, they've had four crashes already.'

A waiter came up. 'Ah', Helen said reverently, '*die Torte*', putting an end to serious conversation.

Mary: As we left Demel's Josef hailed a man who was entering. Later he told me, 'That was Herr Ziegel, the stamp collector whose flat I hid in before escaping in 1938. He had interesting news.'

Sunday 13th August

We were woken by the sound of Stephansdom's bells calling the faithful to mass across Vienna. Johanna and I went by taxi across an almost deserted city to Christ Church, the English church, by our Embassy. A little piece of England, more college chapel than cathedral, but very comforting.

Monday 14th August

Josef: A note at Reception, an invitation to a picnic in the woods, 'Bring swimming costumes', it said. So, after lunch, we were collected by an anonymous black Mercedes. 'You remember Standish', Heslop said, nodding towards the driver. 'We're off to a delightful spot in the Wienerwald, Mrs Bramminger, where I will steal your husband away for five minutes.'

It was good to take in the exhilarating air of the Wienerwald again, its stands of pines, the beech trees, purple and white autumn crocuses, the invigorating air, the stillness... so many memories.

'The western edge of this road, *Amundsenstraße*, is the Russian sector,' said Heslop. We turned off it at the very same spot as all those years ago. 'You might want to open the hamper that's in the boot', he said to Mary, 'over there perhaps, further in.' A jeep appeared – it had shadowed us all the way – and two Redcap SNCO's got out, carrying Sten guns in a purposeful way. He introduced them. 'Sergeants Garner and Kinloch, they've worked with me before. They'll be within shooting distance.'

Sergeant Kinloch came forward with outstretched arm, 'Sergeant Bramminger, you probably don't remember me, but we met in Rendsburg and...'

'and Flensburg, you were a private in the infantry, you helped arrest Dönitz.'

'What a good memory you have. I was Herefordshire Regiment then.'

The two of them waved to Mary and Hanni, busy setting out the picnic things in a clearing further in, then moved off into the trees.

'Every move, the exact words', Heslop insisted.

'The trees and bushes have grown, then it was the end of winter, so fewer leaves on the trees, now it's summer, but it all fits...' I ran through the timings, the sequence, the words, they all came back to me like a well-rehearsed play.

At the end Heslop said, 'Antonov-Ovseyenko was the senior man. You knew that, but he was executed in February 1938, in Stalin's great purge.'

'I met our organiser, Orange, in Demel's, he told me Ovseyenko had died. But he knows nothing of my overhearing that conversation, no-one knows of it, other than Mary, you, and Mr Temple.'

I was glad when it was over and we could tackle that picnic.

Mary: Afterwards they drove us to an open-air swimming pool in the hills of the American Sector, Bad Neuwaldegg. Mr Heslop said, 'The US Army runs it and allows my people to use it. You could all do with a break.'

Tuesday 15th August

I'm anxious for Josef and have come to a decision. What with Semmering, those abductions and that outing to the Vienna Woods, he's daily more nervous, hesitating, looking over his shoulder, checking and double-checking every time we cross a street. My two pennies' worth? To pull the only string I have – apart from prayer, of course – and ask my erstwhile Prince for his help. If I can find him...

At lunchtime the family met in Tante Maria's flat near Stephansplatz. She'd prepared a truly Viennese meal, *Rindsuppe* - beef soup, *Selchfleisch* - smoked meats, with sauerkraut and dumplings, mince and red cabbage. Conversation roamed widely, Tante Rosa telling us, 'After the Russians came the only work to be had was clearing bomb damage. People were close to starvation, butchers' and bakers' shelves were empty, the only coffee was acorns, ersatz. Imagine, no real coffee!'

His father leaned across to Josef, 'Did you know your Mama went to prison?' From the kitchen Josefa giggled, 'No, Josef, don't say that...'

'No', he said, 'it must be told. She saw Russian soldiers looting shops and told them, "You're worse than the Nazis." They sent her to prison for a month.'

Josefa came out of the kitchen, grinning sheepishly. 'Son, you remember that postage stamp they issued after the anschluß, "*Ein Folk, ein Reich, ein Führer.*" Then rations reduced, eggs were down to one a week. That was too much for us Viennese. People started saying, "*Ein Folk, ein Reich, ein Führer... und nur ein Ei* - One people, one country, one leader... and only one egg!*!*"'

I'd just about followed the conversation and joined in the laughter.

'There you are son, your mother, she opposed the Communists, our other resistance hero.'

I raised my voice, 'A cup of tea, anyone?'

In the kitchen I said, 'Josef, can't you see, by telling that joke your mother was asking forgiveness. She knows how foolish she seems in your eyes, worse than foolish perhaps, but it's her way of saying sorry.'

Josef looked at me. 'Forgive her? I forgave her last year. Forgetting's less easy.'

Later his father said. 'Son, in Favoriten we have a Red soldier billeted on us. Imagine, Pepa and me, your sister, Dolfi her husband, Peter, plus one of those vandals in that tiny flat! Actually he's quite human, he mended Peter's toy train for him last week - although, come to think of it, it's probably yours...'

'Peter's welcome to it', Josef responded, laughing. I was so relieved, at least he could relax with his father.

After lunch we went into the Soviet sector, to the Prater, while Josef disappeared on an errand of his own, which was just as well as there was no way I would have allowed him to run that risk. I saw his 'shadows' following him.

Over waffles and ice-cream Liza started, 'Before the war...' then, realising that might be dangerous waters, she started afresh. 'When Josef was a little boy there were brass bands here, parades, steam-organs, swings, roundabouts, rowboats, variety theatres, every sort of food stall, soft-drinks, sausages and sweets too', she said, looking at Hanni.

Peter chimed in, 'I remember, it was wonderful.'

Two great lines of trees stretched away from us. Liza pointed to them, '*Die Prater-Hauptallee* - The Prater's avenue of chestnuts, used to be a blaze of colour. And during the war', she was becoming bolder, 'we enjoyed potato salad here, it wasn't rationed.'

'By 1945, *Das Riesenrad* - the Giant Wheel, was terrible, a metal skeleton, cabins stolen for firewood, earth torn by artillery, smashed trees... they reconstructed it in 1948 but still', she pointed, 'only half the cabins.'

Well, half-wheel, half-skeleton, whatever it was, Hanni and I thoroughly enjoyed the ride!

Wednesday 16th August

Mr Heslop asked me for a favour, a morning's secretarial help at Schönbrunn; I was surprised, but thought, 'He's been good to us, why not?' So along I went. Getting passes filled in, signed and stamped, mine and Johanna's, took ages. Finally, I sat down at a desk and started typing, 'Dear Sir, ...' when he came in. 'I must apologise', he said, 'it turns out the lady who was ill has shown up. But thanks anyway, you can get back to your holiday.'

So off I went, slightly miffed, I confess, but ran into Rhonna Wookey, who apparently works in the Movements Office, near Heslop's department. 'We have a little plan', she said quietly, 'an illusion, something for the opposition to focus on. Go to the city centre ticket office and tell them your travel plans have changed, your husband intends to buy a stamp dealership in Vienna. Make a fuss, as loudly as possible, demand refunds, get yourself noticed. It will all get back to the Russians, and if they believe you'll be returning to Austria it will lessen their interest in you when you're back to England. Here are the details...'

I did that on my way back to the hotel. I wasn't sure if to tell Josef about all this subterfuge - it felt like something from that film.

Back at the hotel, after lunch, I mis-used Mr Heslop's name and slipped away again.

'Grüß Gott, Fraulein Brown, or should I say...', he hesitated, 'Frau ...?'

'Frau Bramminger, Your Serene Highness.'

'Frau Bramminger, welcome to my city, it is my pleasure to see you. But I must tell you at once', he gestured through the half-open door at his secretary in the outer office, 'the post is taken...'

'Oh no, I did not...' I replied, alarmed. Then I saw he was laughing.

'Have no fear, it is my little joke. Daily, you see, I must prove that I am no German but a Liechtensteiner and an Austrian, so I attempt a sense of humour. Now...', he stood up, strode to the door and firmly closed it. He became serious, still charming, but serious. 'Is there some way in which I may be of assistance? An introduction. A door opened? Would you care for a day out? My castle's in ruins – it's in the Russian Sector – but there are other estates, with pleasure gardens', he gestured negligently, 'somewhat overgrown, but you would be most welcome. Or a visit to the art collection? You may recall', he smiled, 'some of its better pieces. Or are you in need of accommodation? We have town houses at our disposal, most in a good state of repair...'

'Your Serene Highness, you are most kind. My husband, through no fault of his own, is in great danger from the Soviets. I believe they wish to remove him from circulation, to kill him even. I am also concerned that our daughter, she's aged eight, might be caught "in the cross-fire", as one might say. We leave Vienna in five days for the Tyrol. If there were a way for us to disappear from our hotel and live for those five days undetected in some property in the British or American Sectors...'

'*Das Gartenpalais*, the Garden Palace, of course! Mary – I insist on calling you Mary – apartments in its old stables fit the bill. In plain sight but shuttered to the public, with obscure entrances that only my staff know of.'

Sharp as ever. I might have been back, thirteen years earlier, in King Street, in Christie's offices. 'He thinks incisively and acts decisively...' Peter Chance had warned me, 'make sure you keep up.'

The Prince, putting his hands together, asked, 'Your hotel ...?'

'The Wienzeile, on Dunklergasse...'

For a moment he sat there, thinking.

Then: 'This evening at eight a *fiaker* – a horse drawn carriage, will collect you from the front of the hotel, like any tourist ride. It will take you to your new accommodation. Do not tell the staff you are departing. Leave your suitcases, someone will pack them and bring them after you. Your bill will be settled, and there will be no trail for the hounds to follow, either to my family or the Gartenpalais. If you need to pass a message to me, or to your friends in Schönbrunn...' seeing alarm on my face he added, 'there are few things in this city that escape my majordomo... he will pass any messages. He is utterly reliable – five generations of his family have served mine.'

He stood up. 'See', a smile wreathed his face, 'it is arranged, and no need to thank me. Years ago, you, most charmingly, helped me acquire some of the finest art and I am happy now to help you. However, I must say farewell, wheels must be set in motion. I hope we meet again in better circumstances.'

Josef had remained in the hotel, it was safer there. I broached the subject rather nervously. 'Josef', I said.

He looked up, 'Are we about to have an argument?'

'Only if you insist, darling. Viennese arguments, Viennese politeness, which will it be, *streitsüchtig* – argumentative, or *gemütlich*? Only you know...' I paused, letting my teasing have its effect. Then, more seriously, 'I've been concerned for you. So many terrible things pressing down on you, on us, and I feel helpless. But then I had an idea. Do you remember, soon after we first met, me saying there'd been an Austrian in my life before you, a prince no less?'

'I remember', he said, 'Herr Liechtenstein.'

'His Serene Highness Prince Franz Joseph II von und zu Liechtenstein, indeed. Peter Chance had me dance attendance on him. He may even remember me.'

'Anyway, I've discovered he's in Vienna, and I plan to approach him and ask his assistance, because we definitely need help. Your Mr Heslop may know the intelligence game but, like me, he's a stranger in a strange land.' I smiled at him, 'Not strange to you, of course, but even you may need a helping hand. Have I offended your Socialist principles, darling?'

Josef had listened attentively. 'Well', he said, 'the Socialist in me cannot stomach royalty but, I admit, I'm out of my depth as a husband and a father and, when up against an irresistible force – and I mean you, darling wife, not those Red thugs – Favoriten's Socialist gives way to London's husband. You must see your Prince. But please take a secret agent's advice', he laughed, 'in a city of secret agents. Tell no one of your plans. Do not use our surname before you see him. Above all, speak only to his private secretary. That's if', he laughed out loud, 'a prince's secretary will condescend to see a mere Miss Brown, or his Serene Highness deign to grant the audience!'

I laughed with him, then, taking him in my arms, I told him the truth, that I'd already seen Franz Joseph, that everything was arranged, all in the utmost secrecy. It sounded like a fairy tale but Josef accepted it. 'Between now and this evening', I said, 'we must say nothing. We'll tell Hanni in the fiaker.'

Thursday 17th to Sunday 20th August

Thank God for past holidays when the weather's been so bad you could only stay indoors, playing endless games, eating too much, getting fretful and discovering ways of surviving apparently endless hours. They probably helped us stay sane over five days entombed in the Gartenpalais, although we never got to see its pictures, stucco and marble halls.

0500 hrs, Monday 21st August

The day started with the alarm-clock. I was awake instantly, but, beside me, Josef slept like a log. I shook him awake. 'I've hardly slept a wink, we're going back through that awful place, doesn't it frighten you? How can you sleep so soundly?' I was on edge and he knew it.

'Army training...', he said, '"sleep at every opportunity!" Anyway, I've a suspicion Heslop has something up his sleeve. Then we're going on a REAL holiday, in the mountains, no soldiers, no politicians, just us!' He turned over in bed, threw his arms around me and kissed me.

Laughing, I rolled out of bed, 'Get yourself up', I said. 'Bath, breakfast then downstairs with those suitcases. I'll get our daughter up.'

Heslop had briefed him. 'A three-tonner will arrive behind the old stables at six. Get in the back. Not the most dignified way to leave a palace, but the least noticeable.'

The two gardeners raking the gravel kept their heads down when the Bedford drove into the yard, apparently not noticing the British soldiers with Sten guns helping the three of us into the truck. They weren't paid to see the palace's comings and goings.

A soldier tied down the canvas tilt and called out to Josef, 'Excuse me, sir, but we've orders to make a detour northwards, for security.' We heard him climb into the cab.

Josef: What did he mean, northwards? I staggered forward in the dark to peer through the canvas's eyelets. A jeep had pulled out ahead of us, two military policemen in the front seats. 'An armed escort', I thought, but kept it to myself. Over my shoulder I started a running commentary for Mary and Hanni, like a tour guide. 'We're heading north, into Heiligenstädt... used to come along here as a butcher's boy on my bike... we're alongside Karl-Marx-Hof, although I can't see it from here.' From the darkness came Mary's voice, 'Neither can we!'

There was an uneasy feeling in my stomach, a tentacle of fear working its way into my head. 'Where are we heading?' It made no sense. Soon we'd be level with Schemerlbrücke, which goes over the *Kanal* into the Russian Sector. Was I to be handed over, just another shabby deal at the fringes of the cold war? Had the Soviets hijacked this lorry? Were those Russians dressed in British battle-dress? They'd sounded right, surely I'd have spotted if they'd been impostors... I wanted to scream out, 'Where are they taking us?'

Just before Schemerlbrücke the jeep ahead turned sharp right, east along Grinzingerstraße, our Bedford trailing in its wake. Thank God! A pole across the road had a Stars and Stripes alongside. The jeep slowed, the barrier went up.

In the dim light I made out my watch, 6.09. I was struggling to keep up. Minutes ago we'd been having breakfast in a palace!

We followed the jeep through barbed wire and pulled up. I made out a hangar, three small aircraft lined up, a windsock hanging limply. Beyond, an airstrip ran alongside the Donaukanal. I remembered Karl Hass, in Demel's, talking about an American strip, used for secret missions. 'Small aircraft only', Karl had said, 'Stinson L5's, fixed landing gear, a pilot, jump seat... curves 40-degrees along the canal... crosswinds... four crashes in eighteen months...'

Still I hadn't shaken off my fear. Would they hand me over to the Russians, entrenched a hundred yards across the canal? If I disappear off the face of the earth what would happen to my 'them', sitting back there, side by side in the lorry's darkness? I checked my watch, 6.11. What is going on?

0611 hrs, USAAF Heiligenstadt airstrip

Hands were loosening the canvas at the back and Heslop's face appeared under it, grinning broadly, 'Guten Morgen, change of plan, let me explain.'

He spoke urgently. 'Josef, you're getting out by air, your wife and daughter going by Medloc, your sister from Südbahnhof. By lunchtime we'll re-unite you all in southern Austria.'

Seeing our bewilderment, he went on, 'Why this airstrip? Well, the Americans owe me a favour and they fly people in and out from here they'd rather the Russians didn't know about. They call it their "Flivver Strip." If I'd used our British strip at Schönbrunn too many people would know. You'll be flying to RAF Zeltweg, its British battalion will drive you to Kapfenberg.'

'Your wife and daughter will take the Medloc from Aspangbahnhof and meet you at Kapfenberg.' He turned to Mary, 'You'll be fine, 50 British soldiers travel on it.'

He continued, 'Your sister's family leave at 9:05 from Südbahnhof as planned, but a King's Messenger will meet her there and stay with them through Semmering to Kapfenberg.'

'And the best news... your holiday's been extended, eleven days at Aflenz in Styria and on to the Grossglockner, not just six in the Tyrol. You will re-join the Arlberg Express at Zell on the last day of the month. At no cost, everything's attended to.'

'So, Josef, debus here, you two continue in this luxurious conveyance', a grin flashed across his face as he took in the bare insides of the lorry.

So I'd climbed down from the truck.

Mary: My head was in a whirl, but I managed to ask, 'Why change the plan?'

'Nothing new. You regained the initiative with your disappearing act, I want us to stay one step ahead, to keep the initiative. Not knowing your connection to Prince Liechtenstein they lost sight of you and, outside their own Zone, they can't easily track people. You've vanished into thin air.'

'So...' he threw the canvas fully back. We were behind the hangar, out of sight of the Donaukanal. An aircraft engine started up.

Over Heslop's shoulder I saw a single-engined olive green plane, its propeller turning. I remembered 'my' Tiger Moth, all those years ago. Despite its open cockpit it had looked more substantial than this tiny thing.

I was distracted from my fears by Hanni giggling and pulling at my coat. 'Look, Mummy', she said, pointing to a white wooden sign in the grass: Salzburg 1½ hrs, Linz 1 hr, Latrines 30 sec.

An American officer appeared. 'Howdy', he said, 'I'm Major Earl B Kelly, I control ops out of our little strip.' He handed Josef a set of overalls, flying hat and goggles. 'These defeat even their telephoto lenses. Them Russkis across that canal would love to know who's coming and going.'

The pilot was gesturing impatiently and, above the noise, Heslop shouted, 'Let's be having you.'

Josef pulled on the flying kit, came back to the truck, embraced us, then, with a smile that was all at once cheerful, grave and defiant, walked to the aircraft. A crewman opened a flimsy triangular door in the fuselage and crammed him in behind the pilot. He gave a wave, the door slammed shut and the plane started taxiing towards the runway.

Heslop smiled reassuringly, 'They call it the Flying Jeep, Mrs Bramminger, it's as safe as houses. "We"...', he paused, nodding towards Hanni. My mind, and my heart, was following the engine noise, but I realised he wanted Hanni distracted. I turned to her, 'So darling, Daddy's the lucky one, he gets a plane ride, we're going in the boring old train. He didn't take your suitcase by mistake, did he?'

Hanni looked anxiously around inside the lorry. In the background, out of sight – as if in another world – the aircraft's noise receded as it taxied away. Then it grew to a crescendo and I saw the plane speeding down the airstrip. All of a sudden, the noise fell away and it was in the air. He was gone.

After what seemed like hours, as if from a great distance, I heard Heslop speaking, '...gained some time on "them." It's 6.15. You'll leave at 7.15, to sail through Semmering at 9. They think you're leaving Vienna at 9.05. Not that it matters. In twenty minutes your husband will be out of Russian airspace and, until his sister arrives at Semmering, they won't even know they've lost him.'

He handed me a manila envelope. 'It's all here, the grey pass for Semmering. Forgive the subterfuge, but because you worked for me at Schönbrunn, however briefly', he grinned, 'it's pukka – plus tickets and hotel bookings for your holiday. Miss Wookey's name's on the paperwork, we don't want an Austrian policeman asking awkward questions involving the name Bramminger, do we?'

Behind his head that tiny plane was disappearing over the Vienna Woods.

'It's alright, Mummy', Hanni said, 'Daddy didn't take my suitcase.'

.....

1 Field Intelligence Unit: Report 61. **SECRET** – RAF ZELTWEG, STYRIA – SUITABILITY FOR CLANDESTINE OPS: Occupied by Br inf bn. Airfield in care & maintenance, ringed by hills rising to 4,500 ft 4 miles fm perimeter. Rarely used. No sigs capability.

.....

Josef: After twenty minutes the pilot mouthed, 'Reds', jabbing his thumb backwards, then downwards, stabbing at his chest, 'Americans.' Then left, 'Brits.' He held up three fingers and formed an O, then swooped his hand down, 30 minutes to landing. We headed for the Alps.

.....

0700 hrs, Zeltweg

Josef: That pilot didn't wait on ceremony. Moments after I was off his plane he was in the air and I was being escorted to an officers mess – regimental colours, oil paintings, silver, a tiger skin, the usual trappings. Waiting there for the battalion to drum up a vehicle the CO joined me. 'I was at school with old Heslop, always glad to help a friend of Ronnie's', he confided. 'Strange cove, but you're in the same line of work and must know that. I'm more run-of-the-mill, commanding an infantry battalion on an out-of-use RAF aerodrome, a company detached to Vienna, another to Spittal. Your plane's the first in weeks. Ronnie signalled, top secret, "CO's eyes only", "expect a friend", didn't even give your name...' he paused, hoping – I just knew it – that I'd volunteer it, but I gave a slight shake of my head. His disappointment showed in his face.

'*Danke, Herr Oberst*. I think Ronnie would say the less said about this trip the better.' No need to disillusion him by revealing my entirely amateur status, a mere glancing acquaintance of his chum 'Ronnie.'

The colonel frowned in conspiratorial agreement, reminding me of Captain Barrass, both hungry for any link with the secret world. For years to come, I thought, he'll be embellishing and re-telling this tale, 'Of course you mustn't pass this on, old boy, but...'

The door to the ante-room opened and the RSM marched in. 'Sir, the escort's outside.'

'Send them round the back, I'll take my guest out that way. And, Mr Bassett', fixing the man with his gaze, 'No need to mention my visitor to anyone, not to the staff, not in the sergeant's mess. All strictly between ourselves.'

'Yessir!'

0705 hrs, Aspangbahnhof

Mary: 'The British contingent's private station', Heslop announced. He'd brought a bemused Hanni and me to this deserted terminus. It felt sad somehow, which matched my mood; he clearly read my mind... 'The Nazis sent the Jews to the camps from here in the war.'

A sign, MEDLOC →, pointed towards a small crowd milling around a train of two carriages. '*Die Blauer Blitz,* the Blue Lighting,' Heslop said, 'They'll look after you from here. Safe journey!' and he was off. My jovial, dependable, quick-thinking 'civil servant', one moment here, gone the next. Part of his job, I suppose, the disappearing act. It set me thinking, 'Josef used to vanish like that.

Perhaps they're trained to dematerialize, like Indian fakirs...'

'Madam... Madam', someone broke into my thoughts, a towering redcap, a sergeant. He was asking, 'Your grey pass, please, the Russians demand them at Semmering.'

At seven-fifteen we were off.

As Heslop promised, we were surrounded by British military and families, plus an RMP escort who wouldn't let us out of his sight, all very reassuring. But, foolishly, I rehearsed my worries... 'What if something goes wrong with that little plane. Will the Russians vent their fury on the two of us? How will Liza react?' I needn't have. At Semmering the Russian officer - a different one, thank God - merely glanced at the grey passes and, moments later, so it seemed, the train pulled up at Kapfenberg.

0905 hrs, Südbahnhof

Miss Wookey: Of course I wasn't there - I'm an office-wallah, not a field-wallah - but our man Bulmer told me about it later. On the platform Frau Liza, Josef's sister, was surprised to find, instead of Josef, a well-dressed, middle-aged Englishman flourishing a magnificent burgundy passport emblazoned with KING'S MESSENGER - COURRIER DIPLOMATIQUE.' Bulmer had explained, in passable German, that her brother was travelling under different arrangements. 'Madam, I can only say, in the strictest confidence, that the British High Commissioner has arranged that I and...' indicating a burly man nearby, 'accompany you into the British Zone.'

1006 hrs, Bahnhof Kapfenberg

Mary: Thank God, there was Josef, safe and sound. He took us to the station café. 'Look Daddy', Hanni said, pointing at the military jeep across the square, 'soldiers. Are they British?'

'They are, darling. They escorted me from the airfield, with orders to stay here until Liza arrives.'

1115 hrs, Monday 21st to Saturday 26th August

After Liza, Dolfi and Peter had disembarked from Die Blauer Blitz we took a bus into the mountains, to sun-drenched Aflenz Kurort, the famous health resort. It certainly looked the part: white-painted houses, winding streets, shops filled with sauerkraut, capons and Bismarck herrings, a church towering over all, and ski-lifts across tree-covered slopes. Outside a café, young men sat drinking coffee while older men in *Jägerhüte* - hunters' hats, drank beer. The waitress brought water, and newspapers on those now-familiar bamboo frames. Even I felt at home.

A taxi took us up the mountainside to Gasthof Pierergut, an old Styrian inn that's our home for the next few days. Herr Karlon, the inn-keeper, welcomed us with home-made plum brandy. His family have owned the Pierergut for generations - the silver buttons on his green velvet jacket impressed Johanna no end.

Inside it's so cosy: double doors and window shutters, a little shrine at the top of the stairs that reminds me of our Christmas crib at home. Everywhere the smell of beeswax and lavender.

It was on our third day that I saw Josef properly relax for the first time since Semmering. The strain no longer showed on his face, he seemed himself once more. Perhaps the sunshine and mountain air helped. 'At long last', he said, smiling, '"*Sommerfrische*."' He and Liza used that word so often I asked what it meant. 'It's an old word for summer, summer escape, summer freshness, maybe a touch of summer madness.'

It's so good to hear him talking like that, that's the Josef I love. I'm not much one for describing emotions, but our love is deep, enduring, it won't be thwarted by time or age or distance. It will overcome. Whether it's his love for me, or mine for him I can no longer tell, it's all one.

Enough! Moving on... it's idyllic here. We've tucked into fresh trout from the mountain stream, hiked and ridden out through the pine forests and alpine meadows around Pierergut, ventured into the mountains by coach. We visited the Mariazeller waterfall and the Bürgeralpe, and climbed to the *Gipfelkreuz* - Summit Cross, which simply demanded photos of Peter, Hanni, Liza, and me. As I write my diary, I'm looking at one Josef took, Liza and me looking so smart in our white blouses and dirndls. Dirndls, of all things! Lovely.

But, that same day, Dolfi took photos of us picnicking on the grass slope by Pierergut. Afterwards Hanni asked, 'Doesn't Daddy like having his photo taken any more?' Why are children so observant? I knew the answer but daren't give it. I'd even been ignoring how, every time Dolfi went to press the shutter, Josef had turned away, fumbling in his rucksack, half-hiding his face; but Hanni had spotted it. Suddenly I have a terrible foreboding: will he - will we - ever escape these haunting fears?

Sunday 27th August

Our last day. We walked down to Aflenz's parish church, Pfarrkirche Sankte

Peter. It looks glorious, everything gilded: altars, pulpits, chandeliers, statues, paintings. Josef took Johanna and me forward to communion. No-one objected. Perhaps they hadn't spotted the two interlopers amongst them. Or is it three, is Josef now Catholic or Anglican? Not that it matters one bit, of course.

Monday 28th August

After those glorious days in Aflenz we've travelled 200 kilometres cross-country to Villach, Josef having arranged to see a man here. It's all shrouded in mystery. Leaving us in the town centre he'd only say, 'It's about a stamp, a rumour, no more', and he was strangely quiet on his return.

Tuesday 29th August

Today we made the three hour journey to the Grossglockner, Austria's highest mountain, to stay overnight near the summit, in the Alpenhotel Franz-Josefs-Haus, just glorious!

Wednesday 30th August

At midday Liza et al headed eastwards back to Vienna while we took the Postbus northwards, down the Die Großglockner-Hochalpenstraße's endless hairpins. At the bottom the driver called out, '*Hier wechseln Sie nach Bischofshofen, Berchtesgaden und Salzburg. Bleiben Sie an Bord für Zell* – Change here for Bischofshofen, Berchtesgaden and Salzburg. Stay on board for Zell.' Josef said something strange: 'I might have gone there, Berchtesgaden, that is, in the war', but would say no more. Secrets!

I'm writing this in The Grand Hotel at Zell-am-See, on a peninsular jutting out into the lake. Our next night on *terra firma* will be in London. I feel exhausted!

Thursday 31st August

Josef: We boarded the Arlberg Express at Zell-am-See. The moment we were in our cabin an Englishman appeared and introduced himself. 'My name's Bulmer, I'm the King's Messenger who was with your sister on the Blauer Blitz. Mr Heslop asked me to see you through to Victoria. Your cabin's next door to mine and this,' indicating another solid-looking man beside him, 'is our security.'

'The Russians', he continued when alone with me, 'have a long arm in Austria and aren't afraid to flex it', handing me a recent newspaper. It read, 'MURDER ON ARLBERG EXPRESS? US Naval Officer dead in tunnel. When the Arlberg-Orient sleeper pulled out of Salzburg, Captain Eugene S Karpe, on his way home after three years as Naval Attaché in Rumania, was in Compartment 2...'

Bulmer told me the rest. 'He was found by the track, some said a door had opened accidentally, but an American investigation suggested assassination. They knew the Reds had a man on the train, and Karpe had vital information for Washington about another American jailed for espionage in Hungary.'

'I suggest you stay close to your wife and daughter, Sir. Shout if anything sets alarm bells bringing.'

'Finally, Sir, Mr Heslop asked me to relieve you of his pistol and ammunition. Somewhen before Victoria Station will be fine.'

'Somewhen?' I thought to myself, then something Mary had said about childhood holidays in Herefordshire popped into my head, 'Sometimes', she'd said, 'they have their own words for things; to them a butterfly is a flutterby.'

But soon I was too busy to think: night must have fallen near Strasbourg, by then I was too busy looking after Mary - and Hanni - to notice. She'd developed a fever and sore throat and was having problems swallowing and breathing. The conductor took one look, hurried away, and returned with an elderly gentleman carrying a black bag. He said, 'Frau Bramminger, this is Dr Strauss, he's returning to London and has kindly offered to examine you.'

Mary was too weak to object.

He looked grave when he emerged. 'Herr Bramminger, superficially your wife is suffering from a bad case of flu, stiffness in the limbs, back and neck, tenderness in the muscles, some spasms. Yet my diagnosis indicates the initial symptoms of poliomyelitis. I have seen it before, four years ago in Vienna. They last from two days to two weeks.'

'She needs bed rest, moist heat, warm towels to reduce the spasms, penicillin to prevent infections and painkillers to reduce the muscle pains. The conductor must arrange the first, I will supply the medicines. Once back in London, a visit to her GP. He can decide if further treatment is needed.'

Friday 1st September

Mary: I can see the Swiss stamp in my passport, 'Basle, 1 Sept, 1950', but my recollection is largely of a day and a half's agony and confusion. Only later did the fever begin to abate.

Josef manfully carried us through it all, and our King's Messenger proved invaluable. He regaled us - me when I was *compos mentis*, at least - with a fund of stories, conjuring all manner of things from his diplomatic bags. I vaguely recall kippers and fruit supplementing the meals the steward kindly served in our compartment.

Mr Bulmer's travelling security officer was an ex-army sergeant-major with a gruff façade, but he had a knack for entertaining Hanni with cards and magic tricks. His excuse, 'She's my nipper's age.'

Perhaps my problems helped Josef forget his own. I realise now that he's had to make most of this journey alone since Semmering, I could only be there for him. At one point he gallantly said, 'I have you and Hanni, what more could a man need?' But I do wonder.

Saturday 2nd September

We docked at Folkestone and, at 14.05, parted company with the delightful Mr Bulmer and his colleague on Victoria's Platform 2.

Home, sweet home!

Chapter 12

From London to Toronto, by way of New York City

5th September 1950

Josef: Immediately we arrived home I asked our GP to see Mary. There was no argument, 'I'm sending you to hospital straight away...' waving down her protest. 'This is the initial stage of poliomyelitis, in the acute stage it becomes unpredictable. You will be in a specialist ward with iron lungs, dedicated doctors and nurses.' A phone call later and an ambulance was taking her to Lambeth's South Western Hospital.

Mary: This was the strangest thing, no two ways about it. By the time I was home it felt as though the illness was trying to invade my body, from my legs upwards, like numbness with shooting pains. Josef and Hanni had left me to 'get some rest', before the doctor turned up and I thought, 'I'm going to fight this.' I managed to get myself onto the floor and dragged myself around the room, convinced that movement would keep it at bay. Whether it was working or not I have no idea, but then the really strange thing happened. As I crawled about the floor, probably looking like a caterpillar - a very determined, angry caterpillar - I found myself praying. About what I have scarcely any idea, for myself and this sickness, perhaps, I don't remember, for the children, of course, but what I do recall was demanding, urgent prayer for Josef's safety. And then, out of nowhere, or so deep inside myself that I cannot place it, a voice spoke, that slow, utterly imperturbable voice that I - and all Christians, I think - sometimes hear, even if we usually dismiss it as our conscience speaking. It wasn't debating, or bargaining with me, just saying it as it is, and will be... 'Child', it said, 'if you will suffer this, allow it, for Josef's sake, for My sake, then I will protect him wherever he may go, and bring him back to you at the end.' Every part of me wanted to argue, to answer back, my leaden legs wanted to kick out. But what could I say? This way (which didn't sound very appealing), or mine? But mine had even less appeal, I had no resources to fight back with, except more crawling around that floor followed by ... what? And anyway I knew, and know, His way is perfect, so ended up saying yes.

Sunday 8th October

Josef: The phone calls started when Mary was in hospital, so it was me who answered. I remember the words exactly: 'We know you we know where you live and if you don't shut that stupid mouth of yours we'll come for you and your wife and child. They'll pay for your loose tongue.'

I said nothing and put the phone down. Johanna had come into the room. Maybe she saw how shaken I was.

Monday 9th October

From a phone box I rang Five, requesting an urgent meeting.

So, at lunchtime, with Joseph Wendehals looking after the shop, I approached the door of a dull flat in the City, as dull as dull can be, but it was the right address, it opened as I approached. 'Come in, Josef', Mr Temple said, 'take a seat.' No time for ceremony, I noticed.

I told him, a man's voice, foreign, possibly Russian, rough, uneducated. That Mary was in hospital, our children with their grandmother, but Johanna still going to school. I wouldn't use the telephone from home, or the shop, for fear I was being listened in to.

Looking me in the eye he said, 'I've spoken to Mr White. He'd hoped the game we played in Vienna - your interest in buying a stamp dealership there - would give us more time. He proposes we make your home phone ex-directory and put a trace on the line in the shop. Remind me of its address...'

'71 London Wall.'

'That's convenient. Past the Post Office, at 72A, passers-by see "Telephone Exchange" in brass lettering over the door but, on the 1st floor, above the Post Office and your shop, is one of 5's telephone monitoring units. Within an hour they'll have a trace on the line. The ungodly will call the shop, but, very quickly, with police cars turning up at every telephone box, office and house they use, they'll run out of numbers to call from and they'll give up. Until your house number goes ex-directory we'll have a trace on that too.'

'As to your family, Mr White has made arrangements...' he looked at a file, 'Your wife is being moved. The consultant will say it's for a change in treatment, and her destination will get lost in the files; in fact she'll be taken to East Surrey Hospital in Reigate. As for your children, Mr White has booked them into a children's school and nursery called Kinnersley Manor, three miles from Reigate. Mrs Bramminger will be relieved to hear the Matron was at school with her... SMB, was that it?'

Astonished by all this behind-the-scenes activity I just nodded.

He carried on... 'You'll ask why. Well, you're a valuable asset to DW. The MGB and Gestapo both used threatening calls: in 1941 Frau Litten spoke out against Hitler in London; she received them, even in wartime Britain, but it didn't stop her. In Karpe's case - which Bulmer told you about on the Arlberg - the MGB used them against his widow. It's thuggery, yes, which matches their mentality, but it's also an own goal since it tells us their priorities. DW's sufficiently senior these days to be able to pull strings, and together we're going to get you all through this, no bones broken.'

Not the happiest way to put it, but I got his drift.

'By the way, we think now and again we'll have the odd piece of work for you. I'll keep you posted.'

They kept to their word. The shop received two threatening calls, one taken by a flabbergasted Joseph whilst he was running the shop for me. In the two days before we were ex-directory at home there were three more, one heard by an astonished Johanna when she got to the phone before me. I comforted her, but I shall have to explain all this to Mary.

23rd February 1951

Metropolitan Police Special Branch: Naturalisation application. Josef Johann BRAMMINGER, 8 Linden Court, Anerley Park, SE20, correctly registered with the police. Austrian passport LP-948/47, issued London 11.7.1947.

BRAMMINGER, born Vienna, served in British Army, Class Z reservist. He was in the Military Government of Germany's Interpreters Pool until June 1947.

Discharge papers: Seen.

On returning to England the applicant, a keen philatelist, began buying and selling stamps privately, making a fair living at this for a year. In August 1948 with a family friend, James Seagrove, he bought the stock and goodwill of a dealer trading at 71 London Wall, in the City, for £500 from F 'Freddie' Buck, manager of Harmer's in Berkeley Street. The purchase price was put up by Seagrove. In October 1948 it was incorporated as London Wall Stamps Limited, capital 1,000 £1 shares, held by Seagrove, Bramminger and his wife, directors.

It does a fair trade and the applicant is well known and of good repute in philatelic circles. At the moment, unfortunately, his wife, who assisted in running the business, is in hospital with poliomyelitis, so he must do everything himself. The company's account at Westminster Bank, Blomfield Street, is £110 in credit. Business volume is above the previous period.

The applicant is a man of good character, with moderate views and loyal to this country. His knowledge of English is adequate. Nothing to his detriment has been traced in Metropolitan Police records

To MI5. BRAMMINGER has applied for naturalisation. Enquiry is made as to whether anything is known or recorded about him/~~her~~. Reply: NOTHING RECORDED AGAINST. D T (MI5) 22 6 1951.

Signed: B H Masters, Chief Inspector.

Friday 25th May

Herbert Lowit: 'My wife and I were lucky. In 47 we escaped again from Czechoslovakia, before the Reds were fully in charge, back to London. 1951 was my last meeting with Josef, at Schmidt's in Charlotte Street, where the German-speaking community met: "Like Piccadilly Circus", people say, "if you sit in Schmidt's long enough every German and Austrian in London will pass you by." North Soho was an easy-going place, like Greenwich Village; bohemian, Jewish, Italian, French and Greek émigrés, all sorts, actors, criminals, academics, students, artists, writers. Josef wasn't serving in the restaurant upstairs, he was behind the delicatessen counter downstairs, selling sausages, cheese etc. We simply said "Hello, how are you", that sort of thing, the usual exchange of pleasantries.'

Josef: MI5 have me working for them at lunchtimes at Schmidt's, keeping an eye on a Foreign Office man, Mr Maclean, who lunches there. Believing he was onto their man in Schmidt's they put me in instead. He's started varying the station he uses, sometimes Charing Cross, sometimes Victoria, and altering his walking speed erratically; all rather schoolboy-like behaviour, just like he is in Schmidt's, where he loves baiting the waiters (they're surly enough as it is). Five's used to watching in Schmidt's: English Nazis and the Gestapo used it as their unofficial headquarters pre-war, and Mosley's Fascists regularly met there. Five have clearly got Frau Schmidt - who's English, from the East End - under their thumb: she gave me this job without an interview.

Perhaps Maclean uses Schmidt's thinking he's anonymous there, in its great cavern always full of noise and activity. With scrubbed wooden floors, long tables, thick tablecloths, silver service, waiters in white aprons, it's reminiscent of Vienna's cafés, but the hospitality's distinctly Teutonic, rather than gemütlich; Viennese waiters were never as rude as Schmidt's.

I reported in: '25th May. Maclean seemed in good spirits, less nervous. I spotted him outside with his friend, Lady Campbell, speaking with a writer, Cyril Connolly. Then Maclean and Campbell came in, went upstairs and joined her husband at Maclean's usual table, Maclean had booked it earlier. He had potato soup, Eisbein und Sauerkraut, a bottle of cold white and crusty rolls. They stayed until 2.30. The waiter on their table – I know him from Vienna – overheard their conversation. From his notes: "They toasted his birthday. Unhappy in his present job, thinking of applying for transfer. Feeling much better, hasn't visited psychoanalyst in weeks. He'll call them about staying while his wife – Melinda? – has the baby." On his way out he stopped in the delicatessen for the first time and bought salami. He made a show of it, he wanted people to notice. Then he headed south down Charlotte Street – I saw your two pick him up outside, they'll know where he went.'

Monday 28th May

That task's over. Their watchers saw him board his usual train on Friday evening, nothing suggested anything amiss. But that night he and a man named Burgess took a ferry to France and disappeared. Only on Saturday morning, when MI5's watchers met the usual train and failed to see Maclean, did telephones begin to ring.

As Mary would say, they've skedaddled.

July

Richard: The defection of Maclean and Burgess having cast suspicion over him, Philby resigned from MI6. Not that he had much choice.

27th July

Oath of Allegiance: I, Josef Bramminger swear by Almighty God that I will be faithful and bear true allegiance to His Majesty King George the Sixth, His Heirs and Successors, according to law. Sworn this day 27th July 1951 before me, John Fogg, Commissioner for Oaths, Solicitor, Salisbury House, London Wall EC2.

13th August

London Gazette: Naturalization granted. Bramminger, Josef; Austria; Managing Company Director; 8 Linden Court, Anerley Park, London SE20.

3rd November

Josef: Mary and children home, released from hospital and rehabilitation. 'This is my happy day!'

Mary: 15 months, the longest-ever gap in my diary, but at last I'm home and can catch up on hosts of things. I gallivant about on crutches and a calliper, free from iron lungs and fresh air on the verandah!

I scarcely remember the early treatment. In hospital I was put straight into an iron lung, I was too weak and muzzy to understand much around me. When I was *compos mentis* the Consultant saw me. 'Mrs Bramminger', he said, 'Polio isn't fully understood yet, but the risk of catching it is increased by travelling in areas that have had a recent outbreak, especially bathing in infected water – and you were in Vienna, which fits the bill. Also extreme stress, which compromises the immune system's function...'

'"Stress!" I can't tell Josef', I thought, 'he'd blame himself, and he has enough to handle just now.' My attention flicked back to the Consultant...

'...polio has no cure. However, we can treat the symptoms while the infection runs its course. So, your reflexes have diminished, you've suffered muscle pains, severe spasms and some paralysis, but all are responding to treatment. Since you arrived this delightful contraption', giving my iron lung an affectionate pat, 'has done your breathing for you, it's your "breath of life!" You'll stay in it for a while longer. Many find they can sleep in it, which helps, old-fashioned rest being vital. Heating pads and warm towels ease the muscle pains, physiotherapists will work on the weakness in your leg muscles, there'll be therapy for your breathing and more fresh air. Soon you'll join the patients being wheeled out onto the verandah.'

'Then you'll be fitted for a caliper, special shoes, crutches and...', he glanced at my notes, 'a wheelchair. But, something very positive: you will walk again, that I'm certain of, although walking any distance will be tiring, hence the wheelchair.'

They moved me to Reigate, the consultant saying I needed a change of treatment, then Josef turned up with the children, and explained about those wretched phone calls and Mr White pulling strings. Things became clearer. They'd stowed me safely away in Surrey, with the children in the woods nearby – it sounds like a fairy tale! – looked after by Winnie (Winifred to the uninitiated!), who I knew at SMB. She's now an SRN and matron, living, by a lovely coincidence, at Kinnersley Manor, where Josef and I honeymooned!

The iron lung dominated my life. I was on my back, head outside, propped up on a cushion, a mirror showing me what was going on behind while a clever frame above held a newspaper or book. Every time the page needed turning a nurse was always there! But much of the time I just drifted off to sleep to the 'rumble, thump, rumble, thump' of the machinery beneath.

Coughing was a trial, it's difficult to cough in rhythm with an iron lung. Eating was easier (ha!) because you're fed through a tube, but when it comes to swallowing you have to wait till 'it' breathes out... then swallow.

Eventually they pulled me halfway out and sat me up for a cup of tea, sliding me back in when my fingers started turning blue. Gradually I was left out for longer until, one day, they took me fully out and sat me in a chair. I felt dreadfully weak – just being washed drained me completely – but things improved.

The nurses and doctors, so hard-worked, were always patient with us. We were totally immobile, utterly helpless. Few illnesses bring them closer to the patient, they say: anticipating our every wish, almost as if they were sharing our thoughts. Initially you have the sole attention of a nurse, watching over you, feeding you, treating you. Later, despite being frantically busy, they'd still come over to wipe your brow or turn a page, then off to another patient, comforting a child or swatting a fly from someone's face.

I can't begin to write how I've felt about Josef and the children. Every week they came to see me, but I'll never get used to being the patient and them the visitors. It should be the other way round!

20th November

'Free at last'... the Ministry of Pensions have given me an invalid carriage. Three-wheeled, tiny, but handles like a ice-blue hippopotamus, especially around roundabouts; she'll be 'hot in summer, freezing in winter', the delightful man told me when he delivered her. She gets me everywhere. Quite extraordinary, if I pull up outside a shop then usually someone comes out, asks what I want, and fetches it for me – people are so kind.

And the timing was just right... next week I start work at Anerley Town Hall, half a mile away, too far to walk or for my wheelchair, but Tootie – my name for her – just whizzes me up there. It's something secretarial, in a ground floor office. Tootie wouldn't do for Stirling Moss, but thank you anyway Lord.

Johanna: How did she manage? Her bad leg always having to be raised, for the circulation, there was a caliper on one leg, two crutches, a folding wheelchair that tried to bite your fingers off whenever you went near it, a wooden leg-rest, travelling rug, ... well, the whole paraphernalia, heavy, awkward, painful to use, would have tried the patience of a saint. But somehow she carted it around. A flight of stairs might defeat her, but kerbs or a few steps, never!

11th May 1952

Mary: Josef started reading to me from a letter from Austria, and I could tell he was truly excited, 'Do you remember that mysterious appointment I had in Villach, before we all headed up to the *Großglockner*? Well, the man I met there,

Ingo Waste, he's the president of Klagenfurt's Stamp Collectors Association, he's announced to the world the stamp he told me about. A friend has sent this cutting: 'The oldest stamp in the world has been discovered', Herr Waste says, 'I have before me a letter with a stamp from Villach to Klagenfurt, dated 20 February 1839.' Do you realise what that must mean? That would be older than the Penny Black! This could turn the world of stamps on its head.'

4th July

The Daily Chronicle: Significant Philatelic Find in Klagenfurt. Stamp experts who had the opportunity to check the postage 'stamp' that has been found in Carinthia, suggest it should be given technical tests. It purports to have been printed in 1839, and they agree that, in appearance at least it gives the appearance of being valid, but they recommend that it be subjected to technical tests.

This is not the first 'stamp' that has been claimed to pre-date the Penny Black of 1840, but these experts are agreed that it must tested by an international expertising committee, rather than that in Austria.

1st August

Mary: Josef's as pleased as Punch. 'The stamp' is coming to England for 'expertization.' In my diaries I see it all started two years ago when he met his friend Herr Ziegel in Demel's. I saw them talking animatedly but, when I asked, Josef simply said, 'Oh! Just stamp talk.' Later, en-route to the Grossglockner, he went to a mysterious meeting in Villach saying, 'It's merely a rumour.' Now it's more solid and serious, it's coming to London.

I'm as pleased as he is, it has bucked him up so. It'll be a long haul, the English elite dealers will hate giving it precedence over the Penny Black but, for now, it's giving Josef room to breath, so to speak. The shock of Semmering, playing hide and seek in his own city, and those phone calls seem to be behind us.

4th August

Following long talks the owner signed a contract: 'Mrs Sophia Heiliger of Sattendorf appoints Mr Bramminger her agent for the Villacher one-cruiser stamp from February 20, 1839, the oldest stamp in the world, for sale, once agreed by London's Expertizing Committee, at a mutually agreed purchase price of not less than $52,000.'

Now we're looking forward, planning for our future, intending to buy a house, while Joseph is both working and looking after me and the children. My polio brought out the best in him, but every visit to me in hospital, collecting the children to and from Kinnersley, must have eaten up his time. On top of that, the house and business to run, the costs of expertizing 'The Stamp' plus the naturalization process - at least that's been successful - now he feels he belongs.

5th August

Brief history of the Villach stamp: Produced for the Owner and her Agent:

1837. LORENZ KAMESIVIC proposed a new system for postal reform to the Austrian Government - an adhesive stamp to collect postage payment.

1839. JOSIP HARTNER, Hereditary Postmaster in Villach, decided to give the idea a trial in his area. This office, held by the Hartner family from the early 1700's, held powers on running postal services and collecting taxes in their area, their responsibility being to hand over the correct amount to the Ministry. As people sometimes tried to evade payment when letters were delivered, Hartner's family had been badly hit financially due to evasion and embezzlement.

20.2.1839. FIRST VILLACH COVER with Stamp (the only known copy). This came into the possession of the current owner on the death, after the 1939-1945 war, of a relative, the daughter of Lina Hartner, the little post-girl who had delivered it. The cover and stamp were kept in an old prayer book, a sentimental link with the family's history. Belonging to Empress Maria Theresa for her personal devotions she gave it to the Hartner family on their child's christening. The present owner, sorting out the possessions bequeathed to her, came across the prayer book. Without realising its possible value, her husband carried it around, showing it to friends as a family memento, until Ingo Waste, a philatelist, realised that it might have value and historical interest.

Postmaster Hartner had hoped that pre-payment of carriage for letters would ease the difficulty of collecting his taxes, so he had several stamps printed, in three colours by Treker, a lithographer. Despite contemporary prints from Austrian collections of three-colour lithographs made by Treker, being brought to England to show to the Expertising Committee, but they said that three-colour printing was unknown at this time.

Hartner had a daughter living away from home, and her mother wrote her a letter (The First Villach Letter), saying the Hebemarke on the cover was a 'try-out' of its merits. A younger, nine-year old daughter, Lina, acted as 'postman', taking in letters, collecting fees, and delivering them. Micro-chemical analysis discovered that Lina had made the cross-cancellations on the face of the stamp and letter as part of her duties.

The Second Villach Cover is similar, but without the stamp, sent a few weeks later. A postscript, in Lina's handwriting, using the same ink used for the cancellations of the stamp, told her sister that the Hebemarke had not proved itself and had been discontinued. Under tests both covers, the stamp and the dye used were all found to be genuine and of the age stated. This stamp came down to us intact because it was a relic of family interest, not because it had any actual philatelic interest for them.

There was possibly a communication of ideas to England and Sir Rowland Hill. In 1836 Galloway, an English Trades Representative, was known to be in Villach and interested in Kamesivic's idea. Possibly he conveyed the idea to Rowland Hill, linking the appearance of the Penny Black in 1840 with that of the Villach stamp in 1839. 'Galloway' may have been the 'Captain Galway' of the Board of Trade who was in touch with Rowland Hill on several occasions.

6th November

Josef: James Seagrove asked me to his London club. 'Someone from the Foreign Office had a word in my ear. You know how things are in Vienna just now, Renner's government deep in negotiations for a State Treaty, hoping to get the Russians out of Austria once and for all. They fear an Austrian stamp knocking the penny black off its perch would ruffle British feathers.'

'Josef, I know the Yard's forensic boys have given the paper and ink the green light, there's even a majority on the committee to admit it as a valid stamp. Despite all that, people say Robson Lowe will override them, majority or not, come what may. He's a strong personality - a polite way of putting it - who brooks no opposition. He doesn't want to go down in history as the man who killed off the Penny Black. And now the Foreign Office has got at him. I do not believe he will let the stamp stand a chance.'

8th December

Mary: Now it's out. That wretched man, Robson Lowe, has said no, 'it's not a stamp, it's a forgery!' It's not yet published, but that's his verdict. I heard this on a weekend that's been depressing enough as it is. We're in the worst smog London has ever known, more than just a pea-souper, it's horrendous, foul to breathe and women are wearing silk scarves over their faces like gas-masks. On Sunday night visibility was nil, nurses said they couldn't see to the end of their wards, conductors walked ahead of their buses carrying lamps. Tonight seems worse, the fog's turned a disgusting yellowy-brown. People abandoned cars, things ground to a standstill.

It might have distracted Josef, but it only added to his burden. He is so bitter about the stamp.

9th December

Wind off the Atlantic has swept that obnoxious cloud out to the North Sea. Hallelujah! If only it could have taken that 'Committee' and its poisonous findings with it. That Robson Lowe, he ... Lord, I'm sorry, but he wasn't being fair, he'd made his mind up before they began and he made the rest fall in behind him. It wasn't justice, it wasn't scientific, it wasn't... Lord, it simply wasn't right!

But, I have some really good news, I'm pregnant again! Estimated date: 10 September. We are so pleased.

14th January 1953

A philatelic newsletter has given the findings of the BPA's Expertizing Committee, saying they did not accept that it was a postage stamp at all. The journal noted that the stamp had not been examined outside Austria since it being found last year.

31st January

At last I have found an account that tells the whole and shabby story. An Austrian newspaper's headline, **Sensation! The oldest stamp in the world. Villach Stamp beats London Conference**, tried to paint a Austrian victory out of defeat, but their story, which I struggled to translate - Josef being too despondent to help, he being under the weather, seemingly stunned by the whole proceedings - told the tale. The Klagenfurt Volkszeitung made a noble effort to show what a travesty it had been, and I certainly can't blame them for trying. I disentagled these points:

1. A member of the London committee on the Villach stamp, reported to the newspaper: 'By the request of the Director of the London Wall Stamp Company, Mr Bramminger, an expertization conference, presiding over by Robson Lowe, was held in London by the British Philatelic Association.

2. The Director of Styrian Land Archives, Prof Dr Fritz Popelka, and Dr Drinklage, represented the Austrian side. They reported: "A detailed agenda providing for the examination of this precious piece was not kept to from the very start. Robson Lowe was entirely preoccupied with examining the stamp under a quartz lamp and, if possible, finding a hair in the gum, thereby proving, in his view, that the stamp had been

stuck on the letter at a later date. He announced that he had found a blue hair in the gum by which the stamp had been affixed to the letter. The statement of the other members, both British and Austrian, that the hair was actually coloured black undermined his finding, so he paid it no attention.

3. Less than a quarter of the agenda was carried through, so...

    a. Neither the paper nor the stamp's watermark were examined
    b. The pre-philatelic letters with Villach hand-stamps of the period were belittled
    c. Samples from Austrian state archives of three-coloured printing were simply dismissed
    d. After less than two hours the conference was prematurely dissolved
    e. No conclusive decision was reached at that time

4. However, the finding in the Committee's report that the stamp was a forgery was contrary to Scotland Yard's conclusion. That world famous institution, working with Professor W H S Cheavin, the co-inventor of the Watson-Cheavin philatelic microscope, used the most modern equipment, and reached the concludsion that the stamp, paper and watermark were genuine.

5. It was characteristic of the proceedings of the whole of the conference or, rather, of Robson Lowe's chairmanship of it; that considerable evidence was simply not allowed and even what limited evidence that he allowed was ignored.

6. Throughout the other British members either remained neutral or, in the case of the well-known London stamp expert, Mr Houtzamer, decided in favour of the genuineness of the stamp. The opinions of Robson Lowe's fellow committee members went unheard, and the committee's findings were essentially his and his alone.

7. With no reason given, other than the simple statement that 'elements of it had been later than the date of issue and so it was a forgery,' the Committee or, rather, Mr Lowe, found that the Villach stamp was not genuine.

5th February

Jim Seagrove: 'Josef, I've heard that Her Majesty isn't much interested in the Royal Stamp Collection. Mention horses, they say, and you have her complete attention, stamps, barely a flicker. One rumour says the Villach was bought by people connected to the Royal family as a present for her coronation, another that your own government purchased it for three million schillings. It's probably in a safe deep under either the Alps or Windsor Castle!'

22nd April

Josef: I wish I could keep this from her, but I must tell her. Any other wife would be scared silly, but she's such a remarkable woman that I know she'll find a way to cope, better than me.

'Mary', I said, gingerly, 'something awful happened today at London Bridge tube station. Don't be alarmed, darling, but someone tried to push me under the tube train as it approached. Somehow I braced myself and by the time I'd recovered my footing he, or they, had disappeared.'

She took it more calmly than I could have dreamt of. 'You know, darling, ever since those telephone calls I've been wondering what would come next. This must be it. The first thing to do is tell your friends.'

23rd April

I'd have done that straightaway but I had a lunch long arranged with Johann Svitanics, back in London from Vienna for some political conference. As soon as we met I could see he was anxious then, having made sure we were not overheard, he said in a hushed voice: 'Most urgent news Josef. You remember Herr Karl Haas, you met him in 1950. Have you heard? Yesterday he was killed in a road accident on Rotenturmstraße. A car veered onto the pavement, crushing him against the wall. He died before an ambulance got to him.'

'And Frau Hass?'

'She was nearly killed with him, both legs broken, lucky to survive. Their son and daughter were walking with them and were also injured. The car was stolen in the Russian Sector. The driver ran off. Such a waste! In the SPÖ we were considering Karl for Minister for the Interior when it becomes vacant.'

'Where did the driver go?'

'He ran across Marienbrücke, into the Russian Sector. A passing Red Army patrol did nothing to stop him and we all know what that means.'

That decided me, never has a meeting been more urgent. As I walked away from lunch my mind was racing... 'Why Karl? Why now? Would we be next? How can I protect Mary and the children from this?' Mary was right, I must meet again with 'my friends', as she calls them.

So, this evening, I found myself sitting in a comfortable armchair in yet another anonymous flat, but this time with bigger guns than Mr Temple.

Heslop spoke first. 'Josef, it's fortunate that I'm just back from Vienna and DW has asked me to lead.' From his armchair across the room, Dick White nodded. 'We know about your tube attack, and my people in Vienna have confirmed the attack on Herr Hass, but we'll never prove a link to the Soviets.'

'It leaves us with one unanswered question: "Why did the Soviets try arresting you at Semmering?"'

I gave what answer I could: 'Only nine people knew of that Wienerwald meeting: Bauer, Hass, Bauer's driver, the other Schutzbündler sentry (Kirsche, that is), the doctor, myself and the three Red's. Only two ever saw me: Kirsche and Haas, and only two of us saw Philby: myself and Hass. Most who were there that day are dead... Bauer, Philby's two Red comrades, Kirsche, all died before 1950. The Schutzbund kept no records and, before 1950, I never spoke of it, not to family, friends or comrades, nor my Czechoslovak controller, other than to two people, my wife and Mr Temple. You yourself', I looked at Heslop, 'saw how astonished she was at Semmering.' Mr Heslop nodded. 'That leaves just your Mr Temple who could have given me away. He's known of this since January 1945, at Blenheim.'

'Temple's not mine, he's Five's', Heslop said, glancing at Mr White.

DW thought for a moment. 'Temple joined us during the war. He's not an Oxbridge man, he's no Red, and he's as true as they come. I vouch for him. But, as you say, he is the only possible source. So, this morning, I spoke to him again. He bitterly regrets laughing off your warning at Blenheim, and he recalled an occasion, much later, when he let something slip. Someone in Five was taking the "party line", vigorously defending Philby. Temple, in the heat of the moment, said "But I've heard one of our own, from Vienna, state that he witnessed Philby taking orders from a senior OGPU officer in 1934..."'

'"And who was that?" the other man asked, rather too sharply in Temple's opinion, but then, suddenly realizing that he'd said too much himself, Temple walked away without giving any answer. The other man never pursued it... he must also have realised what a key moment it was, and could only hope Temple forgot...'

Heslop interrupted, 'Who was this? When?'

In my few meetings with him I'd never seen DW ruffled, but now he came close. He shrugged, took a breath then replied, 'This is all off the record, but it fits. We must pursue the right lines and...', there was a long pause, 'the right traitor. It was Gerald Hoddell, in June 1950.'

'Hoddell's long been a friend, I've trusted him but, unfortunately, it all fits. Prague's information arrived in Moscow in March, so Hoddell's input three months later narrowed the field, leading them directly to you.'

'But this', he looked straight at me, 'explains something I've wondered about, why you resigned from SOE in January 45, so abruptly. But that brought you back to us, thankfully, and it's why we're all here.'

Mary: That night – the memory still hangs over me like the darkest of clouds – Josef told me about Karl Haas, murdered on the street in Vienna, Helen, legs broken, their children injured. 'They won't stop until I am silenced', he said, he must leave. He asked me, 'Do you remember how, at Semmering, I said, "You and Hanni have a better chance if I'm gone"? That's even truer now, now there's,' he paused, 'our unborn child.'

I sat silent for, oh, I don't know how long. I should have known, perhaps I had known from that moment at Semmering. J is no indestructible object while they seem to be an irresistible force – of course they're not, but I don't know how to stop them. I'd never seen the look there was in his eyes that night – was it terror? No, not terror at all, flint-like determination, more like. Josef carried on, 'Darling, you, all of you, are the world's most precious thing to me, but I don't know how to protect you, or the children. The only way I know to get you out of the firing line is to disappear.'

'Mr White has a plan. He said, "We need a clean break to keep you all safe, one they can't follow, so we're providing a ticket on a freighter sailing from London for New York, but actually you will go on into Canada. So far there's no sign that the opposition are about to make an immediate move."'

We talked and talked, the bleakest discussion I've ever had. Up against brutal facts – with Karl and Helen's faces in Vienna looming in my mind – I was desperate to protect Josef, and the children. Long into the night we talked, examining every fact, every possibility, the love that unites us, our fears... their grip on us so vice-like that every exit seemed closed off. It was tearing me apart, I was crying inside but, deep down, both heart and head knew there was no other way. I and the children could not escape with Josef. To be brutal, you might hide a man in Canada's vastness, I could trust Mr White for that, but a man, with three children and a wife in a wheelchair?

3rd May

The battle - inside my head - raged on and on; it's still raging, if I'm honest. I must take account of our unborn child, what part will he, or she, play in this? I may not be thinking quite straight. After six months I'm feeling as if I've been pregnant forever, but this child is at least as real to me as Johanna and David, and this seems the only way to keep all of them safe. The threat is immediate, they might try again tomorrow.

Johanna: Looking back I think, from things she has said, the nagging doubts and fears, the pressure on Mary, desperate to protect her beloved, even at enormous emotional cost to herself, almost overwhelmed her. She said that Josef even urged her to divorce him, to remarry, even though his Catholic upbringing argued against this, but this was impossible according to her own convictions, marriage was for life, she would not let go of that. Years later, she confessed to me - not that she had anything to confess to - the promise God had made her. I suspect that that was what supported her at that moment, and in all the years that followed.

Mary: The morning sickness has come and gone, I've put on nearly a stone, so everyone spots I'm pregnant before I tell them. Baby is over a foot long, weighs almost two pounds and it feels as if it's climbing a ladder up a steep wall inside you, then scampering down and running up the other side of the wall. It will be nice when it's over!

Josef, and even Mother, have tried to help in every way, but with Johanna, David and the baby to feed, clothe and provide for the questions come tumbling in... 'What will we do when he's gone?' - 'Will I have a job to go back to?' - 'And who will look after the children, take them to school...?' They rattle around my head. Then there's the daily worry of seeing Joseph going out of the front door - 'Is this to be my last sight of him?' All in all, my faith is certainly being sorely tested. Nancy and Jim, Stella and Roy, Marjorie and her Jim, yes, they're all lining like guardsmen on parade to help - but that's just for the baby. Not one of them, not even Mother, yet knows that Josef is going to be gone. Mr White was absolutely insistent that we tell no one, not even when Josef has landed in the United States, and even then another week after that. I know, I know, I know just how important secrecy must be, every extra day puts a wider gulf between him and those trying to track him down, but it's not easy keeping this from my closest friends, ones I absolutely know would never betray a secret.

12th May

Josef: I hated giving the shop up, Mary and I have put everything into building it up, but it's gone, sold to Joseph Wendehals. Pre-war he had a stamp dealership in Vienna's 8th Bezirk. In 38 they fled, and in 49 came to England, to Tulse Hill, near us. He's been a good friend – we even get mistaken for one another, both being 'Josef's', of one sort or another – and he's run the shop when we were away. I needed to sell in a hurry and there was no-one better to sell to. I've kept some of the choicest stamps from the stock for myself – so my time in ISRB wasn't entirely wasted!

22nd May

Johanna: From this day on the story became more disjointed, like clips from an old film on some rackety projector. In the foreground, Mary, largely keeping her own counsel, and Josef occasionally glimpsed, but mostly off-stage. To him it must at times have been an all-too-real nightmare, but to us, watching and waiting, with cherished memories fading away, what little hope remained we buried deep.

After hours and days of packing – it felt as if the flat had been ransacked, the reason never fully explained – it started at four one morning. We all crept silently along the corridors, us two children helping (getting in the way, more like) as Josef lugged a trunk and two suitcases to the back door of Linden Court, Mary, finger to lips, bidding silence. Outside stood a large black saloon, lights off, its driver, apparently known to Josef, helping stow the luggage. Then everyone aboard, Mary in front, leg up on the dashboard, draped in her travelling rug, Josef in the back with us. In the back, not knowing the destination, we soon nodded off.

Mary: We went north, through Dulwich, over Tower Bridge and into the docks as dawn was rising. At the head of one quay sat a similar black car, another Rover, four men in overcoats beside it. As our car rolled past them onto a deserted quay, two moved off, left and right, into the shadows. The other two came to meet us where we stopped. A ship loomed above us. I recognised Mr White, who shook hands and introduced us, 'Mr Temple, Mrs Bramminger.'

Josef: Leaving was every bit as hard as I had ever feared. To face life without Mary, without Johanna and David, without even seeing our new child. We hope to be reunited, but, for now at least, must be apart.

Mary: Josef's trunk and two suitcases disappeared into the ship and now Josef was approaching. 'I really have to go, *liebling*.' He took me by the shoulders and kissed me, a quick kiss on the lips, then said, 'Mary, you are the strongest woman in the world, what can I say... is it "all shall be well?"'

Mr Temple, aboard the ship, talking with a ship's officer, suddenly turned and hurried down the gangway. 'Come along, Josef, you have to get going, quickly now.' For a moment I was horror-struck; had 'they' stumbled on the plan? Could they snatch Josef, even here, in London, in front of the children? Then I remembered those two men in the shadows, our sentries. I forced myself to look calm, for the children's sake.

Josef made as if to go, then turned again and gathered me in his arms, kissing me as fully and passionately as he ever had. Letting go of me he crouched down, gathering Johanna and David in his arms, kissing them too. Reluctantly letting go he stood up, 'I'll return to you somehow. We will be together again' he shouted - over the sound of the ship's horn - waved to us and ran for the gangway. On board he turned for a final wave, and disappeared into the ship. Almost immediately came the rattle of chains.

Josef on that gangway, boarding a huge ship was David's abiding memory. Then that gangway, detached from the ship's side, was lifted away by a dockside crane. Two long blasts from the ship's horn echoed around the docks.

I remember watching as the ship slid sideways from the quayside - my moment of heartbreak, I think - moving slowly further from the quay. In mid-channel foam boiled at her stern, then gave me the view I'd hoped never to see, her stern as she pulled away. All too soon she was out of sight.

Mr White broke into my thoughts, 'Mrs Bramminger. I watched Josef coming off the ship at Harwich, it seemed only right I be with him as he leaves. He's safe away. I wish you goodbye, only hoping we may meet again in happier circumstances.'

Hopefully I thanked him, old habits die hard, but it's all a bit hazy.

The driver did a three-point turn. As we drove away David, looking out of the back window with Johanna, said in a hushed voice, 'Mummy, when he reversed, I thought we were all going to fall over the edge and into the water. It was very scary!'

I wanted to burst into floods of tears but held myself together for them - for all of them. Oh Lord, you say you are with us always, but at times it seems awfully lonely; how much more for Josef, he has no-one with him...

From deep inside I heard, 'Except me... Child, I have walked the path he must tread, and yours. Do not be afraid.'

'Thank you, Lord.' It was all I could say, if through gritted teeth.

'Hanni and David', I said out loud, 'now listen, we must keep this to ourselves,

Daddy needs to be alone for a while, we don't want those naughty people following him, do we? So, no mention of the ship, or of Canada...'

'Where's Canada, Mummy?'

'A long way away, darling, so we won't mention it to anyone else.' Josef's words came urgently back to me: 'Ask any magician, it's called misdirection', so I changed tack, 'Anyway, he's going to America, the United States. That's where I went when I was, well, younger than you, with Grannie to Cuba, I'll show you in that old photo-album at home.'

Driving away, through a waking London, gave time to think. Maybe that small trick, landing in New York, will keep the opposition busy for months, even years to come. What Russian, having failed to track him down across the United States, would be brave enough to admit to his lords and masters that they'd been looking in the wrong country?

That trail will go cold.

22nd May to 3rd June

Ship's Log, SS American Commander: Master, A T Messenger, tonnage 5,028, 47 crew, 10 passengers. Inbound Passengers Manifest (Aliens):... John Bramminger. Class 1. Travel Document, British, V143884. Stamp Dlr. Age 37. I Trunk 2 Suitcases. Departed London Docks. Docked New York, Pier 30, North River.

Mary: My poor, poor darling Josef. You escaped the Nazis in Vienna and Prague, you survived what the War Office, the Admiralty and the Home Office could throw at you. I remember you saying, 'We went through Vienna like sand through a sieve'; you'll outwit the Communists, I know you will. But, dearest Josef, I miss you already.

The End

Epilogue

1950 to 1972

Somehow, and I never worked out how, through all those years Mary managed to raise us three children on next to no income. It wasn't easy, struggling about on crutches or in a wheelchair, but she somehow managed. And the holidays we went on: to the seaside, Somerset and Glastonbury, Cheddar Gorge, the Norfolk Broads, stays in a caravan park near Hastings; most astonishing, a holiday afloat in a canal narrow boat. Off we children would go by bus or train, she in pursuit in that wonderful, awful invalid tricycle, her beloved 'Tootie', never complaining, always resolutely positive, cheerful, outwardly, to us at least. But there must have been doubts, fears, despair and (definitely) physical pain, but the truest of her friends and her faith somehow carried her through.

1955

Johanna: Philby was publicly exonerated. He resumed his career as a journalist, and part-time spy for MI6 in Beirut; although, come to think of it, that tiny word, 'for', realistically should be a much larger one: 'against.'

21st January 1963

Mary: From the floor a discarded newspaper shouted at me. I grabbed it, the headline read, '**GAITSKELL DIES.** Leader of the British Labour party, Hugh Gaitskell, aged 56, has died after a sudden deterioration in his heart condition...' Something, I have no idea what, was ringing alarm bells in my head, then I recalled Josef talking about him in Vienna in 1934, on the side of the angels, what had he done to die so soon?

'Convenient for some' I thought.

January

Philby finally moved on, after admitting under questioning in Beirut to having been a Soviet agent, without revealing who else had spied for the Soviet Union, he escaped from Beirut to Moscow, where he lived out his life.

March

People are saying Gaitskell died of a form of 'lupus erythematosis', a rare and incurable tissue disease. Later still the story went round of a KGB plot to provide Harold Wilson the chance of being prime minister. Many thought it so far-fetched: 'the Russians poisoning people in London? What nonsense.'

10th August

The London Gazette: State Intelligence. Honours and Awards. Central Chancery of the Orders of Knighthood. St James's Palace, London SW1. The Queen has directed that the appointment of Mr Harold Adrian Russell Philby to be an Officer of the Civil Division of the Most Excellent Order of the British Empire, dated the 1st January 1946, shall be cancelled and annulled, and his name be erased from the Register.

22nd August 1968

Newspapers: Headlines around the world screamed the story...

- **CROWD OF MANY THOUSANDS GATHERED IN BRATISLAVA MAIN SQUARE TO DEMONSTRATE PEACEFULLY**
- **CZECHOSLOVAKIA INVADED BY RUSSIANS, WHO OPEN FIRE ON CROWDS IN PRAGUE**
- **SOVIET TANKS CRUSH PRAGUE SPRING**
- **SHOUTS OF RUSSIAN MURDERERS GO HOME**
- **WHERE IS ALEXANDER DUBČEK? WORLD ASKS**

28th August

Sir Dick White: 'Hoddell...', that surprised him, but even for old times' sake I couldn't bring myself to call him Gregory, 'I have washed my hands of you, but I'm under orders to close the case. We now know you've been a traitor since the forties, probably even before you entered the Service. With your masters having displayed in Prague just what monsters they are, to speed you on your way I'll pass on a nugget of intelligence which your Soviet masters certainly will not have told you. The world believes Dubček was flown to Moscow on the 21st, conducted negotiations with Brezhnev, then was flown back to Prague. That's what they saw on the television, after all. But the bleak truth? In Moscow they pulled him off the military aircraft, threw him inside a BMP, slammed the door shut and left him there for five days. No food, no drink, no light, no sanitary arrangements, no contact with his guards, nothing. For five days! Then they unlocked the armoured car, dragged him out, stripped him off, hosed him down, gave him new clothes, bread and water, put Czechoslovakia's surrender document under his nose, made him sign, pushed him back onto an aircraft and flew him back to Prague. He never left the airport, there were no negotiations, nothing, they simply debased him, treated him like an animal.'

'And for such people, a foul bunch running a system that stank to high heaven from the very beginning, you betrayed your country, the Queen, your service... let alone such friends as you once had? Aren't you ashamed of yourself?'

He'd looked crushed from the moment I'd started speaking. I didn't know what was going through his head, didn't want to, but I think he'd lost the will to resist. He must have watched events unfold on television, perhaps he'd been asking himself the same question. But his next words did surprise me...

'I don't suppose I'll be missed much.'

I hardened my heart. 'No, not by many. The great and the good will turn out for the funeral, if only to be seen. There again, they'll believe your death was suicide, and they won't know just how shameful your whole ghastly life has been, will they?'

Early September

Sunningdale and Ascot Record: 'The body found in a railway cutting in Berkshire has been identified as that of Sir Gregory Hoddell, KBE, CB. A friend of the family tells this newspaper, "He believed he was suffering from terminal cancer, it may have affected his mind."'

A national newspaper: Obituary. Sir Gregory Hoddell, KBE, CB. '... nothing but praise for his services to this country...'

Johanna: It was around about that time that Mummy asked me to drive her to a church near Sunningdale for a funeral, no word of whose. She was insistent she didn't want to go into the church, just to sit outside in my Mini, watching. We saw people arriving, people one half-recognises from the papers or television. A hearse arrived, a coffin was carried inside. She said nothing, so I asked, 'Was it someone you or Daddy knew?' 'No', she replied, somewhat sternly. A long pause then, more gently, 'I didn't know him at all, although Daddy may have worked with him. I'm not exactly sure why I needed to come. To lay a ghost perhaps.'

People started to leave the church and I was about to drive off when a tall, slim man detached himself from the crowd, and made straight for Mummy's side of the car. She, clearly surprised, slid open her window. 'Mrs Bramminger, I hope you remember me...' 'Sir Dick, how could I forget? Let me introduce you, Sir Dick White, this is my daughter, Johanna.'

'How do you do Johanna? You won't recognize me, but 15 years ago we met, on London's Docks, on a far sadder occasion than today.'

I probably replied, 'How do you do?', I cannot recall but I can clearly remember Mummy's face, her look of astonishment, no, I'm wrong, it was joy. Addressing Mummy he continued, 'Back then I said I hoped we might meet again in happier circumstances, and the fact that you are here suggests you also have realized that this...', he negligently waved a hand over his shoulder, 'is just such a happy occasion. Not something I'd normally say at a funeral of someone I worked with, but I long since ceased regarding him as a colleague. The public thinks his death was suicide, but it certainly came as no surprise to us. You and I, Ronnie Heslop for that matter, Josef even, will privately celebrate his passing. I think you understand me...' Looking back at the milling crowd of mourners, he said, 'I must be off.'

'I fully understand, Sir Dick. And thank you for coming over, that's very comforting.'

Off he went.

'Come on, darling, let's be going. We'll be home in time for tea.'

She wasn't giving much away. Only years later did it make sense.

Mary: Oh, Josef, I hope you get to hear of this. Might it even mean, my darling, that you're no longer a threat to those ghastly people in Moscow? Might you be able to come home? I wish, how I wish you were here!

Johanna: Well! If that was bizarre, what followed four years later was even more so.

Anyway, for years one question niggled at me: why, after 1963 and Philby's flight to Moscow, did Josef not find a way of reuniting himself, in Canada or in England, with Mary and us children? It was what they had decided on before he left, and we now know it remained their intention for years afterwards and, having worked for years to re-establish his fortunes, he was on the verge of success. In London, Dick White and others' hopes of bringing Philby down were delayed for an almost unbelievable decade or more by the vigorous defence made of him by his erstwhile colleagues in MI6. But eventually it dawned on me, even after 1963 Josef would have known he was still not safe, since he knew the identity of Hoddell, who had not only betrayed his identity to the Soviets, but might well have still been working inside MI5.

Also, years later, having seen the 1972 medical documents, it came to me. By 1968, when he may or may not have heard of Hoddell's death, when, in theory, the KGB may (or may not) have given up any intention of eliminating him, had his underlying but as yet undiagnosed illness sapped him of the strength and vitality he'd have needed to ask Mary to join him, or to rejoin her in England?

Anytime, always...

Richard: And a piece of gratuitous advice for anyone researching family history:

'Never, ever, destroy anything your nearest and dearest give you. Always find somewhere (preferably dry) to store it, you never know when you'll want to come back to it.'

The times I walked down the garden with things for the incinerator doesn't bear thinking about. In her last years Mummy downsized several times, from house, to bungalow, to flat, to a room in a residential home. Each move yielded more black bags, "Would you be a dear and burn these for me?" she'd ask. She was such a private person, wary of 'identity theft' before the phrase was even invented. I could kick myself, any of those pages rapidly charring before my eyes might have contained hidden secrets that years of research failed to unearth.

And I never once thought to look!

Pause, while I kick myself.

October to December 1971

Josef: I investigated Coober Pedy and Euduna in Australia for Gérard Pacquet, my prospecting partner, then, after eight weeks in Colombia – South America this time – he has sent me back, to Mount Isa, Australia's biggest mining town.

I'm finding flying increasingly difficult. Even South America was a struggle, but 36 hours of Canadian Pacific to Sydney was so painful. I've seen doctors in both countries and when I get back to Toronto I'm determined to get myself sorted out.

2nd January 1972

Flew Sydney-Vancouver-Toronto International. Booked myself into Ontario General Hospital.

5th January

Hospital Medical Records: SUMMARY ON SELF-ADMISSION:

Name: BRAMMINGER, John
Born: 18 Mar 1916, Austria

This 56 year-old man admitted with a complaint of lower back pain. He denied history of back injury. The pain became gradually worse, radiating into thighs and legs; also pain in neck and ribs. Admits to loss of appetite and weakness.

Past Illnesses: During WW2 was hospitalized for Malta Fever, also suffered a marked pharyngitis. He had a fracture of the right wrist and fracture of the left humerus several years ago. In 1952 he had an incidental splenectomy. There are no other hospitalizations, operations or diseases of note.

1965-1971, resident of Quebec, so no hospitalization coverage. A mineral prospector, he visited several countries overseas to examine and purchase properties. October-December 1971, visiting Colombia, he was treated by doctors after lower costal and mid-low back pain. He began taking pain pills. In mid-December (last worked about this date), prospecting in Australia, where Mount Isa Hospital advised he had arthritis because x-rays showed bony changes.

Systems Review: Admits to weight loss of 30 lbs and appetite loss over 2 months, also for past few weeks neck pain, aggravated by movement of the neck, with no radiation.

Neurological: Admits to weakness of both legs. He can walk but feels weak on walking.

Examination on Admission: A pleasant, intelligent, Austrian gentleman, with a good command of English, generally sallow and already slightly jaundiced, in no acute distress, but rolls about in bed in obvious discomfort from low back pain. His consumption of alcohol is small, usually orange juice during last year, and contact pills as a cure for a deep hurting feeling which he describes as a rheumatic pain. He attributes some of it to vibrations from long air travel, which fatigue him greatly.

12th-20th January

Patient was given blood transfusions on 12 and 15 Jan. On 19 Jan he was taken to Surgery...

On 20 Jan patient developed a slight degree of jaundice. He never had it before despite being exposed near Elliot Lake in 1960's. Dr Drayson thought the jaundice to be secondary to tumour infiltration of the liver.

Reflexes: Patient well oriented, alert and comprehensive of his situation. He asked after his prognosis and inter-alia was advised that he might well prepare a will.

18th March

Johanna: I came across this in a stamp dealers magazine: 'It is our sad duty to announce the death of Joseph Wendehals, for many years proprietor of the London Wall Stamp Co Ltd, City of London. He died in Graz, Austria, earlier this month, having been knocked over by a motor car in late January and failing to recover from his injuries. Mr Wendehals retired three years ago to his native country to live in a charming house he had built in rural Styria.'

10th April

Hospital records continued: SOCIAL HISTORY REPORT:
Information source: Patient
Family: Patient – insists he is known as John, not Josef – has not had contact with his relatives for many years. A brother lives somewhere in the United States and two sisters in Vienna. Patient has no idea of their addresses and does not wish to locate them.
Financial: Mr Bramminger advised me that as a prospector, if he finds anything valuable, he would be owed about $25,000 by his partners. As things are they provide him with spending money when required. They are still hopeful that he will assist them when he is well.
Comfort Allowance: I asked Mr Bramminger to apply for this. Initially he did not wish to do so, but agreed.

In Summary: He seems to be a proud, independent man, very outgoing. Speaks English with little German accent, also French and German (native language). Most anxious to return to work, even if only to give advice.

Signed, L P Scott, Hospital Social Services.

26th May

PLAN: Mr Bramminger would have been moved from my service in due course but will be followed in the out-patient Urology Clinic. I encouraged him to exercise, limiting factor being pain. We will attempt to adjust his analgesia for maximal symptomatic and functional improvement. Prognosis is grave and treatment can only be symptomatic. 26 May. Frances Breadon, MD. Attending Physician.

SELF-DISCHARGE: To whom it may concern. This is to certify that I am leaving Ontario General Hospital on my own responsibility. Date: 23.5.72. Signature: John Bramminger.

DISPOSITION: Patient signed himself out of hospital on 24 May 1972. Signature: R Warnock, MD. 12 June 1972.

24th May

Richard: When Josef discharged himself from the hospital on 24th May he walked to 3C Leopold Avenue, 15 minutes away, and rented an apartment.

16th to 21st July

Office of the Registrar General, Toronto-Bureau du registraire général, Toronto: STATEMENT OF DEATH

PLACE OF DEATH: Toronto, #311, 3 Leopold Avenue, Metropolitan Toronto
Age: 56 years
OCCUPATION: Trade or profession: Unknown. Type of industry: Unknown
BURIAL: Westminster Cemetery, Borough of North York. 20th July 1972

MEDICAL CERTIFICATE OF DEATH (LONG DEATH CERTIFICATE)

FULL NAME OF DECEASED: BRAMMINGER. John
CAUSE OF DEATH: ....
Disease or condition directly leading to death: Myocardial Infarction
I am satisfied as to the correctness of this medical certificate and statement of death.

I register the death by signing the certificate this: JULY ~~24~~ 21 1972.
Signature: Deputy Division Registrar.

Thursday 1st March 1973

Johanna: The way that Mary came to hear of Josef's death was the oddest thing. One morning I answered the door of our home in Bromley to a rather solemn policeman. 'Excuse me, miss, but am I speaking to Johanna Bramminger?'

'Well... yes, I was, but I'm married now.'

'Do you mind if I come in, there's something I must tell you.'

My face must have gone white, I remember asking, fearfully, 'Has something happened to my husband, my daughter? What...'

'If I might come in...'

He left twenty minutes later and I immediately was on the phone: 'Mummy, I have some dreadful news, I've just been told that Daddy has died in Toronto, on...'

She said, 'I know, darling, on the sixteenth of July last year, wasn't it?'

'How on earth did you know that?' I asked. Then, angrily, 'And how could you have known and not told me? How...'

'It's a long story, darling, and I'll tell you all about it, when we see each other. There'll be a lot of things I need to do first. I must put it in the newspaper, letters to write, and, well, any number of things. Do please come up and stay next week.'

Years after that grim telephone call, when I came across the report of Joseph

Wendelhay's death I couldn't help but wonder... was it the most terrible coincidence, two Joseph/Josef's, both former owners of the London Wall Stamp Company, dying within months of each other? Or could it have been yet another bungled assassination attempt by the KGB, or whatever they were calling themselves at the time? It took that Joseph three months to die which, of course, doesn't suggest the mark of professional assassins. But, if true, does it suggest that 'they' confused one for the other, missing their true target, the Josef they were really after? If true, then DW's aim to disguise his escape to Canada had succeeded for nearly two decades, for our Josef at least.

2nd March

The Times: BRAMMINGER. In the Ontario General Hospital, Toronto. JOSEF JOHANN, much loved husband of Mary and father of Johanna and David. "Whether we live or die, we are the Lord's."'

5th March

Sir Dick White, by now head of the Cabinet Office's Intelligence Co-ordinating Committee, summoned his secretary. 'Alison', he asked, 'this file in my in-tray, Bramminger's File No 4 from the Home Office, the one covering 41 to 48. Why have MI5 sent it to me?'

She replied hesitantly, 'Well, sir, its subject having died last July, they'd normally dispose of it themselves. But there's a note from 1941 inside, "No action to be taken on this file without reference to D G White (B.8)." They'll have been afraid to take action without your say-so. I think they're slightly in awe of you...'

'Of me, Alison? I hardly think so.' He laughed, then flipped through it. 'If the rules say it must be destroyed then you must instruct 5, and the Home Office – it's their file after all – to mark it up as destroyed by fire, the usual routine.'

'Yes, sir.' She turned to go. Half-way through the doorway she looked back and said, 'And...?'

'And?' he said.

'And do you actually want me to destroy it by fire, sir?'

He looked surprised, almost hurt. 'Alison, how could you ask?' he said, a touch of disappointment in his voice. 'You know we never do that sort of thing.'

'No, sir,' she said dutifully, closing the door firmly behind her; in the corridor she repeated it, sotto voce, 'We never do that sort of thing!'

6th March

Johanna: Five days after that terrible phone call I managed to get away to stay for a few days in Herefordshire, and soon I was sitting with my brothers David and Richard, back from university, in the well-remembered living room. Miracle of miracles, shortly before they died Uncle Bernard and Auntie Bea had rewritten their wills so that Mary inherited Woodleigh, air-raid shelter and all – and here she was, wheelchair, crutches, the whole caboodle, clearly bursting to tell us the news.

'Darlings, there's so much to say, and I'll tell you all I know. I managed to contact our Consulate General in Toronto. They put me on to Ontario's Registrar General, who kindly air mailed me a death certificate. It seems that Daddy died of a sudden heart attack at his flat in Toronto's suburbs, before anyone could get him to hospital.

'They didn't explain why it took six months to tell us, however, and how that policeman ever found you, under your married name, at a different address from where we used to live, I cannot fathom. The whole thing's so extraordinary and mysterious that I think I detect something numinous about it.'

'But before I tell you both about my strange experience last year, I want to read from two letters which I've found most comforting. The first is from Roy and Stella Foster – do you remember him as our vicar in Brixton? They'd known Josef from when he arrived in London and had read the announcement in the Telegraph. All three of you know something of why Daddy had to leave, his life being under threat, his Austrian friend assassinated in Vienna and someone trying to push him under a tube train at London Bridge; all that, plus his own country having treated him as a traitor, our own intelligence services having ridiculed his warning about treachery in their ranks, the deaths of all those in the Czech army he'd admired, all those things cut very deep. Johanna and David, both of you were too young, thank God, to really see how damaged he was by all that, and I tried to shield you from it as best I could. Then, on top of that, he felt badly treated about the Villach stamp... anyway, listen to what Roy wrote: "the real Josef was not the broken and in some ways sick man that he was in the latter years. I believe he fled not only from his beloved ones but also from himself, escaping into isolation. As you yourself told me, it was his wish to be alone. But we, you and Stella and myself, have the firm assurance to see that if everything can't be put right in this world, then it will be in the next, with our clearer vision of God. I think you can be happier to feel he is now in God's hands and all will be well. Darling Mary, I shall always remember you and Josef standing before me on your wedding day."'

'Then your Austrian cousin, Peter, in the loveliest of letters, wrote this, "But, nobody is alone, God is with them - and was with Josef, even in those last hard hours, when a man is taking the last step from this world into another one."'

'But I must tell you the strangest thing of all. You'll find it hard to believe, so I will tell it exactly as it happened. That day, the day Daddy died in Toronto, the 16th of July last year, was glorious here: a bright, beautiful, summer's day, clear skies, the birds singing away. Across the lawn, through the apple trees, the St John's Wort was in full flower, there were irises and nigella, and the roses blooming. It was all so perfect that, mid-afternoon, I decided to take a tray into the garden and have a cup of tea. Both dogs came running after me and lay down on the grass, hoping for a biscuit, I suspect. I was pouring the tea when I heard the click of the latch on the field gate - you know, it's so distinctive there's no mistaking it. Immediately, Jones and Dai were up and running pell-mell towards the gate, thirty yards away through the trees and bushes. The thought was flashing through my mind, "That's unusual. Why aren't they barking?", when suddenly Josef appeared through the shrubbery, walking over the lawn towards me, the dogs gambolling all around him, they clearly loved him.'

'I staggered to my feet, my mind reeling. Other, wild thoughts came jostling in - only later did I piece them together: "He's wearing modern clothes, not the jacket and trousers he was wearing back in 1953, the last time I saw him, on that horrid dockside in London..." and, "he must have died, and he's come to see me!" - then, the next moment, we were together.'

'His last words on that dock also came racing back: "I'll return to you somehow. We <u>will</u> be together again", even though he'd had to shout them over the noise of the ship's horn. My first words were, "Oh! Josef, Josef, you returned!" - but whether I whispered, said or shouted them escapes me completely, I may have sung them, for all I know.'

'The next moment he was holding me - no, I lie, we were holding each other.'

'"Do you remember our first meeting", he said, with the broadest of smiles. "I said, *Der Tee ist sehr gut*, and you told me your German was *wenig und rostig*, little and rusty? That was the moment I fell in love with you. I somehow knew I could put all my trust in you. Now I must trust you again, to not let go of our love, even though I have to be going, away from you, I know that much. I have no understanding of where or what I'm in for, but just knowing that you have loved me all this time is enough for me."'

'I had to ask him, "So, now you've found that other world, my darling - or maybe it's found you - what is it really like? I'd love to know", and his reply told me that Josef was once more the man I first knew... "I've scarcely had a chance to find out, and I'll let you know, if I ever get a chance. But I already know this, there's none of that skulking around in the dark, no hiding in cupboards, no more looking over the shoulder. There's as much light here as I ever imagined there could be in this life... well", he laughed, and I joined in, we both saw the funny side of what he'd just said. "Well, not THIS life", he gestured at the garden all around us, "but in the <u>real</u> life that I think I'm going to thoroughly enjoy."'

'Then we talked and talked - he even hummed those lines from Bless the Bride, *This is my lovely day. This is the day I shall remember the day I'm dying.* Do you remember them, Hanni darling, heaven knows we sang them often enough in the flat? Richard, even you must remember, I played that record for years afterwards.'

But before I could answer she went on... 'but you won't want to hear the rest. It's all so maudlin, not for your ears, darlings...'

Johanna: Mummy sat there for quite some moments, silent, clearly thinking back to that moment. But she couldn't have been more wrong, I'd never wanted to hear anything <u>more</u> - although I'm sure I'll never find the courage to ask her what else passed between them in those next few minutes.

Anyway, eventually Mummy gathered herself together and carried on.

Mary: After that I waited, every day expecting to hear this terrible news 'officially', so to speak. But the days and weeks and months went by, no policeman at the door, no official letter, no telephone call, so I just had to treasure up that extraordinary scene and hope... until, God bless you, darling Hanni, <u>you</u> rang. I'm so sorry that you had to take the brunt of the shock, but I hadn't seen a way to finding out more, and I couldn't tell anyone of that 'experience', I'd have been hauled off to the madhouse!

But, all that to one side, I can't stop asking myself, how did Daddy know to come here? He never came to Herefordshire in all the years he was in England, how did he even know about the gate into the field? I had even asked him, 'But Josef, you never visited Herefordshire, you never came here, to Bernard and Beatrice's house. How did you know where to find me?'

For a moment he had looked puzzled, then he laughed, 'I have no idea, I just saw the light and stepped forward, there was a gate in front of me and I went through it and, suddenly there you were, here you are...'

Johanna: I remember how, as a child, that book, The Railway Children, and the film, both films in fact, greatly affected me. The mother's struggle to earn a living as a writer, those frequent returned manuscripts, the rare celebratory 'buns for tea', and the father absent, unjustly so, all had echoes for us, but in particular the closing scene. I suppose I always lived in the hope, hope beyond hope, that one day Daddy would reappear in our lives, and, in a funny sort of way, that's exactly what he did.

But I didn't get a chance to say that to Mummy, I realised she was still speaking...

Mary: He said, 'I must go, I won't say goodbye, as what I mean is auf Wiederschau'n - I look forward to seeing you again.' Then he smiled - oh, I shall never forget that smile - and held my eyes. The very last thing he said to me was, 'All shall be well, and all shall be well.'

I had to dig deep to complete the saying, but out it came, 'And all manner of thing shall be well - ALLES möge sich zum Guten wenden.'

Then he was gone.

Author's note

It started years ago, sitting at my computer, looking through the National Archives website. I'd been to Kew many times over the years, researching professionally, but this was the first time I'd accessed their website. It occurred to me, 'Start with what you know' so for my first search I typed in, '*bramminger.*' Up came sixteen wartime files, *mv Bramminger* this, *mv Bramminger* that – the RAF tracking German blockade-runners, the Royal Navy sinking them – then, '*Bramminger, J, Date of birth 15.02.1916*', so familiar that for a minute or two I didn't take it in. Then it dawned, it was his name of course, his date of birth! But the words that followed, 'Closed for 100 years', almost stopped my enthusiasm in its tracks. It took a Freedom of Information request and four long months before I found myself looking at five thick files stacked on a desk in the Reading Room at Kew.

Passing by, for now, the awkward fact that the five files were numbered 1-6, I was immediately assailed by 'doubts'; what would I find in them? Good or bad? Illusions shattered, hopes confirmed? All was well, it turned out, reinforced by seeing Mary's often seen signature, although it was some time before the early and unfamiliar 'Mary Brown' was replaced by the more familiar 'Mary Bramminger.' Josef's handwriting and signature also appeared, entirely new to me, but somehow bringing him to life.

Later a dusty old trunk in the attic, some letters, diaries. Then, almost too late, acquaintances' reminiscences, told hesitatingly, even reluctantly, and, all too often, followed by the silence of the grave. Then more archives raided, to Kew again – there's always something more to find at Kew, you just have to persist – London's Imperial War Museum (especially its audio archives), national, military and other archives in Vienna, Prague, Bratislava, Toronto, Ottawa, a sentence here, a paragraph there. I asked after his Viennese school reports – '*Nein, das halten wir nicht, sie wurden bei der Bombardierung der Stadt zerstört…*', 'No we don't keep those, they were destroyed in the bombardment of the city...' the current Head's words had me in two minds, whose bombardment? RAF and American bombs or Red Army shells? Then, a fortnight later: 'Ah! Suddenly my caretaker has found those reports in the basement, I will send them to you.' Eventually, from so many sources, if all too rarely, reams of reports, letters, memoranda, and the odd one or two gems of intelligence, came my way.

I am most grateful for the advice of a wise old man, Eric Koch, an internee with Josef in Britain then Canada and on the same horrific voyage in the Ettrick.

Settled in Canada, an excellent and witty writer with a lively blog, he answered my first question by email in 2012, 'To write or not to write?': '*The only really difficult thing about writing a book is the decision to write it. Listen to your inner voice.*'

Let's start with the title and sub-title: *All shall be well, and all manner of thing shall be well.* It's the best known saying from *Revelations of Divine Love*, thought to be the earliest surviving book in English written by a woman. The mystery starts with her name - '*Julian of Norwich*' (with its several variations... *Juliana, Dame J..., Mother J..., Lady J...* and *The Lady J...*). For starters she was neither, that we know of, 'a Lady', nor 'Julian' - a man's name adopted from St Julian (more cautious commentators say '*probably* adopted...'), the patron saint of the church in Norwich where she lived in the 14th and 15th centuries in its attached anchorite cell. The cell is still there, rebuilt after being destroyed by Luftwaffe bombs, so at least 'of Norwich' is certain. Her book is well worth reading, but you must make of it what you will, not least in deciding if her story is fact or fiction. A bit like this one.

Which takes me to the next question, 'As fact or fiction?' Eric answered that firmly: '*The invaluable advantage of fiction over non-fiction is that all that matters is inner truth, you don't have to waste time on tiresome facts'*; Sir Andrew Motion - the former Poet Laureate - gave similar advice at a book-signing: '*Definitely fiction, it liberates you from the facts.*' Those helped enormously. Then, reading *The Hare with Amber Eyes* drew me firmly into 1930's Vienna, that strange mixture of glory and ugliness, and seeing its author, Edmund de Waal, talking on television about writing, in 'Make Pots or Die' (with some scenes filmed in the London Library), decided me... I simply had to get on and write.

So, is this book fiction? Yes - although woven around strands of fact. So, what type or fiction - or 'genre', as publishers will insist on? *Spy thriller*? In a minor way. *Family history*? Some elements. *'Dear Diary'?* It certainly draws on some journals and letters, but that's not a genre you find a label for on many bookshop shelves. *Historical fiction*? That's more like it. It has some really grim parts - the Nazis doing their bit in the 1930's and the Soviets theirs in the 1950's (not to mention Prague 1968 - why stop there, why not Crimea and Ukraine in 2014 and 2022, and on, and on...) - that might have come out of the Dark Ages. Certainly in the ten or more years of writing it has sometimes seemed more like current affairs than historical fiction, sometimes with crowds across the world, and their puppet masters, apparently heading back to the totalitarian evils of those times.

Be that as it may, I certainly wasn't thinking the book came under the genre of *Romance* until, in the middle of the night I woke up with the words 'a love story' ringing through my head, slightly muffled, but definitely ringing. I never intended to write one, but at the very least it has given me the book's beginning and end.

Then I spotted – hidden in plain sight – a dry-as-dust, very bureaucratic secret. From the National Archives' Home Office records I had read five Bramminger files, late in the day noticing that they actually numbered 1 to 6. The clue was on the dreary beige cover of File 5, nestled amidst printed instructions, minutes, rubber stamps in many colours, date stamps, initials, signatures, crossings-out and all the usual civil service codes and hieroglyphs: including a barely visible inscription in red crayon, '·/**4 destroyed**' it said. For those whose less than razor-sharp eyes missed – as mine initially did – that dot in '·/**4**' seems to be Civil Service shorthand for 'Number 4.'

What was going on?

I drew up a chronological table of ever document in every file. The fourth file, the missing one, covered from December 1941 to 1948, the period when Josef worked variously for MI5, SOE and pre-Soviet Czechoslovakian military intelligence. Two humdrum letters from that period had been skilfully 'retro-fitted' backwards into File 3, otherwise, for six years, there was nothing. Averaging the files suggested 25-30 documents had gone AWOL.

A member of staff at Kew commented helpfully: 'A file saying "destroyed" doesn't necessarily mean it was. It's not unknown for MI5 to have retained files, whilst recording them as destroyed.' Also, even more helpfully: 'they have, however, left you two valuable clues. Firstly, there's the "Traffic Index sheet", the long slip attached to the cover of File 5. It shows "Date of Dispatch – Destination – Received. Date or Initials" for the entire period, i.e. the missing years, the period covered by File 4 itself. Secondly, "destruction" must have occurred before 1952, i.e. when file 6 was closed.' Those remarks were spot on. In those missing years File 4 had whizzed around the Home Office Alien Department's A Div, B Div, CR, the PA, Stats, various sub-sections of B Div, and MI5. One can track its journey, it's only the contents that are hidden from view. Later a nameless academic muttered about many similar files lurking in a long-lost, disused railway tunnel, deep in rural Berkshire, saying: 'Never give up hope.' So, who knows, one day the missing file 4 and its hidden contents may surface in the public domain. Or was it Oxfordshire? I forget.

It reminded me of Sherlock Holmes's 'curious incident of the dog that didn't bark in the night', but in this instance the unexplained 'black hole' confirmed, albeit tenuously, that the tale I'd been teasing out was along the right lines.

I need to thank Josef's friends and colleagues, sadly few even when I started, and most having since died, for providing personal memories and comments. Meeting Eric Koch at his favourite Japanese restaurant in Toronto was one of the highlights of all the years of research. Herbert Lowit's first words on the telephone, 'I remember him well', were surely the best any researcher could hope to hear. From 1941 he and Josef had served together in the Czech anti-tank battery. Over coffee in the British Library's café, and several letters and emails later, I felt I knew Josef so much better. Then there were Steve Braham's reminiscences of Josef, *'Josef, always Josef, never Joe! He made the most excellent sausages'*, and the several occupants of Brixton Hill Court who let me see the flats where some of the story took place.

Before the writing came the researching, using the usual run of sources including, more than any others, the London Library and the National Archives at Kew. Plus places new to me, the Österreichisches Staatsarchiv, the Royal Maritime Museum at Greenwich, Leamington Spa's library, London's Wiener and Quaker libraries; hospitals and police stations, libraries and provincial record offices across Ontario and Quebec, not least Toronto's magnificent Reference Library, nor forgetting the mining registry in Sault Ste Marie and Toronto's hospitals. My gratitude goes to all their staff and volunteers for their help, often above and beyond the call of duty. Thank you.

For a book some 10 years in the writing, covering locations in, inter alia, Austria, Britain, Canada, the then Czechoslovakia and Germany, there are numerous other people who need thanking for their advice, support and patience, and I apologise to several others whom – through failing emails systems and computers – I lost track of. For reasons of discretion most are shown solely by their first names and include... Josef and Mary, Peter and Gerti, Stephen, Rachel; Karen – for eliciting a story never-before told, and for putting up with me – Alice, Carol, Chris, Christopher, David, Eleanor, Graham, Juliet and Jeremy, June, Laurence, Matt, MBT and Victoria, Paul, Peter, Rich, Robin, Ruth, Sandy, Sarah, Sara, Sean, Teresa and Tracy. Also Clemence and Martin for access to her father's internment letters. Alenka, and John and his friend, for translating some vital Czech documents – no easy matter as it turned out. Another John, closer to home, for translation of lengthy German and official documents – Fraktur script and Sütterlinschrift handwriting making that also not as simple a task as it sounds. Dr Pischl and Hubert Prigl in Austria, Heinz Vogel, Anthony Glees, and Richard Gaskell (for digging in Czech archives), Kateřina Čapková, PhD in Prague's Institute of Contemporary History, also PhDr Jiří Plachý. Brian of Movement Control, Věra Benyovzská, and Dr Helen Fry; Sue, granddaughter of the SS Thysville's captain, Brian Birch, Stephen Walton of the Imperial War Museum, Miss Rhona Wookey of Weston-under-Penyard, whose name I borrowed, Father Martin Smith, Rector of, and Father Luke Penkett, Honorary Librarian of, the Julian Shrine in Norwich and, of course, Julian herself. But my deepest and heartfelt words of praise and thanks go to those Quakers, and others, usually unnamed, who helped refugees across Europe when help was needed.

Also to Michael Sessions my publisher, the Sessions Book Trust and the William Adlington Cadbury Charitable Trust - all Quakers - for their very practical support. And Rachel Hopkins, Michael's editor, for her cheerful assistance in getting this book into shape.

And finally to family members, whose memories helped fill many a gap, and whose support, in many ways, carried me through to the end.

 Thanks are given for the several items from the national archives of Austria, Canada, the Czech Republic and Slovakia, and to their friendly and helpful staff.

A reduced bibliography

I'll spare you footnotes, or the full bibliography of over 700 books and 1,500 or more unpublished sources. But fifty or so of them – two being musical rather than textual – deserve to be noticed and, if you ever have the opportunity, to be read or listened to...

Of Vienna pre-war until the Anschluß...

- *Leb', waiß nit wie lang* – The 'nursery rhyme' that Josef's mother recites to him as a baby, and which he, slightly guiltily, recites to himself in the sheer joy of having escaped across the border to Czechoslovakia in 1938, is variously attributed. Paddy Leigh Fermor takes the more romantic view, of a drunken Emperor as its author, and he unexpectedly, in an unusual footnotes, gives the name of the castle in which it was written: 'Stop press! I've just discovered that the castle is called Schloss Tratzberg. It is near Jenbach, still standing, and not very far from Innsbruck.' Others, including an unamused Martin Luther, attribute it to the German theologian, Martinus von Biberach. I'm happy for either to be the case since, for me – and I could well be wrong – the poem, or nursery rhyme, catches something at least of the saying in Julian of Norwich's *Revelations of Divine Love*, 'All shall be well', this book's title
- Österreichische Staatsarchiv/Austrian State Archives – www.oesta.gv.at/ www.statearchives.gv.at
- Richard Bassett – *The Austrians, strange tales from the Vienna Woods*
- Gordon Brook-Shepherd – *Anschluss, the rape of Austria*
- Joseph Buttinger – *The twilight of socialism, a history of the Revolutionary Socialists of Austria*
- George Clare – *Last waltz in Vienna, the destruction of a family*
- Edmund de Waal – *The hare with amber eyes, a hidden inheritance*
- Muriel Gardiner – *Code-name 'Mary', memoirs of an American woman in the Austrian underground*
- George Eric Rowe Gedye – *Fallen bastions, the central European tragedy*, and his papers in the IWM
- Helmut Gruber – *Red Vienna, an experiment in working-class culture*

- Erich Hackl - *The wedding in Auschwitz, an incident*, translated by Martin Chalmers
- Alexander Lassner - *The invasion of Austria in March 1938, blitzkrieg or pfusch?*
- John Lehmann - *Down river, a Danubian study*, and *The whispering gallery*
- Patrick Leigh Fermor - *A Time of Gifts*, for every word of it and the other parts of his trilogy, but especially for the mention of the 'Emperor's nursery rhyme'
- Igor Lukes, for helpful advice and for his three books - *Czechoslovakia between Stalin and Hitler, the diplomacy of Edvard Beneš in the 1930's; The Munich Crisis, 1938, prelude to World War II;* and *On the Edge of the Cold War, American diplomats and spies in Postwar Prague*
- McDermott, Rodgers and Williams - for their biographies of Hugh Gaitskell
- Naomi Mitchison - *Vienna diary*
- Douglas Reed - *Insanity fair*
- Sheila Spielhofer - *Stemming the dark tide, the story of the Austrian Quakers*

Of Prague and escape to England...

- Kateřina Čapková, PhD and Michal Frankl - *Unsichere Zuflucht, Die Tschechoslowakei unh ihre Flüchtlinge aus NS-Deutschland und Österreich, 1933-1938 / Insecure Refuge, Czechoslovakia and its Refugees from Nazi Germany and Austria, 1933-1938*
- William Chadwick - *The rescue of the Prague refugees, 1938-39*
- Národního archiv/Czech National Archives - www.nacr.cz
- Marcel Fodor - *South of Hitler*, and his many pieces as a journalist, especially in the Manchester Guardian
- Mark Jonathan Harris and Deborah Oppenheimer - *Into the arms of strangers, stories of the Kindertransport*, Bloomsbury Publishing, 2000. A wonderful book from which I have used an element of Norbert Wollheimer's particularly wonderful story. If I knew the name of that immigration officer at Harwich I would happily have included it. He comes close to deserving beatification
- Hans A Schmidt - *Quakers and Nazis, inner light in outer darkness*

- Hanns Skoutajan - *The road to peace, memories and reflections along the way*
- Doreen Warriner - *Winter in Prague, 1938-39*

Amongst many vivid items on internment in Britain and Canada, and three journeys across the Atlantic...

- Library and Archives Canada/Bibliotheque et Archives Canada - www.library-archives.canada.ca
- Ancestry - www.ancestry.co.uk - Outgoing Passenger Lists, 1890-1960
- Heinz Bing - diaries and letters of internment in the Weiner Library and the Imperial War Museum
- Paul Elwell - *Paul Elwell's Story*, and the valuable contribution of his son Derek
- Hans Gal - *Huyton Suite for flute and two violins, opus 92*
- Peter Coleman, Selwyn Cornish & Peter Drake - *Arndt's story, the life of an Australian economist,* published by the open access ANU Press, Canberra
- Peter and Leni Gillman - *Collar the lot! How Britain interned and expelled its wartime refugees*
- Eric Koch - *Deemed suspect, a wartime blunder.* Also his online memories and a gripping blog
- Siri Lawson - *www.warsailors.com*, a site of convoy diaries under a Creative Commons Licence
- Alfred Lomnitz - *Never mind, Mr Lom!*
- Alexander Paterson's report at Kew - *Report to the Home Secretary, Civilian internees sent UK to Canada*
- Ronald Stent - *A bespattered page? The internment of His Majesty's 'most loyal enemy aliens.'* - One of the best of the many books on internment. It is the only source to state that the SS Ettrick, like the Arandora Star before her, was, initially at least, flying a swastika below the Blue Ensign, to warn German naval commanders that she was carrying their nationals. In a book festooned with footnotes it is, regrettably, one of the few stories to be given no source. Yet more unfortunately, years after his death his family eventually destroyed his notes for the book, so no trail back to the source of that story is to be found, other than in Stent's text, and the author's family memories

Of wartime Britain, refugees, the Free Czechs...

- Slovenský národný archív/Slovak National Archive - www.minv.sk/?slovensky-narodny-archiv-1
- Charmian Brinson and Richard Dove - *A matter of intelligence, MI5 and the surveillance of anti-Nazi refugees*
- Jiří Friedl - *Příběh generála Lukase, The story of General Lucas*
- Anthony Grenville and Marian Malet - *Changing countries, German-speaking exiles from Hitler in Britain*
- Alan Griffin - *Leamington's Czech patriots and the Heydrich assassination*
- Arthur Koestler - *Darkness at noon*
- Edith Milton - *The tiger in the attic, memories of the Kindertransport and growing up English*
- Anthony Powell - *The military philosophers*, in his series: *Dance to the music of time,* in which Colonel Kalla appears as Colonel Hlava
- Neil Rees - *The Czech connection, the Czechoslovak government in exile in London and Buckinghamshire*

Of SOE, resistance and intelligence (among many others)...

- Norman Bentwich - *I understand the risks*
- Tom Bower - *The perfect English spy, Sir Dick White and the secret war, 1935-90*
- Michael R D Foot - For his valuable comment on this book, made, unfortunately, just prior to his death, and all his books, chiefly *SOE, an outline history*
- Helen Fry - *Denazification, Freud's war,* and *The King's most loyal enemy aliens*
- Samuel J Hamrick - *Deceiving the deceivers*
- Peter Leighton-Langer - *The King's Own Loyal Enemy Aliens*
- Radomír Luža and Christina Vella - *The Hitler kiss, a memoir of the Czech resistance*
- Fritz Molden - *Fires in the night, the sacrifices and significance of the Austrian resistance*
- Airey Neave - *Saturday at MI9*
- Sven Sømme - *Another man's shoes,* referred to on the BBC's *Antiques Road Show* in 2013
- Bickham Sweet-Escott - *Baker Street irregular*
- Peter Wilkinson - *Foreign fields, the story of an SOE operative*

Of post-war Europe...

- Madeleine/Mrs Robert Henrey - *A journey to Vienna*
- Fred Pelican - *From Dachau to Dunkirk*
- Masha Williams - *White among the reds*

I have drawn on numerous sources, and received enormous help from friends and others, but responsibility for any faults, not least for the format, the translations and the text itself, are mine alone. Richard Essberger.